HAWAII

HAWAII

CONTENTS

DISCOVER 6

EXPERIENCE HONOLULU 66

EXPERIENCE HAWAII 118

NEED TO KNOW 236

Left: Brightly colored sign in Hale'iwa
Previous page: Beach in Mākena State Park
Front cover: Coastline of Kauai Island

DISCOVER

Looking over Diamond Head and Honolulu

WELCOME TO HAWAII

Golden sands fringed by swaying palms and laid-back bars; emerald valleys tumbling toward an azure ocean teeming with tropical fish; shore-side towns serving up some of the world's best surf: Hawaii is an island paradise. Whatever your dream trip to these idyllic isles includes, this DK travel guide is the perfect companion.

1 *Ki'i* carvings at Pu'uhonua O Hōnaunau.

2 Lookout in Waimea Canyon State Park.

3 A green sea turtle in the island's clear waters.

4 A surfer on one of the islands' beautiful beaches.

Made up of six main isles sprinkled across the Pacific Ocean, Hawaii is famed for its stunning natural beauty. Sweeping arcs of sugary sand, crescent-shaped bays, and fluted sea cliffs line a coast lapped by turquoise seas, while the interiors are blanketed with lush rainforest and smoldering volcanoes. Such stunning landscapes, coupled with a sunshine-filled climate, mean that life on Hawaii is lived firmly outdoors. Here, you can stroll along white-sand beaches, eat alfresco beneath swaying palms, or jump into warm, cobalt seas to snorkel and surf – all year round.

The islands' diverse towns and cities are just as enticing. Multicultural Honolulu, the state's capital, is home to the world-famous Waikīkī Beach, historic Chinatown, and poignant Pearl Harbor, while oceanside towns like Lāhainā and Hilo feature intriguing museums, historic sights, and excellent restaurants. Throughout the year, lively festivals celebrating such things as Chinese New Year, Thanksgiving, and Hawaiian dance showcase Hawaii's multicultural heritage, which blends Polynesian, Asian, and European influences. These varied cultures are also evident in the islands' cuisine, which offers up a delicious fusion of Pacific Rim flavors.

So, where to start? We've broken Hawaii down island by island into easily navigable chapters, with detailed itineraries, expert local knowledge, and colorful, comprehensive maps to help you plan the perfect visit. Whether you're staying for a week, a month or longer, this DK travel guide will ensure that you make the most of all that this enchanting archipelago has to offer. Enjoy the book, and enjoy Hawaii.

REASONS TO LOVE HAWAII

This remote archipelago is blessed with incredible natural beauty and diverse wildlife, mouthwatering cuisine, and an abundance of outdoor activities. There are so many reasons to love Hawaii; here are some of our favorites.

1 MARINE WILDLIFE ENCOUNTERS

The balmy waters that encircle Hawaii are awash with marine life, including schools of bright yellow tang fish, elegant manta rays, *honu* (green sea turtles), and majestic whales.

HONOLULU 2

Hawaii's capital has it all: super-cool neighborhoods, delectable fusion food, and plenty of intriguing museums. Plus, it's home to Waikīkī *(p96)*, one of the world's best beaches.

3 VARIED COASTLINES

A stunning medley of different landscapes, Hawaii's coast includes champagne-colored sands, black lava-rock tidal pools, and soaring, ridged sea cliffs covered in green foliage.

THE LŪ'AU 4

These traditional feasts see guests dine on Hawaiian dishes such as *poi* (mashed taro root) and *haupia* (coconut pudding), accompanied by performances of Polynesian music and dance.

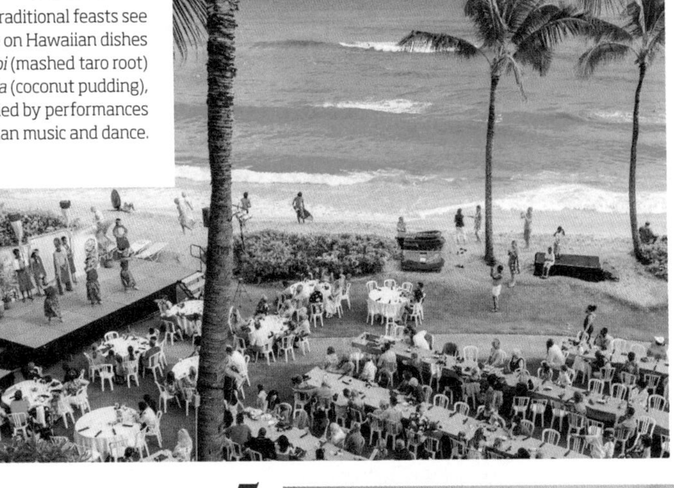

VOLCANIC LANDSCAPES 5

Home to some of the world's most active volcanoes, Hawaii has some truly eye-catching volcanic scenery, including barren lava flats, smoldering craters, and red-hot lava flows.

POKE BOWLS 6

This Hawaiian dish is made from raw diced fish, usually tuna, marinaded in sesame oil and soy sauce, mixed with spring onions, and accompanied by rice and other veggies.

HIKING THE KALALAU TRAIL 7

This challenging trail *(p220)* weaves along cliff-hugging jungle footpaths, offering spectacular views of the rugged Nāpali Coast State Wilderness Park *(p218)* on the way.

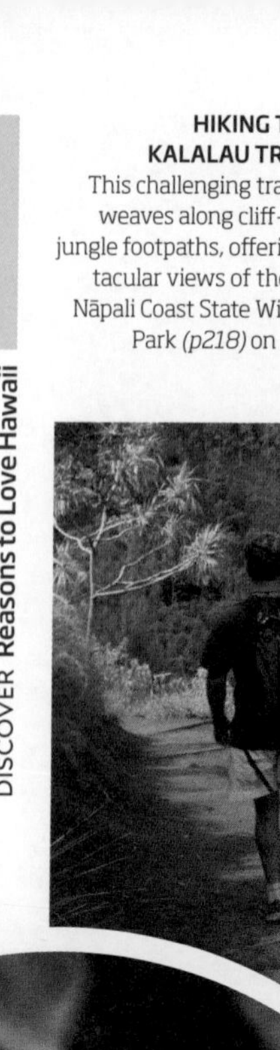

IMPORTANT HISTORICAL SITES 8

From ancient Hawaiian petroglyphs and sacred temple complexes to royal palaces and World War II monuments, Hawaii has an impressive array of historical sites to discover.

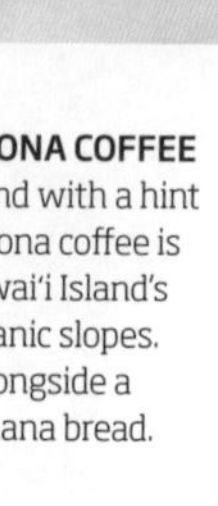

9 A CUP OF KONA COFFEE

Smooth, fruity, and with a hint of smoky spice, Kona coffee is cultivated on Hawai'i Island's mineral-rich volcanic slopes. It's best sipped alongside a slice of warm banana bread.

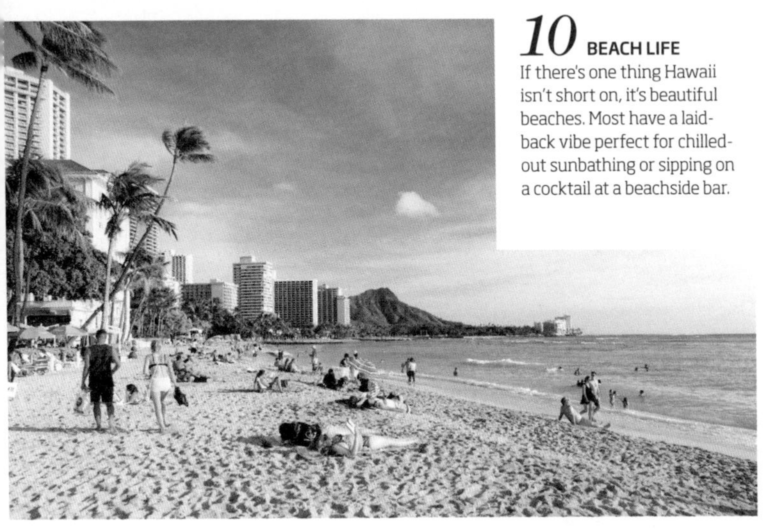

10 BEACH LIFE

If there's one thing Hawaii isn't short on, it's beautiful beaches. Most have a laid-back vibe perfect for chilled-out sunbathing or sipping on a cocktail at a beachside bar.

THE ROAD TO HĀNA 11

Tracking the edge of Maui's lush eastern coast, this iconic road winds past enchanting waterfalls, sandy beaches, and a historic temple. Expect some epic coastal views, too.

SUPERB SURFING 12

Originally an ancient Polynesian sport, surfing was born in the islands. Here, waves can range from a tame swell perfect for beginners to monster pipelines that attract expert surfers.

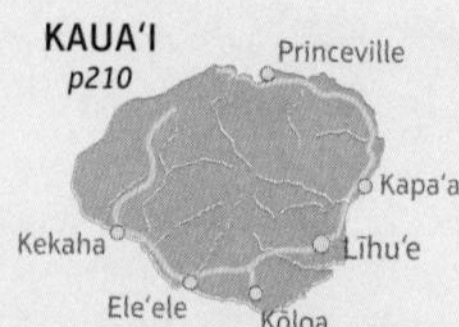

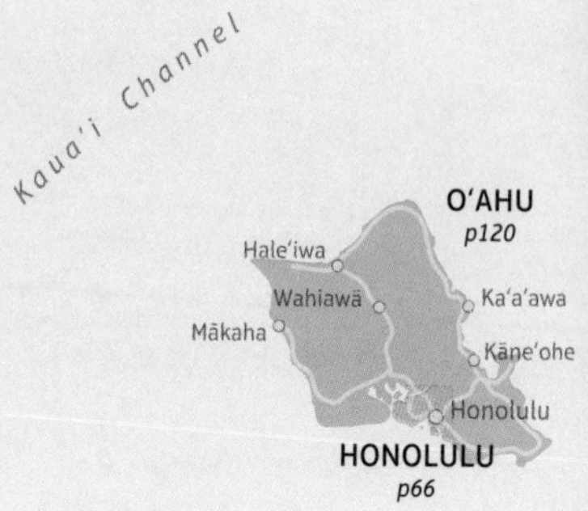

EXPLORE HAWAII

This guide divides Hawaii into six color-coded sightseeing areas, as shown on this map. Find out more about each area on the following pages.

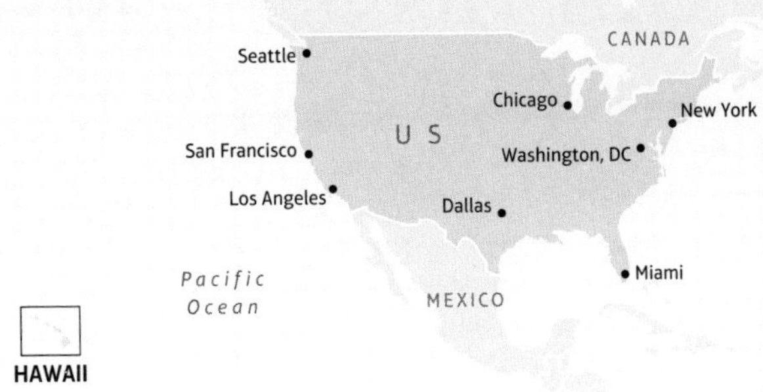

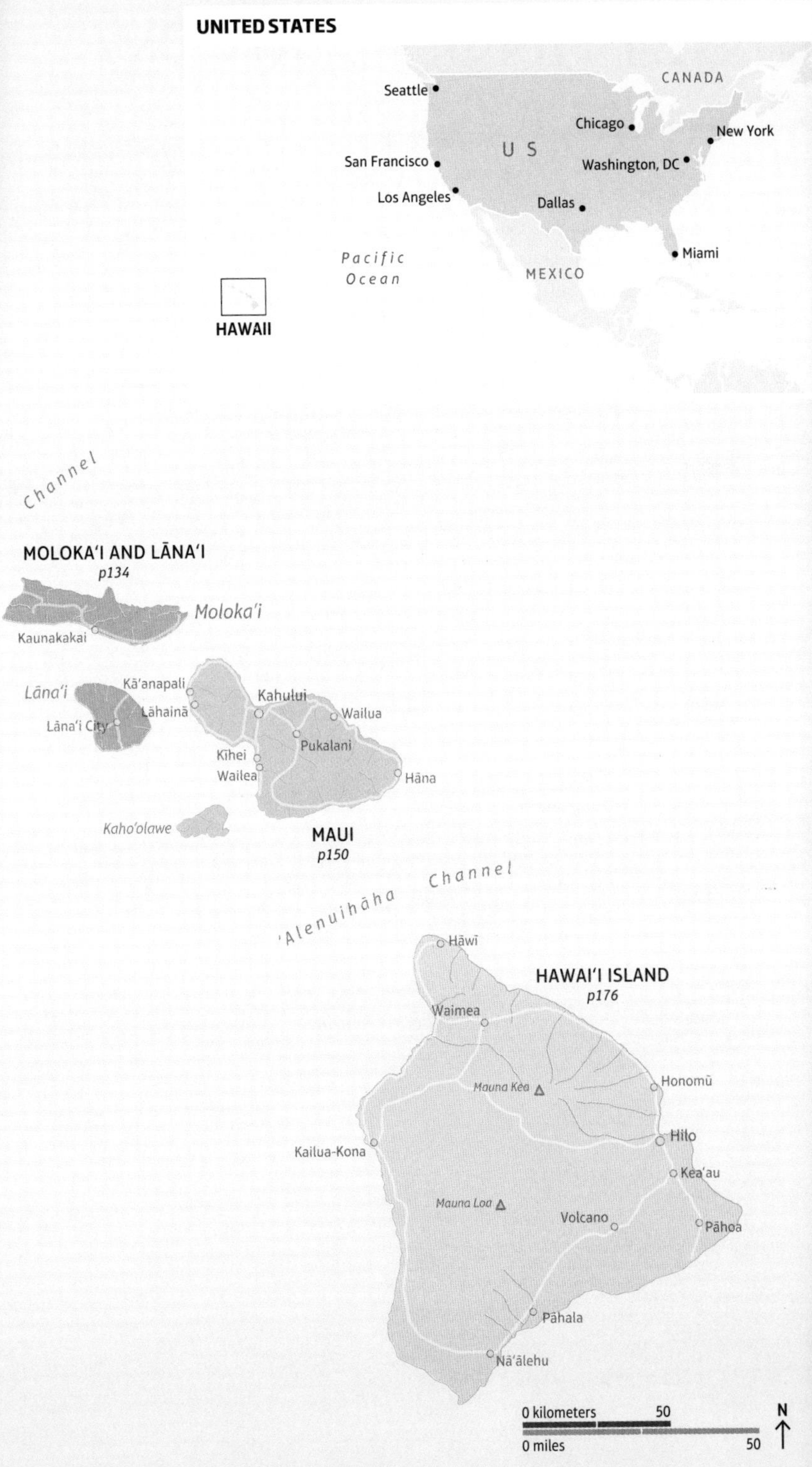
UNITED STATES
CANADA
Seattle
Chicago
New York
U S
San Francisco
Washington, DC
Los Angeles
Dallas
Miami
Pacific Ocean
MEXICO
HAWAII
Channel
MOLOKA'I AND LĀNA'I
p134
Moloka'i
Kaunakakai
Lāna'i
Kā'anapali
Lāhainā
Lāna'i City
Kahului
Wailua
Pukalani
Kīhei
Wailea
Hāna
Kaho'olawe
MAUI
p150
'Alenuihāhā Channel
Hāwī
HAWAI'I ISLAND
p176
Waimea
Mauna Kea
Honomū
Hilo
Kailua-Kona
Kea'au
Mauna Loa
Volcano
Pāhoa
Pāhala
Nā'ālehu
0 kilometers 50
0 miles 50
N

GETTING TO KNOW HAWAII

Set in the middle of the Pacific, Hawaii is an isolated archipelago consisting of six main inhabited islands and over 100 smaller ones. O'ahu, home to the state's capital Honolulu, is the most populated island in the chain, while Hawai'i, aptly named the "Big Island," is the largest.

HONOLULU

PAGE 66

Nestled between forest-blanketed peaks and sparkling ocean, compact Honolulu is both the island of O'ahu's main city and the capital of the state of Hawaii. The city's core is Downtown, an area home to the historic Capitol District and to buzzing Chinatown, with its range of excellent restaurants and cool art galleries. Nearby lies the famous neighborhood of Waikīkī, known for its sublime stretch of beach, routinely recognized as one of the world's best. Just beyond the center are several world-famous sights, including the illuminating Bishop Museum and poignant Pearl Harbor.

Best for
Nightlife and cultural sights

Home to
Chinatown, Waikīkī Beach, Bishop Museum, Pearl Harbor

Experience
A classic Mai Tai cocktail at a beachside bar on Waikīkī Beach

PAGE 120

O'AHU

Thickly forested slopes, tumbling waterfalls, and powder-soft beaches: O'ahu is not short on natural beauty, or on outdoor adventure opportunities. The North Shore is lapped by Pacific waves just perfect for surfing, while the island's interior is criss-crossed by lush volcanic crater trails. O'ahu's southern tip is blessed with one of Hawaii's most striking sights, the half-moon-shaped Hanauma Bay, whose clear, warm waters are a magnet for snorkelers. Found around the island is an enticing mix of outdoor museums, relaxed towns, and tooth-some food trucks serving up fresh, local cuisine.

Best for
Laid-back island life

Home to
Hanauma Bay

Experience
Surfing the big, blue waves of the North Shore

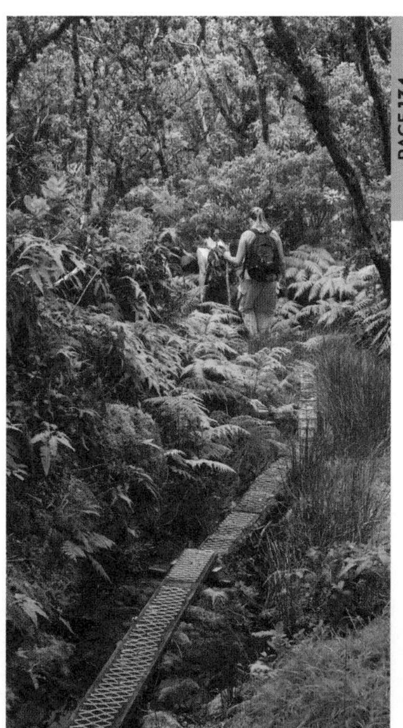

PAGE 134

MOLOKA'I AND LĀNA'I

These less-visited isles might be smaller than the other Hawaiian Islands, but they still pack a punch. On Moloka'i, the larger of the two, you'll find the world's highest sea cliffs and one of the best beaches in the whole state, Pāpōhaku, known for its stunning stretch of white sand. Moloka'i's unusual history, meanwhile, is recounted at the Kalaupapa National Historical Park, a remote peninsula that was once a leper colony. South of Moloka'i, little Lāna'i offers marine-rich reefs and remote crater trails, as well as ancient petroglyphs and historic ruins.

Best for
Off-the-beaten-path adventure

Home to
Kalaupapa National Historical Park

Experience
Diving with green sea turtles, octopuses, and shoals of fish at the Lāna'i Cathedrals

→

PAGE 150

MAUI

Called the "Valley Isle," Maui is dominated by two volcanoes connected by a narrow stretch of land. Haleakalā, a vast shield volcano to the east, is famed for its Mars-like summit area, while the older Mauna Kahālāwai, or West Maui Mountains, are draped in vegetation and home to the historic ʻIao Valley. Beachfront resorts and relaxed towns, including Kīhei and upscale Wailea, dot the island, while the Road to Hāna, one of the world's best driving routes, traces the edge of the winding east coast. The surrounding seas, meanwhile, play host to migrating whales during the winter months.

Best for
Ocean activities

Home to
Haleakalā National Park

Experience
Watching humpback whales breaching the waves along Maui's coast

PAGE 174

HAWAI'I ISLAND

Often referred to as the "Big Island," Hawai'i is the largest of the Hawaiian Islands. Its sun-drenched coast is dotted with colorful beaches, while the interior is a mix of snowy peaks, barren lava fields, fiery volcanic craters, and emerald valleys laced with waterfalls. The island's western side is famed for its coffee farms and historic sights, including ancient temples and old fishing villages, while the east coast is home to a number of verdant gardens, and the quaint town of Hilo, Hawai'i's largest settlement.

Best for
Impressive feats of nature

Home to
Hilo, Pu'uhonua O Hōnaunau National Historical Park, Hawai'i Volcanoes National Park, Waipi'o Valley, Mauna Kea

Experience
The fiery power of the highly active Kīlauea Volcano in Hawai'i Volcanoes National Park

PAGE 210

KAUA'I

The oldest of the Hawaiian Islands, Kaua'i is known as the "Garden Isle" thanks to the dense swaths of emerald forest that cloak its lofty ridges and undulating valleys. A large section of the island's northwest coast is given over to the Nāpali Coast State Wilderness Park, an area of fluted cliffs overlooking remote sandy beaches and teal-colored waters. Around the rest of the coastline lie oceanside towns, crescent-shaped bays, and sugar-sand beaches. Further inland is Waimea Canyon, dubbed the "Grand Canyon of the Pacific," and Kōke'e State Park, a hiker's paradise that overflows with native wildlife.

Best for
Outdoor pursuits

Home to
Līhu'e, Waimea Canyon and Kōke'e State Parks, Nāpali Coast State Wilderness Park

Experience
The remote and stunning Nāpali Coast by sailboat

1 Hanauma Bay's stunning curved beach and blue waters.

2 The USS *Missouri* battleship at Pearl Harbor.

3 View from Diamond Head.

4 Murals in Kaka'ako.

An archipelago known for its stunning natural beauty and easygoing lifestyle, the Hawaiian Islands are bursting with an array of amazing adventures. Wherever you choose to go, our handpicked itineraries will help you plan the perfect trip.

13 DAYS

in Hawaii

Day 1

There's no better spot to start your two-week tour of Hawaii than on Honolulu's world-famous Waikīkī Beach *(p96)*. A few hours of sunbathing on this strip of soft, golden sand and you'll definitely be on "island time." If all this lazing leaves you hungry, pop into nearby Heavenly Island Lifestyle *(p103)* for a delicious farm-to-table brunch. Spend the afternoon wandering round the Bishop Museum *(p108)*, a treasure trove of Polynesian art and artifacts.

Day 2

Rise with the sun and drive to pristine Hanauma Bay *(p124)*, an amazing snorkeling spot. The turquoise-hued sea here is filled with shoals of brightly colored fish, green sea turtles, and even manta rays. Back in Honolulu, grab a bite to eat at Hana Koa Brewing Co. *(p88)*, then wend your way into the Kaka'ako neighborhood *(p88)* to admire its colorful murals. In need of a little retail therapy? The area's SALT shopping mall sells everything from 'ukuleles to locally made chocolate.

Day 3

It's up early this morning to take a muddy but enchanting one-hour hike through dense rainforest to reach the tumbling Mānoa Falls *(p116)*. Afterward, it's over to The Curb Kaimuki *(p115)* for an aromatic cup of locally roasted coffee and a pastry before visiting Pearl Harbor *(p110)*. This poignant national memorial is filled with museums and monuments that recount the infamous World War II attack.

Day 4

For 360-degree panoramas over Honolulu and beyond, start the day with a pleasant hike up Diamond Head *(p117)*, a stunning volcanic crater to the east of the city. Once you've descended, the Hawaiian-Japanese plate lunches at the Pioneer Saloon *(p115)* are a great way to re-energize. Enjoy a couple of hours relaxing on Kahanamoku Beach *(p98)* before taking a short flight to Hawai'i – aka the "Big Island" – in the evening.

Day 5

Waipi'o Valley *(p192)* is an impressive introduction to your time on Hawai'i. Laced with cascading waterfalls, this lush green valley was Kamehameha I's playground as a boy. When hunger strikes, make for the Waimea Coffee Company *(65-1279 Kawaihae Rd, Waimea)* for a lunch of organic salads and Kona-grown coffee. See out the day by chilling on the beach next to your hotel, the luxury Mauna Kea Beach Hotel *(p201)*.

→

1

2

3

Day 6

Dedicate today to exploring the barren, lunar-like landscape of Hawai'i Volcanoes National Park *(p184)*. The scenic Crater Rim Drive *(p185)* takes you to the edge of the smoldering Kīlauea Caldera, Hawaii's most active volcano, and past several other excellent viewpoints. On the way you can pull in and descend into the Thurston Lava Tube *(p186)*, a lava-carved tunnel known for its shimmering, mineral-rich walls. In the evening, continue west to Hilo *(p178)*, a pleasant, characterful town.

Day 7

Spend an easygoing hour or two browsing the collection of Hawaiian cultural items at Hilo's Lyman Museum *(p180)*. A short drive away is Suisan Fish Market *(p181)*, where you can enjoy the island's best ahi tuna poke for lunch. In the afternoon, take a short, easy walk to Rainbow Falls *(p180)*, a pretty waterfall whose spray creates shimmering rainbows. While away the rest of the day at the Hawaii Tropical Botanical Garden *(p203)*, a beautiful spot overflowing with tropical plants and colorful birds.

Day 8

Fly out of Hilo's airport on to Maui, an island famous for its magnificent shorelines. Your first stop is Kā'anapali *(p160)*: sink your toes into the white sands of its 3-mile (5-km) beach before grabbing a refreshing treat at Ono Gelato Co. *(Whalers Village, 2435 Kā'anapali Pkwy)*. As evening rolls in, head down to Ma'alaea and go on a sunset dinner cruise with PacWhale Eco-Adventures *(pacwhale.com)*; if you're lucky, you might even spot a humpback whale or two.

Day 9

Today is all about the otherworldly beauty of Haleakalā National Park *(p154)*, home to a vast shield volcano. Take in the views of the Mars-like scenery from the Pu'u'ula'ula Summit, the highest point on Maui, then traverse the Halemau'u Trail, which winds its way across the barren landscape to an arid crater floor. You'll need to refuel after all that exploration, so round the day off with a belly-filling Hawaiian dinner at Hali'imaile General Store *(900 Hali'imaile Rd, Makawao)*, a true farm-to-table restaurant.

1 The Thurston Lava Tube. ↑

2 Snorkeling with tropical fish off the coast of Molokini.

3 Hiker walking the Kalalau Trail.

4 Sunrise over Hanalei Pier and Bay.

5 Hanapēpē's beautiful Glass Beach.

Day 10

A short hop, skip, and a jump away by catamaran is Molokini *(p166)*, a crescent-shaped volcanic crater ridge found off the southwest coast of Maui. The teal-colored waters surrounding this tiny islet are teeming with shoals of tropical fish, including reef triggerfish and yellow tang. Spend the best part of the day here snorkeling and snuba diving (a cross between scuba and snorkeling, without tanks); Pride of Maui *(prideofmaui.com)* offers a five-hour boat tour.

Day 11

Hop on a plane to the Eden-like island of Kaua'i and make for Hanalei *(p226)*, a half-moon bay surrounded by stunning emerald ridges. The historic Hanalei Pier, built in 1892, is a lovely place to stroll; grab an organic sandwich made with a wholesome taro bun from the Fresh Bite food truck *(p226)* set up by the pier. Refueled, make for the golden sands of Lumaha'i Beach *(p228)* to indulge in a bit of beachcombing. As evening arrives, check into 1 Hotel Hanalei Bay *(p229)* for a dose of pure luxury.

Day 12

Devote the day to hiking the first section of the epic Kalalau Trail in the Nāpali Coast State Wilderness Park *(p218)*. Running from Ke'e Beach to Hanakāpī'ai Beach, this 4-mile (6.5-km) out-and-back route follows a cliff-side path lined with lush foliage. On the way are jaw-dropping views of the Nāpali Coast, with its massive fluted ridges plunging down into the blue sea. In the evening, kick back at Hanalei Gourmet *(p226)*, where you can listen to live music and nibble on coconut shrimp.

Day 13

The last day of your grand voyage will be spent on Kaua'i's southern end, starting at the golden sands of Po'ipū Beach *(p234)*. Here you can boogie board, snorkel, or surf the day away (rentals are available at the beach). Then drive up to funky artists' enclave Hanapēpē *(p234)* to visit Glass Beach, a stunning stretch made entirely of smooth sea glass. Complete the day, and your trip, at the Kaua'i Island Brewery & Grill *(4350 Waialo Rd)* with a sample flight of beers and a big plate of Kalua pork nachos.

1

2

3

4 DAYS

on O'ahu

Day 1

Morning Visit Honolulu's Capitol District this morning to soak up some of Hawaii's history (it's a quick bus or taxi ride from Waikīkī). Start at the absorbing Hawaiian Mission Houses Museum *(p84)*, which preserves the oldest houses in Hawaii. Across the street is Kawaiaha'o Church *(p86)*, built out of coral blocks for American missionaries in 1842. Next, stroll across to the lavish 'Iolani Palace *(p84)*, home to Queen Lili'uokalani before the monarchy was overthrown in 1893.

Afternoon It's a short walk from the palace along King Street into the heart of the city's Chinatown *(p80)*. Here you can browse the gift shops and grab lunch – sample Cantonese dishes at Mei Sum Dim Sum *(meisumdimsum.com)*, or try The Pig and the Lady *(p82)*, a Vietnamese restaurant. After lunch, wander over to the Izumo Taisha Shrine, an authentic Japanese Shinto shrine. Spend the rest of your afternoon in the free Capitol Modern *(p86)*, which has a superb collection of local contemporary and Polynesian art.

Day 2

Morning Dedicate at least half a day to Pearl Harbor National Memorial *(p110)*, one of America's most venerated military sites. Arrive early to avoid the crowds, and take the tour of the USS *Arizona* Memorial first (make reservations in advance). This floats above the ship of the same name that was sunk during the 1941 Japanese raid – more than 1,100 sailors remain entombed below, making this a very moving experience. Spend time perusing the exhibits in the Pearl Harbor Visitor Center and take an absorbing tour of the USS *Missouri*, on which the Japanese surrendered in 1945.

Afternoon A great spot for lunch is Restaurant 604 *(restaurant604.com)*, a short walk from the Pearl Harbor Visitor Center and right on the water. It serves burgers, sandwiches, and Hawaiian favorites such as grilled *mahi mahi* fish, Kalua pork, and *loco moco* (rice topped with a burger patty, eggs, and gravy). In the afternoon, drive over to the stunning Bishop Museum *(p108)*. You'll need a couple of hours to do justice to this huge collection of rare Polynesian art and artifacts.

1 Kawaiaha'o Church in Honolulu.

2 People snorkeling at Hanauma Bay.

3 The striking USS *Arizona* Memorial at Pearl Harbor.

4 Performers at the Polynesian Cultural Center.

5 Trees over Nu'uanu Pali Highway.

Day 3

Morning Today involves the most driving, so get an early start and head up the Kamehameha Highway to O'ahu's North Shore. Beaches are the main attraction here – family-friendly Hale'iwa Beach Park *(p130)* makes a good introduction. Have a tasty Hawaiian lunch at Haleiwa Joe's *(haleiwajoes.com)* in Hale'iwa itself *(p130)*. A dessert at Scoop of Paradise *(66-145 Kamehameha Hwy)* after is a must.

Afternoon Drive farther along the coast to Waimea Valley *(p131)*, a lush botanical garden just inland, with a short, blossom-draped trail to a plunging jungle waterfall. Afterward, you can swim or snorkel at nearby Waimea Bay Beach Park, or drive up to watch daredevil surfers tackle the world-famous Banzai Pipeline *(p130)*.

Evening It's around 14 miles (23 km) to the Polynesian Cultural Center *(p131)* from Waimea. Aim to get here in time for dinner (you can reserve the Ali'i Luau Buffet) and the spectacular evening cultural show, which features over 100 Polynesian performers.

Day 4

Morning Start by driving the spectacular Pali Highway, or Hawaii Route 61 from Honolulu, which snakes up the Nu'uanu Valley and over the dizzying Ko'olau Range. En route, make time for several scenic viewpoints and Queen Emma Summer Palace *(p114)*, which has a small museum dedicated to the Hawaiian royal family. On the other side of the mountains, travel up the northeast coast to the Byodo-In Temple *(p126)*. From here, head south to Kailua Beach Park *(p127)*, and grab a burger at Buzz's Original Steakhouse *(buzzsoriginalsteakhouse.com)*.

Afternoon Spend the rest of the day making a loop on Route 72 around the eastern Makapu'u region, which bulges out into the Pacific. Highlights include family-friendly Kaupō Beach Park, and the dazzling views over the coast at Makapu'u Point *(p126)*, where you can hike to historic Makapu'u Lighthouse. Finish up at the beautiful Hanauma Bay Nature Preserve *(p124)*, a protected cove renowned for its snorkeling. It's a short trip back to Honolulu from here.

1

2

3

6 DAYS
on Maui

Day 1

Spend your first morning at sheltered Wailea Beach *(p168)* on Maui's leeward coast. The waves are tame so snorkeling is excellent here and you're likely to see green sea turtles in the water. After some beach time, walk up to The Shops at Wailea *(3750 Wailea Alanui Dr)* and pop into Island Gourmet Markets for some snacks for the week. On your way out from the mall, grab a coffee and an açai bowl from Island Vintage Coffee *(islandvintagecoffee.com)*. In the afternoon, drive down to Mākena State Park *(p168)* and go on a kayak tour of the coastline here with Maui Kayaks *(maui kayaks.com)*. Then, as the sun sets in warm peach tones, dine on fresh local seafood at the romantic Nick's Fishmarket Maui in the opulent Fairmont Kea Lani *(fairmont.com)* – your luxurious base in Maui.

Day 2

In the morning, drive north along the coast, stopping at the Olowalu General Store where an easy footpath leads up to 300-year-old petroglyphs, known locally as Pu'u Kilea *(820 Olowalu Village Rd)*, carved into the cliffs. Then continue north to Ka'anapali *(p160)* and stroll along the sugary white beach, keeping your eyes peeled for humpback whales in the distance. Stay put for the afternoon and enjoy a dip in the ocean, or a spot of retail therapy at Whalers Village – the green Ka'anapali trolley will whisk you there for free. Come evening, enjoy a tradi-tional Hawaiian feast and performances of Polynesian song and dance at the beachfront Maui Nui Lū'au *(sheratonmauiluau.com)*.

Day 3

It's an extra-early start today as you drive up to Haleakalā National Park *(p154)* to catch the sunrise from the summit of this enormous volcano. Afterward, hike the full-day Sliding Sands Trail that descends into the otherworldly landscape of the crater, and passes by cinder cones and Kawilinau, a volcanic pit. Revive yourself post-hike with a mouthwatering Hawaiian barbecue chicken plate from L&L Hawai'ian Barbecue *(247 Piikea Av, Kīhei)* and devour it back at your hotel beach. Finish the

1 The golden sands of Wailea Beach.

2 Shops and restaurants at Whalers Village.

3 Harvesting of taro in Halawa Valley.

4 Kalaupapa National Historical Park.

5 A waterfall on the Road to Hāna.

evening with a well-deserved cocktail at the hotel's lounge, Pilina, surrounded by the soothing sounds of the 'ukulele.

Day 4

Fly over to the island of Moloka'i to take a tour of the stunning Halawa Valley with Molokai Outdoors (*molokaioutdoors.com*). You'll spend the day wandering through an ancient Hawaiian village and farm with an informative guide, who'll explain the history of the area, before stopping for lunch at a tranquil waterfall. Don't miss the afternoon treats back at the farm– the local chocolate and fresh fruit smoothies are divine. When you arrive back on Maui, head straight to the lively patio of Esters Fair Prospect *(2050 Main St, Wailuku)*, a tiny bar that serves up locally sourced small plates and a variety of delicious tropical cocktails.

Day 5

The epic Road to Hāna *(p172)*, one of the world's most spectacular driving routes, beckons today. This winding road follows Maui's stunning eastern coast, and passes by waterfalls, lava tube caverns, and lush botanical gardens along the way. And if you get peckish, no problem – there's plenty of snack spots en route, too, including Coconut Glen's *(p171)* which serves delicious organic and vegan ice cream made with local coconuts.

Day 6

First on the list is a drive along the verdant 'Īao Valley *(p167)*, which snakes through the West Maui Mountains. On the way, stop off at the Kepaniwai Heritage Gardens, a pretty county park that celebrates Maui's multicultural heritage via different gardens, including a Portuguese garden and a Japanese one. After, head to Wailuku *(p163)* and pick up a delicious Japanese bento box and dessert from Shikeda Bento Patisserie (*shikedamaui.com*). Next up is the impressive Maui Ocean Center *(p166)*, where you can wander through a glass-tunnel aquarium while sharks and rays glide on by. Round off your trip with beers and pizza at the Maui Brewing Co. *(605 Lipoa Pkwy)* in the lively tourist town of Kīhei *(p166)*.

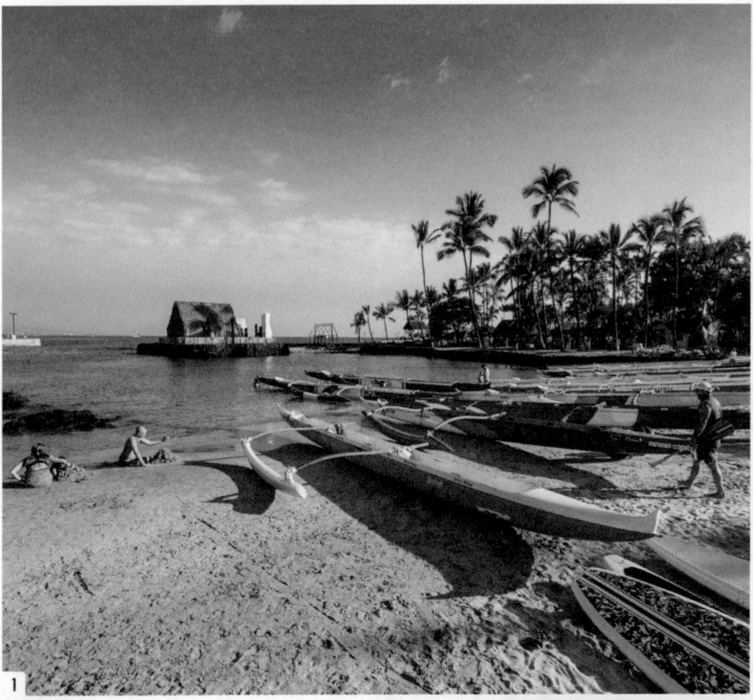
1

2

3

4

←

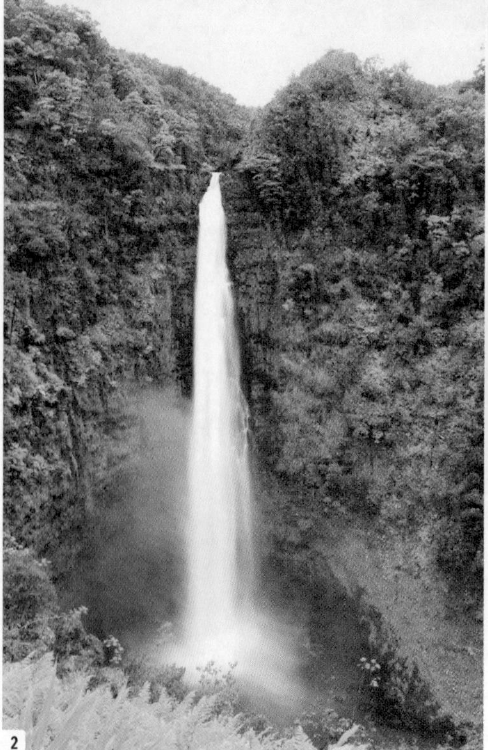

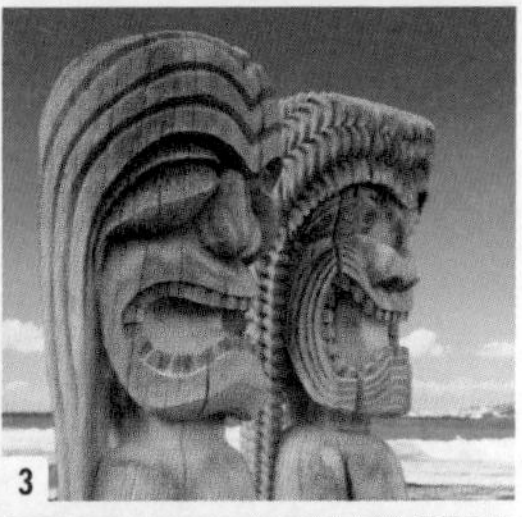

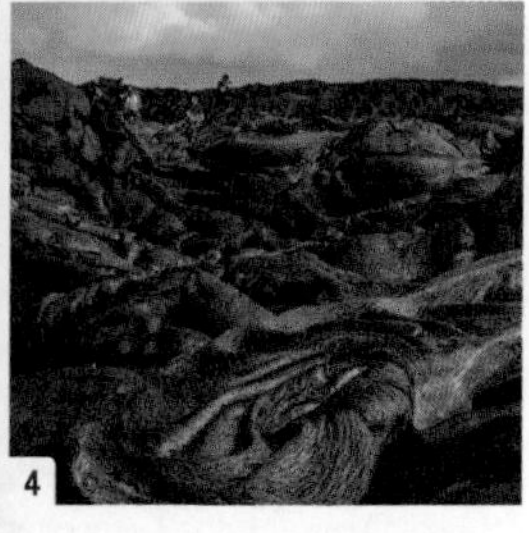

1 The beach at Kailua-Kona.

2 'Akaka Falls State Park.

3 Wooden *Ki'i* at Pu'uhonua O Hōnaunau.

4 Lava landscapes in Hawai'i Volcanoes National Park.

5 DAYS

on Hawai'i Island

Day 1

Landing on Hawai'i, drive straight to Kailua-Kona *(p196)*, a relaxed tourist town known as Kona to the locals. Take a stroll along oceanfront Ali'i Drive, then pop inside the historic Hulihe'e Palace: this former holiday home of the Hawaiian royals is now a museum dedicated to their lifestyle. Afterward, go to the Kona Brewing Company *(p197)* for tasty fish tacos and excellent beer, then work off lunch by snorkeling at nearby Kahalu'u Beach Park just south of Kona. Huggo's on the Rocks *(75-5828 Kahakai Rd)* is a great place to end the day with a sunset cocktail.

Day 2

Drive south and spend a couple of hours wandering around Pu'uhonua O Hōnaunau National Historical Park *(p182)*, a 16th-century sanctuary. Here, you can admire fierce-looking wooden *Ki'i* and a reconstructed *heiau* (temple) that once held the bones of important chiefs. A short drive north is Kona Coffee Living History Farm *(p196)*, which tells the story of the island's first coffee growers, as well as offering tours and tastings. Back in Kona, grab a juicy burger from Ultimate Burger *(p197)* and complete the day with a night snorkel or dive with giant manta rays; Sea Paradise offers organized tours *(seaparadise.com)*.

Day 3

Spend the whole day exploring Hawai'i Volcanoes National Park *(p184)*. It's a two-hour drive from Kona to reach this fiery landscape, so break up the journey with a stop at Punalu'u Beach *(p205)*, a jet-black beach fringed with lush palm trees. Once you reach the park, cruise around the Chain of Craters Road *(p186)*, which will take you from rainforest to lava fields. If you fancy a walk, try one of the hiking trails found along the route, which includes one that leads to thousands of petroglyphs. Then, head east to Hilo *(p178)*, on the verdant side of Hawai'i Island, where a fine seafood dinner awaits at Moon and Turtle *(p181)*.

Day 4

Devour a stack of fluffy pancakes for breakfast at Ken's House of Pancakes *(1730 Kamehameha Av)*, then hit the road. Hilo is the starting point for a scenic drive up the Hāmākua Coast *(p206)*, which winds up the island's lush windward side. There are plenty of great stops along the way, including 'Akaka Falls State Park *(p203)*, famed for its spectacular cascades. Make sure to grab a Hawaiian lunch at the Tex Drive-In *(p204)* in Honoka'a, and finish with a *malasada* (donut) for dessert. At last you'll reach the much drier Kohala Coast, where you'll spend the night at the luxurious Mauna Kea Beach Hotel *(p201)*.

Day 5

Enjoy an oceanside breakfast at the hotel and then spend the morning lazing at the gorgeous crescent beach just steps away. In the afternoon, rent a kayak or SUP and make your way south to Hāpuna Beach *(p200)*, another postcard-perfect bay of champagne sand and turquoise waters. Finish your time on Hawai'i Island at the hotel's own *lū'au*, where you'll be treated to a feast of traditional food, as well as performances of Polynesian music and dance.

1

2

3

6 DAYS on Kaua'i

Day 1

Begin your journey on the "Garden Isle" in the laid-back town of Līhu'e *(p214)*. The Kaua'i Museum is a great spot to learn all about the history of the island and its Indigenous people. After you've soaked up some history, visit the Aloha 'Aina Juice Cafe *(p215)* for a healthy açai bowl, then take a dip at the half-moon Kalapakī Beach *(p214)*, Līhu'e's main swimming spot. As the light fades, grab a seat at Duke's Kauai *(p215)* and enjoy tasty coconut shrimp, a cocktail sipped out of a pineapple, and stunning views of the bay. Then it's off to beachy Wailua *(p222)*, where the elegant Waipouli Beach Resort *(p223)* makes the perfect base for your time on the island.

Day 2

Drive southwest this morning to Po'ipū Beach *(p234)*, swinging by Little Fish Coffee *(p235)* first for a breakfast bagel and fresh smoothie. The beach is a popular one, and for good reason – it's a slice of tropical paradise with pristine waters and golden sands, which rare monk seals like to sunbathe on, too.

After some sunning and snorkeling, continue west to wander around the shady Allerton Garden *(p232)*, whose fig trees starred in *Jurassic Park*. Across the road is a stunning natural blowhole, Spouting Horn *(p235)*, worth a careful peek from the designated lookout. End the day in Līhu'e with a tasty poke bowl from The Fish Express *(3–3343 Kuhio Hwy)*.

Day 3

Wake up early and go on a guided kayak tour up the mellow Wailua River *(p222)* with Kayak Wailua *(kayakwailua.com)*, passing by feral chickens and an ancient Hawaiian village with reconstructed huts. Tie up your boat and explore the village, then continue on foot via spectacular canyons and dense rainforest to the secluded Uluwehi Falls *(p222)*, also known as Secret Falls – it's the perfect place for a dip. In the afternoon, make for Anahola Bay *(p225)*, unroll your towel, and relax on the beach as you watch boogie boarders paddle around in the calm ocean waves. Dinner and drinks are at the casual Lava Lava Beach Club *(420 Papaloa Rd, Kapa'a)*, just an oceanside stroll away from your hotel.

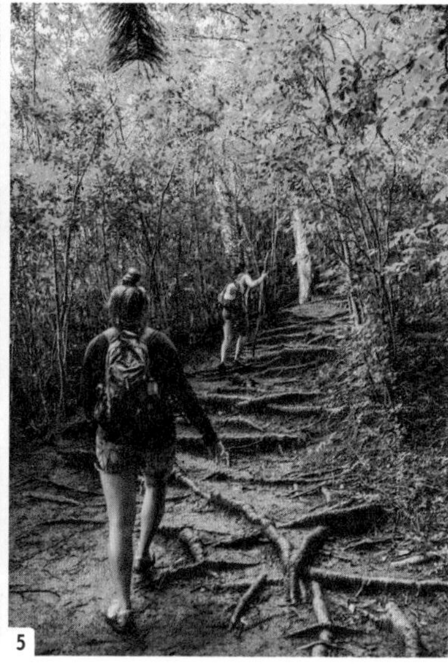

1 The rust-red Waimea Canyon.

2 Kalapaki Beach's sandy shore.

3 The emerald cliffs of the Nāpali Coast.

4 Spouting Horn, a powerful blowhole.

5 A walking trail leading to the summit of Sleeping Giant.

Day 4

Drive north to the picturesque bayside community of Hanalei *(p226)*. Take a walk along the pretty pier here, gazing across the crescent-shaped bay toward the surrounding lush mountains, before popping into the Hanalei Bread Company *(p226)* for a late breakfast – the avocado toast is addictive. Then it's off on an afternoon boat trip to the stunning Nāpali Coast State Wilderness Park *(p218)* with Na Pali Catamaran *(napalicatamaran.com)*. You'll be treated to spectacular views of the park's razor-sharp fluted cliffs and a snorkel in the teal-hued waters. Dinner is at Hanalei's Tahiti Nui *(p226)*, a Tahitian restaurant with live Hawaiian music.

Day 5

Head west to explore the jaw-dropping Waimea Canyon, known as the "Grand Canyon of the Pacific" *(p216)*. The road that winds through this state park is dotted with lookouts offering expansive views of the steep-sided gorge, whose crimson walls are covered in green foliage. Keep following the road to reach neighboring Kōke'e State Park *(p216)*, famed for its unique flora and fauna, and excellent hiking. Discover both on the Pihea Vista trail: this 2-mile (3-km) route skirts along the rim of the Kalalau Valley, winds through dense forest home to the native *'i'iwi*, a scarlet bird with a unique squeaky call, and offers views of the emerald cliffs of the Nāpali Coast *(p218)*.

Day 6

Grab a breakfast sandwich at Java Kai *(javakai.com)*, washed down with an iced coffee, then spend an hour or two hiking to the top of Sleeping Giant *(p223)*. There are several routes to the summit, but follow the west trailhead for a moderate mountain hike with great coastal views. After, drive north, stopping at the Moloa'a Sunrise Fruit Stand *(p225)* for a reviving smoothie before reaching Kīlauea Point *(p224)*. Take a walk out along this rugged promontory toward the simple Kīlauea Lighthouse, keeping an eye out for birds, including the black-winged Laysan albatross, along the way. For dinner, reward yourself with a Hawaiian feast at the Smith Family Garden Luau *(smithskauai.com)*.

Superb Stargazing

Remote and far from big city lights, the Hawaiian Islands offer a nighttime spectacle like no other. Drive up toward the top of Maui's Haleakalā *(p154)* or Hawai'i Island's Mauna Kea *(p194)*, both volcanoes, to see some of the clearest and darkest skies in the world. If you're based on the coast, pick out your favorite constellations while the waves crash on the shore at Moloka'i's beautiful Pāpōhaku Beach *(p146)*.

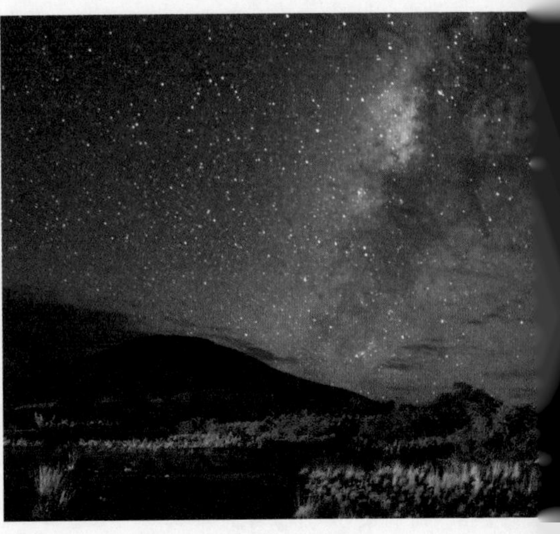

→ A shimmering blanket of stars seen from Mauna Kea, on Hawai'i Island

HAWAII FOR NATURAL WONDERS

It's no secret: this clutch of islands is a natural paradise. Brooding volcanoes, colorful sandy beaches, and tropical rainforests bursting with flora cover the landscape. Up above, the nighttime skies also put on quite a show.

Multicolored Sands

Bored of the same old bland sand? You're in luck – Hawaii is home to an array of beaches with unusual hues. Hit up Papakōlea *(p205)*, Hawai'i Island's green-sand beach, which owes its tint to Mauna Loa's olivine crystals. On Maui, Kaihalulu Beach *(p169)* is lined with red, iron-rich sand, and Wai'ānapanapa State Park is home to a black-sand beach, formed from lava.

↑ The striking black-sand beach in Wai'ānapanapa State Park, Maui

Vehemently Volcanic

Mighty volcanoes loom over this entire archipelago. Lava-laden landscapes can be found in the fiery Hawai'i Volcanoes National Park *(p184)*. If you'd rather swerve the active volcanoes, climb to the top of Pu'u'ula'ula Summit, which offers mind-bending views of the dormant Haleakalā *(p154)*.

→ Lava flowing from Kīlauea Volcano, in Hawai'i Volcanoes National Park

Flowers and Gardens

You'll see verdant plant life everywhere you turn in Hawaii. Botany enthusiasts can head to the Waimea Valley *(p131)*, a giant botanical garden on O'ahu that is covered in rare tropical plants. The Lyon Arboretum *(p116)*, near Honolulu, has over 6,000 plant species, including the bright yellow hibiscus (the official state flower), while Kaua'i's Limahuli Garden *(p229)* celebrates the connection between Hawaii's people and plants.

← A tropical heliconia flower blooming at the Lyon Arboretum, just outside Honolulu

BEST TIME TO VISIT HAWAII

Thanks to its tropical climate, average day-time temperatures in Hawaii seldom drop below 80°F (27°C), making it a great year-round destination. The weather does vary according to season, however: during *kauwela* (summer), which runs from May to October, the weather tends to be drier, while *ho'oilo* (winter), which usually lasts from November to April, sees an increase in rainfall. The ocean is also affected by these seasons, tending to be placid during the summer months, and turning rougher come winter.

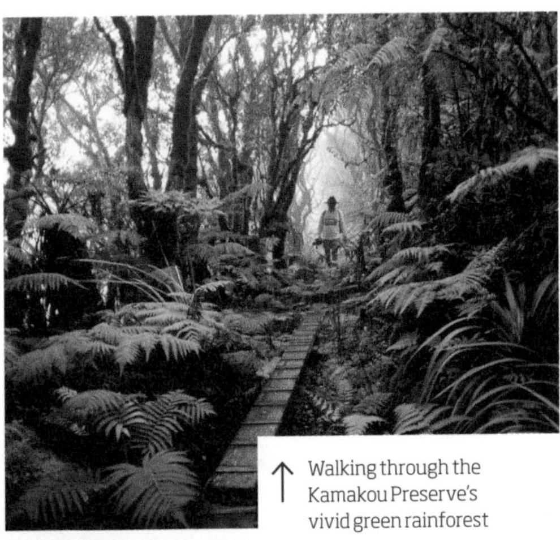

↑ Walking through the Kamakou Preserve's vivid green rainforest

Lush Rainforests

You'll find some of Hawaii's most spectacular tropical rainforests in the Kamakou Preserve *(p144)*, on Moloka'i. This unspoiled landscape, woven with moss-covered paths, is famous for its colorful *'ōhi'a* trees. Elsewhere, the tracts of emerald forest that surround Honolulu are teeming with bird life and exotic flora.

FLORA OF THE HAWAIIAN ISLANDS

By the time early Polynesians had their sights set on the shores of the Hawaiian Islands over 1,500 years ago, this isolated archipelago was already brimming with diverse vegetation. Some 300 immigrant flowering plant species – seeds borne by wind, carried by birds, or drifting on the ocean – arrived on the islands. Over millions of years, many of these species evolved, some into new forms entirely. As a result, native flora is unique here, with over 90 per cent found only in Hawaii.

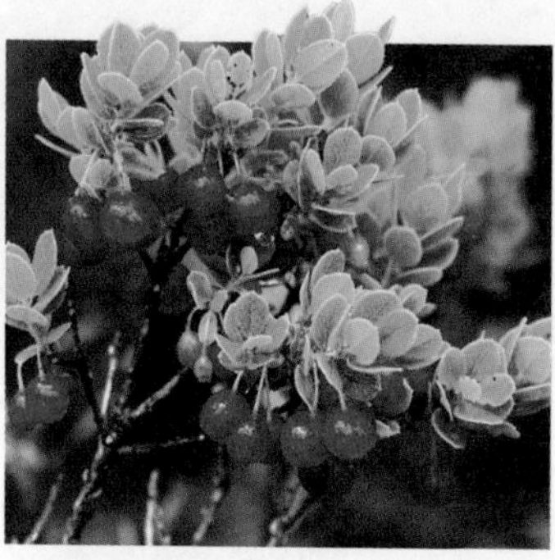

↑ Vibrant red *'ohelo* berries, found throughout Hawaii

EDIBLE BERRIES

An endemic shrub, *'Ākala*, or Hawaiian raspberry, produces juicy, sour berries that can reach the size of a golf ball. Hawaiians would crush them to produce dye for coloring *kapa* (traditional Hawaiian fabric). Another endemic shrub is the *'ōhelo*, a close relative of the cranberry and blueberry, with sweet pink, orange, and yellow fruit loved by the *nēnē* (Hawaiian goose). Both berries are often used to make pies and jams.

MEDICINAL PLANTS

Vivid green ferns, carpeting Hawaii's rainforests and poking out of newly hardened lava, have thrived here since the formation of the islands. The *uluhe* fern, known for its purple coil during its early stages of life, was traditionally made into a drink by Hawaiians and used as a cure for intestinal disorders.

GRASSES AND DECORATIVE FLOWERS

Early Hawaiians frequently utilized the endemic grasses on the islands. One of the most commonly used was *pili* grass, which was ideal for thatching roofs and stuffing mattresses. Local flora, especially the hibiscus flower, has also played a role in Hawaiian culture. Seven species of hibiscus are endemic to the islands. Their flowers were once a symbol of power and respect for Hawaiians. Now they are more often used for fashioning into lei, but the flowers can also be dried and made into tea.

PRACTICAL TREES

One of the most abundant of trees here is the *'ōhi'a lehua*, an endemic species that is part of the myrtle family. Recognizable by their bright red blossoms, though they can also be orange and yellow, these trees flourish in volcanic landscapes. In ancient Hawaii, the tree's hard brown wood was used for building houses, temples, idols, tools, and weapons.

ESPECIALLY RARE FLORA

The silversword, or *'āhinahina*, is a highly endangered plant and is found nowhere else on earth except for Maui and Hawai'i Island, where it clings to cool and dry alpine habitats. A hardy plant, the silversword can live for over 50 years. This species, together with the bog greensword and 25 other shrubs, trees, and a liana (vine), actually evolved in the Hawaiian Islands from one single ancestral immigrant.

VEGETATION ZONES

1 Alpine vegetation
A sparse array of shrubs dominated by silverswords occurs at 9,850–11,150 ft (3,000–3,400 m). This is a harsh, dry zone that can freeze at night.

2 Subalpine communities
These occur in cool, dry zones about 5,575–9,850 ft (1,700–3,000 m) high. Vegetation varies from grassland or shrubland to stunted trees.

3 Montane dry areas
Dry grasslands and forests with a canopy 10–65 ft (3–20 m) high are characteristic of these zones, which occur on leeward slopes at an elevation of 1,650–8,850 ft (500–2,700 m).

4 Montane wetlands
Montane wetlands can occur in areas of high rainfall at elevations of 3,950–7,200 ft (1,200–2,200 m). These zones can include wet herb-lands, sedge-lands, shrublands, bogs, and forests with canopies up to 130 ft (40 m) high.

5 Lowland and coastal communities
These zones include a diverse array of dry, medium, and wet herb, grass, shrub, and forest vegetation that are found occurring below 5,000 ft (1,500 m) elevation.

↑ The striking Kalalau Valley on the island of Kaua'i

◁ Fresh Fruits

With its ideal crop-growing climate, Hawaii is overflowing with fresh fruits. Find groves of strawberry guava trees ready to harvest as a snack along the Kalalau Trail *(p220)* in Kaua'i or savor the juicy yellow star fruit from the KCC Farmers' Market *(p116)* in Honolulu.

▷ Grab a Coffee

For over a century, the slopes of Hualālai and Mauna Loa *(p187)* on Hawai'i Island have been cultivating the world-famous, highly prized (and highly priced) Kona coffee. Enjoy a tasting flight at the Kona Coffee & Tea Company café *(p196)*, or for an informative history lesson, pay a visit to the Kona Coffee Living History Farm *(p196)*, where you can stroll among the coffee trees and peek inside a 1920s farmhouse.

HAWAII FOR FOODIES

Hawaii's cuisine is wonderfully diverse, combining traditional Polynesian dishes with modern, global influences. From the humble, locally grown taro root to fantastic buffet spreads, super-fresh seafood to fluffy donuts, there's much to be enjoyed here.

◁ Food Trucks and Road-Side Delights

Nothing gives you an appetite like an afternoon swimming in the ocean. Luckily, in Hawaii, where there's a beach, there's almost always a food truck dishing up something amazing. Try the taro-based goodies from Hanalei Taro & Juice Co.'s food truck *(hanaleitaro.com)* on Kaua'i. Better yet, attend the Street Eats: A Kailua Village Food Truck Festival in Kailua-Kona every fall.

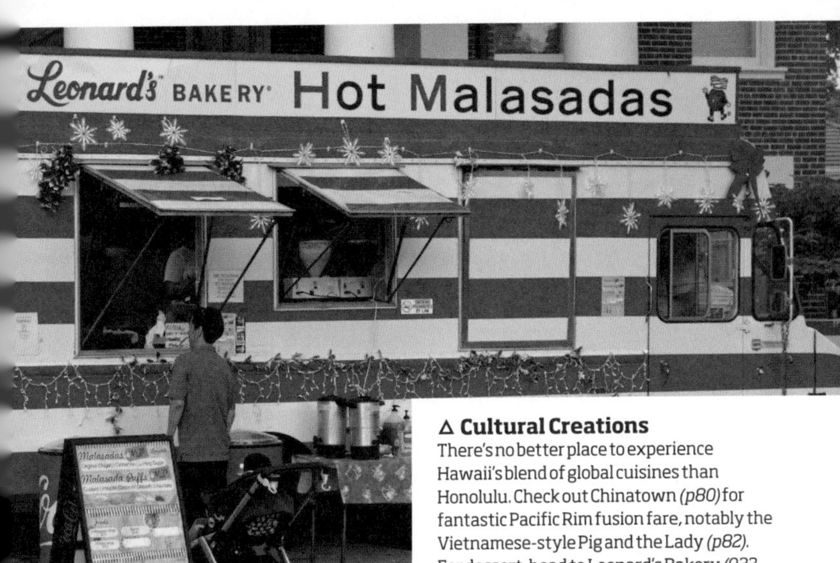

△ Cultural Creations

There's no better place to experience Hawaii's blend of global cuisines than Honolulu. Check out Chinatown *(p80)* for fantastic Pacific Rim fusion fare, notably the Vietnamese-style Pig and the Lady *(p82)*. For dessert, head to Leonard's Bakery *(933 Kapahulu Av)* for cinnamon and sugar-dusted Portuguese *malasadas* (donuts).

▷ The Lū'au

Picture a beachfront restaurant lit up by flaming torches, with the fragrance of plumeria lei in the air, dancers swaying to the sounds of the 'ukulele, and a grand buffet of local dishes on display. This is a *lū'au* - a festive experience with Polynesian origins. Some of the best to attend are the Old Lahaina Lū'au in Maui *(oldlahainaluau.com)* and the Smith Family Garden Luau *(p31)* on Kaua'i.

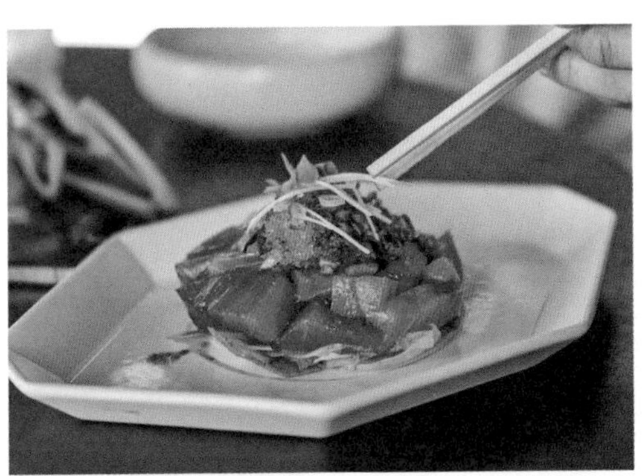

△ Sustainable Seafood

Surrounded by the bountiful Pacific Ocean, it's no surprise that Hawaii is highly acclaimed for its seafood. For sustainably caught ahi tuna poke and buttery sashimi, stop by the Suisan Fish Market *(p181)* in Hilo. Or, for lunch in Ka'anapali, try the *mahi mahi* fish sandwiches at Monkeypod Kitchen *(2435 Kaanapali Pkwy)*.

HAWAIIAN FOODS TO TRY

Shave Ice
Finely shaved ice flavored with fruit syrup.

Poke
Marinated chunks of raw fish, usually tuna, served with various toppings.

Loco Moco
Rice topped with a beef burger patty, a fried egg, and gravy.

Manapua
Hawaiian version of a Chinese bao bun.

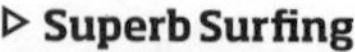

▷ Superb Surfing

Once practiced by royalty, including Hawaii's first king, Kamehameha I, surfing has historically had an honored place in Hawaiian culture. Today, the islands are the ultimate hot spot for the sport, which can be enjoyed by anyone. Po'ipū Beach *(p234)* on Kaua'i is an excellent area for those learning to surf, especially the Kiahuna Beach stretch. Expert wave riders should head to O'ahu's North Shore and Honolua Bay *(p101)* on Maui.

HAWAII FOR BEACHGOERS

From soft sands to wave-lapped shores, Hawaii's beautiful beaches offer an array of different activities. So, hop on your surfboard, order an oceanside cocktail, or simply roll out your beach towel and relax. Pristine turquoise bays and shimmering sands await.

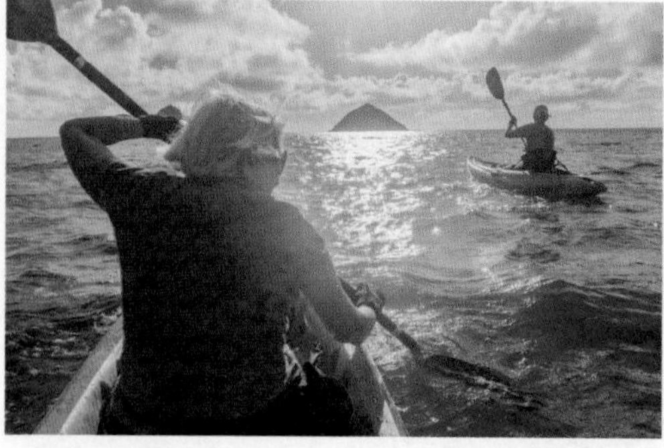

△ Get Active

With balmy climes, crystal-clear waters, and readily available watersport rentals and lessons, getting active out on Hawaii's shores is a breeze. Rent your own watercraft from eco-friendly Kailua Beach Adventures *(kailuabeachadventures.com)* on O'ahu or swim and snorkel at ease in the calm scoop of beach at Mauna Kea Beach on Hawai'i Island.

BEACH SAFETY

The Pacific Ocean is as powerful as it is beautiful. Always pay close attention to the ocean and forecasted conditions, regardless of how experienced a swimmer you are. Watch for rip currents and so-called rogue waves that can appear suddenly, and wear appropriate footwear to protect you from sharp lava rocks, coral, and sea urchins. Check oceansafety.hawaii.gov for current conditions of the beach.

▷ Beach Bars

Dreaming of sipping a tropical cocktail next to a white-sand beach? Hawaii's got you covered. Head to the roomy Duke's Waikiki Barefoot Bar *(dukeswaikiki.com)* for delicious drinks with views of Honolulu's famous Waikīkī Beach *(p96)*. If you're visiting Hawai'i Island, make for Huggo's on the Rocks *(huggosontherocks.com)* to enjoy fresh cocktails on golden sands.

◁ Sunbathing Spots

There's no shortage of sun-kissed sand to lie on in these islands. Majestic scenery can be found at Hanalei Bay *(p227)* on Kaua'i, which features a breathtaking 1-mile (3-km) swath of sugary sand framed by emerald mountains, while Hāpuna Beach *(p200)*, on Hawai'i Island, promises soft champagne sand and all the facilities you might require.

▷ Beachside Events

Hawaii's beaches aren't just about the sun and sand. Attend surfing competitions such as the grand Vans Triple Crown *(triplecrown.vans.com)* on O'ahu, or watch free fireworks shows at Waikīkī Beach *(p96)* every Friday night. If you're feeling peckish, luxuriate in a traditional, beachside *lū'au* feast, such as the Old Lahaina Luau *(oldlahainaluau.com)* on Maui.

△ Secret and Secluded Strands

Hawaii has hundreds of beautiful, and near deserted, beaches to discover. Postcard-perfect Makalawena Beach *(p199)* on Hawai'i Island requires a jaunt across an old lava flow and some sand dunes, but this half-moon strand is rarely occupied. Polihua Beach *(p140)* on Lāna'i has strong currents but its sands are lovely for sunbathing or a stroll.

Road Tripping

Hawaii is home to one of the world's most famous road trips: the winding Road to Hāna *(p172)*. Snaking around Maui's east coast, this route follows curving coastal roads and passes by gorgeous beaches, jungle trails, and waterfalls. That said, Highway 450, which traces a path beneath the verdant peaks of east Moloka'i *(p148)* could give it a run for its money.

↑ The Road to Hāna on Maui, snaking through lush green forest

HAWAII FOR ADVENTURERS

With such a diversity of landscapes and outdoor activities, Hawaii is a great place to get adventurous. Whether you're zip-lining across waterfalls or hiking through an ancient volcanic crater, Hawaii will get your blood pumping.

Seek a Thrill

There's plenty on Hawaii to make your heart rate spike. Soar on zip-lines across beaches, over waterfalls, and above a crater with Skyline Hawaii *(skylinehawaii.com)* on Maui. After a real burst of adrenaline? Go on a cage-free shark diving tour with O'ahu's One Ocean Diving *(oneocean diving.com)*.

← Zooming through the trees high above the ground on a zipline-adventure

Go Beneath the Waves

Explore the depths of O'ahu, Hawai'i Island, and Maui's ocean waters in quiet, battery-powered submarines with Atlantis Submarines *(p98)*. This eco-concious company has also invested in artificial, self-sustaining reefs to ensure that the marine life of these islands can continue to thrive.

→ Passengers on an Atlantis Adventures submarine in Honolulu

Descend into the Earth

Spelunking into the depths of a humid and dark cave is about as adventurous as it gets. Descend into Kazumura Cave on Hawai'i Island, the longest and deepest lava tube in the world, with Kilauea Caverns of Fire *(www.kilaueacavernsoffire.com)*. If you want a slightly more laid-back experience, make for the Hāna Lava Tube *(p169)* on Maui. It's kid-friendly and can be ventured into without a guide.

Descending deep into the heart of the vast Kazumura Cave on Hawai'i Island

TOP 3 HIKES IN HAWAII

Halawa Valley Hike, Moloka'i
A historically rich 3.5-mile (5.5-km) hike that ends with a refreshing waterfall dip. Guide required.

Canyon Trail to Waipo'o Falls, Kaua'i
A moderate 3-mile (5-km) hike through the Grand Canyon of the Pacific *(p216)* to rushing waterfalls.

Munro Trail, Lāna'i
A challenging 13-mile (21-km) hike around the top of the island's caldera rim, offering views of the other islands *(p140)*.

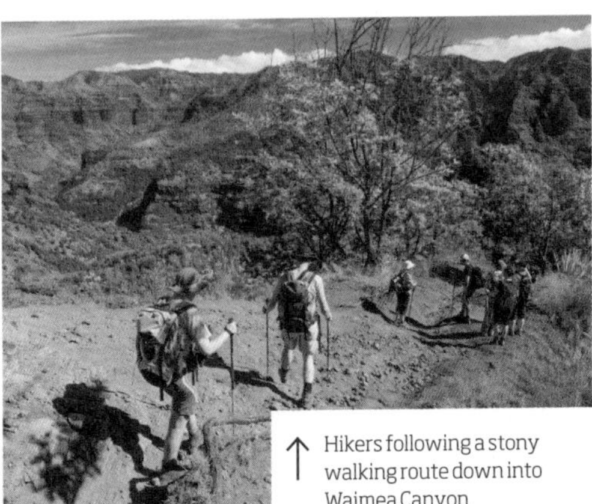

↑ Hikers following a stony walking route down into Waimea Canyon

Head Off Hiking

Hawaii is laced with incredible hiking routes. One of the best is the heart-stopping Kalalau Trail *(p220)* on Kaua'i's lush Nāpali Coast, where expert hikers can dive into dense jungle and scale vertiginous cliffs. Also on Kaua'i is the dramatic Kukui Trail, which plunges into the steep-sided Waimea Canyon *(p216)*, while on Maui, the otherworldly Sliding Sands Trail *(p158)* drops down into a volcanic crater dotted with burned-red cinder cones.

Sporting Events

Countless nail-biting sports events take place on the islands year round. In October, cheer on the hardy competitors tackling Hawai'i Island's grueling Ironman World Championship *(p58)*. Later, in November and December, O'ahu's North Shore hosts the world's top surfers as they take on colossal waves during the Vans Triple Crown *(p59)*.

Taking part in the swim stage of the Ironman World Championship

HAWAII FOR FESTIVALS

Throughout the year Hawaii's calendar is jam-packed with countless festivals that celebrate the state's richly diverse heritage. Expect lively music performances, creative arty events, mouthwatering foodie festivals, and competitive sporting escapades.

Cultural Celebrations

Many of Hawaii's festivals showcase the state's diverse cultural heritage. Head to Hawai'i Island to see hula performances at the Merrie Monarch Festival *(p59)* or visit Honolulu to watch colorful lion and dragon dances during Chinese New Year *(p58)*. Steeped in Buddhist tradition, the Lantern Floating Festival *(lanternfloatinghawaii.com)* sees thousands of lanterns glimmering off the coast of O'ahu.

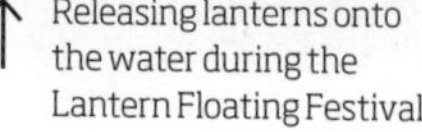

Releasing lanterns onto the water during the Lantern Floating Festival

INSIDER TIP

Events Listings

Check out *HAWAI'I Magazine*'s online event listings for information on other exciting festivals and celebrations taking place throughout the state *(hawaii magazine.com)*.

More Music Please

Known for its cheery notes and poetic lyrics, Hawaiian music celebrates the joys of island life. Laupāhoehoe Music Festival *(laupahoe hoemusicfestival.org)* features live performances by local talents *(p59)*, while the Aloha Festivals *(p59)* has everything from traditional chants to 'ukulele performances. For more 'ukulele tunes, the 'Ukulele Festival *(p59)* on O'ahu is a must.

→

A musician performing at the 'Ukulele Festival

Eat Till You Pop

Hawaii is known for its incredible cuisine, which blends flavors from Polynesia, Asia, and beyond. Sample a range of dishes at the Hawaii Food and Wine Festival *(hawaiifoodandwine festival.com)*, which celebrates both local produce and culinary talent, or enjoy artisanal delights like macadamia nut basil pesto and lavender chocolate at Honolulu's Made in Hawaii Festival *(p59)*. Possibly the islands' quirkiest festival, Waikīkī Spam Jam *(spamjamhawaii.com)* pays homage to the state's favorite canned meat.

←

Serving up Spam-inspired dishes at the unusual Waikīkī Spam Jam

Getting Arty

The Hawaiian Islands play host to a number of creative arty festivals. Admire the works of local painters and crafters at the Big Island Art Fair *(bigislandartfair.com)* and then check out the bright, beautiful landscape paintings at the Hale'iwa Arts Festival *(haleiwaart festival.org)*. In search of artisanal crafts? The Waikīkī Artfest *(gohawaii.com)* is brimming with pieces, including handmade ceramics, jewelry, and clothes.

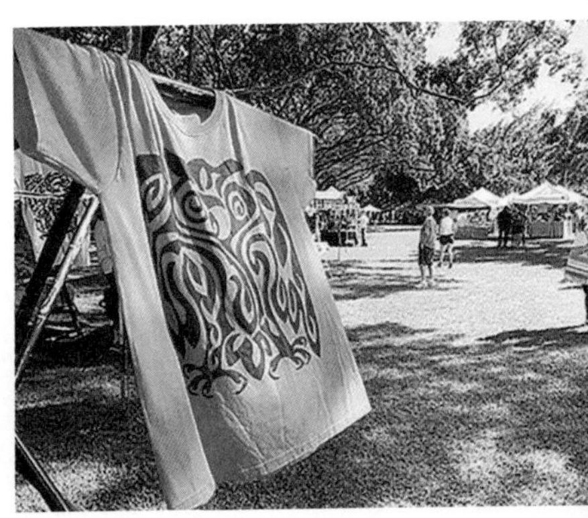

→

Colorful clothes on display at the Waikīkī Artfest

Spot Endangered Species

The Hawaiian Islands are home to many endangered animals, including the warm-water-loving Hawaiian monk seal and the green sea turtle, one of the largest sea turtles in the world. Sunbathing monk seals, known as *Ilio holo I ka uaua* on the islands ("dog that runs in rough water") can pop up anywhere, but a great place to watch them is sandy Po'ipū Beach *(p234)* on Kaua'i. Green sea turtles can also be found throughout the islands; a good viewing area is along the Kohala Coast on Hawai'i Island. Remember to observe these special creatures from a distance, or you risk a heavy fine.

→ A monk seal and a sea turtle lounging on Po'ipū Beach, Kaua'i

Did You Know?

Hawaii has the highest number of endangered native species of any place on the planet.

HAWAII FOR WILDLIFE ENCOUNTERS

Unique species continue to endure on Hawaii's remote shores and protected rainforests. Catch a glimpse of some of these beautiful creatures through one of the islands' many reputable, environmentally conscious operators.

Whale-Watching

Every winter, humpback whales migrate from the North Pacific to the warm waters of Hawaii to breed and bear their young. It's possible to see them from the shoreline, such as from the Pu'ukoholā Heiau National Historic Site *(p200)* on Hawai'i Island, but to get closer, go on a whale-watching tour. PacWhale Eco-Adventures *(pacificwhale.org)*, on Maui, offers some of the best.

← A humpback whale sighting off the coast of Kīhei, Maui

Under the Sea

Hawaii's protected waters and dynamic reef ecosystem are home to over 7,000 marine species, one third of which are unique to the islands. Spy whales, hawksbill turtles, spotted eagle rays, and tropical fish at the longest fringing reef in Hawaii, which lies just off Moloka'i.

→ Endangered green sea turtles swimming in Hawaii's warm waters

Bird-watching

Hawaii is home to more than 30 unique bird species. Though many are endangered, some are easily spotted, so get your binoculars ready. To see the protected state bird of Hawaii, the *nēnē* (Hawaiian goose), take a trip to Hawai'i Volcanoes National Park *(p184)*. Fancy a guided bird-watching tour with local experts? Hawaii Bird Tours *(hawaiibirdtours.com)* offers bird-watching tours on four of the main islands.

← The *nēnē*, or Hawaiian goose, a species of bird endemic to the islands

TOP 4 ECO-FRIENDLY TRAVEL TIPS

Reef-safe sunscreen
Use sunscreens that don't contain the coral-harming chemicals oxybenzone and octinoxate.

Limit single-use plastic
Opt for reusable water bottles and shopping bags instead of plastic.

Protect local species
Refrain from picking flowers or taking rocks, coral, and sand home.

Keep to the path
Stay on designated hiking trails to protect delicate ecological environments.

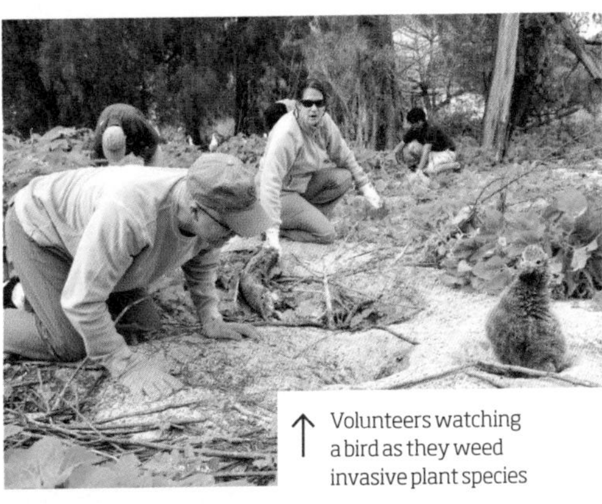

↑ Volunteers watching a bird as they weed invasive plant species

Restoration and Rehabilitation

Be part of the Hawaiian concept of *Mālama 'Āina* (to care for the land). With Hawaiian Legacy Tours *(hawaiianlegacytours.com)*, you can help restore habitats for a variety of species by planting endemic koa trees on the slopes of Mauna Kea *(p194)*. Alternatively, spend some time at Hawaii Wildlife Center on Hawai'i Island – the facility, which cares for injured native birds and the Hawaiian hoary bat, is always in search of enthusiastic volunteers, even for the short term.

MARINE WILDLIFE OF HAWAII

While Hawaii's lofty volcanic ridges and dense forests flourish with flora, the islands' coastlines are brimming with wildlife. Creatures big and small can be spotted here, from tiny hermit crabs scuttling around the coves and tidal pools to seals soaking up the sun on the sand. Reefs are prime habitat for urchins, octopuses, and schools of fish in dazzling colors darting in and out of coral crevasses. Farther out, in the dark depths of the Pacific, sharks, dolphins, and rays scout the waters for their next meal. Much of this incredible underwater world is protected, though its future is ultimately in the hands of its caretakers (locals and visitors).

↑ Endangered green sea turtles swimming in the shallows

SEA TURTLES

Among Hawaii's most beloved creatures are the Hawaiian green sea turtles *(honu)*, which can live up to the age of 80. They can reach lengths of up to 4 ft (1.2 m) and spend much of their day munching away on algae and sea grasses, which is thought to be the reason behind their greenish skin. *Honu* were thought to represent a family's ancestral spirit guide and may have led early Polynesian settlers to Hawaii. Today, the *honu* are an endangered and protected species. They are often seen bobbing their heads out of the water to catch a breath of air or soaking up some sun on the beach, camouflaged in the lava rocks.

FISH

From Hawaii's state fish, the *humuhumu-nukunukuāpua'a* (a reef triggerfish), to the predatory moray eels, over 680 species of fish are known to inhabit the waters of the Hawaiian Islands. Most occupy the coral reefs, and invariably as many as 40 species of shark lurk nearby – including reef sharks, whale sharks, hammerhead sharks, and tiger sharks. Manta rays, with wingspans of up to 20 feet (6 m), can also be found feeding on plankton and small fish near Hawaii's coast. They sometimes breach the waves, performing somersaults for lucky onlookers.

CORAL REEFS

Hawaii's kaleidoscopic coral reefs are complex living structures that provide and support a vital habitat for countless marine species. One of the most notable species living on the reef is algae, an organism that provides nearly 75 per cent of the earth's atmospheric oxygen. Reefs also protect Hawaii's shorelines from erosion by dissipating wave energy and contribute to the beautiful beaches that fringe the islands – the soft golden sand here is mostly made up of tiny pieces of coral.

MARINE CONSERVATION

When Hawaii's Papahānaumokuākea Marine National Monument was expanded in 2016, it became one of the world's largest protected areas. It now includes vast sections of ocean and numerous uninhabited islands that support thousands of species. The monument relies on volunteers to continue conservation efforts; the Mokupāpapa Discovery Center *(p178)* is one of the main facilitators for such work.

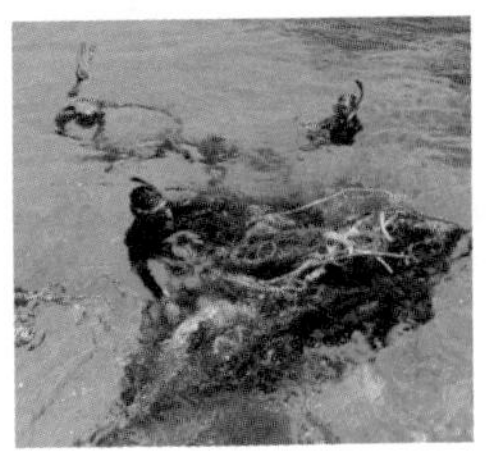

CRUSTACEANS AND CEPHALOPODS

Several species of lobster roam Hawaii's coral reefs. One of these species is the banded spiny lobster, which was used for sacrificial offerings centuries ago. Many species of octopus are also found here, hiding in reef crevices and preying on their crustacean neighbors. Hawaiian octopuses are smaller than the well-known giant octopuses of the Pacific Northwest.

MARINE MAMMALS

The warm Hawaiian waters are a favorite winter destination for migrating humpback whales who come here to rest, mate, and nurse their young. These gentle giants share the waves with bottlenose and spinner dolphins. Closer to the reefs are Hawaiian monk seals. Once hunted to the brink of extinction, these endemic seals now have a population estimate of around 1,600.

← A day octopus *(Octopus cyanea)*, common in Hawaii's waters

↑ Tropical fish darting between the colorful coral reefs that surround Hawaii

Budget-Friendly Activities

Manage your holiday costs by seeking out budget-friendly activities, of which there are plenty in Hawaii. On O'ahu, check out the roaming peacocks at the Byodo-In Temple *(p126)* for a nominal fee of $5 per adult and $2 per child. Teenagers will enjoy the hike to the Diamond Head crater *(p117)*, which costs $5. On Hawai'i Island, the Pana'ewa Rainforest Zoo and Gardens *(p181)*, which has a zoo and butterfly house, and the Mokupāpapa Discovery Center *(p178)*, with its aquarium and hands-on science exhibits, are both free to visit.

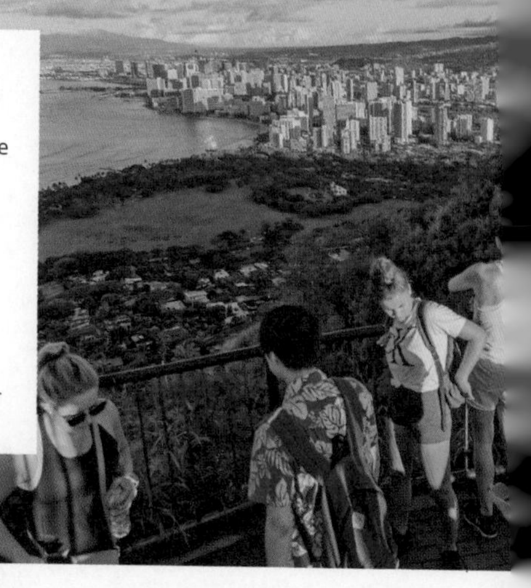

→ Stunning views from the summit of Diamond Head crater, near Honolulu

HAWAII FOR FAMILIES

Hawaii is a great destination for families looking for a bit of fun in the sun. Tranquil lagoons keep little ones sheltered from the waves, intriguing museum exhibits engage young minds, and tons of adventurous pursuits in Hawaii's stunning natural landscapes will keep the whole family entertained outdoors.

STAY

Aulani, O'ahu

This Disney resort offers storytelling, slides, and a 'ukulele-playing Mickey Mouse.

92-1185 Ali'inui Dr, Kapolei
disneyaulani.com

$$$

Grand Wailea, Maui

An upscale resort with a family games room and entertaining *lū'aus*.

3850 Wailea Alanui Dr, Wailea
grandwailea.com

$$$

Fun on the Ranch

The Hawaiian Islands are peppered with ranchland and many of these working farms are open to the public. Visit O'ahu's Kualoa Ranch *(p127)*, the filming location of *Jurassic Park*, where the horseback and e-mountain bike tours (both ages 10+) are highly memorable. On Maui, the Maui Zipline Company *(mauizipline.com)* takes kids (ages 5+) over lagoons and through lush tropical forest.

→ Flying through a dense canopy of trees on a zipline

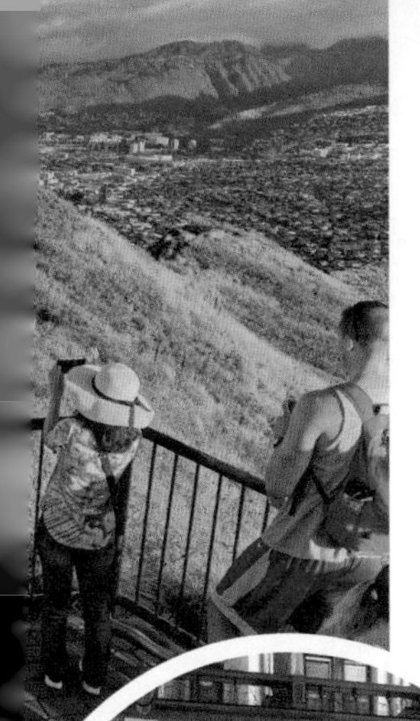

Marvelous Museums

Keep kids amused on rainy days with the incredible exhibits in Hawaii's many museums. The Bishop Museum *(p108)* in Honolulu includes a life-sized model of a sperm whale, a dress-up area, planetarium shows, and a daily volcano demo. The ʻImiloa Astronomy Center of Hawaiʻi *(p180)* brings Mauna Kea to life via a 3-D show. If you're looking for free indoor activities, check out Capitol Modern's *(p86)* hands-on gallery, specifically designed with kids in mind, which offers painting and drawing sessions.

← An exhibit in the Hawaiian Hall at the Bishop Museum

RAINY DAY SUGGESTIONS

Volcanic views
Head above the clouds and explore the craters of Mauna Kea *(p194)* or Haleakalā *(p154)*.

Find fish
Find yourself in a massive fishbowl at the Maui Ocean Center's aquariums *(p166)*.

Fly away
Try out a flight simulator or peek inside a cockpit at the Pearl Harbor Aviation Museum *(p113)*.

Get cultural
Enjoy a free hula or lei-making lesson at the Royal Hawaiian Center *(2201 Kalākaua Av)*.

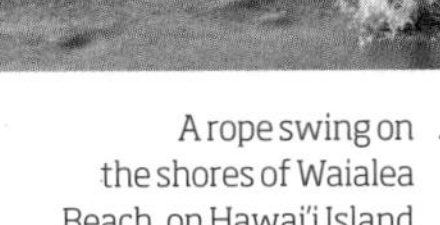

A rope swing on the shores of Waialea Beach, on Hawaiʻi Island ↑

Beaches for Kids

Shimmering sand and teal-colored water beckons families to Hawaii's beaches. The four magical artificial Ko Olina Lagoons *(koolina.com)* on Oʻahu are perfect swimming and snorkeling holes for families; you might even spot a turtle or two. At Poʻipū Beach *(p234)*, on Kauaʻi, is a sandy crescent called Baby Beach where the waters are shallow and the waves gentle. Situated in a protected bay rich in marine life, Waialea Beach on Hawaiʻi Island also offers a slice of paradise.

THE ORIGINAL MAI TAI

A little different to today's rum-and-juice mix, the original Mai Tai was invented by Victor Bergeron in 1944 at his Polynesian-themed restaurant in California. The vintage recipe contained: the juice of one lime, 0.25 oz (7 g) simple syrup, 0.5 oz (14 g) orange curaçao, 0.25 oz (7 g) orgeat syrup, 1 oz (28 g) dark Jamaica rum, and 1 oz (28 g) Martinique or light rum. Shake by hand, serve over ice, and garnish with half a lime and fresh mint.

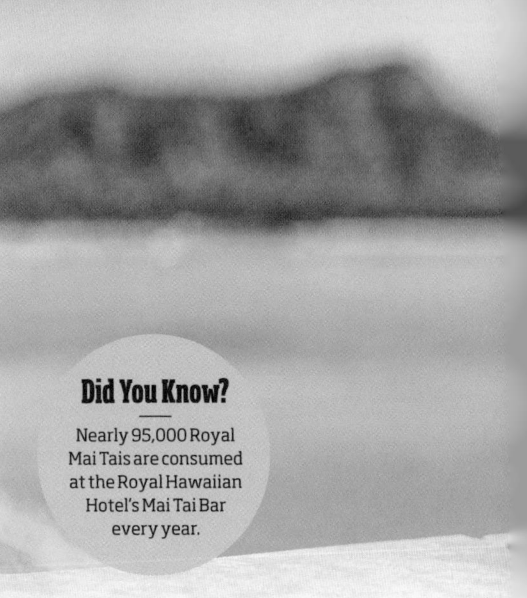

Did You Know?

Nearly 95,000 Royal Mai Tais are consumed at the Royal Hawaiian Hotel's Mai Tai Bar every year.

HAWAII

RAISE A GLASS

Hawaii might be most famous for its cooling tropical cocktails, but these balmy islands offer more than just iconic Mai Tais.There's a mouthwatering selection of tipples to discover here, from superbly crafted local beers to lusciously flavored wines.

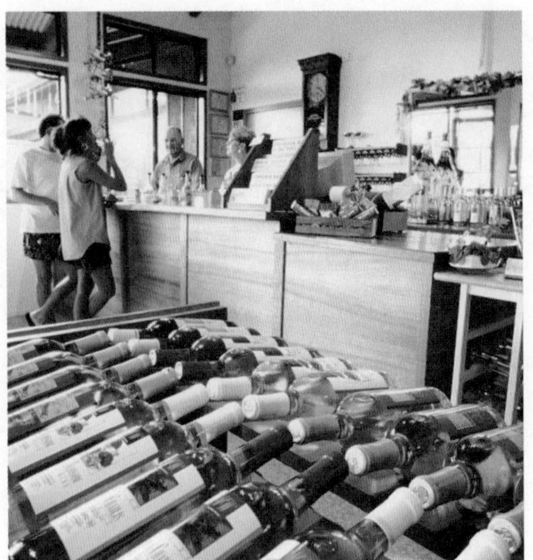

Fine Wineries

Hawaii may not be synonymous with wine like other American states, but this tropical archipelago has some excellent climatic conditions for viticulture – especially on volcanic slopes where grape vines thrive. Savor crisp, light pineapple wine inside an old stone jail at MauiWine *(mauiwine.com)* or, while on Hawai'i Island, ask for a premium flight at the Volcano Winery *(volcanowinery.com)*, which includes its award-winning, golden guava-grape blend wine.

Locally produced wine on display at Volcano Winery on Hawai'i Island

Classic Cocktails

Hawaii is known for its tropical cocktails made with locally sourced ingredients such as coconuts and pineapples. Try a Lava Lava Flow cocktail, which contains fresh strawberries, local bananas, coconut cream, and rum, at the beachside Lava Lava Beach Club *(lavalavabeachclub.com)*. Hawaii's most famous cocktail is the Mai Tai, a fruity drink that includes rum and pineapple juice; sample it at the Royal Hawaiian hotel *(p103)*, the first place in Hawaii to serve this now-iconic drink.

Two quintessential Mai Tai cocktails, served at a beachside bar

Craft Brews

While you might expect the islands to offer sun, sand, and surf, you might not expect suds; yet Hawaii has nearly 30 craft breweries offering up ales, lagers, and stouts. Order a flight at the Kona Brewing Company *(p197)* where the Island Colada Cream Ale is a real standout. If you're on Hawai'i Island in March, partake in the Kona Brewers Festival *(p59)* where revelers can sample a variety of beers.

→

Visitors exploring Kona Brewing Company, on Hawai'i Island

Distillery Tastings

With nutrient-dense soil, an abundance of fresh fruit, and some of the world's purest spring water, Hawaii has all the ingredients needed for concocting delicious spirits. Book a tour at Ko'olau Distillery *(koolaudistillery.com)* on O'ahu to try its whiskey or check out the botanical gin from Hali'imaile Distilling *(haliimailedistilling.com)* in Maui.

←

Tempting, handcrafted spirits from Hali'imaile Distilling, on Maui

The 'Ukulele

The upbeat sounds of the 'ukulele are integral to Hawaiian music. Yet this small, four-string instrument originated on the islands only in the 19th century as an adaptation of the machete instrument, which had been introduced by Portuguese immigrants working on the sugarcane plantations here. For a day devoted to 'ukulele music, attend the annual 'Ukulele Festival *(p59)* in mid-July in Kapi'olani Park *(p117)*. If you'd rather play yourself, attend one of the free lessons at the Royal Hawaiian Center *(2201 Kalākaua Av, Honolulu)* on Mondays from 11am till noon.

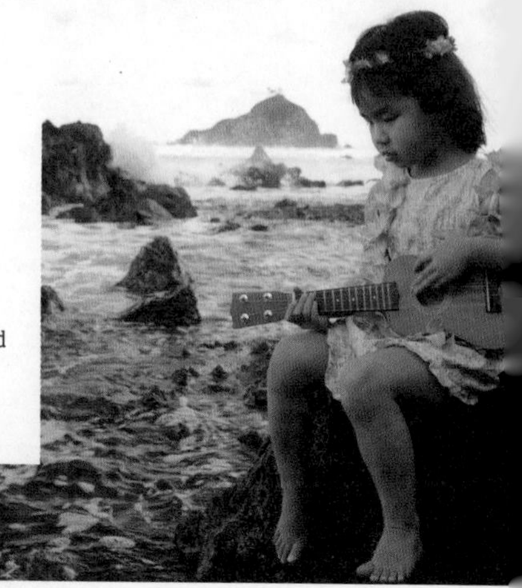

→ A young musician playing the 'ukulele, Hawaii's favorite instrument

HAWAII FOR CULTURE SEEKERS

The people of Hawaii have a culture that can be traced back centuries. Deeply influenced by the land, these philosophies are most keenly expressed through local music, hula, arts, and stories, which visitors will find captivating.

The Hula

As though mimicking the sway of palm trees, the hula acts as a storytelling dance in Hawaii. Two forms are practiced: the *hula kahiko* (ancient) and the *hula auana* (modern). Check out Hilo's Merrie Monarch Festival *(p59)* for a week-long celebration of the dance. For lessons, visit the Polynesian Cultural Center *(p131)*.

→ Costumed dancers performing the hula in Hawaii

INSIDER TIP

Origins of Hula

Visit Ka'ana on Moloka'i, regarded by many as the birthplace of hula. The dance is celebrated in January in Halawa at the Ka Moloka'i Makahiki Festival *(p58)*, with lots of hula performances.

The Talk Story

Originally, Hawaiians had an entirely oral culture, without a written language. This meant that the talk story (simply meaning, "to chat") was an important way of passing down stories, ideas, values, songs, and traditions. Honolulu's annual Talk Story Festival in early October *(honolulu.gov)* honors this longstanding Hawaiian tradition, featuring tales from a range of storytellers. The Mauna Lani hotel on Hawai'i Island *(aubergeresorts.com/maunalani)*, meanwhile, hosts a free monthly talk story event called Twilight at Kalāhuipua'a. Held on the Saturday closest to a full moon at 5:30–8:30pm, it takes place outside with various guests sharing stories, and performances from dancers and musicians.

← A storyteller performing at Honolulu's annual Talk Story Festival

CULTURAL REVIVAL

Ever since the Hawaiian Renaissance *(p65)* began in the 1970s, a revival of Hawaii's hula, music, language, and arts continues to flourish. Both ancient and modern forms of hula are now practiced at dozens of hula schools in Hawaii and abroad, and events such as the Merrie Monarch Festival have been established to promote the dance. During this period, the Hawaiian language, 'Ōlelo Hawai'i, has also come back from the brink of extinction. Thousands are now fluent, encouraged by the establishment of preschools where children can learn the language, as well as free lessons at the University of Hawai'i.

Lei

Lei, Polynesian garlands made from vibrant, scented flowers, have always been important symbols of affection in Hawaii and are bestowed frequently with a kiss. On Lei Day *(p58)*, locals all wear lei and free events take place, including live music, hula shows, and lei competitions. Free lei-making tutorials take place at the Whalers Village's ABC courtyard *(p160)* on Maui on Tuesdays and Thursdays from 11am to 1pm.

↑ Crafting vibrant lei from pink and white flowers

Celebrating a festival dedicated to Lono, the Hawaiian god of agriculture and fertility

STORIES OF HAWAII

Ancient Hawaii produced a wealth of oral literature and myth, which was passed down from generation to generation. These stories of gods and goddesses – often brimming with passion, betrayal, birth, and death – spoke of the creation of the Hawaiian Islands and of Hawaii's people. Today, Hawaiians maintain a profound respect for their deities and associated legends, keeping these narratives alive through such things as chants, music, and hula.

ORAL TRADITIONS

The oral traditions of early Hawaiian culture played a vital role in island life. The literature, committed to memory, was often chanted to the accompaniment of music and dance. There were *oli* (chants), *mo'olelo* (stories and narratives), *mele* (songs), and *'ōlelo no'eau* (proverbs). The *kahuna* (priests) composed and recited poetry to preserve history, genealogies, and the knowledge of crafts. *Haku mele* (composers) often created verses for special occasions, such as the birth of an *ali'i* (royal) child; such songs were considered sacred.

Pu'ukoholā Heiau, a sacred site built by Kamehameha I on Hawai'i Island

LEGENDS OF CREATION

In Hawaiian mythology, the creators of the Hawaiian Islands and the ancestors of

KAPU

A brutal but efficient system of rule, *kapu* was a strictly enforced Hawaiian code of conduct that was instated around the 11th century. Hawaiians believed *kapu* was created by the gods and interpreted by the *ali'i* (royalty). Punishment for breaking a *kapu* was most often death, unless the offender could escape to a *pu'uhonua* (place of refuge). Many *kapu* were associated with keeping men and women separated, especially during mealtimes, but other offences included stepping on a chief's shadow. The system was abolished in 1819 by Kamehameha II *(p62)*.

all the Hawaiian chiefs were the male Wākea (the Heavens) and the female Papahānaumoku (the Earth). A well-known Hawaiian creation chant, Kumulipo, which is over 2,000 lines long, tells of both life and the islands growing up gradually, like a child of Wākea and Papahānaumoku. The Kumulipo also includes a genealogy of the members of Hawaiian royalty and links them to their gods.

HAWAIIAN DEITIES

Hawaiians venerated dozens of gods and goddesses, especially the four main gods: Lono (productivity of the land), Kūkā'ilimoku (politics and war), Kāne (light, life, and water), and Kāne's twin brother, Kanaloa (the sea and the underworld). Each of them had numerous manifestations and their deeds were visible in everyday nature. Kūkā'ilimoku, the god that Kamehameha I revered the most, was the main god, whose worship rituals sometimes included human sacrifices, which took place at such sites as the Pu'ukoholā Heiau *(p200)* on Hawai'i Island. These sacrifices were for appeasing Kūkā'ilimoku, assuring his follower success in combat or in ending famine or disease.

OTHER LEGENDS

A number of stories surround other Hawaiian gods. One tells of Pele, the fiery-tempered volcano goddess who migrated from Kahiki (Tahiti, or simply the "distant homeland") seeking a dry place for her eternal fires. Tracing the geological evolution of the islands, she resided first on Kaua'i and then O'ahu before settling for a time in Maui's Haleakalā Crater *(p154)*. She now lives in Hawai'i Island's Kīlauea Caldera *(p184)*. Māui, meanwhile, is a Hawaiian demigod credited for many life-giving alterations, including lifting the sky and slowing down the sun's pace across the sky, all accomplished from atop Haleakalā.

→ Carved statue honoring Kūkā'ilimoku, the Hawaiian god of politics and war

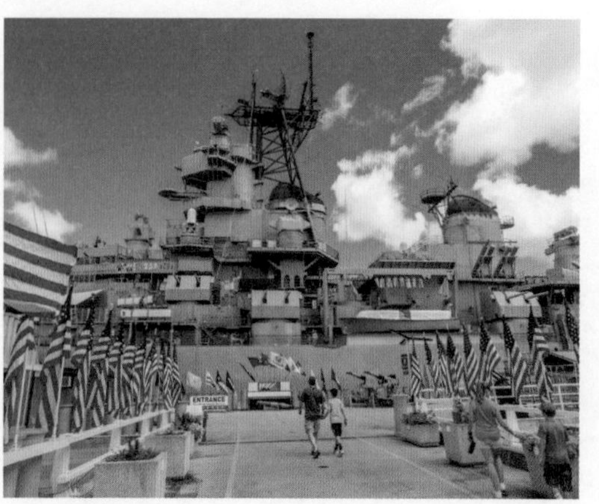

Significant Monuments

Defining historical places are found throughout the islands. Spend a day at Pearl Harbor *(p110)*, and come away with a deeper understanding of the devastating consequences of war. Or trek through the ʻĪao Valley State Park *(p167)* where a great battle took place in 1790 that changed the course of Hawaii's history.

The USS *Missouri*, one of the battleships berthed in Pearl Harbor

HAWAII FOR HISTORY BUFFS

Hawaii has a rich and tumultuous history. Primed for learning, the sacred and commemorative sights here - including temple ruins, royal residences, dazzling museums, and solemn burial places - will immerse you in the islands' compelling past.

Royal Residences

Hawaii was once ruled over by kings and queens who resided in opulent homes. In Honolulu, stroll the grand halls of the residence of Hawaii's former monarchy at ʻIolani Palace *(p84)*, and peruse the fine antiques at the Queen Emma Summer Palace *(p114)*. On Lānaʻi, you can visit the humble ruins of Kaunolū Village *(p141)*, a favorite fishing spot of Kamehameha I.

INSIDER TIP
Take a Tour

Kona Historical Society *(konahistorical.org)* brings history to life with tours of an early 20th-century coffee farm and off-road excursions around Hawai'i Island's historical sites.

Spiritual Sites

No history tour would be complete without discovering Hawaii's spiritual past. Explore Pu'uhonua o Hōnaunau National Historical Park *(p182)* and imagine a time when a broken sacred law meant death unless you reached this refuge. Pi'ilanihale Heiau *(p171)* is also a fine example of an early community structure where deities were worshiped.

→

Imposing wooden *Ki'i* in Pu'uhonua O Hōnaunau National Historical Park

Precious Petroglyphs

Carvings etched into lava rock centuries ago - known as petroglyphs, or *ki'i pohaku* - are found throughout the islands. The largest petroglyph field in Hawaii is Pu'u Loa, which is located in Hawai'i Volcanoes National Park *(p184)* and features over 23,000 images. The Olowalu Petroglyphs along Maui's coast about 300 years old and have remarkable images of sails and warriors.

←

Ancient carvings in Olowalu Petroglyphs giving a glimpse into Hawaii's past

Memorable Museums

Brush up on your knowledge of the Aloha State's past by visiting a museum or two. The Lyman Museum *(p180)* in Hilo is the oldest wood-frame building on the island and details 19th-century missionary life. If you're near Koke'e State Park *(p216)*, pop into the Koke'e Natural History Museum for 19th-century botanical prints.

↑ The decadent exterior of 'Iolani Palace in Honolulu

→

Artifacts on display at the Lyman Museum in Hilo on Hawai'i Island

A YEAR IN HAWAII

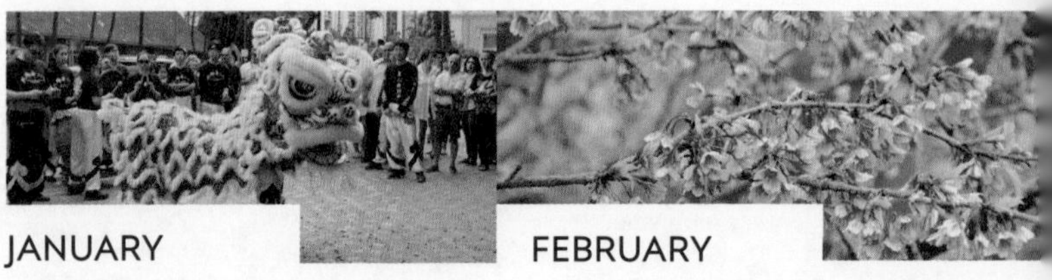

JANUARY

△ **Chinese New Year** *(mid-Jan–early Feb)*. Crimson is the color of this two-week celebration, marked by lion and dragon parades in Honolulu's Chinatown.

Ka Moloka'i Makahiki *(end Jan)*. Week-long cultural festival in Moloka'i with traditional Hawaiian games, fishing competitions, and hula dance performances.

FEBRUARY

△ **Cherry Blossom Festival** *(late Jan–early Feb)*. Festivities in Honolulu celebrate Japanese culture, with tea ceremonies, flower-arranging demos, and traditional Taiko drumming sessions.

Maui Whale Festival *(all of Feb)*. A celebration of these marine mammals, with a film festival, craft fair, charity run, and shoreside whale count.

MAY

△ **Lei Day** *(May 1)*. Everyone is adorned with these traditional flower garlands and lei-making contests are held throughout Hawaii.

Hāmākua Harvest *(late May)*. The annual Farm Fest celebrates the farming community with food vendors, cooking contests, and entertainment in Honoka'a on the Big Island.

JUNE

△ **Kapalua Wine and Food Festival** *(early Jun)*. Wine enthusiasts and foodies will appreciate this event where local celebrity chefs put on a grand dinner on Maui's northwestern shores.

King Kamehameha I Day *(Jun 11)*. Public holiday with parades, hula performances, and craft markets on all the islands.

SEPTEMBER

△ **Hawaii Food and Wine Festival** *(early Sep)*. Over a hundred master chefs and wine producers provide beachside feasts on O'ahu, Maui, and Hawai'i Island over three indulgent weekends.

Kaua'i Mokihana Festival *(late Sep)*. Week-long and island-wide event showcasing contemporary Hawaiian music and hula, with lots of concerts and competitions.

OCTOBER

△ **Ironman World Championship** *(early Oct)*. The ultimate test of endurance, this race takes place on Hawai'i Island and includes a lengthy swim, bike ride, and marathon.

Hawai'i Island Festival of Birds *(late Oct)*. A celebration of native birds and biodiversity, this event holds educational talks, offers birding opportunities, and sells local crafts.

MARCH

△ **Honolulu Festival** *(early Mar)*. A big parade, craft fair, gourmet food vendors, and fireworks are part of this cultural festival that celebrates Hawaii's link to the Pacific Rim.

Kona Brewers Festival *(mid-Mar)*. Enjoy a selection of craft beer from Hawaii's breweries at this lively event. There's also delicious food prepared by top local chefs, plus live music.

Prince Kūhiō Day *(Mar 26)*. Public holiday in celebration of Hawaii's first delegate to the US Congress, with traditional Hawaiian *mele* and hula performances taking place island-wide.

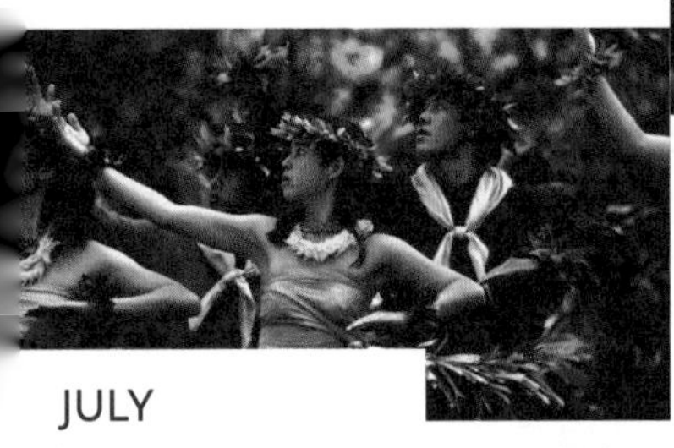

JULY

△ **Prince Lot Hula Festival** *(3rd Sat)*. Local hula schools honor Prince Lot (Kamehameha V) with both ancient and modern styles performed at the Moanalua Gardens in O'ahu.

'Ukulele Festival *(late Jul)*. This energetic festival has been celebrating the 'ukulele since the 1970s, with free concerts throughout the islands.

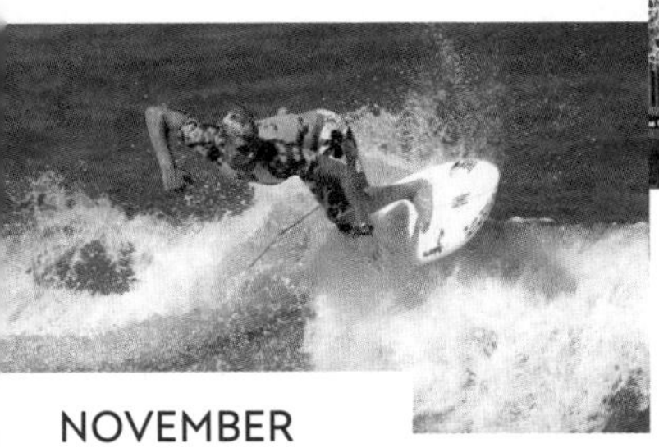

NOVEMBER

△ **Vans Triple Crown** *(late Nov–mid-Dec)*. The world's most prestigious surfing competitions take place on O'ahu's North Shore over three weeks, waves and weather permitting.

Kona Coffee Cultural Festival *(early Nov)*. The Kona district celebrates its famous beans, with a parade, gourmet food, and coffee-picking contest.

APRIL

△ **Merrie Monarch Festival** *(week after Easter)*. Honoring King David Kalākaua, a proponent of Hawaiian culture, with a world-famous hula competition and a parade through Hilo.

Laupāhoehoe Music Festival *(late Apr)*. A full day of live music featuring local bands, food stalls, and family-friendly activities at Laupāhoehoe Point Beach Park.

AUGUST

Made in Hawaii Festival *(mid-Aug)*. Local vendors showcase their fine food creations, artworks, and handicrafts in Honolulu.

△ **The Aloha Festivals** *(end of Aug–early Sep)*. Throughout the islands, dozens of music and dance events, craft fairs, parades, food vendors, and even a royal ball make up the grandest of Hawaii's annual celebrations.

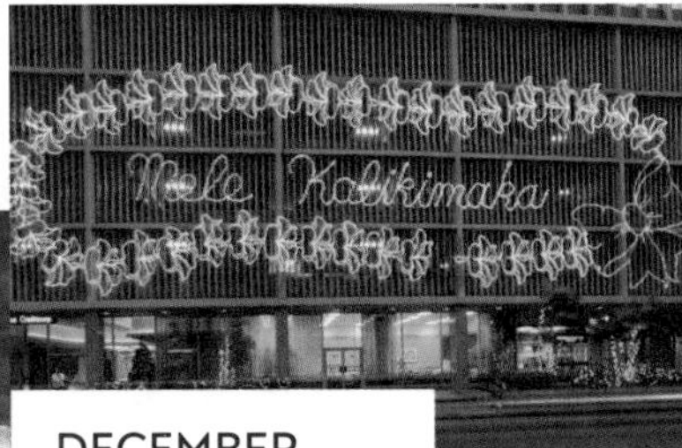

DECEMBER

Honolulu City Lights *(month long)*. A must-see display of holiday lights and one-of-a-kind decorated trees, all created by employees of different county and city departments.

Honolulu Marathon *(mid-Dec)*. With a route stretching along Honolulu's sunny coast, this is one of the most popular and scenic marathons in the US, drawing thousands of runners.

△ **Christmas** *(Dec 25)*. A national holiday where Santa is depicted in shorts carrying a surfboard, sandmen are made instead of snowmen, and people wish each other *"Mele Kalikimaka."*

A BRIEF HISTORY

Forged by volcanic eruptions in the Pacific Ocean millions of years ago, this isolated archipelago has been occupied by humans for over 1,500 years. The islands' history is marked by waves of settlements and invasions that, over time, have made Hawaii one of the most multicultural places in the world.

Polynesian Explorers

The Polynesians, whose culture was established in the island clusters of Samoa and Tonga, possessed remarkable seafaring abilities, which enabled them to explore the vast Polynesian Triangle. They traveled in twin-hulled voyaging canoes that carried up to 100 passengers, as well as pairs of domesticated animals, and crops for planting, such as taro, coconut, and banana. These explorers colonized the Society Islands, including Tahiti, and the Marquesas Islands, in the first century CE. Around 400 CE, the Marquesans risked the 3,000-mile (5,000-km) ocean crossing to discover the Hawaiian Islands.

1 Map of the Hawaiian Islands. ↑

2 Illustration of Tahitian boats.

3 An impressive Hawaiian *heiau* (temple).

4 A Hawaiian chief wearing a helmet.

Timeline of events

40 million BCE

Hawaiian Islands formed by volcanic eruptions in the Pacific; life evolves from wind-borne spores and seeds.

400CE

Marquesans discover and settle the Hawaiian Islands.

1100–1300 CE

Tahitians invade Hawaii.

1250

Heiau (temples) are rededicated by Tahitian priest Paao, some for human sacrifice.

2

3

4

Ancient Hawaii

The early Hawaiians established an advanced, spiritual culture. Farmers and stone-builders, they were the first to alter a landscape that had, until then, evolved in isolation. They divided the land into *ahupua'a*, pie-shaped wedges running from mountain to sea, erected monumental *heiau* (temples), and built some of the largest irrigation systems in Polynesia. Life centered on *'ohana* (family), in which everyone was vital to the whole. Cultural values included *aloha 'āina* (love of land) and *laulima* (cooperation).

New Waves

In the 12th and 13th centuries, new waves of Polynesian settlers from the Society Islands invaded Hawaii. Casting themselves as reformers of a weakened Polynesian race, these new arrivals established a rigid class system of *ali'i* (royalty) who regulated the lives of the *maka'āinana* (commoners) through the harshly enforced *kapu* (taboo) system. *Kapu* designated any activity that interfered with the apportionment of *mana* (supernatural power) as forbidden; punishment for infractions were quick and fatal. This system dominated life in Hawaii for generations.

DISCOVERING THE PACIFIC

Long before the compass was invented, Polynesians were able to traverse the vast Pacific Ocean thanks to the ancient navigation system known as "wayfinding." Using an intricate knowledge of the stars, ocean swells, bird flight patterns, and cloud formations, they discovered new lands and, time and again, found their way back home.

1400

Tahitians control trade routes between Hawaii and Tahiti.

c. 1500s

Pu'uhonua O Hōnaunau built; this sanctuary was a place of refuge for those who had broken *kapu* laws.

1542

A Spanish expedition, led by Joao Gaetano, supposedly finds Hawaii but suppresses the information.

1758

Kamehameha I, the first monarch of the Hawaiian Islands, is born on the island of Hawai'i.

European Arrival

British explorer Captain James Cook landed on Kaua'i in 1778, likely becoming the first European to reach Hawaii. He came back a year later, this time to Kealakekua Bay on Hawai'i Island, where he was greeted by the local Hawaiians. However, relations soon grew hostile, in part because Cook and his men were desecrating sacred sites. Eventually there was a violent confrontation: Cook was killed, and some 30 Hawaiians murdered in retaliation.

Kamehameha I

In the late 18th and early 19th centuries, Kamehameha I, an ambitious chief and skilled warrior from Hawai'i Island, managed to systematically conquer each of the islands, and by 1810 Hawaii had become a united kingdom. Foreign trade, while not new to the islands, took off during this time, with sandalwood a major export to China. When Kamehameha I died in 1819, he left a leadership void that his son Kamehameha II was unable to fill. That same year the inexperienced young king – influenced by Queen Ka'ahumanu, Kamehameha I's favorite wife – abolished the *kapu* system, dramatically altering life in Hawaii.

1 A group of Hawaiians sailing out to meet Captain James Cook. ↑

2 Statue of Kamehameha I.

3 Hawaiians with a Christian missionary.

4 Queen Ka'ahumanu.

Did You Know?

Cook named Hawaii the Sandwich Islands in honor of his patron, the Earl of Sandwich.

Timeline of events

1778

Captain Cook lands on Kaua'i; he is killed a year later on a return visit to Hawai'i Island.

1795

Kamehameha I conquers Maui, Moloka'i, Lāna'i, and O'ahu.

1820

Christian missionaries arrive; cultural practices including the hula are banned.

1825

Kamehameha III becomes king, with Queen Ka'ahumanu as regent.

1825

Sugar and coffee plantations begin on O'ahu.

Christian Missionaries

In 1820, left without a strong leader and clearly defined laws, the weakened Hawaiian Kingdom received its first group of US missionaries, who were intent on "civilizing" the Hawaiians. Following Kamehameha II's death in 1824, Kamehameha III, his 11-year-old brother, was left to rule, but power was ultimately wielded by the formidable Queen Ka'ahumanu, a Christian convert. By the time of her death eight years later, she had engineered the peaceful conversion of the entire kingdom to Christianity.

The Plantation Era

In an attempt to modernize Hawaii, Kamehameha III, guided by his *haole* (foreign) advisors, developed a constitution and, in 1848, announced the Great Mahele (land division), releasing millions of acres for sale to private owners. While intended to help give land rights back to Hawaiians, most deeds went to Western planters. For the next century, sugar ruled Hawaii's economy, attracting contract laborers from China, Portugal, Japan, Puerto Rico, Korea, and the Philippines, who endured dire conditions. Many stayed on after their contracts finished and integrated into island life.

KAMEHAMEHA I

Born around 1758 into Hawaiian royalty, Kamehameha I, also known as Kamehameha the Great, was hidden away on Hawai'i Island for years to protect him from warring clans that saw him as a threat. Trained as a warrior, he gradually conquered each of the Hawaiian Islands in the late 18th and early 19th centuries. By 1810 he was the first king of a united Hawaiian Kingdom.

1840

Kamehameha III proclaims Hawaii's first constitution.

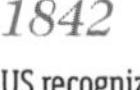

1842

US recognizes independence of Hawaiian Kingdom.

1845–48

A series of epidemics kill thousands.

1848

Kamehameha III proclaims the Great Mahele.

1852

Contract laborers arrive on Hawaii to work the plantations.

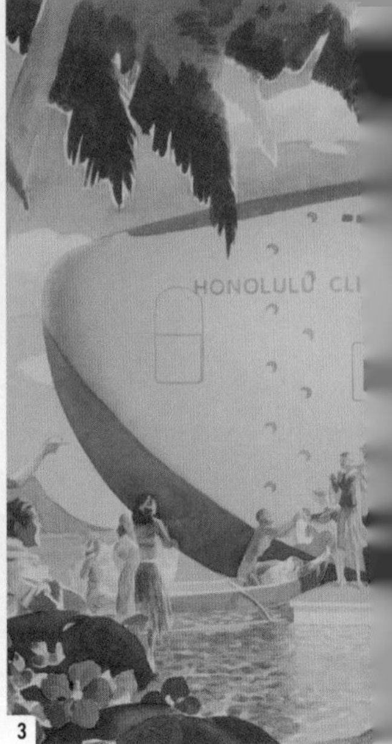

A Shift in Power

In 1874, Kalākaua, son of a high chief and chiefess, took the throne and began a cultural renaissance. However, in 1887, he was forced by white settlers (largely agribusiness owners) to enact the new Bayonet Constitution; signed at gunpoint, it restricted the monarchy's power. The king's sister Lili'uokalani ascended in 1891 and tried to broaden constitutional powers, but was deposed in 1893 by the "Committee of Safety," a group of white settlers. Hawaii was later annexed by the US during the Spanish-American War.

The Territorial Government

Despite opposition from Hawaiians, in 1900 Hawaii became a US territory. It was run by the island's white agribusiness owners, who tightly controlled island life. During World War II, following the 1941 attack on Pearl Harbor, Hawaii was placed under martial law. Five years of direct federal involvement forced territorial leaders to adopt more democratic governing methods. After the war, Hawaii's lower class gained voting rights and were elected to positions of political power. In 1959 a majority of citizens voted for Hawaii to become the 50th state of the US union.

1 Queen Lili'uokalani, Hawaii's last monarch. ↑

2 King Kalākaua visiting the White House.

3 Tourism poster for visiting Hawaii by air.

4 Visitors on the Waikiki Trolley in Honolulu.

Did You Know?

King Kalākaua was known as the "Merrie Monarch" thanks to his love of Hawaiian dance and music.

Timeline of events

1893
The Hawaiian monarchy is overthrown.

1894
Hawaii is declared a republic.

1895
Royalists attempt an armed insurrection to stop annexation by the US.

1898
Hawaii is annexed by the US; royal and government lands are seized.

1941
Japan attacks Pearl Harbor; after, many Japanese Americans are sent to mainland internment camps.

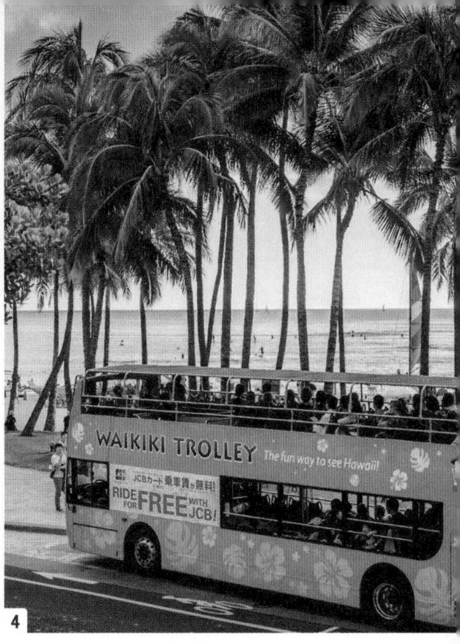

4

Tourism and Cultural Revival

Tourism took off in the mid-20th century, with short, affordable flights to Hawaii from the US mainland. The islands' economy entered a new era with rapid hotel and resort development. By the 1970s, a Hawaiian-led movement was underway to reclaim autonomy in its ancient homeland. It demanded the release of Kaho'olawe (a sacred island used by the US military) and generated renewed interest in Hawaiian culture, language, and crafts. In 1993, the US government apologized for any complicity in the wrongful overthrow of the monarchy, and the "nation of Hawaii" began a movement to re-establish political autonomy.

Hawaii Today

Tourism continues to be the dominant industry in Hawaii, with yearly visitor numbers surpassing 10 million. For many locals, however, overtourism is a grave concern that adversely affects the cost of living, housing affordability, and the environment. Concerns about climate change, especially wildfires and rising sea levels, led Hawaii to commit to becoming carbon neutral by 2045, partly through reforestation efforts and renewable energy.

BARACK OBAMA

Barack Obama was born on August 4, 1961, in Honolulu, O'ahu. He grew up on the island and graduated from the elite Punahou School in 1979 before continuing his studies on the US mainland. A Democrat, Obama was elected to the US Senate in 2004, before becoming the 44th US president in 2008. He is both the first African American president and first Hawaii-born president of the US.

1959

Hawaii becomes the 50th US state.

2002

Linda Lingle elected as the first female governor of Hawaii.

2008

Hawaii-born Barack Obama elected president of the US.

2018

Hawaii is the first US state to commit to becoming climate neutral by 2045.

2023

Wildfires destroy nearly all of the historic downtown of Lāhainā, Maui.

EXPERIENCE HONOLULU

Relaxing at Waikīkī Beach

EXPLORE HONOLULU

This guide divides Honolulu into two sightseeing areas, as shown on this map, plus an area beyond the center *(p106)*.

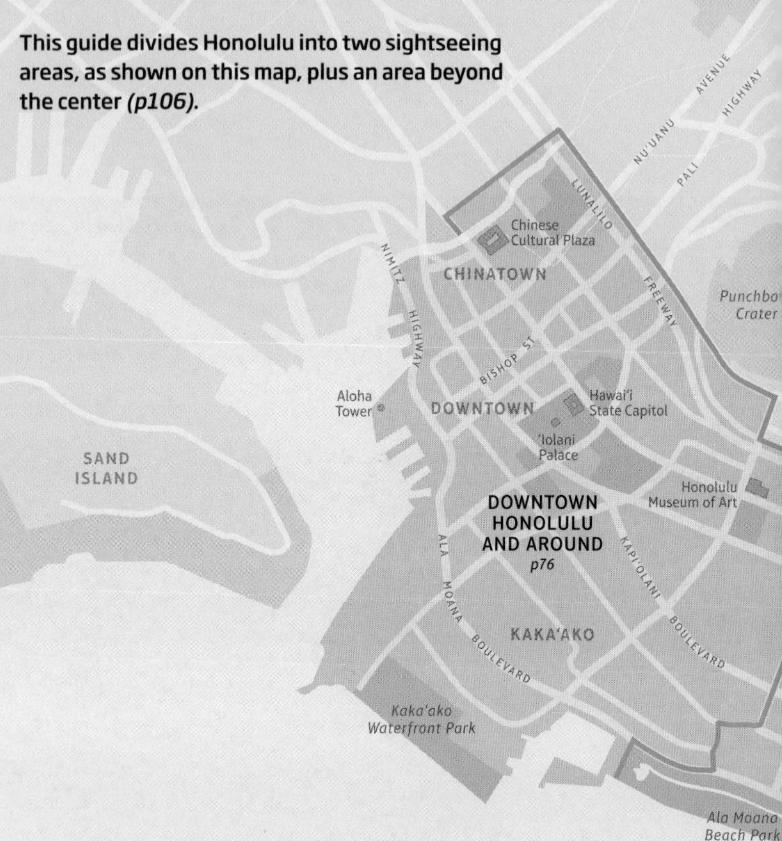

HAWAII
HONOLULU
PACIFIC HEIGHTS
MAKIKI
MĀNOA
LUNALILO FREEWAY
SOUTH BERETANIA STREET
SOUTH KING STREET
University of Hawai'i
ALA MOANA
Ala Moana Center
MCCULLY
ALA MOANA BOULEVARD
KALĀKAUA AVENUE
KAPI'OLANI BOULEVARD
WAIKĪKĪ AND BEYOND p92
Ala Wai Golf Course
KAPAHULU
The US Army Museum of Hawaii
WAIKĪKĪ
Waikīkī Beach

GETTING TO KNOW HONOLULU

Hawaii's oceanside capital might be small in size, but it sure packs a punch. Overlooked by a dormant volcano and lush hills, this compact city has two main areas, the Downtown core and the famed Waikīkī neighborhood, around which lie a mix of pretty parks, residential areas, and historic sights.

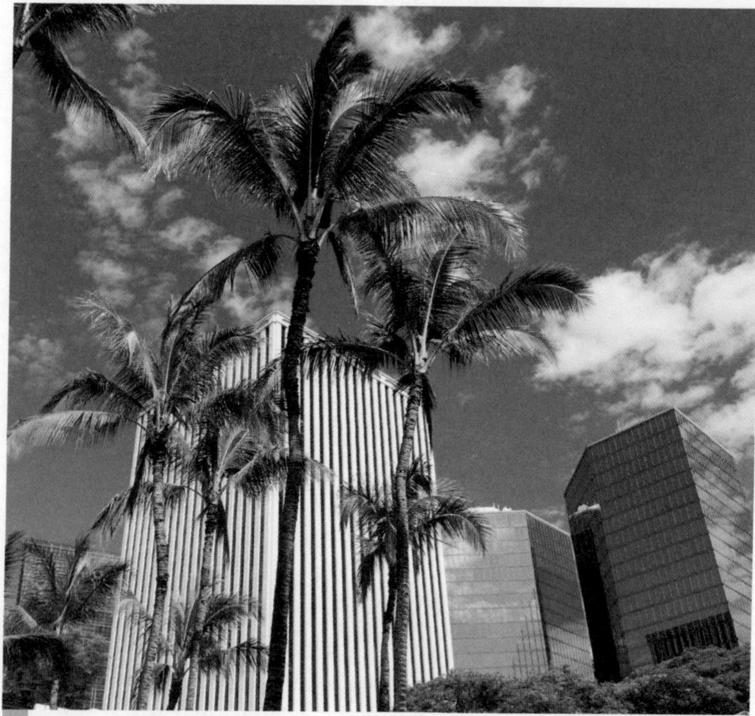

PAGE 76

DOWNTOWN HONOLULU AND AROUND

Split into the fairly distinct areas of Chinatown, the Capitol District, and several smaller neighborhoods, Downtown is a mix of towering skyscrapers, tranquil temples, and arty museums. Chinatown is filled with eat-till-you-pop foodie spots and contemporary art galleries, while the nearby historic Capitol District is home to the regal 'Iolani Palace. Don't miss the Kaka'ako neighborhood, with its cool design stores and colorful street murals.

Best for
Cultural and historical sights

Home to
Chinatown

Experience
Stepping inside the only royal residence in the US – 'Iolani Palace

PAGE 92

WAIKĪKĪ AND BEYOND

Stretching from the Ala Wai Canal to the glittering sea, the Waikīkī neighborhood is best known for its namesake beach. This long curve of soft sand is dotted with sunbathers, lapped by mellow turquoise waters, and fringed with swaying palm trees and hotel beach bars. Lying on either side of this golden strip you'll find even more sandy spots, including pretty Kahanamoku. Beyond Waikīkī Beach lies the busy Kalākaua Avenue, lined with top-notch clothing stores, fine-dining restaurants, and chic condos. To the west is the Ala Moana neighborhood, known for its spacious shopping mall and popular park.

Best for
Laid-back beach life

Home to
Waikīkī Beach

Experience
The exhilarating world of surfing at Kūhiō Beach

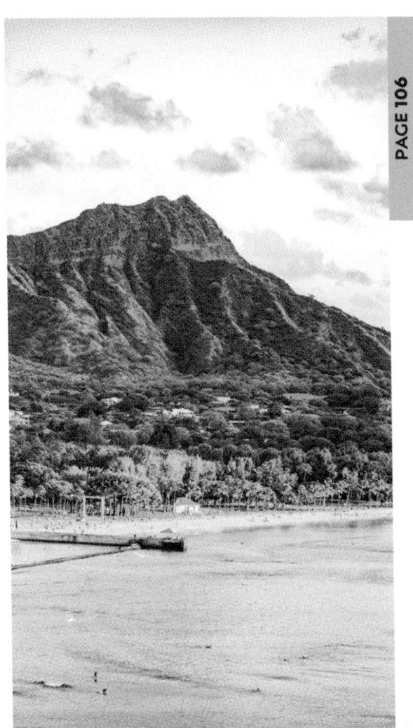

PAGE 106

BEYOND THE CENTER

The city is surrounded by verdant landscapes, including the rainforest-draped peaks and valleys of the Ko'olau Range to the north, the Diamond Head volcanic crater to the east, and the Punchbowl crater to the west. Nestled between this natural beauty and the city center, you'll find sights such as the beautifully furnished Queen Emma Summer Palace, lush Lyon Arboretum, and the intriguing Bishop Museum. Lying on the city's western shore, meanwhile, is Pearl Harbor, a national memorial known for its poignant monuments and museums.

Best for
Pretty green spaces

Home to
Bishop Museum, Pearl Harbor

Experience
Taking the scenic trail up to the emerald-green crater of Diamond Head

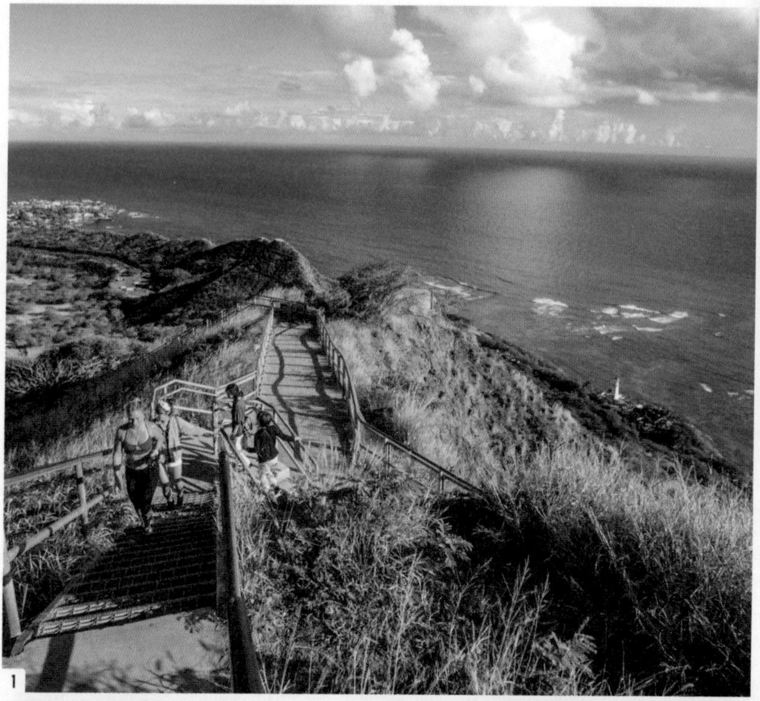

1

2

3

4

←

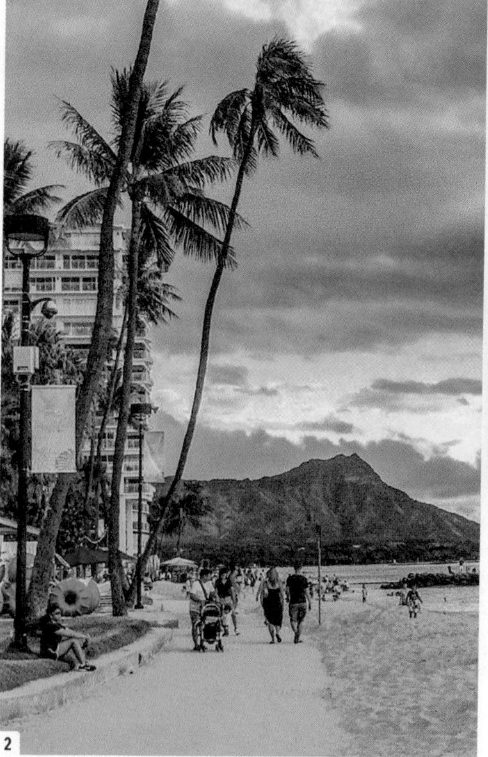

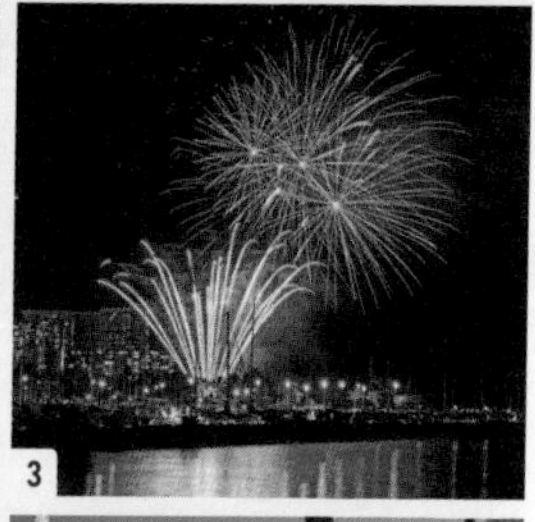

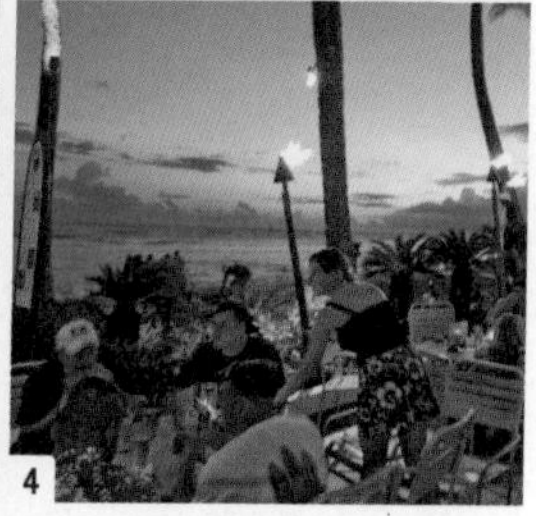

1 Hiking to the top of Diamond Head crater.

2 Stunning Waikīkī Beach.

3 Fireworks display over Waikīkī Beach.

4 Alfresco dining at Duke's Waikiki.

2 DAYS

in Honolulu

Day 1

Morning There's no better way to start your discovery of Honolulu than with a trip to Waikīkī, the city's most famous beach *(p96)*. Here you can take a stroll along the shaded, paved boardwalk before throwing off your shoes, laying down your beach towel, and sinking your feet into the soft, sun-kissed sand. The sea here (wonderfully warm and turquoise-tinged) is perfect for a dip; you may even be tempted to schedule in a surfing lesson with one of the nearby schools. For lunch, refuel with savoury *loco moco* at Hideout at The Laylow hotel *(hideoutwaikiki.com)*.

Afternoon Hop on the marmalade-hued Waikiki Trolley and head to the Honolulu Museum of Art *(p88)*. Among many other things, its impressive collection includes landscape paintings of Maui by the renowned American artist Georgia O'Keeffe, as well as thousands of detailed Japanese *ukiyo-e* woodblock prints and 300-year-old Hawaiian wooden bowls. There's lots to see here, so break things up midway with a coffee in the museum's shady Palm Courtyard.

Evening Once you've had your fill of art, make for Chinatown to eat-till-you-pop at Lucky Belly *(p82)*. This hot spot serves up mouthwatering bowls of ramen noodles, plus other delicious Pacific Rim fusion dishes. Fancy an evening tipple? Lucky Belly stays open late for drinks or you can walk around North Hotel Street for your pick of bars, including Bar 35 *(p81)* where DJs spin the latest hits. Spend the night in complete comfort at the beachy cool and eco-conscious Surfjack hotel *(p103)*.

Day 2

Morning Rise early, grab an organic smoothie from Heavenly Island Lifestyle *(p103)*, and make for the Diamond Head *(p117)* crater trail. Winding its way up to the summit of this once-fiery volcano, this popular walking route offers magnificent views over Honolulu. The trail tends to get very busy, so it's best to start as early as possible (and definitely before 10am). Afterward, if it's a Saturday, pick up breakfast at the KCC Farmers' Market *(p116)* or line up for a tummy-filling brunch at the Koko Head Cafe *(kokoheadcafe.com)*; the cornflake French toast, with bacon and maple syrup, is top-notch.

Afternoon Dedicate an afternoon to exploring the creative Kaka'ako neighborhood *(p88)*. Huge, colorful street murals are splashed across the walls here, including the playful *Aloha Monsters* on 690 Pohukaina Street and eye-catching giant sea turtle, known as *Hilo Honu*, on Auahi Street. You can also pick up souvenirs at the modern SALT shopping mall, take a walk through the waterfront park, or refresh yourself at one of the area's excellent craft breweries, such as the Honolulu Beerworks *(honolulubeerworks.com)*.

Evening Enjoy an evening of Polynesian dance and song, accompanied by delicious local food, at the Diamond Head Luau *(diamondheadbeachluau.com)*. Then take a post-dinner walk along Waikīkī Beach and finish the day with a tropical cocktail at Duke's Waikiki *(dukeswaikiki.com)*. If it's a Friday, gaze skyward to spy fireworks illuminating the night sky over the beach.

Beachside Bars

During the day, the open-air bars lining Waikīkī Beach *(p96)* are pretty laid-back; but when the sun goes down they start to sizzle. With styles ranging from shack to chic, these beachside hotspots serve up refreshing tropical cocktails such as the coconutty Lava Flow and world-famous Mai Tai. Two of the best spots to sip in style are the oceanside lawn at Hale Koa's Barefoot Bar *(halekoa.com)* and the palm-lined patio at Sheraton's RumFire *(rumfirewaikiki.com)*.

→ Overlooking Waikīkī's sandy shore, lined with buzzing beach bars

HONOLULU AFTER DARK

Looking for the best nightlife in Hawaii? Honolulu is unequivocally the winner. Cool watering holes are dotted across the city, so whether you want to sip on a cocktail by the beach, sample world-famous whiskeys in refined digs, or sing the night away at a karaoke bar, Honolulu's got you covered.

Performing in one of Honolulu's karaoke bars ↑

Karaoke Kings

Honolulu loves karaoke. For a lively spot near the beach, look no further than Wang Chung's *(2424 Koa Av)* in Waikīkī. Near the Kaka'ako neighborhood *(p88)*, Café Duck Butt *(p85)* has private rooms as well as delicious Korean snacks and drinks to fuel your performance.

INSIDER TIP
Happy Hour

Almost every bar and restaurant in Honolulu offers happy hour deals in the early evening. Some of the best are found at Deck *(deck waikiki.com)*, a stunning rooftop bar.

Late-Night Snacks

Looking for a midnight snack? Lucky for you, Sikdorak *(honolulukoreanbbq.com)* serves food to your table till 4am each day. Fill up on a tasty Korean barbecue with indulgent dishes like tender beef brisket and *bulgogi* grilled or, alternatively, head to Zippy's *(zippys.com)*. This diner provides bleary-eyed party people with Hawaiian comfort food, including *loco moco* (a burger on a bed of rice, topped with an egg and gravy).

← A plate of mouthwatering and tummy-filling *loco moco*, a popular Hawaiian dish

World of Whiskey

Bored of coconut concoctions? Honolulu's sophisticated whiskey bars will refresh your palate. The intimate Bar Leather Apron *(p85)* is known for its creative whiskey cocktails and locally produced spirits, while the stylish Shanghai Bar *(shanghaibarhawaii.com)* with its vintage 1930s vibes offers a well-curated list of Japanese whiskeys.

↑ The interiors of one of the popular bars with a wide collection of liquors

Palm trees in front of high-rise buildings in Downtown Honolulu

DOWNTOWN HONOLULU AND AROUND

As early as the 11th century, Polynesian sea voyagers began settling in this southeastern part of O'ahu and for centuries resided in thatched huts clustered along its shores. They named their settlement Kou and subsisted on fishing and growing crops such as taro, yam, and sugarcane.

In 1794, Captain William Brown, a British gun and fur trader, came upon the protected bay here and anchored his ship. Kou soon became known as Brown's Harbor – a vital port of call for fur and sandalwood traders and whaling vessels. To serve the throngs of visiting sailors, many Hawaiians, descendants of the original Polynesian settlers, set up taverns and brothels next to the harbor.

In 1795, Kamehameha I, a chief from Hawai'i Island, conquered O'ahu. He settled in Kou 14 years later, building a royal residence and giving the fledgling center its current name, Honolulu ("sheltered bay"). In 1820, Christian missionaries arrived, constructing the Kawaiaha'o Church and attempting to convert the local population to Christianity. Plantation workers from Asia and Europe followed soon after, building homes, establishing neighborhoods, and adding to the city's cultural diversity.

In 1845, Honolulu became the official capital of Hawaii, and in 1882, the magnificent 'Iolani Palace was built here for Hawaiian royalty. In the 1920s, tourism took hold and cruise ships arrived. Today, the area continues to draw in visitors with its historic sights and distinctive neighborhoods, including foodie-haven Chinatown and creative Kaka'ako.

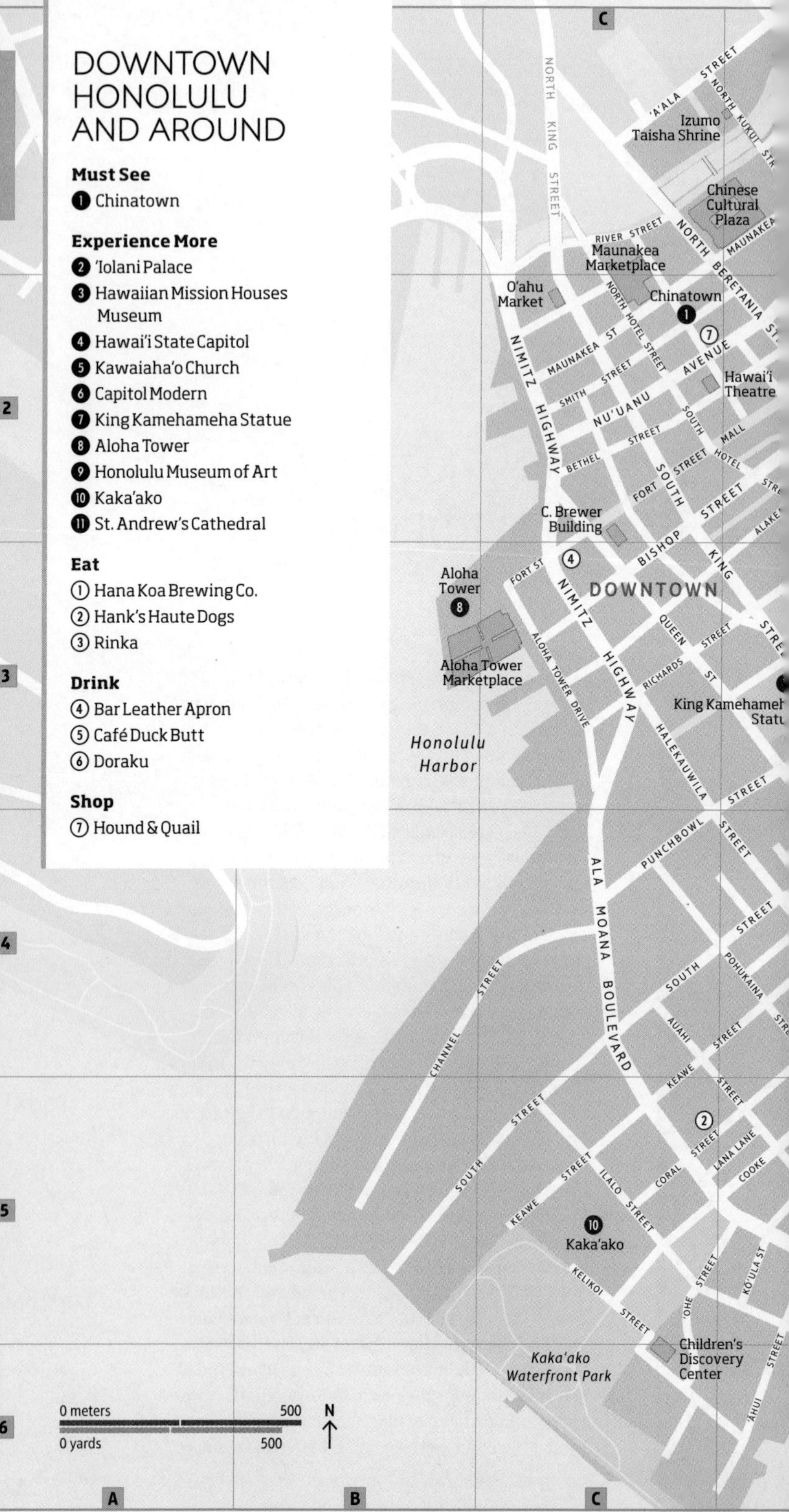

DOWNTOWN HONOLULU AND AROUND
Must See
1 Chinatown
Experience More
2 ʻIolani Palace
3 Hawaiian Mission Houses Museum
4 Hawaiʻi State Capitol
5 Kawaiahaʻo Church
6 Capitol Modern
7 King Kamehameha Statue
8 Aloha Tower
9 Honolulu Museum of Art
10 Kakaʻako
11 St. Andrew's Cathedral
Eat
① Hana Koa Brewing Co.
② Hank's Haute Dogs
③ Rinka
Drink
④ Bar Leather Apron
⑤ Café Duck Butt
⑥ Doraku
Shop
⑦ Hound & Quail
Izumo Taisha Shrine
Chinese Cultural Plaza
Maunakea Marketplace
Oʻahu Market
Chinatown
Hawaiʻi Theatre
C. Brewer Building
DOWNTOWN
Aloha Tower
Aloha Tower Marketplace
Honolulu Harbor
King Kamehameha Statue
Kakaʻako
Children's Discovery Center
Kakaʻako Waterfront Park
NORTH KING STREET
ʻAʻALA STREET
NORTH KUKUI STREET
RIVER STREET
NORTH BERETANIA STREET
MAUNAKEA
NORTH HOTEL STREET
NIMITZ HIGHWAY
MAUNAKEA ST
SMITH STREET
NUʻUANU AVENUE
SOUTH HOTEL
MALL
BETHEL STREET
FORT STREET
SOUTH KING STREET
BISHOP STREET
ALAKEA STREET
FORT ST
QUEEN STREET
RICHARDS ST
ALOHA TOWER DRIVE
HALEKAUWILA STREET
PUNCHBOWL STREET
ALA MOANA BOULEVARD
SOUTH STREET
POHUKAINA STREET
AUAHI STREET
CHANNEL STREET
KEAWE STREET
CORAL STREET
LANA LANE
COOKE
ILALO STREET
KELIKOI STREET
ʻOHE STREET
KOʻULA ST
ʻAHUI STREET
0 meters 500
0 yards 500
N
A
B
C
2
3
4
5
6

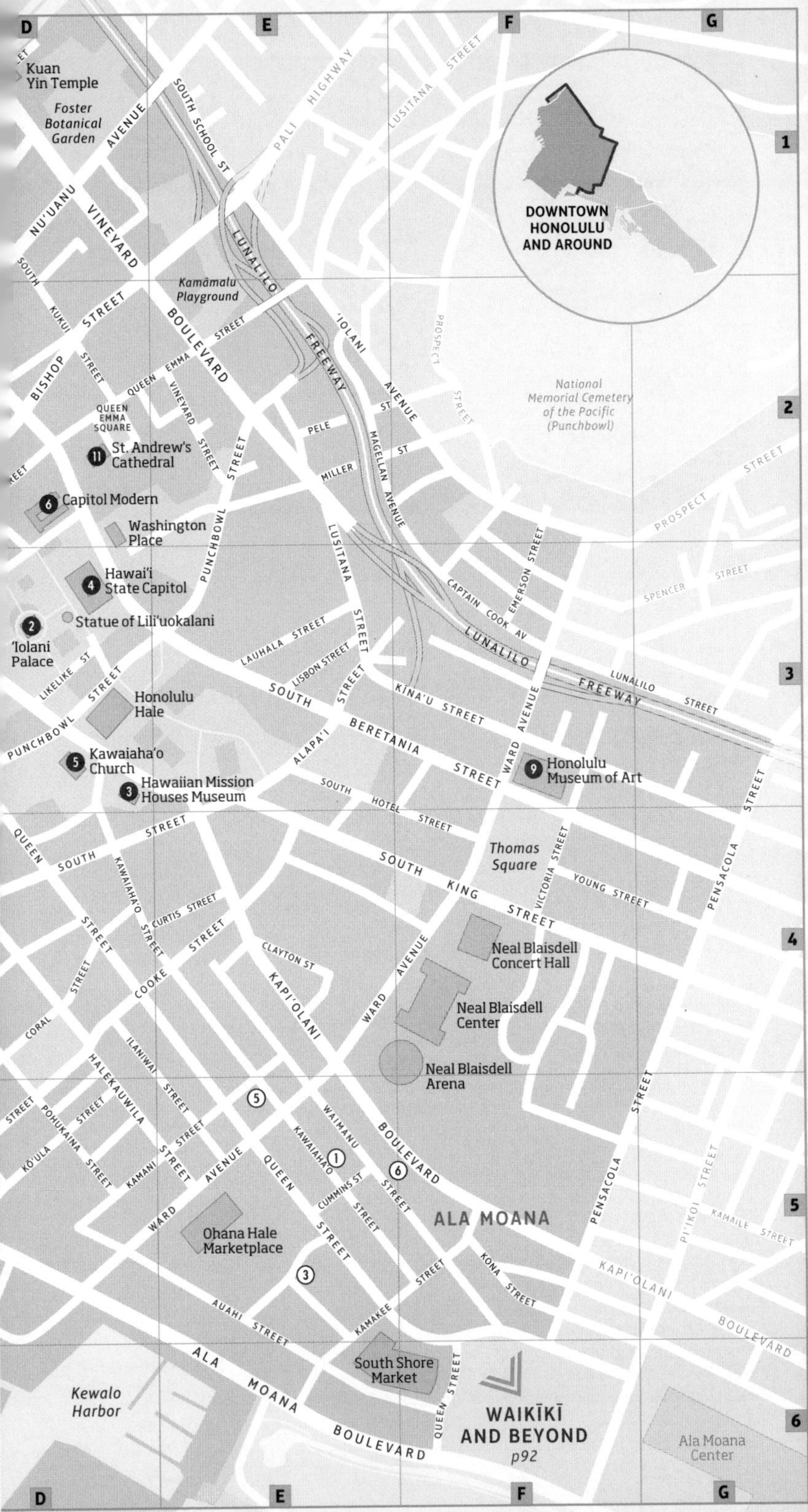
DOWNTOWN HONOLULU AND AROUND
Kuan Yin Temple
Foster Botanical Garden
Kamāmalu Playground
National Memorial Cemetery of the Pacific (Punchbowl)
Queen Emma Square
11 St. Andrew's Cathedral
6 Capitol Modern
Washington Place
4 Hawai'i State Capitol
Statue of Lili'uokalani
2 'Iolani Palace
Honolulu Hale
5 Kawaiaha'o Church
3 Hawaiian Mission Houses Museum
9 Honolulu Museum of Art
Thomas Square
Neal Blaisdell Concert Hall
Neal Blaisdell Center
Neal Blaisdell Arena
ALA MOANA
Ohana Hale Marketplace
South Shore Market
Kewalo Harbor
Ala Moana Center
WAIKĪKĪ AND BEYOND p92
D
E
F
G
1
2
3
4
5
6

CHINATOWN

C2 2, 13 2270 Kalākaua Av, Suite 801, Waikīkī; (808) 524-0722

This neighborhood was established in the late 18th century by Chinese immigrants. Following fires in 1886 and 1900, Chinatown fell into decay. However, today, after much rejuvenation, it is a thriving area with historic shrines, art galleries, and restaurants.

①  

Hawaii Theatre

1130 Bethel St 2, 13 Box office: 9am-5pm Tue-Sat Most federal hols hawaiitheatre.com

Opened in 1922 to present vaudeville, musicals, plays, and silent movies, this beautifully renovated theater today hosts a great selection of films and live performances. Dubbed "The Pride of the Pacific," the theater's Neo-Classical exterior is decorated with designs inspired by Byzantine, Corinthian, and Moorish culture. The lavish interior flaunts ornate columns, marble statuary, and a gilded dome. Excellent tours here cover the history, art, architecture, and restoration of the theater.

Dr. Sun Yat-Sen Statue

100 N Beretania St 4

On the edge of the Chinese Cultural Plaza, just opposite the river, is a statue of Dr. Sun Yat-Sen, a famous Chinese politician, physician, and philosopher. Yat-Sen came to Hawaii in 1879 to study at Honolulu's 'Iolani School and O'ahu College. Here, he learned about Western democracy and the ideals of the American and French revolutions. Years later, in 1911, Yat-Sen played an instrumental role in the overthrow of China's Qing dynasty, and shortly after became the first president of the Republic of China, earning him the name "Father of the Nation."

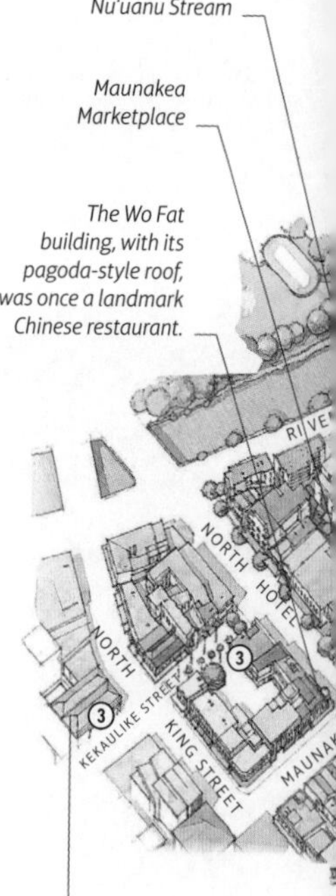

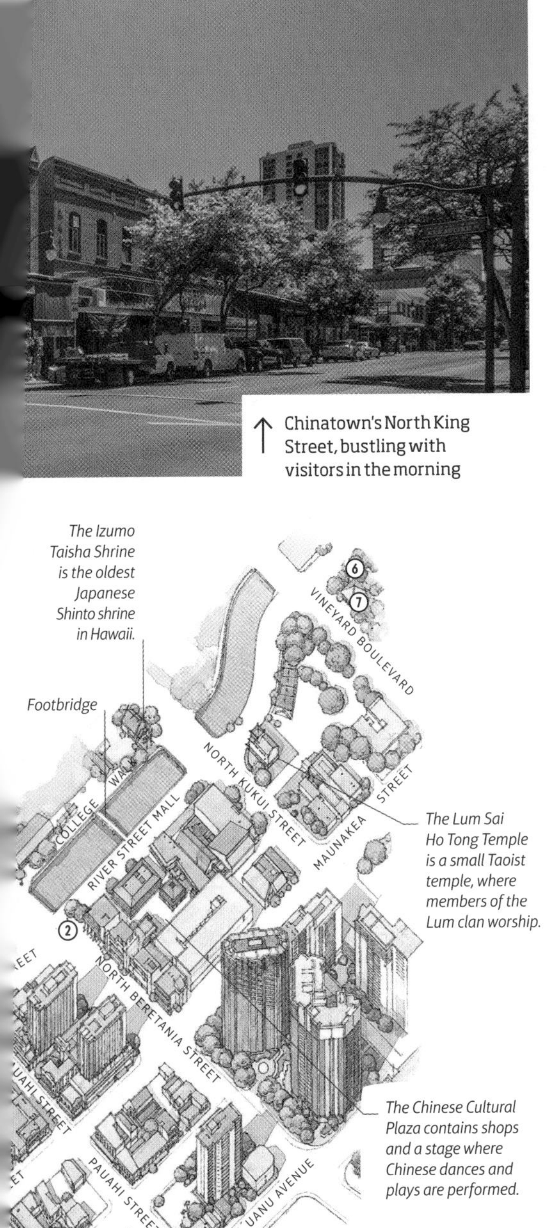

↑ Chinatown's North King Street, bustling with visitors in the morning

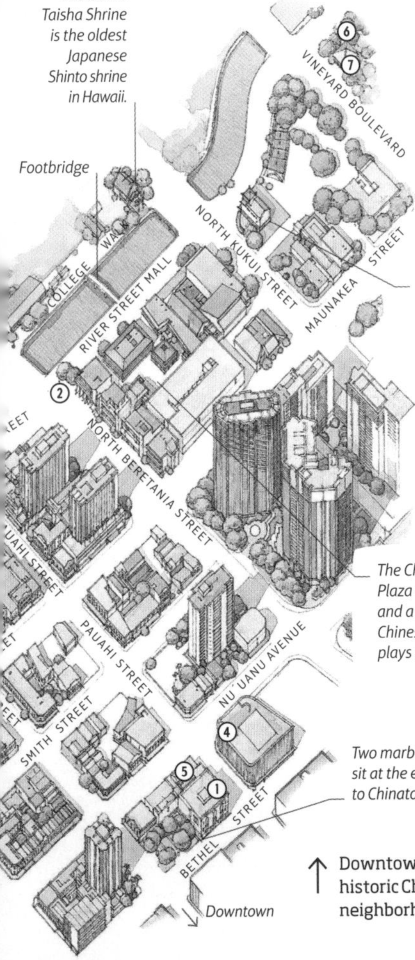

↑ Downtown Honolulu's historic Chinatown neighborhood

DRINK

Tchin Tchin

Fine wine and savory appetizers are served at the cozy rooftop patio of this intimate wine bar.

39 N Hotel St
Sun & Mon **thetchintchinbar.com**

The Dragon Upstairs

Sip on a cocktail and enjoy the live performances at this tiny club. Make the most of the daily happy hours.

1038 Nu'uanu Av
Sun-Wed **thedragonupstairs.com**

Bar 35

Enjoy craft beers, cocktails, and sake alongside gourmet pizzas here.

35 N Hotel St **Sun-Wed** **bar35hawaii.com**

Manifest

This place is a coffee shop by day, and a chic cocktail bar and nightclub by night. Its walls are adorned with works by local artists.

32 N Hotel St
Sun **manifesthawaii.com**

Nextdoor

Spend the evening dancing at this industrial-style nightclub featuring top DJs and live concerts, which range from jazz to heavy metal.

43 N Hotel St
Sun-Tue
nextdoorhi.com

EAT

The Pig and the Lady
This award-winning Vietnamese restaurant offers fresh oysters, amazing pho, and eclectic desserts.
83 N King St Sun & Mon thepigandthe lady.com

Lucky Belly
A modern restaurant specializing in tasty ramen noodle soups.
50 N Hotel St Sun luckybellyhi.com
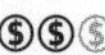

O'Kims Korean Kitchen
Come here to feast on Korean fare. Try the succulent pork belly or the tender braised beef.
1028 Nu'uanu Av Sun okims hawaii.com
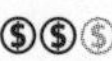

Nami Kaze Hawaii
This creative Japanese restaurant serves delicate hot and cold small plates that you can share.
1135 N Nimitz Hwy Mon & Tue namikaze.com
$$$

Rangoon Burmese Kitchen
Enjoy Burmese dishes inspired by Indian and Thai cuisine at this popular restaurant.
1131 Nu'uanu Av (808) 367-0645 Sun

↑ One of Chinatown's markets, offering a wide variety of goods and produce

Markets

Chinatown's markets are a great place to pick up a snack. Find tropical fruits, seafood, and local vegetables at **O'ahu Market**, and delicious baked goods, meats, and delicacies at the **Kekaulike Market**. Meanwhile, the **Maunakea Marketplace** has a food court serving Asian and Hawaiian dishes, and also sells trinkets.

O'ahu Market
145 N King St
(808) 841-6924 7:30am-4pm Mon-Sat, 7am-2pm Sun

Kekaulike Market
1039 Kekaulike St
(808) 259-7100 7am-3pm daily

Maunakea Marketplace
1120 Maunakea St
(808) 441-9757
6:30am-4pm daily

The ARTS at Marks Garage

1159 Nu'uanu Av
Noon-5pm Tue-Sat
artsatmarks.com

Known as the center of Honolulu's burgeoning art scene, Chinatown is dotted with more than 20 art galleries. One of the best is The ARTS at Marks Garage, where new art shows by local and international talents are exhibited every month. It also hosts art performances, lectures, workshops, and special film screenings.

Downtown Art Center

1041 Nu'uanu Av 11am-6pm Tue-Sat (to 4pm Sun)
downtownarthi.org

Located on the second floor of the Chinatown Gateway Plaza, Downtown Art Center is a bright and modern multipurpose gallery that offers local artists a space for showcasing their work, be it fine art, music, or even creative writing. The center also offers art classes for all ages and hosts art performances, art demonstrations, and other creative events regularly.

Did You Know?

The sidewalks here are made from the ballast stones once used to weigh down visiting Chinese cargo ships.

INSIDER TIP
First Friday Art Walks

On the first Friday of every month, Chinatown's streets are pedestrianized and its art galleries stay open late to showcase the latest exhibits. There are also art demonstrations and live music.

6   

Foster Botanical Garden

180 N Vineyard Blvd
(808) 768-7135 6
9am-4pm daily
Jan 1 & Dec 25

Located right at the edge of Chinatown, the Foster Botanical Garden is an oasis of tranquility in the heart of a fast-paced city. The oldest botanical garden in Hawaii, this site was planted by a pioneering botanist in the 1850s. In the 1880s, it was nurtured by an amateur gardener, before being donated to the city in 1931.

The garden features some of the oldest trees to be found on the island, a dazzling collection of orchids, and a selection of rare and endangered tropical plants. To learn more about the exotic flora here, take a free guided tour of the gardens. There is also an open-air Butterfly Garden where you can spot some of Hawaii's colorful butterflies. Right next to the Butterfly Garden is a small-scale replica of the Great Buddha of Kamakura, which is a 44-ft- (13-m-) tall statue located in Kamakura, Japan.

7  

Kuan Yin Temple

170 N Vineyard Blvd
(808) 533-6361 4
8:30am-2pm daily

Found on the western edge of the lush Foster Botanical Garden, Kuan Yin Temple is the oldest Buddhist place of worship in Hawaii. It is dedicated to Kuan Yin, the Chinese goddess of mercy and a bodhisattva (someone who has achieved nirvana but has forgone it through compassion for those who suffer). Designed in traditional style, the temple has a green ceramic-tile roof, striking red columns, and a peaceful, ornate interior filled with the aromatic smell of burning incense. Devotees often bring fresh fruit or flowers to the temple as an offering. On New Year's Eve, the temple brims with locals who come to seek the blessing of the goddess.

The temple is free but donations are gratefully accepted.

Entrance to the Foster Botanical Garden, and *(inset)* the garden's Great Buddha statue ↓

The decadent throne room at 'Iolani Palace and *(inset)* the beautiful facade

EXPERIENCE MORE

2   

'Iolani Palace

D3 364 S King St 2, 9, 13 9am–4pm Tue–Sat Federal hols iolanipalace.org

King David Kalākaua *(p64)* was inspired by English Victorian architecture when he commissioned this royal residence. Drawing heavily on sugarcane profits, Hawaii's "Merrie Monarch" tried to re-create the pomp and circumstance of the English court in the palace's luxurious interiors.

The only royal palace in the US, 'Iolani ("Royal Hawk") Palace served that function for 11 years. Kalākaua took up residence in 1882, followed by his sister, Lili'uokalani, who reigned for only two years before the monarchy was overthrown in 1893.

The palace became the seat of government, and in 1895, Lili'uokalani was imprisoned here for nine months. The first governor used Kalākaua's bedroom as his office, and the legislature met in the chambers downstairs. After the government moved to the Capitol building, the palace became a set for Jack Lord's office in the television series *Hawaii Five-0*. Fans will recognize the arched floor-to-ceiling windows. Both the first and second floors of the palace are open to the public.

The grounds make a very pleasant place for a stroll. The barracks of Kalākaua's royal guard, which date from 1871, serve as a gift shop and visitor center. The grass near Kalākaua's coronation bandstand makes an ideal picnic spot, and every Friday at noon – except in August – the Royal Hawaiian Band gives a free concert.

Did You Know?

Honolulu's 'Iolani Palace got electric lighting four years before the White House did.

3   

Hawaiian Mission Houses Museum

D3 553 S King St 2, 9, 13 10:30am–4pm Tue–Sat Federal hols missionhouses.org

This bucolic enclave of the past contains the oldest timber-frame house in Hawaii, built by New England missionaries. In 1821, one year after their arrival, Kamehameha II allowed Reverend Bingham to construct a Christian house and to establish Hawaii's first printing press here. A more elegant house followed, part of which contains a replica press. The interiors have been lovingly preserved.

A number of items are on display here, including clothes worn by the missionaries,

such as long underwear. Also on display are original diaries, vintage kitchen crockery, and family heirlooms that reflect the prolific trade of goods with China. Tours focus on missionary history, architecture, and the perspective of Hawaiians and their interactions with the missionaries. The gift shop sells locally crafted artwork that includes jewelry, ceramics, and woodworks.

Hawai'i State Capitol

D3 415 S Beretania St 2, 13 7am–5pm Mon–Fri Federal hols capitol.hawaii.gov

Crossing under the canopy of banyans stretching from 'Iolani Palace to the Hawai'i State Capitol feels like a trip from the old to the new, from Victorian monarchy to the contemporary crossroads of the Pacific.

America's youngest state boasts the most imaginative statehouse, its architecture symbolizing Hawaii's majestic environment. The building rises from a reflecting pool just as the islands rise from the blue Pacific. Fluted columns, suggesting lofty palms, circle the veranda, and two volcano-shaped chambers contain the houses of the legislature. The building can be explored on a self-guided tour.

At the rear, by the Capitol veranda, stands a statue of Queen Lili'uokalani, holding the music to "Aloha 'Oe," a famous ballad she composed. The statue is often decked with lei. In front of the building is a modern statue of Father Damien *(p142)* by Marisol Escobar.

Across Beretania ("Britannia" in Hawaiian) Street is the Eternal Flame, a memorial to World War II soldiers. Farther down the street is **Washington Place**, formerly the governor's mansion and Hawaii's oldest continuously occupied dwelling. This Georgian-style frame house was built by John Dominis, Queen Lili'uokalani's father-in-law, in 1846. After release from imprisonment in the palace, the queen lived out her days in this house, now a museum in her honor. Hawaii's governors reside in a new house on the property.

Washington Place
320 S Beretania St
Tours: 10am Thu (reservations required)
washingtonplace.hawaii.gov

DRINK

Bar Leather Apron

This intimate, high-end bar serves up an extensive and ever-changing menu of cocktails, as well as an excellent choice of whiskeys. There's also a mouthwatering selection of tapas, so you can sate your hunger pangs as you sip.

C3 127A-745 Fort St 5pm–midnight Wed–Sat barleatherapron.com

Café Duck Butt

This lively Korean karaoke bar serves its cocktails inside watermelons. There's also a range of Korean nibbles to snack on, including kimchi fries and *bulgogi* (beef) tacos.

E5 901 Kawaiahao St (808) 593-1880 5pm–2am daily

Doraku

Head to this fun Japanese bar during happy hour (4–6pm Mon–Fri) when there are deals on sake and sushi. As night falls and the offices close, watch this establishment fill up with locals sipping lychee martinis.

F5 1009 Kapi'olani Blvd 11:30am–10pm daily (to 11pm Fri & Sat) dorakusushi.com

The striking Hawai'i State Capitol, the official statehouse of Hawaii

Did You Know?

Casual Fridays, when company employees have a relaxed dress code, began in Honolulu in the 1970s.

Kawaiaha'o Church

D3 957 Punchbowl St 2, 9, 13 8:30am-4pm Mon-Fri, 9:30am Sun for services Federal hols kawaiahaochurch.com

Built in 1842, this imposing edifice – the first Christian Church built on O'ahu – is a monument to Hawaii's missionary days. With the collapse of the old Hawaiian religion around 1820, shortly after Kamehameha I's death, the missionaries soon gained influential converts, including the formidable Ka'ahumanu, the king's favorite wife.

The name of the church refers to the legend of a sacred chiefess who caused water to flow here, but it's also a biblical reference to "living waters." The church, known as "Hawaii's Westminster," was built out of 14,000 hand-cut coral blocks from ocean reefs, hauled from the sea. The New England-style architecture of the church is softened by the coral-block construction. The upper gallery has 21 portraits of Hawaiian monarchs and their families, most of whom were baptized, married, and crowned here.

Outside are two cemeteries for missionaries and their early converts, and a mausoleum where King Lunalilo is buried. This popular king wished to be buried "among his people" at Kawaiaha'o Church. Apart from Kamehameha I, whose bones were hidden so that no one could steal his *mana* (spiritual power), most of the other royalty are laid to rest in the Royal Mausoleum *(p114)*.

Capitol Modern

D2 2nd floor, No.1 Capitol Building, 250 S Hotel St 2, 9, 13 10am-4pm Mon-Sat Federal hols capitolmodern.org

The Capitol Modern museum is housed on the second floor of a Spanish Mission-style building. It is dedicated to Hawaiian art, including bark cloth items, embroidery, quilts, and pottery. Many items blend Western forms and traditional folk art. The museum is also home to Art in Public Places, which has a collection of over 5,000 works of art by more than 1,400 local artists.

Outside the museum, in the pretty sculpture garden, pathways and water features provide a pleasant and tranquil space for reflection. The on-site café, Artizen, offers local farm-fresh salads and delicious Hawaiian sandwiches and smoothies.

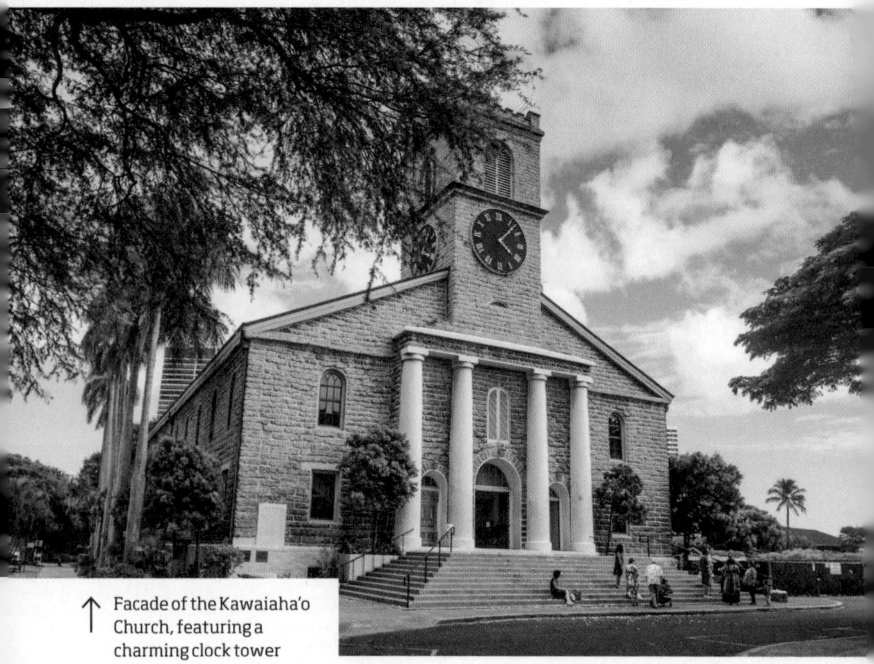

↑ Facade of the Kawaiaha'o Church, featuring a charming clock tower

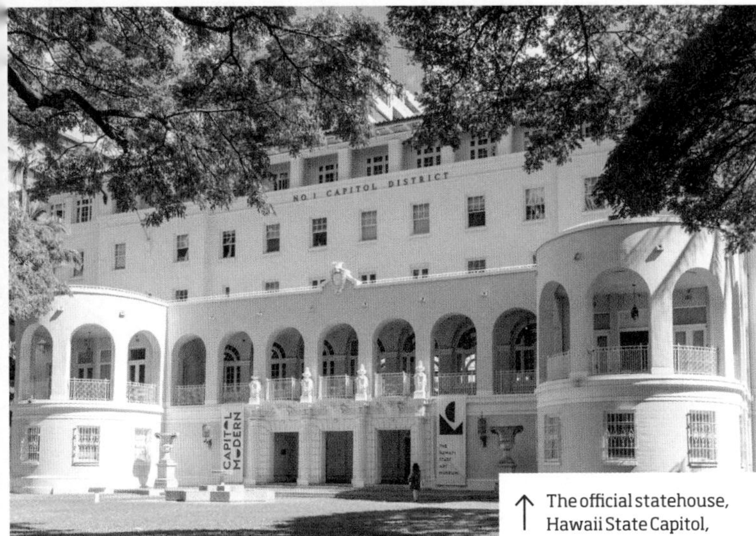

↑ The official statehouse, Hawaii State Capitol, in Honolulu

On the first Friday of every month, the museum remains open until 9pm and features a program of live entertainment suitable for the whole family. Throughout the month, Capitol Modern also hosts art workshops for kids of all ages. Look out for the museum's "meet the artist" lecture series as well. Entry to the museum and all special events is free.

SHOP

Hound & Quail

This curio shop is filled with bric-a-brac, quirky taxidermy, fine art, and unusual gifts. It also hosts art shows and workshops in the basement.

D C2 1156 Nu'uanu Av houndandquail.com

7 King Kamehameha Statue

D3 Corner of King St & Mililani St 2, 13

Kamehameha I, who ruled the islands from 1795 to 1819, is Hawaii's most revered monarch. This Hawai'i Island chief united the islands into a single kingdom and established a respected monarchy. As a young warrior, Kamehameha met a number of foreigners, including Captain Cook in 1778. He soon grasped the importance of Western technology and incorporated ships and cannons into his attempts to unite the Hawaiian Islands. After consolidating the kingdom, Kamehameha I turned his attention to looking after his people.

With its gold-leaf feathered helmet and cloak, the bronze statue in front of Ali'iōlani Hale is one of the most famous sights in Hawaii. The original statue was lost when the ship carrying it sank in a storm, and this replica was unveiled by King Kalākaua in 1883. The original was recovered by divers the same year and erected in Kapa'au *(p202)*.

→ Striking statue of Kamehameha I, Hawaii's first monarch

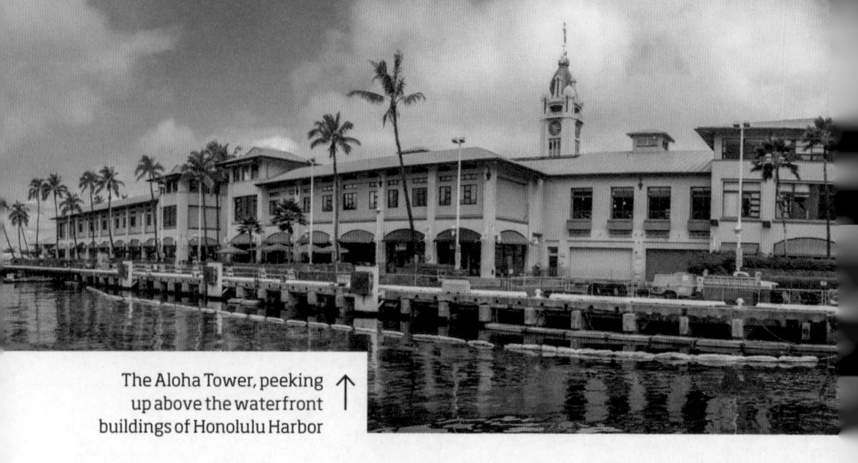

The Aloha Tower, peeking up above the waterfront buildings of Honolulu Harbor

EAT

Hana Koa Brewing Co.
This brewery serves more than 15 craft beers on tap, along with delicious daily specials like Taco Tuesdays.

E5 962 Kawaiahao St hanakoa brewing.com

Hank's Haute Dogs
From genuine Chicago-style all-beef hot dogs to lobster dogs and rabbit sausage, this fast-food joint is a hit.

C5 324 Coral St hankshautedogs.com

Rinka
Modern and spacious Japanese restaurant with excellent lunch specials, including *donburi* (rice) bowls, chicken *karaage* (deep-fried), and sushi combos.

E5 1001 Queen St rinkahawaii.com

8

Aloha Tower

B3 1 Aloha Tower Dr 2, 3, 9, 13 9am–5pm daily alohatower.com

This tower was built in 1926, in the days when tourists arrived by steamship. Locals flocked to Aloha Tower and terminals to sell lei to the passengers and dance the hula – a tradition that lasted until the mid-20th century, when more tourists began traveling to Hawaii by air.

Ten stories high, with four clocks facing the points of the compass, what was Honolulu's tallest building is now dwarfed by skyscrapers.

The building has reinvented itself as part of the Hawai'i Pacific University, with restaurants, shops, and spaces for events. The *Star of Honolulu* ship sails from the tower's harbor, and features dinner with Hawaiian entertainment while it sails around the coast.

Honolulu Museum of Art

F3 900 S Beretania St 2 10am–6pm Wed–Sun (to 9pm Fri & Sat) Federal hols honolulu museum.org

Housed in an impressive building, the Honolulu Museum of Art (HoMA) has been in existence since 1927. The permanent collection includes more than 20,000 works of Asian art, with the highlight being the James A. Michener Collection of more than 10,000 Japanese *ukiyo-e* woodblock prints. The collection also features European art; most noteworthy are the Italian Renaissance paintings, and works by Van Gogh, Monet, and Picasso. American works on display include pieces by Mary Cassatt and Winslow Homer, among others.

A guided tour to the Shangri La, the home of American heiress Doris Duke, starts at the museum. This architectural landmark displays an extensive Islamic art collection from Iran, India, Morocco, and Syria.

Visitors can enjoy the cafés, gardens, concerts, and films in both locations for a single admission fee. On Friday and Saturday evenings, the museum hosts HoMA Nights, where guests can mingle among the art exhibits, listen to live music, and attend art workshops. In the courtyards, stargazing is also possible. Admission is free for children aged 18 and under.

Kaka'ako

C5

First an area of fishing villages and salt ponds, then

PICTURE PERFECT

Art Attack

Each spring, artists from around the world get creative on Kaka'ako's walls, producing striking murals that are ideal for a photo op. Check the website for the current locations *(powwow worldwide.com)*.

an industrial and residential hub, this neighborhood has blossomed into a bustling, contemporary community. Designers have set up shop, brewpubs are thriving, and murals adorn the cement walls.

On the area's southern shoreline there is a pleasant waterfront park and two shopping malls: SALT and Ward Village. Both offer weekly events, including calming courtyard yoga and relaxed art exhibitions. SALT also hosts the Honolulu Night Market, which takes place on the third Saturday of every month, and includes art exhibits and live music, plus food trucks. For local farmers' produce, stop at Kaka'ako Farmers' Market, which takes place on Saturday mornings on Auahi Street.

For Hawaiian books, Hawaiian language and music classes, and lei-making workshops, check out **Nā Mea Hawai'i**. This store also sells locally produced tea, coffee, and chocolate, as well as items made by local artisans.

Nā Mea Hawai'i

1200 Ala Moana Blvd
10am-6pm Mon-Thu, 10am-7pm Fri & Sat (to 5pm Sun) nameahawaii.com

St. Andrew's Cathedral

D2 229 Queen Emma Sq 2, 13 9am-5pm Tue-Fri, 7am Sun for services cathedralhawaii.org

The oldest Episcopal edifice in Hawaii, St. Andrew's was built as an Anglican cathedral in 1867. (It turned Episcopalian in 1898, when Hawaii became an American territory.) Alexander Liholiho (Kamehameha IV) brought Anglicanism to Honolulu following a trip to England during which he was enchanted by English church rituals. His wife, Queen Emma, the granddaughter of Englishman John Young, an advisor of Kamehameha I, was baptized by the first Anglican clergymen to arrive in the islands.

After the death of the king in 1863, Emma traveled to England to raise funds and to find an architect for the cathedral. Kamehameha V, her husband's brother and successor, laid the cornerstone four years later. Much of the stone was imported from England, although the arched walkways are more suggestive of Gothic churches in France.

The cathedral was not consecrated until 1958, when the final phase of construction, including a huge stained-glass mural, was completed. Outside, a striking statue of St. Andrew appears to preach to fish rising from a surrounding pool. The carved message reads "Preach the Gospel to every creature."

← Beautiful stained glass inside St. Andrew's Cathedral and *(inset)* a statue of St. Andrew outside the cathedral

A SHORT WALK CAPITOL DISTRICT

Distance 1 mile (1.6 km) **Time** 25 minutes
Nearest bus S King St & Alakea St

The architectural contrasts in this compact area mirror Hawaii's cultural medley and trace its fascinating history. A short walk takes you from clapboard missionary homes to a sophisticated, Victorian-style palace where Hawaiian kings hosted lavish parties and the last queen of the islands was imprisoned. This majestic survivor of the island monarchy soon gives way, though, to a nearby symbol of 20th-century democracy – one of the few domeless state capitol buildings in the United States.

Did You Know?

The 'Iolani Barracks were constructed with 4,000 coral blocks chiseled by hand from O'ahu's reefs.

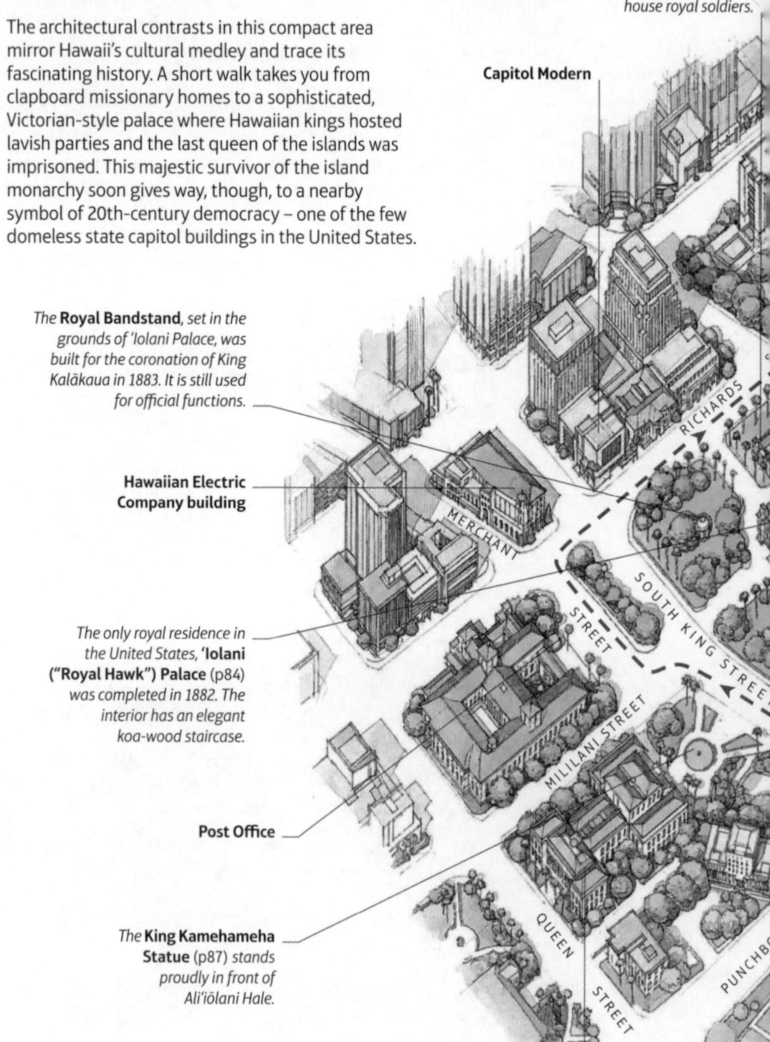

The **'Iolani Barracks** *were built in 1871 to house royal soldiers.*

Capitol Modern

The **Royal Bandstand**, *set in the grounds of 'Iolani Palace, was built for the coronation of King Kalākaua in 1883. It is still used for official functions.*

Hawaiian Electric Company building

The only royal residence in the United States, **'Iolani ("Royal Hawk") Palace** (p84) *was completed in 1882. The interior has an elegant koa-wood staircase.*

Post Office

The **King Kamehameha Statue** (p87) *stands proudly in front of Ali'iōlani Hale.*

Ali'iōlani Hale *("House of the Heavenly King") was designed as a palace and built in 1874. It now houses the Supreme Court and the Judiciary History Center.*

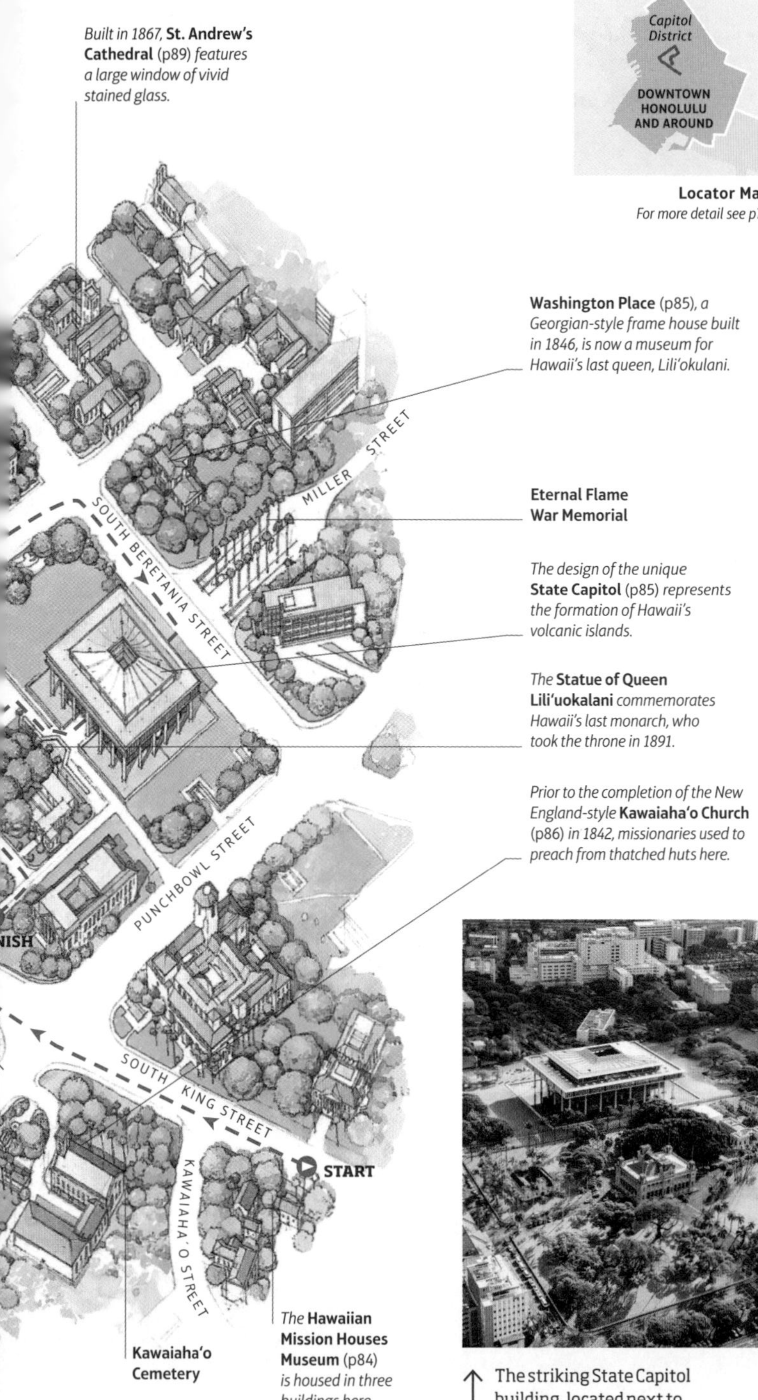

Locator Map
For more detail see p78

↑ The striking State Capitol building, located next to the smaller 'Iolani Palace

Waikīkī Beach at dusk

WAIKĪKĪ AND BEYOND

Waikīkī was once a swampy marshland, irrigated as early as the 1400s by Polynesian settlers who established taro patches and rice paddies. These pioneering newcomers also constructed fishponds along the shore, and for several centuries the area supported the surrounding local communities with its abundant harvests.

In 1809, Kamehameha I, the first king of the Hawaiian Islands, built a royal residence in Waikīkī and his successors followed his lead, establishing summer homes among the fertile coastal fields. Farming continued until the land was reclaimed in the early part of the 20th century; large areas were filled in and the Ala Wai Canal was dug to drain the area by diverting streams from the hills above Waikīkī to the sea. Seawalls and groins were also built to protect the coast from erosion.

Tourists began to flock to Waikīkī in the late 19th century, and in 1901 the area's first hotel, the Moana Hotel (today the Moana Surfrider), was built. It included a wooden pier that extended 300 ft (90 m) into the sea. Tourism accelerated in the 1920s with the opening of the Royal Hawaiian Hotel, which was host to movie stars and the well-heeled crowd. During the first half of the 20th century, sand was imported to help bolster Waikīkī Beach, a strip of golden sand that became popular with sunbathers and – in particular – surfers. Previously discouraged by Christian missionaries, this watersport flourished once again after Duke Kahanamoku, a Waikīkī resident and Olympic gold medalist, popularized it in the 1930s. Today, Waikīkī remains one of Hawaii's most popular spots for sun, sand, sea, and surfing.

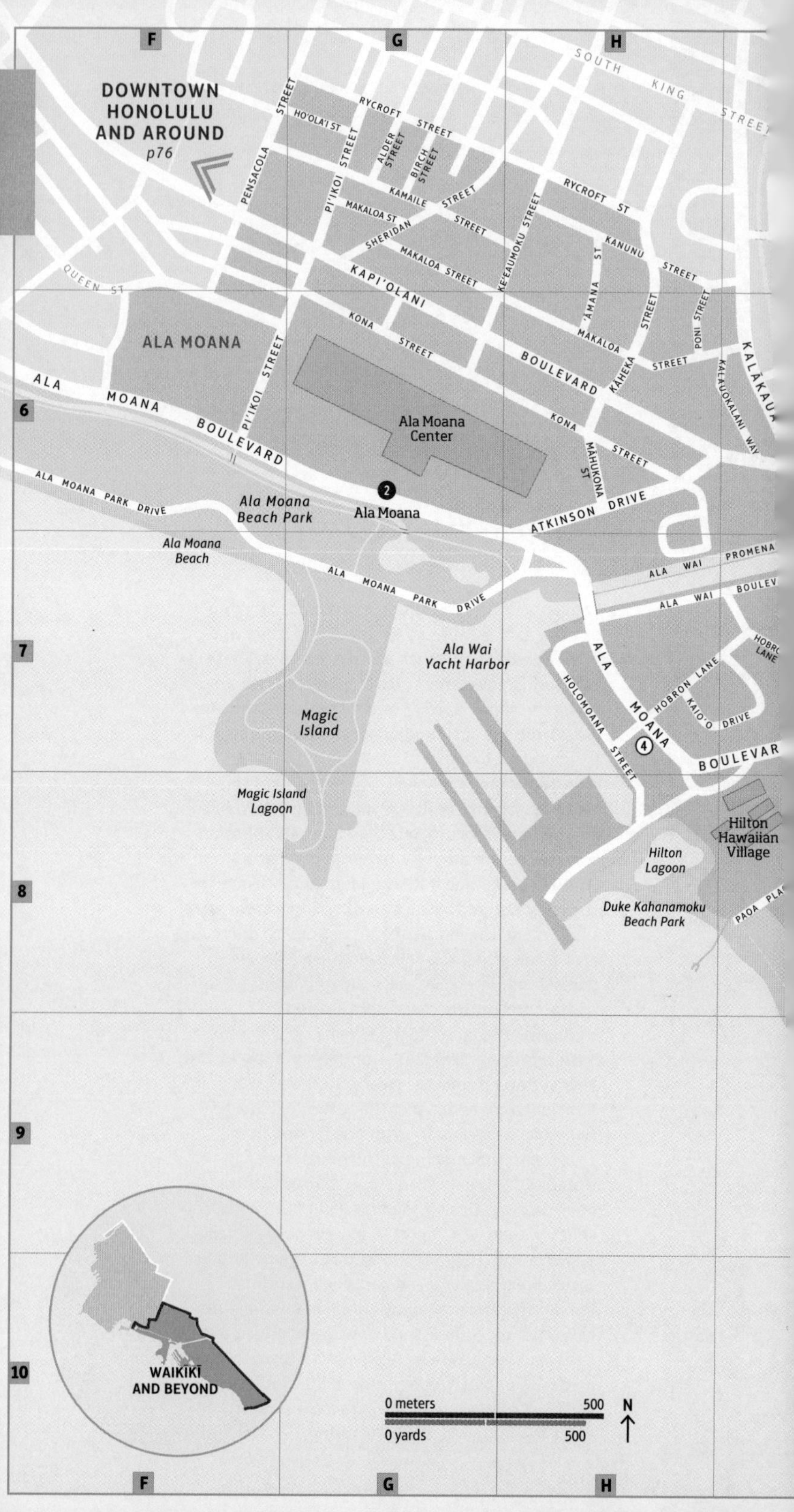

F
G
H
DOWNTOWN HONOLULU AND AROUND
p76
ALA MOANA
Ala Moana Center
Ala Moana
Ala Moana Beach Park
Ala Moana Beach
Ala Wai Yacht Harbor
Magic Island
Magic Island Lagoon
Hilton Hawaiian Village
Hilton Lagoon
Duke Kahanamoku Beach Park
SOUTH KING STREET
RYCROFT STREET
HO'OLA'I ST
PENSACOLA STREET
PI'IKOI STREET
ALDER STREET
BIRCH STREET
KAMAILE STREET
MAKALOA ST
SHERIDAN STREET
MAKALOA STREET
KE'EAUMOKU STREET
RYCROFT ST
KANUNU STREET
'ĀMANA ST
KAPI'OLANI BOULEVARD
KONA STREET
MAKALOA
KĀHEKA STREET
PONI STREET
KALĀKAUA
KALAUOKALANI WAY
QUEEN ST
ALA MOANA BOULEVARD
ALA MOANA PARK DRIVE
MĀHUKONA ST
ATKINSON DRIVE
ALA WAI PROMENA
ALA WAI BOULEV
HOBRON LANE
HOLOMOANA STREET
KAIO'O DRIVE
PAOA PLA
6
7
8
9
10
WAIKĪKĪ AND BEYOND
0 meters 500
0 yards 500
N

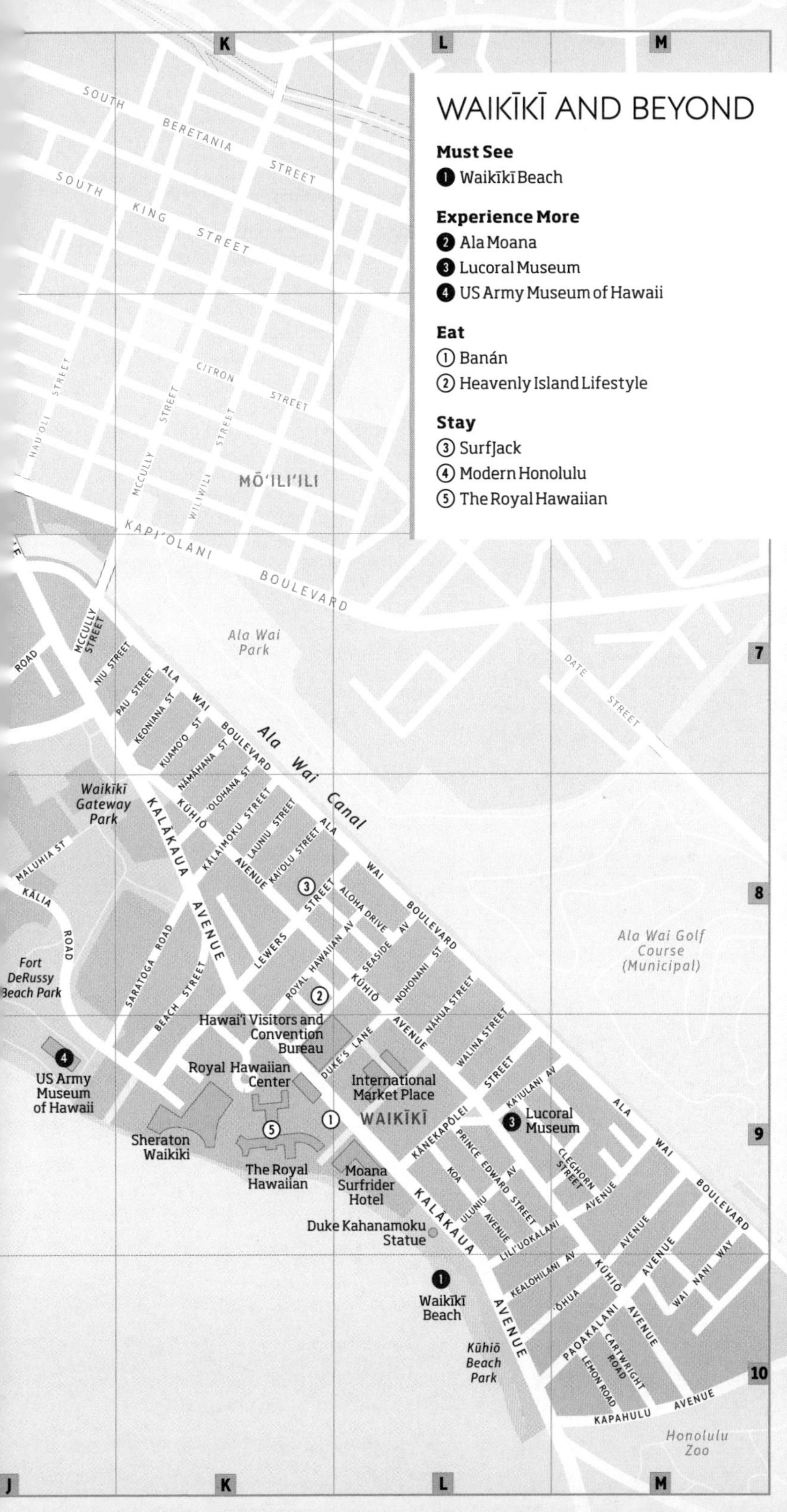

WAIKĪKĪ AND BEYOND
Must See
1 Waikīkī Beach
Experience More
2 Ala Moana
3 Lucoral Museum
4 US Army Museum of Hawaii
Eat
① Banán
② Heavenly Island Lifestyle
Stay
③ SurfJack
④ Modern Honolulu
⑤ The Royal Hawaiian
K
L
M
J
7
8
9
10
SOUTH BERETANIA STREET
SOUTH KING STREET
CITRON STREET
HAU'OLI STREET
MCCULLY STREET
WILIWILI STREET
MŌ'ILI'ILI
KAPI'OLANI BOULEVARD
Ala Wai Park
DATE STREET
Ala Wai Canal
ALA WAI BOULEVARD
NIU STREET
PAU STREET
KEONIANA ST
KUAMO'O ST
NĀMĀHANA ST
'OLOHANA ST
KALAIMOKU STREET
LAUNIU STREET
KA'OLU STREET
KŪHIŌ AVENUE
KALĀKAUA AVENUE
Waikīkī Gateway Park
MALUHIA ST
KĀLIA ROAD
Fort DeRussy Beach Park
SARATOGA ROAD
BEACH STREET
LEWERS STREET
ROYAL HAWAIIAN AV
ALOHA DRIVE
SEASIDE AV
NOHONANI ST
NĀHUA STREET
WALINA STREET
Ala Wai Golf Course (Municipal)
Hawai'i Visitors and Convention Bureau
Royal Hawaiian Center
DUKE'S LANE
International Market Place
WAIKĪKĪ
US Army Museum of Hawaii
Sheraton Waikiki
The Royal Hawaiian
Moana Surfrider Hotel
Duke Kahanamoku Statue
Lucoral Museum
KA'IULANI AV
KĀNEKAPŌLEI
PRINCE EDWARD STREET
KOA
ULUNIU AVENUE
CLEGHORN STREET
LILI'UOKALANI AVENUE
KEALOHILANI AV
'ŌHUA
PAOAKALANI AVENUE
CARTWRIGHT ROAD
LEMON ROAD
WAI NANI WAY
KAPAHULU AVENUE
Waikīkī Beach
Kūhiō Beach Park
Honolulu Zoo

1

WAIKĪKĪ BEACH

L10 20 2270 Kalākaua Av, Suite 801; (808) 524-0722

Overlooked by Honolulu's glittering skyscrapers and fronting a calm turquoise bay, Waikīkī is among the most famous beaches in the world. Attracting over five million visitors every year, this 2.5-mile (4-km) stretch of soft white sand is actually made up of several different beaches, including surf-spot Queen's and family-friendly Kūhiō.

Royal Hawaiian Beach

This buzzing stretch of sand runs from the iconic salmon-pink facade of the Royal Hawaiian hotel *(p103)*, all the way to the lei-draped bronze statue of surfing icon Duke Kahanamoku. Despite making up only a small section of the main Waikīkī strip, this beach is occasionally – and somewhat confusingly – referred to as Waikīkī Beach.

The Royal Hawaiian Beach is a great spot to enjoy water-based activities, including stand-up paddleboarding, surfing, and canoeing. Several companies also offer catamaran rides that start from the beach.

Found just off the Royal Hawaiian Beach are four volcanic boulders, a tribute to the quartet of healers who came from Tahiti centuries ago and helped to heal the maladies of the locals; the boulders are said to possess the special healing powers of these Tahitian visitors.

Kūhiō Beach

This large swath of golden sand is a relaxed and family-friendly spot. Two seawalls here – built to protect the sand from erosion – have divided the sea in front of Kūhiō into a pair of placid pools, and have given the beach its nickname of "Kūhiō Ponds." These enclosed and protected swimming spots are ideal for families with children. The facilities are good, too, and include washrooms and showers. Plus there's a lifeguard on duty here.

The beach offers outrigger canoe rides during the day as well as hula and music shows at sunset. On Tuesday and Saturday evenings, you can catch a free Hawaiian hula performance at the Kūhiō Beach Hula Mound, found to the northern edge of the beach, where it joins with the Royal Hawaiian Beach. The show commences with a ceremony that features the light-ing of a torch along with the traditional blowing of a conch shell.

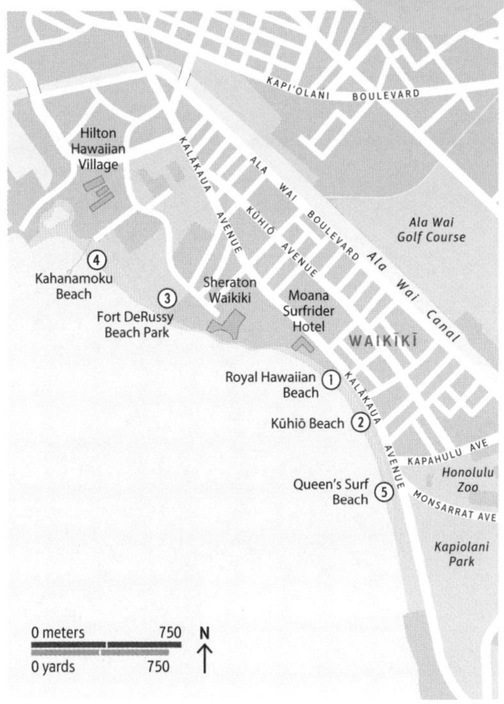

↑ Waikīkī Beach, backed by hotels and resorts, and *(inset)* taking a canoe ride just off the beach

DUKE KAHANAMOKU

Duke Kahanamoku (1890–1968) first swam into fame at the 1912 Olympics, when he broke the world record for the 100-m freestyle. It was as the father of modern surfing, though, that "the Duke" really made his name. He popular-ized the Hawaiian pastime, called *he'e nalu* (wave sliding), by giving demonstra-tions in the US, Europe, and Australia.

The palm-shaded Kūhiō and Queen's Surf beaches, divided by the Waikīkī Wall

Fort DeRussy Beach Park

The property of Chinese millionaire Chun Afong during the 1850s, Fort DeRussy Beach Park is now an active military reservation that's largely open to the public. The fine white-sand beach here is bordered by a pretty park laced with shady paved paths to the north, and is lapped by gentle waves to the south, making it an ideal spot for families. Facilities include washrooms, a playground, and picnic areas; the free US Army Museum of Hawaii *(p103)* is close by, too.

Kahanamoku Beach

Named after the legendary Duke Kahanamoku *(p97)*, this wide stretch of beachfronts the Hilton Hawaiian Village and the Duke Kahanamoku Lagoon, a sparkling, human-made saltwater pool. This sandy spot is one of Waikīkī's more popular and busier beaches – and it's easy to see why. Kahanamoku has a gentle slope and a protected seawall, and so is perfect for relaxed and leisurely swimming. Its spectacular lagoon, meanwhile, offers an array of fun-filled activities for families and is a great place to lounge on a beach chair, enjoy a tranquil swim, or ride an aqua-cycle.

From the nearby Hilton Pier, **Atlantis Submarine** tours depart and take guests down to the ocean floor to explore the marine life that lives here. Expect to see yellow tangs, moray eels, stingrays, and green sea turtles – if you're really lucky, you might even spot a reef shark. The submarines are eco-friendly: being battery-powered, they emit little noise and no pollutants. The tour company has also been instrumental in creating artificial reefs – including sunken ships and concrete pyramids – allowing the marine life here to continue to thrive.

INSIDER TIP

Light Up the Night Sky

Every Friday night at about 7:45pm (weather permitting) the Hilton Hawaiian Village puts on a fabulous fireworks display. Find a spot on Kahanamoku Beach to watch the show.

Atlantis Submarine
252 Paoa Pl atlantisadventures.com

Queen's Surf Beach

This sandy spot is named after the last monarch of Hawaii, Queen Lili'uokalani *(p64)*, who used to have a beach house at this location. It offers up excellent surf,

SURF SCHOOLS

Waikiki Beach Services
waikikibeachservices.com
Teaching locals and visitors how to ride the waves since 1955.

Big Wave Dave Surf Co.
bigwavedave.com
Coffee shop and surf shop all in one, with lessons for experts and beginners alike.

Gone Surfing Hawaii
gonesurfinghawaii.com
Surfing lessons for all age groups, with an option of taking lessons at sunset.

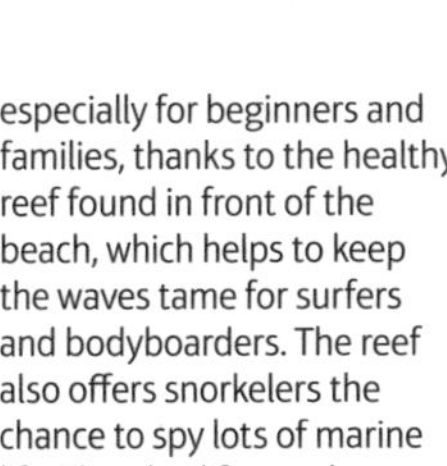

especially for beginners and families, thanks to the healthy reef found in front of the beach, which helps to keep the waves tame for surfers and bodyboarders. The reef also offers snorkelers the chance to spy lots of marine life. There's a lifeguard on duty here.

The south end of the beach has been popular with the local LGBTQ+ community since the 1980s. It is a quieter, more secluded beach with no hotels and only the leafy green expanse of Kapi'olani Park *(p117)* situated behind it.

Occasionally, special movie nights known as **Sunset on the Beach** are hosted here. This event is free and includes live music, entertainment, and food stalls, followed by a movie screening on a giant 1,000-ft (300-m) outdoor screen.

Sunset on the Beach
sunsetonthebeach.net

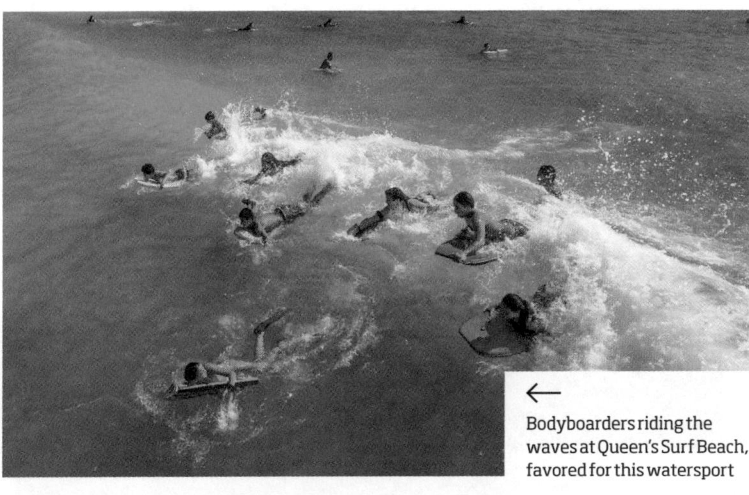

←
Bodyboarders riding the waves at Queen's Surf Beach, favored for this watersport

SURFING IN HAWAII

Practiced by Polynesians for centuries, the art of "wave sliding," aka surfing, is now a thriving watersport in Hawaii. Athletes from around the world flock to the Hawaiian Islands to test their swell-carving skills in some of the world's best surfing conditions. Surfing can be pursued throughout the year, but the waves reach their peak from November through April, when the north shore of the islands can be dangerous for experienced surfers, let alone beginners. Be sure to avoid big surfs and never go surfing alone.

SURF SPOTS FOR BEGINNERS

With its bounty of protected bays and outfitters offering lessons and rentals, Hawaii is ideal for surfing novices. One of the best spots to test the waters is Waikīkī Beach *(p96)*, on O'ahu. This sandy beach features gentle breaks and plenty of lifeguards who can offer advice if you're struggling. The Cove in Kīhei on Maui is another popular spot for beginners. It offers consistent surf and is best attempted in the early mornings before the winds kick up. Over on Kaua'i, Po'ipū Beach is an excellent place for those learning to surf – the Kiahuna Beach stretch in particular promises mellow waves close to shore. Kahalu'u Beach Park in Keauhou, on Hawai'i Island, has dependable surfing conditions year-round and crystal-clear waters overlooked by the ruins of the Ku'emanu Heiau – an ancient temple. The north end of the beach is especially popular with beginners; stand-up paddleboarders, or *hoe he'e nalu*, gather here as well.

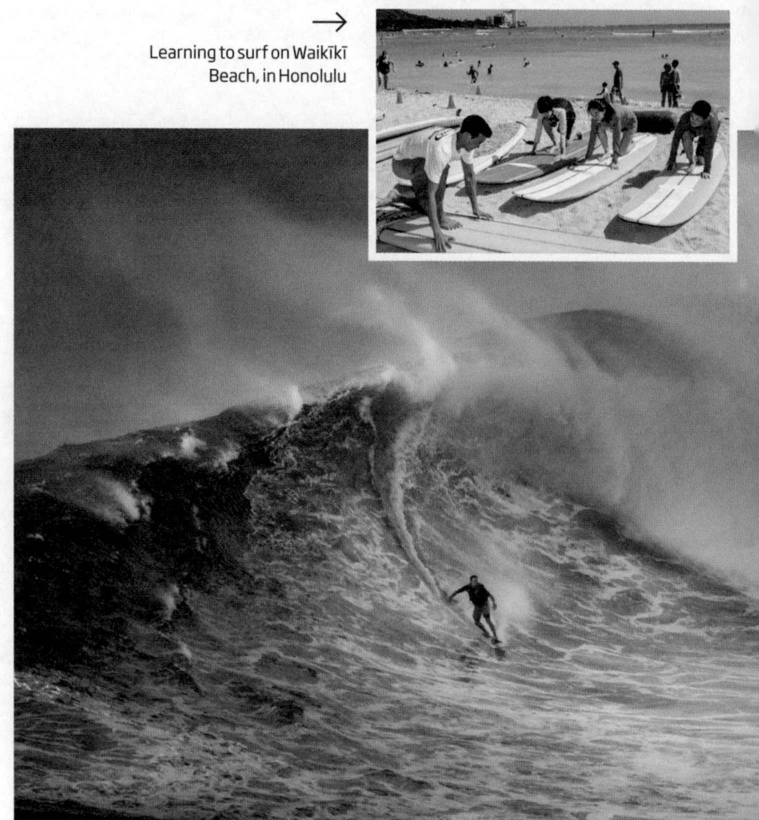

→ Learning to surf on Waikīkī Beach, in Honolulu

Catching a wave off the coast of O'ahu

SURF SPOTS FOR EXPERTS

Hawaii features many world-famous and iconic surfing locations. O'ahu's legendary North Shore is a hub for experienced surfers. Dubbed locally as the "Seven Mile Miracle," with 7 miles (11 km) of excellent surf spots between Hale'wa and Sunset Beach, this area is the surfing capital of the world, and the site of the annual Triple Crown surfing contest. During the big wave season, from November to April, waves can reach over 40 ft (12 m) high. Over on Maui, surfers head to the reef-rich cove of Honolua Bay to test their skills along the three main breaks of the wave: the point (farthest out, with powerful waves), the cave (thick barrels), and keiki bowls (where young surfers congregate). Also on Maui, Pe'ahi, better known to locals as "Jaws," is where surfers seeking a real adrenaline rush are towed out by jet-skis to catch huge waves reaching 50–60 ft (15–18 m) high.

SECRET SURF SPOTS

Hawaii's coastlines are awash with lesser-known surfing locations, ideal for those who prefer to share the ocean with only a handful of wave riders. On Hawai'i Island, just south of Kealakekua Bay, lies the secluded rocky cove of Ke'ei Beach. While the swells remain relatively small, it's the long wave ride and serene atmosphere that surfers appreciate best here. Kaua'i's west side features Pakala's Beach, which is popular with expert surfers and known for its "Infinities" surf break. On Lāna'i, the white sands of Lopa Beach see more fishers than surfers. Expect challenging swells for expert surfers here. Hālawa Bay Beach Park, on Moloka'i, offers sizable and thrilling winter waves with few visitors.

"Jaws," a surfing spot in Maui known for its monster waves

HAWAII'S SURFING HISTORY

Though its exact origins are unclear, *he'e nalu* (wave sliding) has been practiced here for centuries. The sport was dominated by the *ali'i* (royals), who used surf breaks denied to commoners. In the 19th century, surfing declined after missionaries discouraged it, but it experienced a revival in the early 20th century when Olympic medalist Duke Kahanamoku *(p97)* helped popularize the sport. By the 1960s daredevil surfers, including American surfing legend Mike Doyle (1941–2019), had begun to visit Hawaii for challenging surf.

EXPERIENCE MORE

Ala Moana

G6

Straddling the gap between Kaka'ako and Waikīkī, the Ala Moana neighborhood is best known for its **Ala Moana Beach Park** and **Ala Moana Center**. The Ala Moana Beach Park is a local resident favorite, and attracts swimmers and picnickers who come to relax on the park's beautiful golden-sand beach and splash in the natural lagoon. The park is also home to an artificial peninsula, Magic Island, which offers beautiful views over Waikīkī Beach *(p96)* and Diamond Head *(p117)*, a volcanic crater.

INSIDER TIP
Waikiki Trolley

With lines stopping at key sights, this trolley is a handy alternative to driving or taking the bus around Honolulu and beyond. Purchase a one-, four-, or seven-day pass for unlimited hop-on, hop-off access.

Paved trails around the park are perfect for strolling or biking with one of Honolulu's Biki Bike rentals *(p133)*, a bike-sharing program – just look for the turquoise bikes anywhere in the city. On Memorial Day (end of May) the park hosts the Lantern Floating Ceremony where thousands of paper lanterns are lit at sunset.

For shoppers, the upscale and open-air Ala Moana Center is a definite highlight, as it has over 300 stores to choose from, including top luxury brands such as Gucci and Prada and high-end department stores such as Macy's and Nordstrom. The center also has a children's playground and an excellent food court with a huge range of choices, from *gelato* (ice cream) to poke (diced raw fish), burgers, and ramen.

Ala Moana Beach Park
1201 Ala Moana Blvd
(808) 768-4611
4am-10pm daily

Ala Moana Center
1450 Ala Moana Blvd
Hours vary, check website alamoanacenter.com

Lucoral Museum

L9 2414 Kūhiō Av (808) 922-1999 2, 8, 13, 19 9am-5:30pm Mon-Fri

Established in 1989, this unusual museum celebrates the natural world through an eclectic mix of exhibits. The main focus is a collection of Hawaiian corals, shells, and pearls, including examples of jewelry and other things made from these natural resources. The museum also contains an extensive collection of gemstones, rocks, and ancient fossils, including one of a dinosaur egg. Other notable exhibits include taxidermied Hawaiian birds, displays on local flora, and an area exploring the island's volcanic history.

Visitors can watch jewelry makers transform pearls and coral into creative pieces (a selection of which can be bought at the gift shop), and can join jewelry-making workshops held here on Tuesday and Thursday afternoons. Weekly lectures, on topics such as gemstone identification and the history of pearls in Hawaii, are also offered. The museum and lectures are free, but the workshops have a small fee.

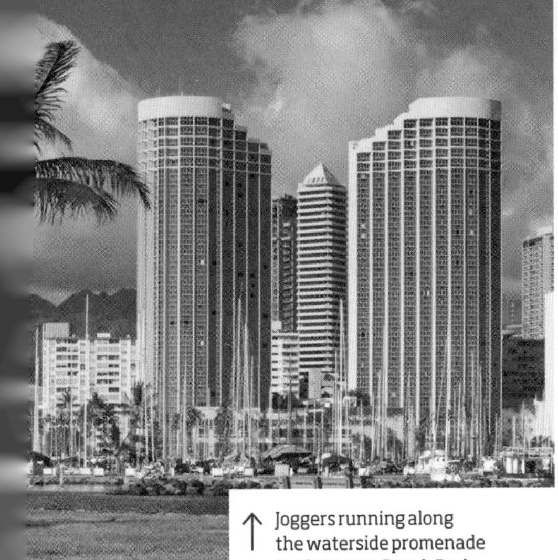

Joggers running along the waterside promenade in Ala Moana Beach Park

4

US Army Museum of Hawaii

J9 Battery Randolph, 2131 Kālia Rd, Fort DeRussy Beach Park 8, 19, 20 10am–5pm Tue–Sat hiarmymuseumsoc.org

The fascinating US Army Museum of Hawaii is housed in a cavernous concrete bunker. Built in 1911 as a key part of the "Ring of Steel," which encircled the island of O'ahu, the bunker's primary mission was the defense of Pearl Harbor and Honolulu from attacking battleships.

The well-designed museum memorializes the US Army's multifaceted history in the Pacific. Detailed exhibits cover Hawaii's military past, stretching from early warfare through to World War II, and the Vietnam, Korean, and Iraq wars. The collection includes weapons and a retired army helicopter from the 1960s. The museum also features a "Gallery of Heroes" honoring recipients of the Medal of Honor and the Distinguished Service Cross.

Outside, further relics are displayed within the military reservation of Fort DeRussy Beach Park, including Japanese tanks from World War II.

One of the excellent exhibits found at the US Army Museum of Hawaii

EAT

Banán

This former food truck offers delectable soft-serve desserts, made with local bananas.

K9 2301 Kalākaua Av banan.co

Heavenly Island Lifestyle

A busy spot for organic, farm-to-table Hawaii-inspired brunch, including eggs benedict.

K8 342 Seaside Av heavenly-waikiki.com

STAY

SurfJack

This modern, eco-friendly boutique hotel is just a quick stroll from the beach.

K8 412 Lewers St surfjack.com

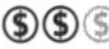

Modern Honolulu

A sleek harborfront and sustainability-focused hotel.

H7 1775 Ala Moana Blvd hilton.com

$$$

The Royal Hawaiian

Dating from 1927, this salmon-pink, luxury beachfront hotel is one of Honolulu's most famous landmarks.

K9 2259 Kalākaua Av royal-hawaiian.com

A SHORT WALK
WAIKĪKĪ HISTORIC TRAIL

Did You Know?

Waikīkī means "spouting waters" in Hawaiian.

Distance 2 miles (3 km) **Time** 45 minutes
Nearest bus Kalākaua Av & Monsarrat Av

Best known today for its long stretches of sand, stylish hotels, and laid-back beachside bars, Waikīkī also has a rich history that dates back centuries. Visitors can uncover it by taking a stroll along the Waikīkī Historic Trail, which starts near the imposing volcanic cone of Diamond Head. The route consists of a collection of 23 bronze, surfboard-shaped markers, each of which narrates an aspect of the area's rich history, whether its time as a place of sprawling taro fields and fishponds, its role as a royal retreat, or its part in the revival of surfing.

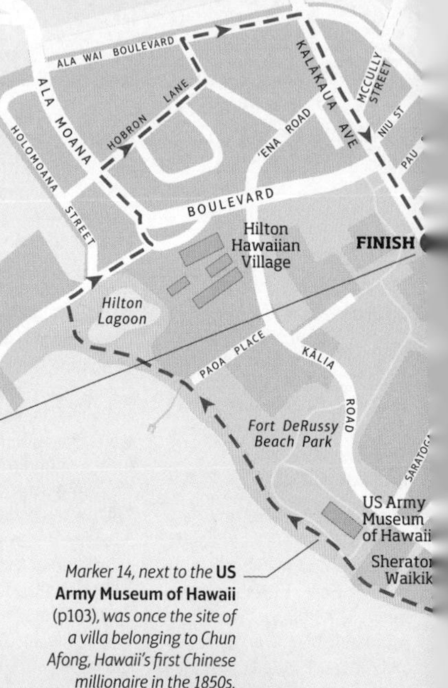

Toward the end of the trail, near the Hilton Hawaiian Village, marker 21 stands in front of a large **statue of King David Kalākaua**, *the last king of Hawaii. He was often called the "Merrie Monarch" because of his passion for music and dance.*

Marker 14, next to the **US Army Museum of Hawaii** *(p103), was once the site of a villa belonging to Chun Afong, Hawaii's first Chinese millionaire in the 1850s.*

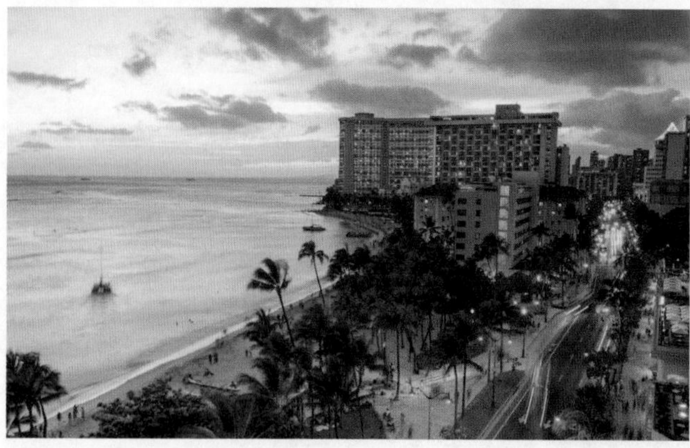

↑ Waikīkī Beach and Kalākaua Avenue, illuminated by a pink-hued sunset

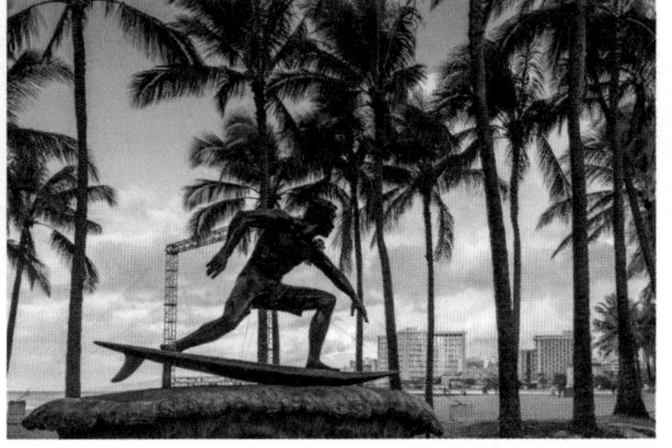

Statue of Duke Kahanamoku surrounded by palm trees on Queen's Surf Beach ↑

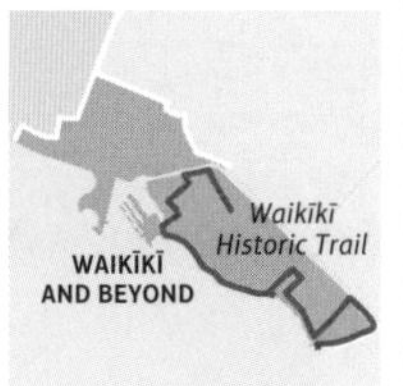

Locator Map
For more detail see p94

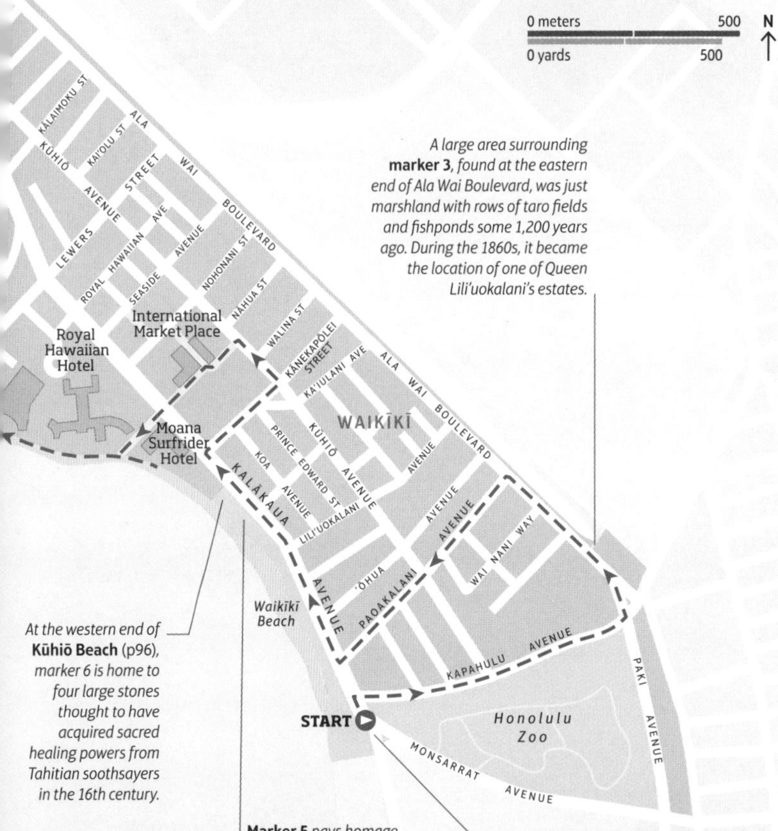

0 meters 500
0 yards 500
N

A large area surrounding **marker 3**, *found at the eastern end of Ala Wai Boulevard, was just marshland with rows of taro fields and fishponds some 1,200 years ago. During the 1860s, it became the location of one of Queen Lili'uokalani's estates.*

At the western end of **Kūhiō Beach** (p96), *marker 6 is home to four large stones thought to have acquired sacred healing powers from Tahitian soothsayers in the 16th century.*

Marker 5 *pays homage to Hawaiian icon Duke Kahanamoku* (p97). *Nick-named "The Big Kahuna," he was famous for winning five Olympic medals and for introducing surfing to the mainstream.*

Where Monsarrat Avenue and Kalākaua Avenue merge, look for **marker 1**, *with brief descriptions of legendary surf spots Queen's Surf Beach (p98) and Sans Souci Beach.*

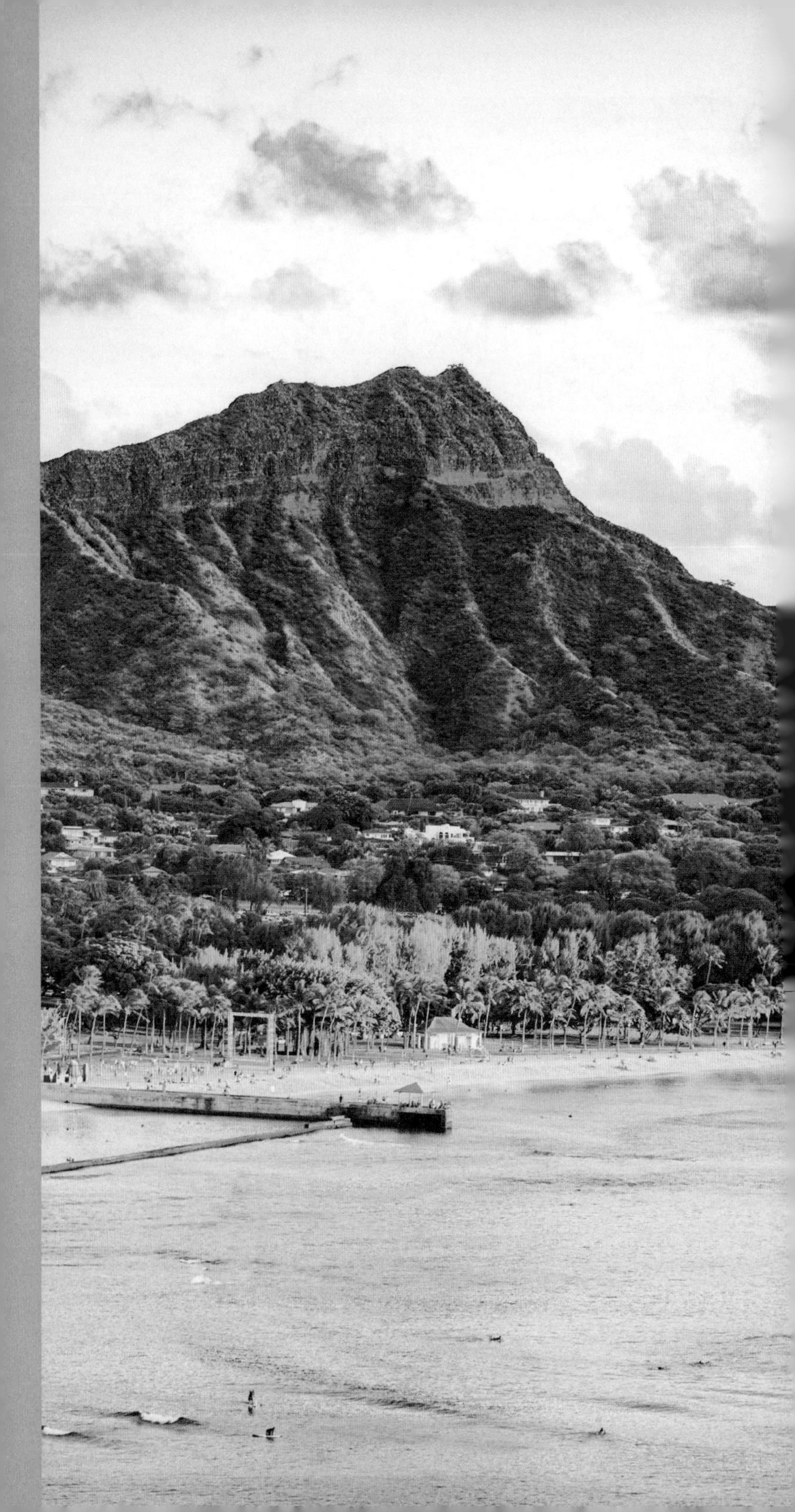

Diamond Head looming over the coast

BEYOND THE CENTER

Must Sees

1. Bishop Museum
2. Pearl Harbor

Experience More

3. Royal Mausoleum
4. Queen Emma Summer Palace
5. National Memorial Cemetery of the Pacific
6. O'ahu Cemetery
7. Mānoa Valley
8. Mānoa Heritage Center
9. Lyon Arboretum
10. Kapi'olani Park
11. Diamond Head

Less than a million years ago, a series of volcanic eruptions created some of the well-known landmarks around Honolulu, including Diamond Head, a volcanic crater regarded as sacred by O'ahu's Polynesian settlers. Just north lies the Mānoa Valley, a rainforest area that became prime agricultural land for early settlers; it was here that O'ahu's first sugarcane plantations sprung up in the 1800s. In 1848, Queen Emma constructed her summer palace to the west of the valley and, just over 50 years later, the Bishop Museum was established nearby to house royal heirlooms. In 1941, the area west of the city became the focus of World War II, when Pearl Harbor was attacked. Today, the area contains a mixture of historic sights, interesting museums, and stunning nature.

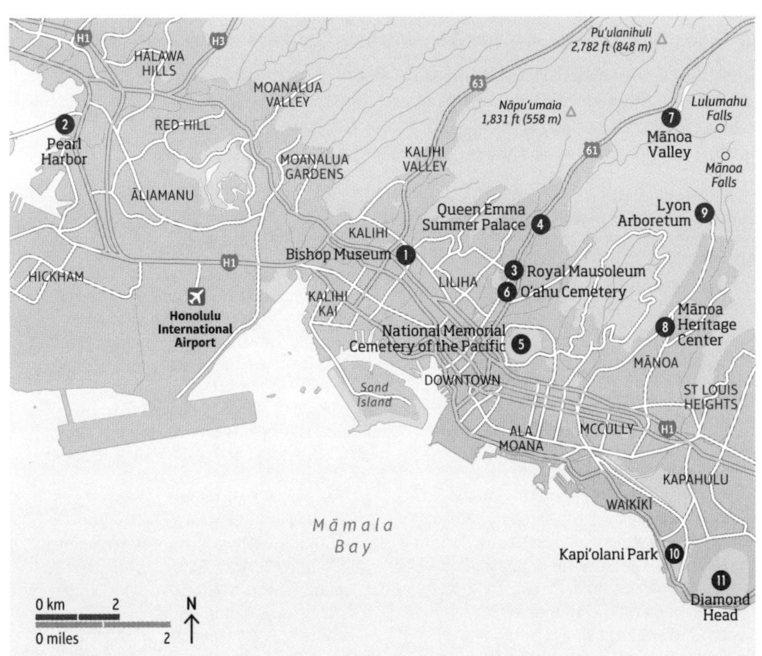

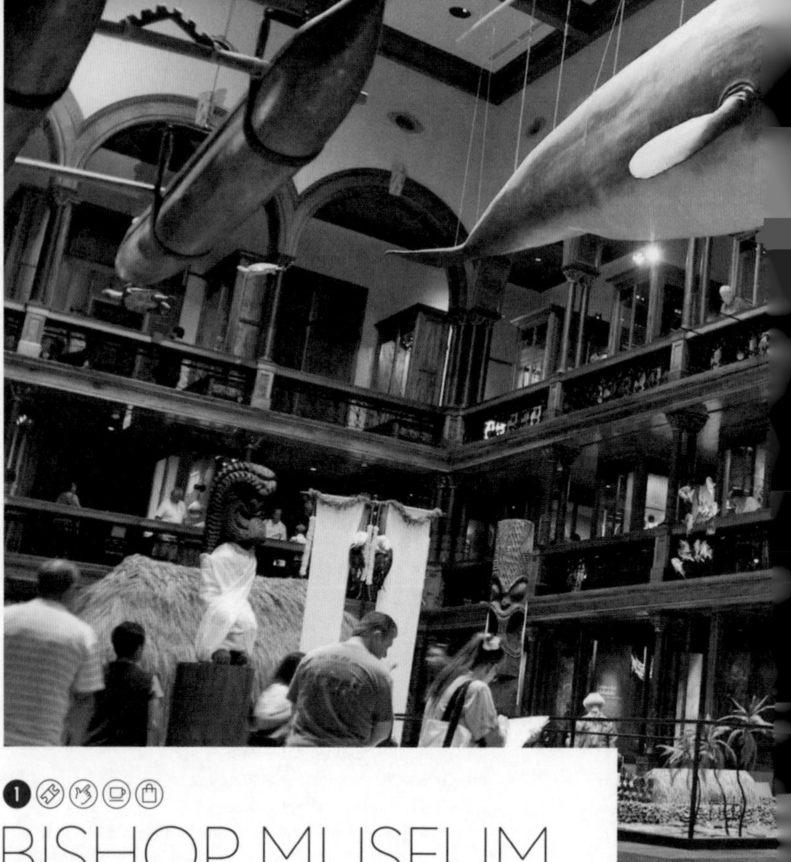

1

BISHOP MUSEUM

1525 Bernice St 2 9am-5pm daily Dec 25 bishopmuseum.org

Considered the world's finest museum of Polynesian culture, the remarkable Bishop Museum has over a million Pacific artifacts, and an array of specimens of regional fauna and flora. It is also home to an interactive science center and an immersive planetarium.

This museum was created as an American businessman's farewell to his beloved wife. When Princess Bernice Pauahi, the last royal descendant of Kamehameha I, died in 1884, she left all her family heirlooms to her husband, Charles Bishop. Her cousin, Queen Emma, died shortly afterward and bequeathed her own Hawaiian artifacts to Bishop. He immediately set about building a home for the priceless collection, and the Bishop Museum opened in 1902.

Unmissable highlights at the museum include an impressive sperm whale skeleton with a papier-mâché body and a traditional *hale pili* (thatched grass house), both found in the Hawaiian Hall, as well as replica Polynesian canoes in the Pacific Hall. There are also lava demonstrations in the Science Adventure Center, and excellent shows in the planetarium multiple times each day.

MUSEUM GUIDE

The Bishop Museum is made up of several halls and buildings. The Hawaiian Hall has three floors: the first covers pre-contact Hawaiian culture, including a replica *heiau* (temple); the second illustrates the importance of nature to Hawaiians in daily life and culture; and the third deals with Hawaiian gods, *ali'i* (royalty), and history. Artifacts from the whole Pacific region can be seen in the Pacific Hall, while the Kāhili Room displays the treasures of Hawaii's monarchy. Other parts of the complex include a Science Adventure Center, a planetarium, a library, and the Castle Memorial Building, which usually houses contemporary traveling exhibitions.

Life-sized model of a sperm whale hanging in the Bishop Museum

When Princess Bernice Pauahi, the last royal descendant of Kamehameha I, died in 1884, she left all her family heirlooms to her husband, Charles Bishop.

The striking Victorian facade of the Bishop Museum

Wooden statues of Hawaiian gods in the Hawaiian Hall

PEARL HARBOR

7 miles (11 km) NW of downtown Honolulu 20, 42 1 Arizona Memorial Pl; nps.gov/perl

This key US naval base was the site of one of World War II's most infamous attacks, a devastating event that brought America into the conflict and forever changed its course. Today, this site is a national memorial, where warships, museums, and monuments scattered around the harbor tell the story of that fateful day and commemorate those who lost their lives.

USS Oklahoma Memorial

Langley Av, Ford Island For tours: 3pm Mon, Wed, & Fri (reservations required) nps.gov/perl

This memorial is dedicated to the 429 people who lost their lives when the USS *Oklahoma* got hit by nine Japanese torpedoes and capsized during the 1941 attack on the harbor. It has 429 white marble columns, one for each soldier, that stand 7 ft (2.1 m) high. There are shuttle buses from the Pearl Harbor Visitor Center.

Battleship Missouri Memorial

63 Cowpens St, Ford Island 8am–4pm daily Jan 1, Thanksgiving & Dec 25 ussmissouri.org

On September 2, 1945, General MacArthur, aboard the massive USS *Missouri*, accepted the signed Japanese Instrument of Surrender that ended World War II. Now a memorial to that pivotal moment, the *Missouri* offers self-guided audio tours as well as engaging guided walks that are often led by US military veterans. Both tours explore parts of the ship, such as the engine rooms. Shuttle buses run from the Pearl Harbor Visitor Center.

HIDDEN GEM

Ford Island Trail

A 4-mile (6.5-km) trail runs around the island that was ground zero for the 1941 attack. The trail has interpretive signs along the route, which include information on Ford Island's history, from the plantation era to the Cold War.

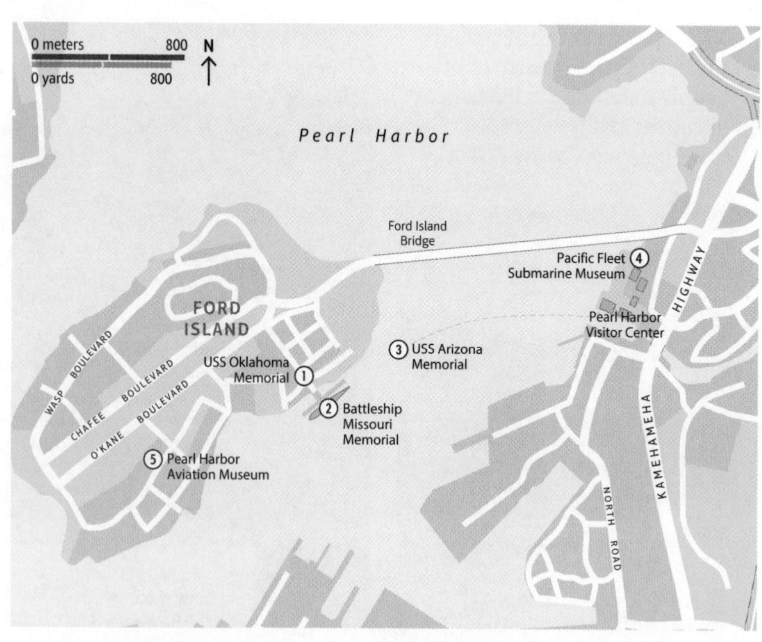

↑ USS *Missouri* docked at Ford Island, an islet in Pearl Harbor

USS Arizona Memorial

1 Arizona Memorial Pl
8am-3:30pm daily Jan 1, Thanksgiving & Dec 25
nps.gov/perl

Perhaps the most significant site at Pearl Harbor is the USS *Arizona* Memorial, a stark-white, rectangular structure perched just above the ship of the same name that was sunk during the Japanese bombing on December 7, 1941. The wreck of the sunken ship, where more than 1,100 soldiers are entombed in the hull, still leaks engine oil into the shallow harbor.

Today the open-air memorial is one of Hawaii's most-visited sights. Inside, visitors can watch a film about the historic event, see the battleship's bell, and pay their respects at the shrine room where the names of the fallen are carved in stone. The memorial is accessed by boats that leave from the Pearl Harbor Visitor Center, and requires an entry ticket, which can be booked online *(recreation.gov)*.

Pacific Fleet Submarine Museum

11 Arizona Memorial Dr
7am-5pm daily Jan 1, Thanksgiving & Dec 25
bowfin.org

The award-winning Pacific Fleet Submarine Museum is a tribute to the role that the submarine plays in both war and peacetime. This fascinating museum covers the history of submarines, beginning with the first attempt to build one in 1776. Visitors can view the inner workings of a Poseidon missile, inspect the control panels and bells from retired submarines, and see how the crew whiled away their time in the often very cramped quarters of submarines.

The 312-ft- (95-m-) long USS *Bowfin* submarine is moored near the museum. It is open for public viewing. Tourists can take informative, guided tours of the submarine to explore the compact crew quarters, the control room, and the galley. The surrounding park contains a

SHOP

Pearl Harbor Gift Shop

This shop, located in the Pearl Harbor Visitor Center, has a great collection of books on World War II, especially related to Pearl Harbor, and other mementos.

1 Arizona Memorial Pl
pacifichistoricparksbookstore.org

Did You Know?

Pearl Harbor's Hawaiian name is *Pu'uloa* ("long hill").

An aircraft displayed at the Pearl Harbor Aviation Museum

waterfront memorial that is dedicated to more than 3,600 officers and crewmen of the 52 US submarines that were lost during the course of World War II. There are also missiles, Japanese Kaiten (manned torpedoes), and other fascinating war relics on display.

The poignant USS Arizona Memorial at Pearl Harbor

5

Pearl Harbor Aviation Museum

319 Lexington Blvd, Ford Island 9am-5pm daily pearlharboraviationmuseum.org

Housed inside two World War II hangars, this museum features dozens of aircraft and exhibits from the 1941 attack, as well as displays on other conflicts, including the Korean War, the Vietnam War, and the Gulf Wars.

Between the two hangars is the Raytheon Pavilion, which showcases temporary exhibits covering everything from the heroes of World War II to the future of aviation.

The museum also has fun STEM (science, technology, engineering, and mathematics) exhibits for children. Other attractions include 360-degree flight simulators and a gift shop, where you can buy World War II model airplanes and other interesting collectibles. There is also a World War II-themed café. Note that access to the museum is via the free shuttle buses that leave from the Pearl Harbor Visitor Center.

HISTORY OF THE HARBOR

During the reign of Kamehameha I, the harbor - then just an inlet - supported oysters that were farmed for their pearls. In the 19th century, it transformed into a port that was crucial for whalers, trade with China, and both the sugar and pineapple industries. Leased to the US in 1887 as part of a trade treaty, it was used by the Americans as a military base, with a US naval station officially established in 1898. Then, on December 7, 1941, the harbor became one of the most infamous sites of World War II when it was attacked by over 350 Japanese war planes. The bombers crippled US military installations on O'ahu, killing 2,403 officers and civilians. The US officially entered World War II the following day.

EXPERIENCE MORE

Royal Mausoleum

2261 Nu'uanu Av (808) 587-0300 4 8am-4:30pm Mon-Fri Federal hols, except Mar 26 & Jun 11

The Gothic-influenced Royal Mausoleum, enclosed by a wrought-iron fence with gold crowns on each post, is the final resting place of the kings and queens of Hawaii. Only two royal names are missing from this sanctuary: Kamehameha I (1758–1819), who was buried in secret, and Lunalilo (1835–74), who is buried in the grounds of Kawaiaha'o Church *(p86)* in downtown Honolulu.

Other notable people buried here include John Young, the English advisor to Kamehameha I, and Charles Bishop, founder of the Bishop Museum *(p108)*. The original mausoleum building, built in 1865, is now a chapel. The interior is made entirely of rich, dark koa wood.

Did You Know?

The Royal Mausoleum is the only place in the US where the Hawaiian flag is allowed to fly alone.

GREAT VIEW
Nau'uanu Pali

Just up the Pali Highway from the Queen Emma Summer Palace, the Nau'uanu Pali Lookout offers a stunning, if windy, vantage point overlooking O'ahu's Windward Coast and the lush Ko'olau ridges.

4   

Queen Emma Summer Palace

2913 Pali Hwy (Hwy 61) 4, 55, 56, 57 10am-3:30pm Wed-Sat Federal hols daughtersofhawaii.org

Built in the 1840s, this airy retreat in the Nu'uanu Valley was the summer home of Queen Emma and her husband, Kamehameha IV. It is a combination of Greek Revival architecture and local touches, such as the *lānai* (porch). Set in extensive gardens, it is a cool oasis surrounded by huge trees, some planted by the royal family over 100 years ago. The mango trees planted at their wedding in 1856 are now 100 ft (30 m) tall and still bear fruit. The tamarind tree was planted by the couple's only son, Prince Albert, who died at the age of four.

The building houses many of the royal couple's personal belongings, including valuable period pieces, jewelry, household items, and artifacts from their Hawaiian heritage.

The National Memorial Cemetery of the Pacific, set within a volcanic crater ↑

Among the fine koa-wood furniture is the couple's large bed and their son's cradle, famous for its wave design.

The gift shop is run by a group of women descended from missionary families, who rescued the house from demolition in 1913, restored it, and reopened it two years later. They also give daily tours.

5 

National Memorial Cemetery of the Pacific

2177 Pūowaina Dr
(808) 532-3720 15, then short walk 8am-6pm daily

Looming above downtown Honolulu is Punchbowl, an extinct volcanic crater. Within it lies a massive US military cemetery, dedicated in 1949. By 1991, the plot was filled to capacity with over 33,000 graves, nearly half of them for World War II dead, including victims of the Pearl Harbor attack in 1941 *(p110)*.

Dominating the grounds is the Honolulu Memorial (dedicated in 1966), which consists of a chapel, marble slabs with the names of over 28,000 soldiers missing in action, and a staircase topped by Columbia, a huge memorial statue.

6 

O'ahu Cemetery

2162 Nu'uanu Av
(808) 538-1538 4
6:30am-6pm daily
oahucemetery.org

Founded in 1844, the O'ahu Cemetery was one of the first cemeteries established in Hawaii. It was created to bury foreigners who did not belong to Kawaiaha'o Church, including members of prominent 19th-century missionary and merchant families. The cemetery is still in use, and many notable people of Asian, European, and Hawaiian descent are buried here.

Veterans of the American Civil War (1861–65) are laid to rest here, as are many of the casualties of the bombing of Pearl Harbor on December 7, 1941. Elaborate headstones dot the garden-like setting.

Just behind the parking lot is a grassy trail that leads to several petroglyph spots. Nearby, another short trail along the west bank of the Nu'uanu Stream passes by 40 or so rock carvings, made by Hawaiians centuries ago.

EAT

Pioneer Saloon
Get a Hawaiian plate lunch (rice, macaroni salad, and an entrée) with a Japanese twist at this take-out spot.

3046 Monsarrat Av
pioneer-saloon.net

Diamond Head Market & Grill
Pick up warm scones, hearty Hawaiian breakfasts, and sandwiches from this gourmet deli counter and bakery.

3158 Monsarrat Av
diamondheadmarket.com

South Shore Grill
Tasty fish tacos that are easy on the wallet are available from this family-run diner.

3114 Monsarrat Av
southshoregrill.com

DRINK

Ars Cafe
This cozy café offers well-brewed coffee, house-made *gelato,* and walls decorated with funky art.

3116 Monsarrat Av
ars-cafe.com

The Curb Kaimuki
Cozy spot featuring a rotating selection of locally roasted coffee and a delicious macadamia milk option.

3408 Waialae Av
thecurbkaimuki.com

Mānoa Valley

The richly vegetated neighborhood of the Mānoa Valley was the site of the first coffee and sugarcane plantations in Hawaii in the early 1800s. The area is best known today as having several waterfalls to hike to, including the ever popular Mānoa Falls. These falls are reached via a gently sloping but rocky and muddy trail that winds through groves of bamboo, eucalyptus, edible mountain apple, and tangled *hau* trees. The 150-ft (46-m) waterfall at the end is spectacular after a heavy rainfall. There's no fee for the hike, but parking is $5.

Additional waterfalls nearby that are also worth visiting are the Lulumahu Falls and Aihualama Falls.

STAY

Lotus Honolulu

Rooms at this contemporary boutique hotel have a Zen vibe and views of either the ocean or Diamond Head.

2885 Kalākaua Av
lotushonoluluhotel.com

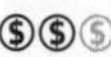

SHOP

KCC Farmers' Market

Pick up picnic supplies or stay for dinner at Kapi'olani Community College's market.

4303 Diamond Head Rd
hfbf.org

Bailey's Antiques and Aloha Shirts

For vintage aloha shirts and collectibles head to this iconic store, open since 1980.

517 Kapahulu Av
alohashirts.com

Aloha Stadium Swap Meet & Marketplace

A large, open-air flea market for clothing, art, souvenirs, and snacks.

99-500 Salt Lake Blvd alohastadium.hawaii.gov

Mānoa Heritage Center

2856 Oahu Av 5
9am-4pm Mon-Fri
manoaheritagecenter.org

Surrounded by a large private property in the Mānoa Valley suburb, this center is dedicated to promoting and preserving Hawaii's rich natural and cultural heritage.

Situated on the property are botanical gardens filled with native Hawaiian plants and species brought over by early Polynesian settlers. There's also a sacred agricultural temple, which dates back at least a thousand years, and a historic Tudor-style home from 1911. The latter is not currently open to the public; future plans are to open it up as a museum.

The center welcomes visitors but pre-booked tour reservations are required.

Lyon Arboretum

3860 Mānoa Rd 5
9am-3pm Mon-Fri
Federal hols manoa.hawaii.edu/lyon

Only a short drive from busy Waikīkī, this retreat is an ideal tonic for the weary sightseer. Verdant trails wind through the trees and reveal botanical delights at every turn.

Founded in 1918 in an effort to reforest land made barren by cattle grazing, the arboretum is now home to over 6,000 plant species, both native and introduced. It is nationally recognized as a center for the conservation of Hawaiian plants, and its 194 acres (78 ha) support over 80 endangered and rare species. These include the state flower, *ma'o hau hele* (a yellow hibiscus), and the tree gardenia, *nānū*, whose scientific name, *Gardenia brighamii*, honors W. T. Brigham, the first director of the Bishop Museum *(p108)*. The arboretum also features around 600 varieties of palm, more than any other botanical garden in the world.

A substantial part of the arboretum is open to the public (reservations are required); the rest has been set aside for research. The on-site hybridization program has resulted in more than 160 new cultivars, including hybrids of hibiscus and rhododendron.

There are three memorial gardens and an aromatic spice and herb patch near the main building. A little farther away, the Beatrice H. Krauss Ethnobotanical Garden displays plants that have been used by Hawaiians as medicine, food, and building materials.

↑ Heliconia, one of the many species thriving at the Lyon Arboretum

Walkers admiring the extensive views out to sea from Diamond Head

Kapi'olani Park

Entrances on Kalākaua, Monsarrat, and Paki Avs 2, 13, 20 Daily

This large expanse of green offers a 2-mile (3-km) jogging path, tennis courts, barbecues, and shady picnic spots, plus designated areas for softball, archery, and kite-flying. It is also the site of craft fairs and many celebrations. In addition, the park provides a gateway to the extinct volcanic cone, Diamond Head, which looms above the city. King Kalākaua gave the park to the people in 1887, who named it after his wife Queen Kapi'olani.

The north end of the park is devoted to **Honolulu Zoo**. The highlight here is an extensive African savanna section. There's also the small but excellent **Waikīkī Aquarium**, on the southwest side of the park, which features various species of sea life including seahorses, stingrays, and octopuses. The park's amphitheater, the **Waikīkī Shell**, hosts live concerts and theatrical entertainment. See the website for information on performances and tickets.

Honolulu Zoo
151 Kapahulu Av 10am-3pm daily Dec 25 honoluluzoo.org

Waikīkī Aquarium
2777 Kalākaua Av 9am-4:30pm daily Dec 25 waikikiaquarium.org

Waikīkī Shell
2805 Monsarrat Av
Hours vary, check website
waikikiamp.com

Diamond Head

Diamond Head Rd & 18th Av 23 6am-6pm Thu-Tue hawaiistateparks.org

Watching over Waikīkī, this 300,000-year-old volcanic crater is called *Lē'ahi* (brow of the tuna) by Hawaiians as the formation's ridgeline resembles the tuna fish's dorsal fin. The crater's slopes are shadowy green in the rainy season and a dusty parched brown at other times of year.

To see the extinct volcano, take the scenic circle drive to Diamond Head lighthouse, where the lawn is a popular spot for weddings and watching sunsets. Or you can hike to the summit from a parking lot in the crater. The entrance to the crater is marked by a sign on Diamond Head Road, the continuation of Monsarrat Avenue. The trail is rather steep, but it is paved and the sweeping view is worth the hour-long ascent.

The trail was originally built in 1908 as part of the US Army Coastal Artillery defense system. You'll go through tunnels on the way up and, at the second lookout point, you'll find a World War II bunker. In addition to the trail within the crater, a 3-mile (5-km) loop walk allows you to see the peak from a full circle. Start the walk where Monsarrat Avenue meets Diamond Head Road and from here you can proceed in either direction.

GREAT VIEW
Epic Cityscapes

Drive along the winding Tantalus-Round-Top, a tree-lined route with great lookouts, including the one at Pu'u Ualaka'a State Park, which offers epic vistas over Honolulu and Diamond Head.

EXPERIENCE HAWAII

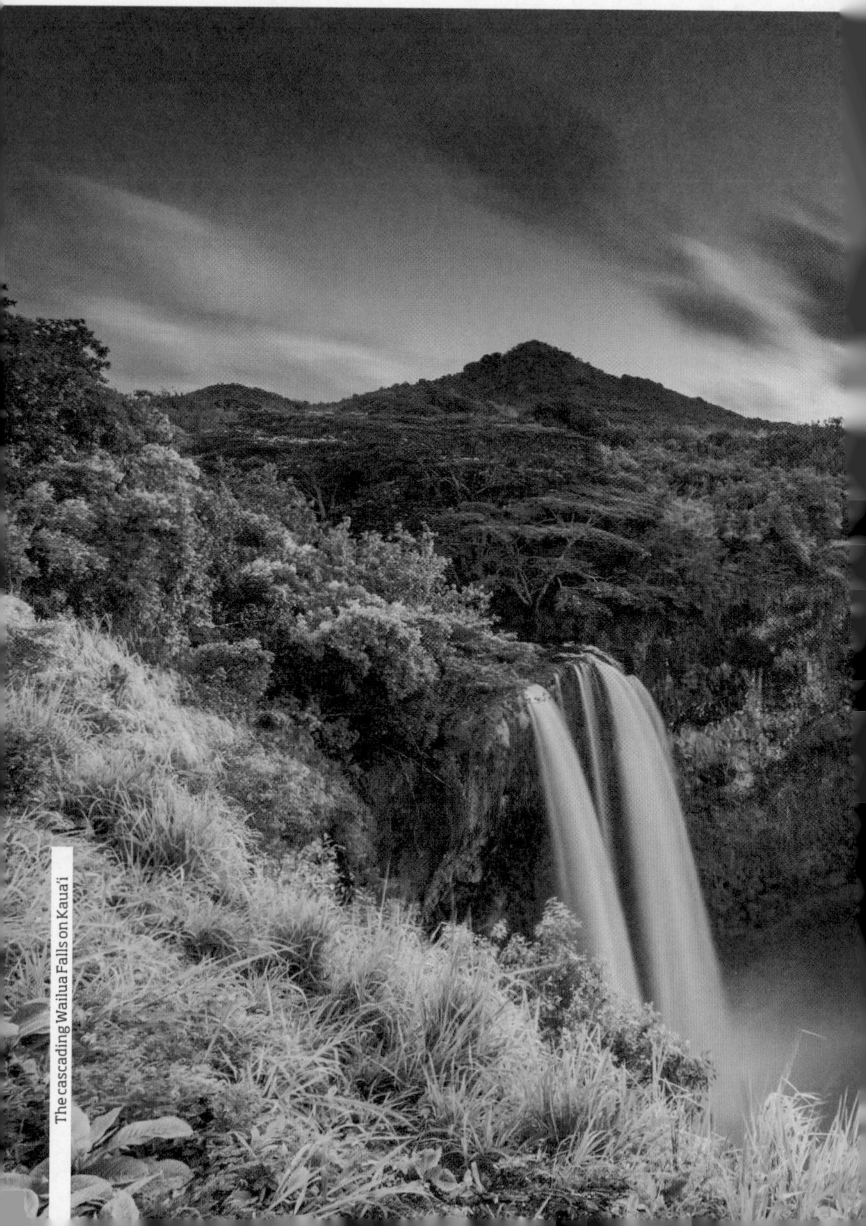

The cascading Wailua Falls on Kaua'i

Surfing off the coast of O'ahu

O'AHU

The third-largest island in the archipelago, with an area of 600 sq miles (1,550 sq km), O'ahu was born of two volcanoes that formed the Wai'anae Mountains to the west and the Ko'olau Range to the northeast. Around 1200–1300 CE, travelers began to arrive on O'ahu from a number of other islands in the South Pacific, including today's Tahiti and the Marquesas Islands. These first settlers built communities around the island's resource-rich perimeter.

For centuries after this, O'ahu was organized into chiefdoms, with the population living quiet, agricultural lives. Then, in 1795, the island was conquered by Kamehameha I. His forces chased rival chiefs Kai'ana and Kalanikūpule and their men back into Nu'uanu Valley on the southwest of the island, forcing them off a precipice at the top. The battle was an important victory in Kamehameha's campaign to unify all of the Hawaiian Islands.

In the 1800s, farmers began growing pineapples in O'ahu's highlands, and by the middle of the century, sugarcane plantations – largely owned by foreigners – had become big business. Workers came from China, Japan, Portugal, and elsewhere to work on these plantations; despite being separated along ethnic lines, these workers developed a universal language known as Hawaiian Pidgin.

In the late 19th century, O'ahu and the rest of Hawaii became American territory, and fertile fields slowly gave way to hotel grounds. By the 1950s, tourism was taking hold, and thousands of visitors started to arrive each year, including surfers who made for the island's North Shore. Today, O'ahu remains one of the most popular Hawaiian Islands thanks to its buzzing capital city and stunning natural beauty.

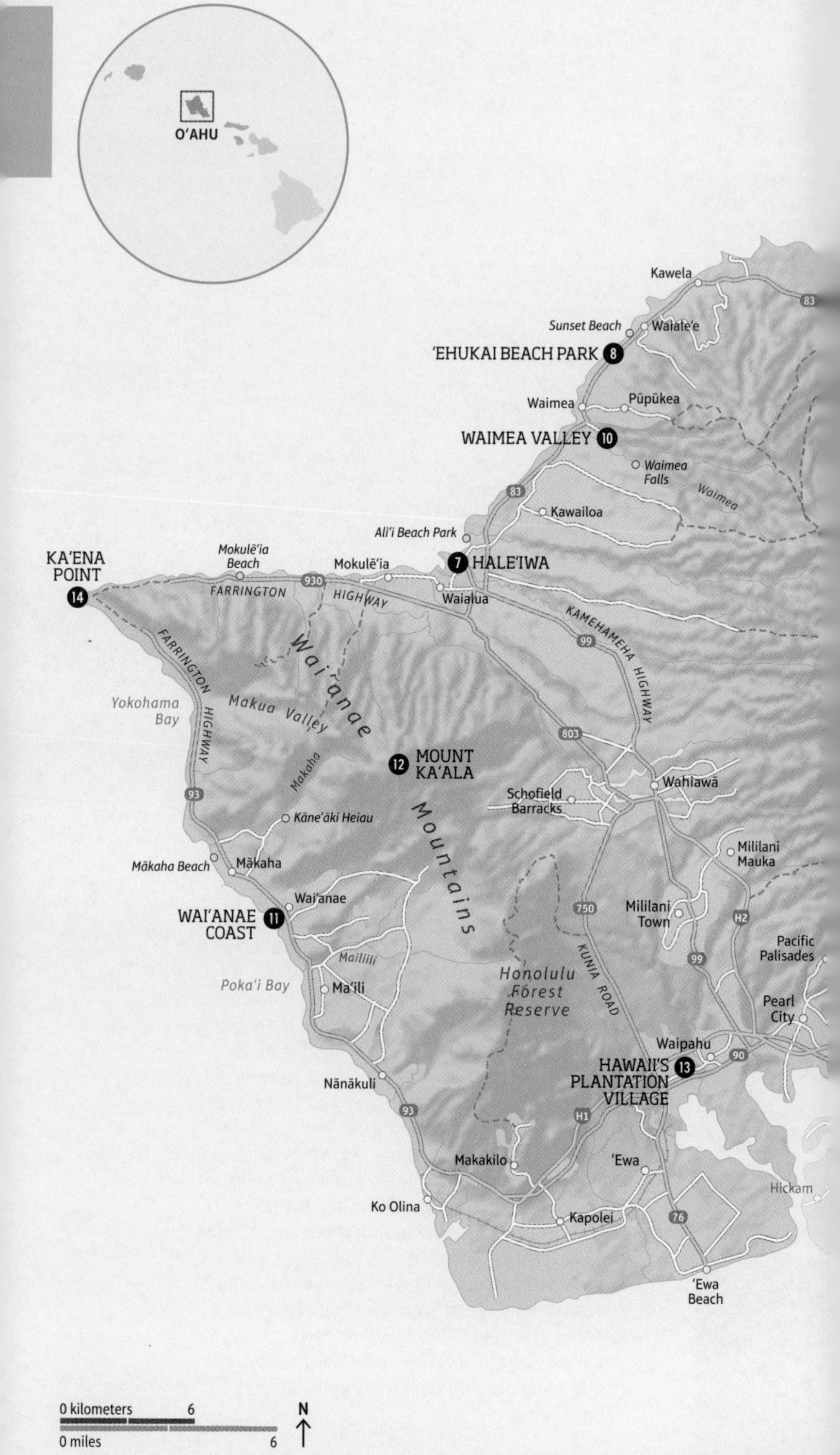

O'AHU

Kawela
Sunset Beach
Waiale'e
'EHUKAI BEACH PARK 8
Waimea
Pūpūkea
WAIMEA VALLEY 10
Waimea Falls
Waimea
83
Kawailoa
Ali'i Beach Park
KA'ENA POINT 14
Mokulē'ia Beach
Mokulē'ia
7 HALE'IWA
930
FARRINGTON HIGHWAY
Waialua
KAMEHAMEHA HIGHWAY
99
FARRINGTON HIGHWAY
Wai'anae Mountains
Yokohama Bay
Makua Valley
803
12 MOUNT KA'ALA
Makaha
93
Wahiawā
Schofield Barracks
Kāne'āki Heiau
Mililani Mauka
Mākaha Beach
Mākaha
Wai'anae
WAI'ANAE COAST 11
750
Mililani Town
H2
Pacific Palisades
Mailiili
Poka'i Bay
Ma'ili
Honolulu Forest Reserve
KUNIA ROAD
99
Pearl City
Waipahu
90
HAWAII'S PLANTATION VILLAGE 13
Nānākuli
93
H1
Makakilo
'Ewa
Hickam
Ko Olina
Kapolei
76
'Ewa Beach

N

O'AHU

Must See

1 Hanauma Bay

Experience More

2 Koko Crater
3 Makapu'u Point
4 Byodo-In Temple
5 Kualoa Ranch
6 Hau'ula Trails
7 Hale'iwa
8 'Ehukai Beach Park
9 Polynesian Cultural Center
10 Waimea Valley
11 Wai'anae Coast
12 Mount Ka'ala
13 Hawaii's Plantation Village
14 Ka'ena Point
15 Ka'au Crater

1

HANAUMA BAY

7455 Kalaniana'ole Highway (Hwy 72), 10 miles (16 km) E of Waikīkī
22 6:45am-4pm Wed-Sun Dec 25 hanaumabaystatepark.com

This pristine keyhole-shaped nature preserve is one of the world's most spectacular snorkeling spots. Lined by an arching sandy beach, the bay's warm, brilliantly turquoise waters are bursting with diverse marine life.

Hanauma Bay owes its unique shape to a series of violent volcanic eruptions that occurred here some 32,000 years ago. Now a flooded crater, the sheltered bay's shallow, sandy bottom is studded with fragile coral and dark basalt rock, providing an ideal environment for marine life. Here you'll find more than 400 species of colorful fish, green sea turtles, and moray eels, as well as the occasional curious spinner dolphin or manta ray. This abundance of marine life, plus the bay's calm waters, makes it the perfect snorkeling spot, especially for novices. The beach here also has restrooms, a snack bar, and a snorkel equipment rental booth.

Hanauma is such a popular spot that the state has had to take action to protect it from overtourism. The number of daily visitors is limited to 1,400 (online reservations must be made in advance), an entry fee is charged, and there are only 300 spaces at the parking lot ($3 charge, cash only). All visitors must watch an orientation video shown at the bay's award-winning Marine Education Center before entering the park.

The stunning keyhole-shaped Hanauma Bay, with its white-sand beach

1 Green sea turtles are one of the regular inhabitants of Hanauma Bay.

2 Several people snorkeling in the clear turquoise waters above the bay's coral reef.

3 Shoals of brightly colored reef fish, including yellow tang and raccoon butterfly, swimming in the blue waters of Hanauma Bay.

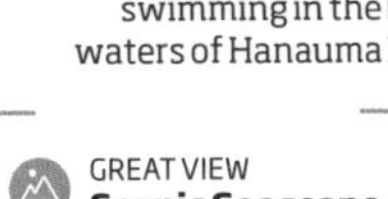

GREAT VIEW
Scenic Seascape

For an unforgettable view, head to the parking lot situated high above Hanauma Bay. From here, you can take in the panoramic vista of the sparkling blue bay, half-moon beach, and coral reef.

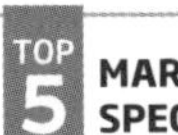

TOP 5 MARINE SPECIES

Green Sea Turtles
An endangered species, Hawaii's *honu* (green sea turtles) are the world's largest hard-shelled sea turtles.

Parrotfish
These colorful fish are easily recognized by their unique, parrot-like beak of fused teeth.

Moray Eels
Ubiquitous in Hawaii, these grouchy fish like to hide in rock and coral crevices. Be warned – they can bite.

Yellow Tang
The brightly colored yellow tang is the easiest to spot of all Hawaiian reef fish.

Reef Triggerfish
The official state fish of Hawaii, also known by its local name *Humuhumunu-kunukuapua'a*.

EXPERIENCE MORE

Koko Crater

Off Kalaniana'ole Hwy (Hwy 72), 10 miles (16 km) E of Waikīkī

Found on a jutting headland, the volcanic Koko Crater rises to 1,200 ft (366 m). Inside the basin lies the **Koko Crater Botanical Garden**, with a collection of drought-tolerant, rare, and endangered plant species from around the world. An easy but hot 2-mile (3-km) interpretive loop trail winds through the gardens, or you can book a guided tour where a horticultural expert will guide you round. Tours of the garden are by appointment only; call (808) 768-7135 to book ahead.

Beyond the crater, you can tackle the more grueling Koko Head Stairs trail that follows an old, steep railroad track, offering panoramic views.

Koko Crater Botanical Garden

7491 Kokonani St
22 Dawn-dusk daily
honolulu.gov/parks

HIDDEN GEM

Blowing a Gasket

Found at the shores of the Koko Crater, the Hālona Blowhole is a lava tube that sends jets of seawater into the air. Observe with care; many who have ventured too near have been injured or killed.

Makapu'u Point

Kalaniana'ole Hwy (Hwy 72), 14 miles (23 km) E of Waikīkī 22

The most eastern point on O'ahu, Makapu'u Point offers stunning views over the rocky coast, ocean, and the islands of Rabbit and Kāohikaipu, both of which are seabird sanctuaries. The Makapu'u Lighthouse is an excellent spot from which to enjoy whale-watching during the winter months.

Nearby Makapu'u Beach is a pocket cove that claims the island's best bodysurfing waves, which require precise timing and skill to avoid being dragged onto the rocks.

Hiking trails lead upward into black mountains, but you do not need to climb beyond the first 100 ft (30 m) or so for spectacular photos.

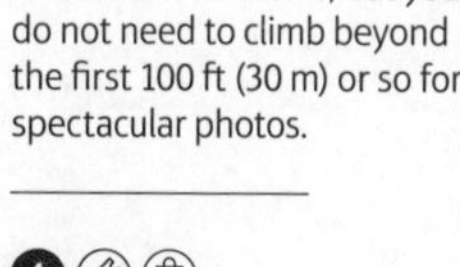

Byodo-In Temple

47-200 Kahekili Hwy (Hwy 83), Kāne'ohe 65, on Kahekili Hwy (Hwy 83), then ten-min walk
8:30am-4:30pm daily
Dec 25 byodo-in.com

This replica of a 950-year-old Japanese temple cannot be seen from the highway. The only marker is a Hawai'i Visitors and Convention Bureau sign for a historic sight. Once you turn into the Valley of Temples, a non-denominational

↑ The elegant red Byodo-In Temple, situated beside a tranquil lake

cemetery, the road winds into the valley to reach this hidden treasure, its walls red against fluted, green cliffs. Remove your shoes before entering the shrine, where a 9-ft (3-m) gold and lacquer Buddha presides.

Visiting the temple at sunset is a tranquil experience. You will not be able to see the Buddha (the temple closes at 4:30pm), but you will get to enjoy the profound silence here, which will be punctuated only by the singing of birds.

Kualoa Ranch

49-560 Kamehameha Hwy (Hwy 83), Kāne'ohe, 23 miles (37 km) N of Waikīkī 55, shuttles from Waikīkī 7:30am-6pm daily kualoa.com

Established in 1850 by an American doctor, Kualoa Ranch was purchased for $1,300 from King Kamehameha III. Today, the ranch serves as both a working cattle ranch and a day excursion for those looking for a taste of the *paniolo* (Hawaiian cowboy) lifestyle.

Activities are scattered between the two major areas: Ka'a'awa Valley and Hakipuu Valley. A popular attraction is the guided movie tour that takes visitors on a ride through the scenic Ka'a'awa Valley, sometimes referred to as Hollywood's "Hawaii Backlot," to see the film locations used for more than 50 Hollywood blockbusters and TV shows, such as *Jurassic Park* and *Lost*. In Hakipuu Valley, visitors are taken by boat to an ancient Hawaiian fishpond and a secluded beach. Other activities include horseback riding, ATV rides, and an electric mountain-bike tour. The ranch is very popular so excursions should be booked well in advance.

BEACHES OF SOUTHEAST O'AHU

Kāne'ohe Bay
A short drive from Byodo-In Temple, this pretty bay, protected by a barrier reef, is inhabited by green sea turtles.

Lanikai Beach
Found north of Makapu'u Point, this white-sand beach is one of the most beautiful on O'ahu.

Kailua Beach Park
This pretty park on O'ahu's east coast has full facilities and reef-protected waters.

Waimānalo Beach
Just 3 miles (5 km) from Makapu'u Point, this beach has safe seas and gently sloping sand.

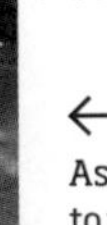

Ascending the access road to the Koko Crater, with gorgeous views behind

A boat bobbing on crystal-clear waters on Lanikai Beach

6

Hau'ula Trails

Kamehameha Hwy (Hwy 83), 20 miles (30 km) NW of Kāne'ohe, approximately 2 miles (3 km) past Punalu'u hawaiitrails.ehawaii.gov

The three trails that make up the Hau'ula Trails area – Hau'ula Loop Trail, Ma'akua Ridge Trail, and Ma'akua Gulch Trail – provide everything that hikers love best about Hawaii's finest trails. They are wide with excellent footing and offer spectacular valley, mountain, and ocean views. You should allow around two hours for a round-trip of any of the trails, all of which begin beyond the end of Ma'akua Road, off Hau'ula Homestead Road, which is just beyond the tiny town of Hau'ula.

EAT

Matsumoto's

Since 1951, this place has offered rainbow-colored and candy-flavored shave ice.

66-111 Kamehameha Hwy, Hale'iwa matsumotoshave ice.com

Kahuku Farms Café

Here, dig into a healthy açai bowl and fresh smoothies made with the café's own farm-grown ingredients.

56-800 Kamehameha Hwy, Kahuku Tue & Wed kahuku farms.com

$$$

Giovanni's Shrimp Truck

This graffiti-clad food truck is a familiar face on Hawaii's snacking scene, serving up plates of sautéed garlic shrimp.

66-472 Kamehameha Hwy, Hale'iwa giovannisshrimptruck.com

$$$

Hale'iwa

Kamehameha Hwy (Hwy 83), 30 miles (48 km) N from Waikīkī 52 66-434 Kamehameha Hwy, Hale'iwa; gonorthshore.org

Formerly a small plantation town, Hale'iwa is now a popular hub for the North Shore surfing community. The town has a creative and alternative feel and consists of a single main street lined with art galleries, boutiques, general stores, restaurants, and coffee shops.

Flanking a picturesque boat harbor are well-appointed public beaches. Ali'i Beach Park is famous for big waves and surfing contests, but the adjacent Hale'iwa Beach Park, protected by a breakwater, is one of the few North Shore spots where it is usually safe to swim in winter.

Besides the annual surfing festivals, including the Eddie Aikau Big Wave Invitational at Waimea Bay, the town is known for the Obon Festival. Held every summer at a seaside Buddhist temple, the festival involves folk dancing and the release of thousands of floating lanterns into the sea.

Driving west from Hale'iwa, you travel past a former sugar plantation at Waialua and arrive at Mokulē'ia, where polo fields border empty, white-sand beaches. Here you can while away a very pleasant afternoon watching parachutists from nearby Dillingham Airfield float down across the surf like clouds of colorful butterflies.

'Ehukai Beach Park

59-337 Ke Nui Rd, Hale'iwa 52

At 'Ehukai Beach Park, expanses of sand fringe the rocky shore, over which the surf boils. The most famous of the surfing breaks here is the tubular Banzai Pipeline, which throws up waves of tremendous steepness and power, some reaching heights of over 30 ft (9 m). The name Banzai comes from the battle cry of Japanese kamikaze pilots, and was first applied to the waves here during the narration of the late 1950s film *Surf Safari*.

Lifeguards at the beach are kept very busy because of the steeply sloping ocean bottom and the irresistible allure of huge winter surf; the summer waves are more tame, but may still not be suitable for inexperienced surfers.

Sunbathers also flock to the beach park to enjoy the soft sand and picnic facilities.

→ Hanging out in the surfing town of Hale'iwa on the North Shore

→ A tropical waterfall in Waimea Valley, home to an abundance of varied bird life *(inset)*

Polynesian Cultural Center

55-370 Kamehameha Hwy (Hwy 83), Lā'ie 55 12:30-9pm Thu-Tue Thanksgiving & Dec 25 polynesia.com

The village of Lā'ie was founded by Mormon missionaries in 1864 after a failed attempt to settle on the island of Lāna'i. Lā'ie now contains a Mormon temple, a branch of Brigham Young University, and one of O'ahu's most popular attractions, a large educational theme park known as the Polynesian Cultural Center.

At the center, students from all over the Pacific demonstrate crafts and dancing in six Polynesian "villages": Fijian, Tongan, Hawaiian, Samoan, Tahitian, and Māori (Aotearoa). The instruction, whether it be Tongan drumming or Samoan fire-making, is delivered in almost continuous mini-shows, and audience participation is encouraged. There is also a cinema showing a program of films.

The afternoon show, Huki: A Canoe Celebration, presents legends from all the islands, with singing, dancing, and martial arts performed on double-hulled canoes. The evening show, Hā–Breath of Life, meanwhile, sees performances of Polynesian music and dance, complete with fire-knife dancing. Visitors can also book an entertaining *lū'au* show with a fabulous buffet of Polynesian specialties, such as Kalua pork and *lomi-lomi* salmon salad (raw and salted salmon chopped up with tomatoes and onions), or opt for an indulgent prime rib buffet.

Waimea Valley

59-864 Kamehameha Hwy (Hwy 83), Waimea 52, 55 9am-4pm daily Thanksgiving & Dec 25 waimeavalley.net

This lush valley is one of a few intact examples of an *ahupua'a* – a Hawaiian land division from mountain to sea. A beautiful, unspoiled environment, it is a sacred place for Hawaiians, and a key educational resource.

The valley was previously run as an attraction, with glitzy hula shows, and was then used as a facility by the Audubon Society (a bird conservation group). Today this stunning valley is operated by the Office of Hawaiian Affairs. The large area includes a waterfall, a 5,000-plant botanical collection, a refuge for endangered wildlife, and archaeological sites, including a 15th-century *heiau* (temple) dedicated to Lono, god of peace, agriculture, and music. Walking tours and cultural activities such as lei making, hula lessons, and storytelling are included in the cost of admission. It's also worth bringing binoculars, as the park has great opportunities for bird-watching.

After your visit, enjoy a swim or a snorkel at Waimea Beach Park, just across the street.

GREAT VIEW

Pu'u o Mahuka Heiau

Made up of the ruins of three sacred rock terraces, Pu'u o Mahuka is the largest *heiau* (temple) on O'ahu. Set 300 ft (90 m) above Waimea Valley, it offers spectacular views of the valley and beach below.

11

Wai'anae Coast

Farrington Hwy (Hwy 93), 33 miles (53 km) NW of Waikīkī C (Country Express) to Nānākuli, Wai'anae, and Mākaha Beach 2270 Kalākaua Av, Suite 801, Waikīkī; (808) 524-0722

O'ahu's sunny Leeward coast remains largely undiscovered by tourists, partly due to its remoteness and partly due to the fact that its shoreline – made up of some of the oldest lava on the island – is quite rough. The main town here, also called Wai'anae, is a good place to stock up on supplies.

One of the coast's prettiest beaches is Pōka'ī Bay, where a breakwater shelters an aquamarine lagoon with soft sand. Around 3 miles (5 km) northwest lies Mauna Lahilahi, a little mountain standing only 230 ft (70 m) high. A sacred Hawaiian site for centuries, it is dotted with ancient temple remains; petroglyphs depicting human and dog-like figures can also be found on its eastern side. A short distance farther north is Mākaha Beach, famous for its massive waves.

South of Wai'anae, at Kaukama Road, is the trailhead for the Pu'u O Hulu hike, also known as the Pink Pillbox hike. The moderately challenging 1-mile (2-km) climb takes around an hour to complete. At the top, you get breathtaking views of O'ahu's western coast. You'll also spy the pink pillbox. This graffiti-covered structure functioned as a small observation bunker during World War II.

One of the coast's prettiest beaches is Pōka'ī Bay, where a breakwater shelters an aquamarine lagoon with soft sand.

Mount Ka'ala

End of Wai'anae Valley Rd (trailhead) C dlnr.hawaii.gov

Rising to 4,025 ft (1,227 m), Mount Ka'ala – O'ahu's highest mountain – dominates the Wai'anae Coast. Its fog-bound plateau is home to an ancient rainforest protected by the Mount Ka'ala Natural Area Reserve, where wild boar roam and the crimson 'apapane bird fills the air with its song.

Only advanced hikers can attempt to reach the summit of Mount Ka'ala. The tough 6.7-mile (11-km) hike takes a full day and includes navigating some boulders and steep ridges. Once at the top you'll discover a fenced-in military facility, which contains a dome structure that is part of a US Army tracking station.

13   

Hawaii's Plantation Village

94-695 Waipahu St, Waipahu E (Country Express) to Waipahu 9am-2pm Mon-Fri (occasional Sat, check website) Federal hols hawaiiplantationvillage.org

Restored at a cost of 3 million US dollars, Hawaii's Plantation Village portrays over 100 years of sugar plantation culture in an outdoor setting. The excellent museum shows how the plantation owners segregated workers along strict ethnic lines and how, in spite of this, a common pidgin language developed.

The village contains some re-created buildings from the major ethnic groups that worked the plantations, including Korean, Puerto Rican, and Japanese homes, a Japanese bathhouse, Chinese cookhouse, and a Shinto shrine. Personal objects placed in the houses give the impression that the occupants have just left.

14

Ka'ena Point

**Beyond end of Farrington Hwy (Hwy 930), 7 miles (11 km) N of Mākaha**

Located at O'ahu's western extremity, Ka'ena Point has a stark, mountainous coastline and spectacular sunsets. A hot but relatively easy 2-mile (3-km) trail leads to the point. Legend tells that the rock off the point is a chunk of Kaua'i that the demigod Maui pulled off when he was trying to unite the two islands. On clear days, Kaua'i can be seen to the north. It is also possible to spot rare monk seals, green turtles, and humpback whales. The world's highest waves slam against the rocks here, but attempting to surf them is not advised. The point can be reached from either Highway 930 or Highway 93. The two roads do not connect.

15

Ka'au Crater

End of Waiomao Rd in Palolo Valley (trailhead)
**1 and 9S**

Three volcanic craters (tuff cones) are located within the vicinity of Honolulu: the iconic Diamond Head Crater *(p117)*, the exposed Koko Crater *(p126)*, and the lesser-known Ka'au Crater. Unlike the first two, you can't drive up to the Ka'au Crater, but there is a gorgeous – yet arduous – hike that leads to the marshy crater caldera and crater rim.

The 5-mile- (8-km-) long trail, which begins at the back of Palolo Valley, goes round in a loop and passes through thick forests and beside three stunning waterfalls. Although very challenging (the hike requires scrambling up muddy and slippery rocks) the amazing panoramic views of the Windward side of O'ahu – including Olomana, Nā Mokulua, and Mokoli'i – and beyond make it well worth it.

INSIDER TIP
On Your Bike!

O'ahu has a network of designated bike lanes; Hawaii's Department of Transportation publishes route maps online *(hidot.hawaii.gov/highways/bike-map-oahu)*. Bikes, including electric bikes, can be rented in Waikīkī. The Biki bike-share program *(gobiki.org)* in Honolulu is also a convenient option to move around.

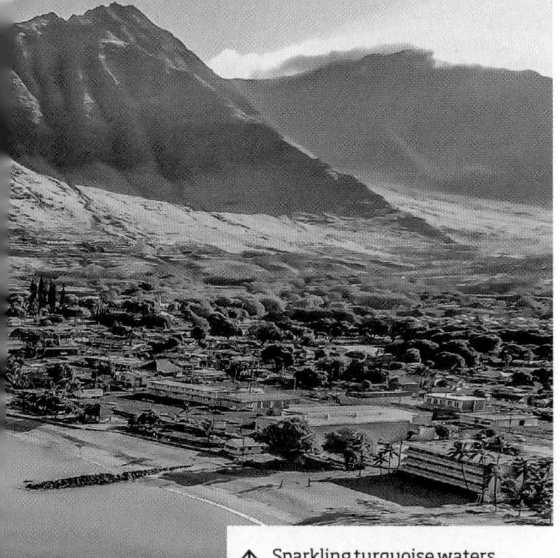

↑ Sparkling turquoise waters lapping against Mākaha Beach, on the remote Wai'anae Coast

STAY

Turtle Bay Resort

Family-friendly and fairly remote, this modern resort has a huge pool complex, including a 70-ft (20-m) main pool and a kids' pool, plus a golf course and tennis courts.

57-091 Kamehameha Hwy, Kahuku
turtlebayresort.com

$$$

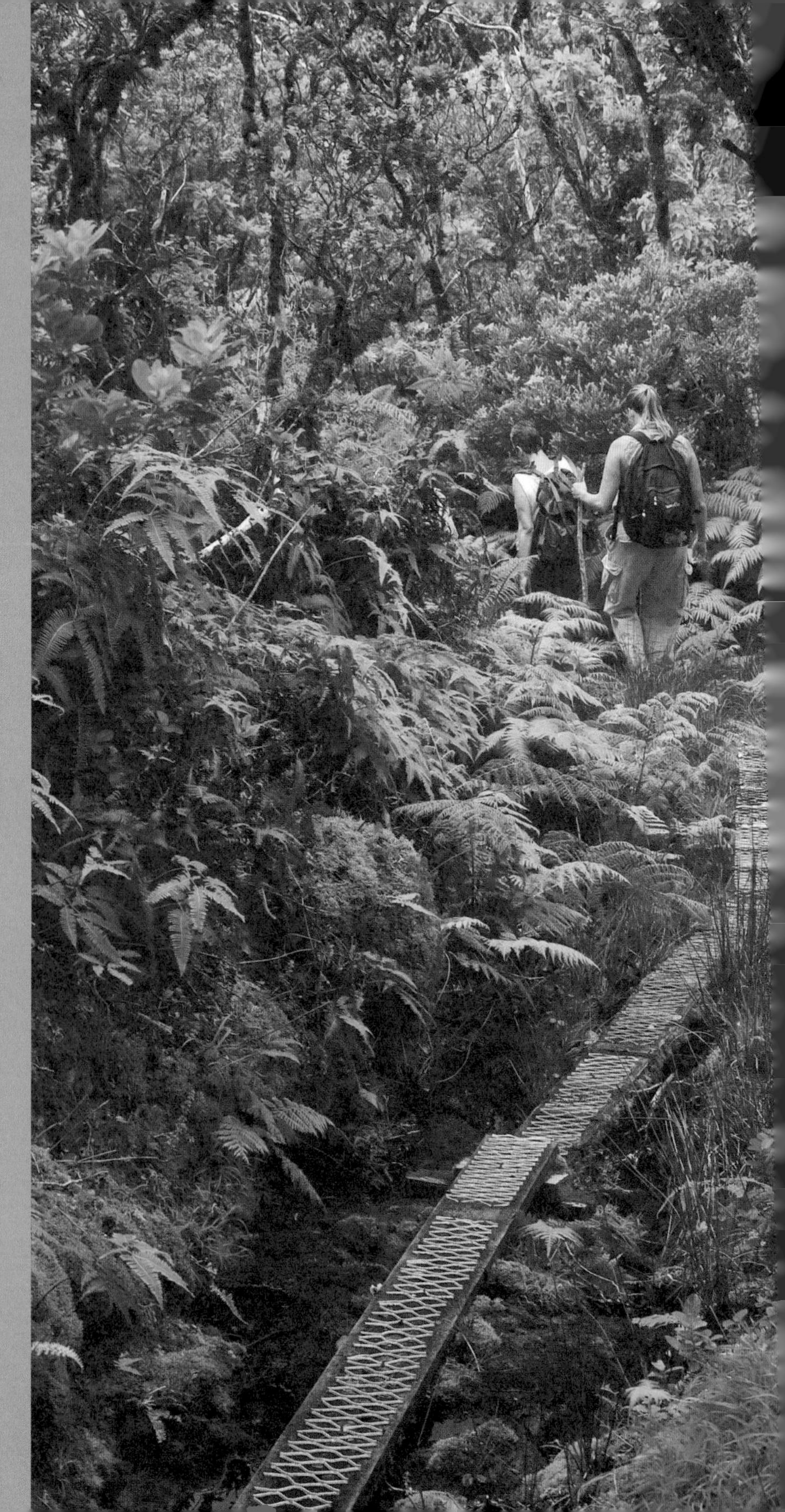

Hikers walking through the rainforest at Kamakou Preserve

MOLOKA'I AND LĀNA'I

Moloka'i is formed from two extinct volcanoes that were once, along with Lāna'i and Kaho'olawe, joined to Maui. The island's sheltered southern slopes held the bulk of its inhabitants, who planted crops along the coastline and raised fish in rocky enclosures just offshore. During the 1500s, despite repeatedly falling to invading armies from O'ahu, Maui, and Hawai'i Island, Moloka'i acquired a reputation for great spiritual power due to its resident religious leaders, including the divine prophet Lanikaula. In 1795, as part of his Hawaiian unification strategy, Kamehameha I took control of Moloka'i. In the 1860s, his grandson Kamehameha V built a vacation estate here and planted over 1,000 coconut trees, which still stand in the Kapuaiwa Coconut Grove. During his reign, the island's Kalaupapa Peninsula was also set aside as a leprosarium.

Though Polynesian settlers inhabited many of the Hawaiian Islands, Lāna'i was not one of them, due to its reputation for being haunted. In the 1500s the island had its first resident, a man named Kauluaau, who was banished there after breaking a *kapu* law on Maui. As with the other Hawaiian Islands, Kamehameha I came to rule Lāna'i in the 1790s and used it as a fishing retreat. In 1922, James Dole, an American and president of the Hawaiian Pineapple Company (later the Dole Company), bought Lāna'i and developed it into the world's largest pineapple plantation. When pineapple harvesting ended 70 years later, the Castle & Cooke Corporation (the parent company of Dole) built two luxury hotels here. In 2012, most of Lāna'i passed to American businessman Larry Ellison, who is said to be transforming it into an eco-friendly destination.

Polihua Beach

MOLOKA'I AND LĀNA'I

Must Sees

1. Lāna'i
2. Kalaupapa National Historical Park

Experience More

3. Kaunakakai
4. Kamakou Preserve
5. Hālawa Valley
6. Maunaloa
7. Pāpōhaku Beach
8. Pālā'au State Park
9. Kualapu'u
10. Mo'omomi Beach

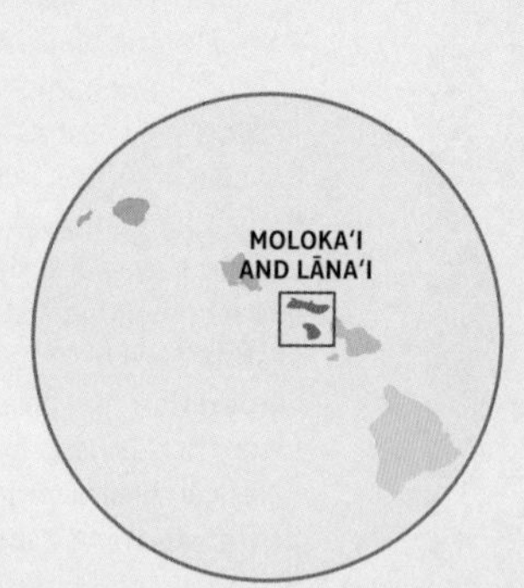

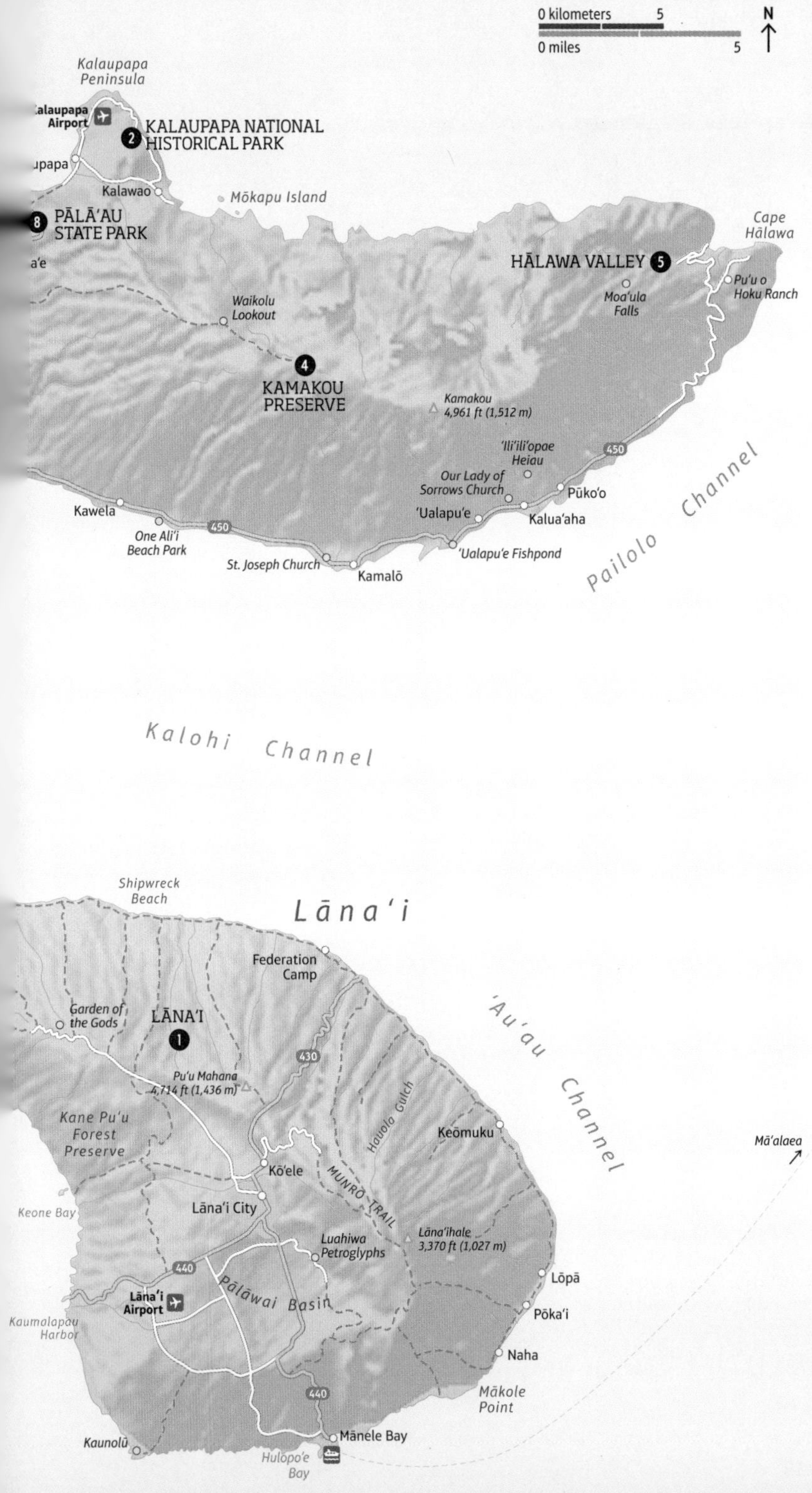

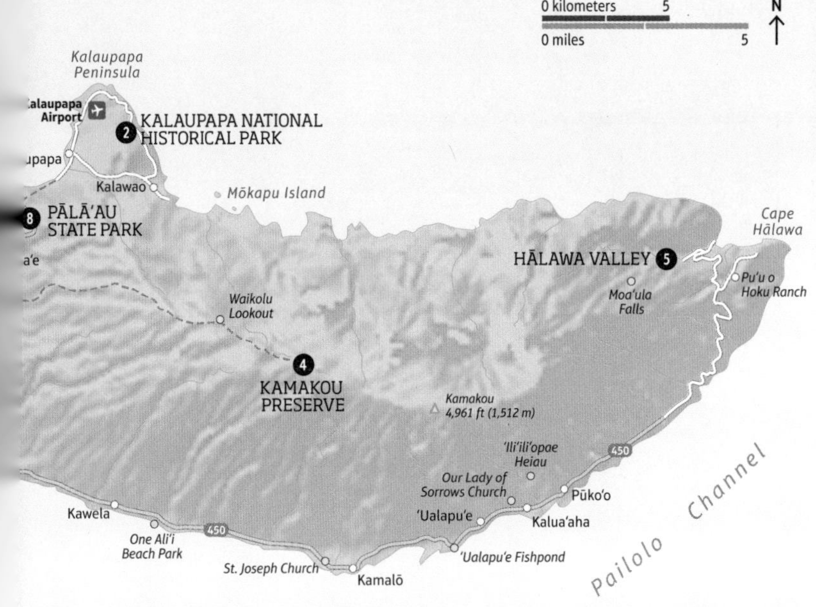

0 kilometers 5
0 miles 5
N
Kalaupapa Peninsula
Kalaupapa Airport
2 KALAUPAPA NATIONAL HISTORICAL PARK
Kalawao
Mōkapu Island
8 PĀLĀ'AU STATE PARK
Cape Hālawa
HĀLAWA VALLEY 5
Pu'u o Hoku Ranch
Moa'ula Falls
Waikolu Lookout
4 KAMAKOU PRESERVE
Kamakou 4,961 ft (1,512 m)
'Ili'ili'opae Heiau
Our Lady of Sorrows Church
Pūko'o
450
Kawela
One Ali'i Beach Park
450
'Ualapu'e
Kalua'aha
'Ualapu'e Fishpond
St. Joseph Church
Kamalō
Pailolo Channel
Kalohi Channel
Shipwreck Beach
Lāna'i
Federation Camp
Garden of the Gods
LĀNA'I
1
430
'Au'au Channel
Pu'u Mahana 4,714 ft (1,436 m)
Kane Pu'u Forest Preserve
Hauola Gulch
Keōmuku
Mā'alaea
Kō'ele
MUNRO TRAIL
Keone Bay
Lāna'i City
Luahiwa Petroglyphs
Lāna'ihale 3,370 ft (1,027 m)
440
Pālāwai Basin
Lāna'i Airport
Lōpā
Pōka'i
Kaumalapau Harbor
Naha
440
Mākole Point
Kaunolū
Mānele Bay
Hulopo'e Bay

1

LĀNA'I

✈ 4 miles (6.5 km) SW of Lāna'i City ℹ Lāna'i Culture & Heritage Center: 730 Lāna'i Av; lanaichc.org

Sun-baked Lāna'i was once the world's largest pineapple plantation, owned by the Dole Company. In 1991, the Castle & Cooke Corporation (Dole's parent company), opened two luxury resorts and re-employed the island's farm workers as hotel staff. This identity shift opened the island to visitors to come and explore its many beaches, cliffs, and ancient ruins. In 2012, the tech magnate Larry Ellison purchased 98 per cent of the island and made several eco-friendly and sustainability-focused changes.

Lāna'i City

Home to virtually all of the island's 3,100 residents, Lāna'i City offers a first-hand experience of a Hawaiian plantation town. Built in the 1920s to house Dole's contract workers, this friendly town centers on rectangular Dole Park, which is lined with frontier-style shops. Visitors can browse around the Lāna'i Culture & Heritage Center for free, which is located in the Old Dole Administration Building. The center has a small museum with vintage photographs of the area's plantation past and display cases full of historic artifacts belonging to the island's first residents. For feline fans, a visit to the Lanai Cat Sanctuary is a must. Here there are over 650 feral cats – rescued from areas where native birds are nesting – who have been given a safe home at the sanctuary.

Luahiwa Petroglyphs

⌂ Off Hō'ike Rd, 2 miles (3 km) S of Lāna'i City, near the water tower

The broad, hazy expanse of Pālāwai Basin is actually the remains of Lāna'i's extinct volcanic crater. Its eastern wall bears one of Hawaii's richest collections of petroglyphs. Visible from quite a distance, a cluster of 34 black boulders

LĀNA'I'S COOK ISLAND PINE TREES

Groves of Cook Island Pine, which give the island its characteristic look, were planted in the early 1900s by New Zealander George C. Munro, the manager of what was then the Lāna'i Ranch. Freshwater is Lāna'i's most precious resource, and Munro realized that these trees increase the island's water-drawing capacities. Mountain mists collect in the trees' tightly leaved branches and drip onto the thirsty ground - on a good day, as much as 40 gallons (150 liters) of water fall per tree.

Coconut palm trees dotting a golden stretch of beach on the island of Lāna'i

stands out against a red hillside dotted with dry white patches of *pili* grass. Some of these stones were thought to possess the *mana* (sacred power) of the Hawaiian rain gods Kū and Hina. Starting at least 500 years ago, Hawaiians decorated them by carving figures of humans and dogs. More recent images of horses, surfers, and leashed dogs were carved by students in the 1870s. The petroglyphs are best viewed early or late, when the sun is not directly overhead.

Did You Know?

There's only 30 miles (48 km) of paved road on Lāna'i and no traffic lights.

③

Mānele and Hulopo'e Bays

End of Mānele Rd (Hwy 440), 8 miles (13 km) S of Lāna'i City

These adjacent bays form a marine life conservation district, home to spinner dolphins. Mānele Bay is the only small boat harbor here and Hulopo'e Bay is the island's best swimming and snorkeling spot. The bay is off-limits to all boats except those of excursion and charter companies. Camping is permitted here.

Between the bays lies Pu'u Pehe, or Sweetheart Rock. In legend, Pehe was kept by her jealous husband in a nearby cave until she drowned in a storm. He buried her here, then jumped to his death.

EAT

Blue Ginger

Generous portions of Hawaiian favorites, such as *loco moco* (rice topped with a burger patty, eggs, and gravy).

409 7th St, Lāna'i City
bluegingercafe lanai.com

Lāna'i City Bar & Grill

Housed inside the historic Hotel Lāna'i, this casual, charming restaurant serves top-notch American fare.

828 Lāna'i Av, Lāna'i City (808) 565-7212

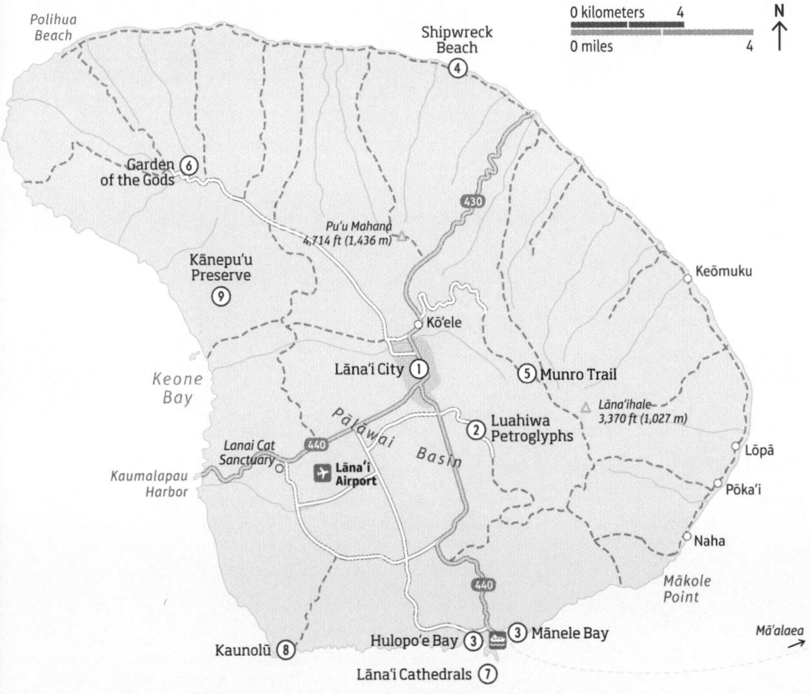

④

Shipwreck Beach

 **Keōmuku Rd (Hwy 430), 8 miles (13 km) NE of Lāna'i City**

Lāna'i's northern shore is lined with an 8-mile (13-km) stretch of beach that takes its name from the rusting hulk of a World War II supply ship that is wrecked on the reef. Many other ships have come to harm in these shallow, hazardous waters, including an oil tanker that is visible 6 miles (10 km) up the beach. To reach the beach, follow Keōmuku Road (Hwy 430) until the asphalt ends; then take the dirt road on the left that rambles over sandy ground for about a mile (1.5 km). From here, a beachcomber's trek offers isolation and beautiful views of Maui and Moloka'i – a day's hike northward will bring you to the secluded red sands of Polihua Beach. Note that swimming is dangerous at both Shipwreck and Polihua beaches.

HIDDEN GEM
Ghost Town

Found en route to Shipwreck Beach, Keōmuku has been a ghost town since the 1950s when it was abandoned following droughts. It has a lovely century-old wooden church and other relics to peruse.

⑤

Munro Trail

 **Turn off Mānele Rd (Hwy 440) 5 miles (8 km) S of Lāna'i City**

This pine-studded, 13-mile (21-km) rugged dirt trail can be biked or hiked (vehicles are no longer allowed). It ventures along the volcanic ridge of Lāna'ihale, whose summit reaches 3,370 ft (1,027 m), offering sensational views of five of the Hawaiian Islands on a clear day. After a significant rainfall, the trail can be alarmingly muddy and is at times closed. To reach the trailhead, follow Mānele Road south out of town, and just after the Pālāwai Basin, turn left onto a dirt road and then follow the most worn track up the hill. Alternatively, begin the trail past the horse stables at Sensei Lāna'i, A Four Seasons Resort, north of town.

⑥

Garden of the Gods

 **Polihua Rd, 6 miles (10 km) NW of Lāna'i City**

The Garden of the Gods is a visual oddity – a reddish lunar landscape dotted with boulders made of compacted sand. They range in color from reds and oranges to browns and blues, and the effect is most intense at sunset, when the rocks seem to glow. This peculiar dry and rocky landscape is reached by an easy 30-minute drive along a dirt road from Kō'ele, which passes through a hunting zone for axis (spotted) deer and native dryland forest.

Continuing on, the road to the island's northern tip gets rougher, ending at long,

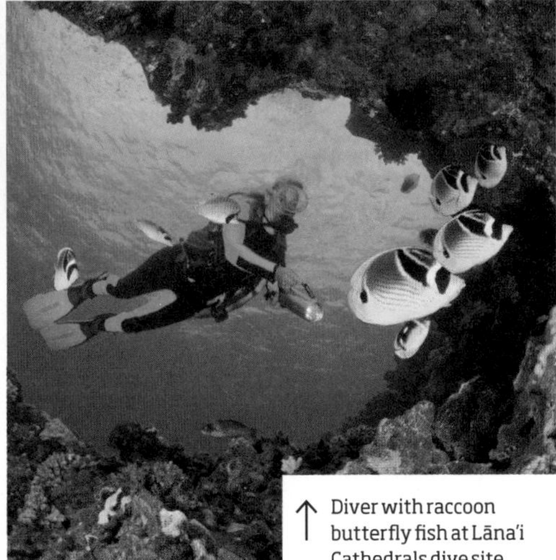

↑ Diver with raccoon butterfly fish at Lāna'i Cathedrals dive site

wild Polihua Beach. At this remote strand, one hour from Kō'ele, a visitor's footprints may be the only ones of the day. The ocean currents can be dangerous.

Lāna'i Cathedrals

Scuba divers flock to these underwater caverns, found southeast of the island's Hulopo'e Bay. Formed from lava tubes and standing two-story tall, they are home to green sea turtles, white-tip reef sharks, octopuses, and an array of colorful fish and pristine coral. The caverns have holes in the ceilings, allowing natural light to pour in like a skylight and illuminate the water below. Lāna'i City-based **Lāna'i Ocean Sports** can take experienced scuba divers on a guided diving tour to these caverns and they'll provide all the gear, plus a gourmet picnic lunch made by the Four Seasons hotel onshore.

Rocks dotting the rust-colored landscape of the Garden of the Gods

Lāna'i Ocean Sports
Mānele Small Boat Harbor lanaioceansports.com

Kaunolū

Kaunolū Trail, a dirt track off Kaupili Rd, which leaves Mānele Rd (Hwy 440) 4.5 miles (7 km) S of Lāna'i City

Few sites evoke the drama of ancient Hawaiian life like the ruins of this seldom-visited fishing village, abandoned in the mid-19th century. The rough drive to this naturally fortified clifftop takes an hour from the city in a 4WD vehicle.

Early Hawaiians excelled in building with unmortared stone, and you can see well-preserved examples here, including the stone platform of the Halulu Heiau on Kaunolū Bay's west side. On the east there is a cliff-side platform, once home to Kamehameha I. There are also ruins of a canoe house and a fishing shrine.

Just west of Kaunolū, there is a diving platform, known as Kahekili's Leap. Here, the former chief of Maui, Kahekili, proved his mettle by hurling himself more than 60 ft (18 m) down – clearing a 15-ft- (4.5-m-) wide rock outcrop – into 10-ft- (3-m-) deep water. Cliff-jumping was one way ancient Hawaiians showed their bravery.

Kānepu'u Preserve

Polihua Rd Dawn-dusk daily

Northwest of Lāna'i City, on the west side of the island, the expansive Kānepu'u Preserve is home to nearly 50 species of native plants that thrive in the dry forest. The preserve offers a rare opportunity to view such species as the Hawaiian ebony, sandalwood, and *'aiea*, a tree used for building canoes.

Access to the preserve is via a rough path; self-guided maps are provided at the entrance kiosk. The **Nature Conservancy of Hawaii** offers tours for large groups.

Nature Conservancy of Hawaii
gohawaii.com

ADVENTURE ACTIVITIES

Book any of the below adventures through the Lāna'i Adventure Park *(lanaiadventurepark.com)*, conducted by the island's Four Seasons resort.

Zip-lining fun
Enjoy panoramic views as you soar through the Kaiholena valley.

Go mountain biking
Traverse miles of trails and dirt roads on an electric mountain bike.

Aerial activities
Test your fitness on this challenging off-ground obstacle course.

2

KALAUPAPA NATIONAL HISTORICAL PARK

From Ho'olehua, Moloka'i, or Honolulu Sun nps.gov/kala

Sealed off from the rest of Moloka'i by a wall of mighty cliffs, the Kalaupapa Peninsula was once a settlement for those with Hansen's Disease (leprosy). Today, the park is dotted with the poignant remnants of this remote settlement.

In 1865, when the imported disease of leprosy seemed to threaten the survival of the Hawaiian people, the Kalaupapa Peninsula was designated a leprosy colony, and those afflicted were exiled here. The main settlement was at the village of Kalawao, on the eastern side of the peninsula. The policy of enforced isolation ended in 1969 thanks to new medication that meant that patients were no longer contagious; despite this, many patients chose to continue living on the peninsula.

Today, the area – now a national park – serves as a memorial and a handful of the original patients still live here, voluntarily. The settlement is made up of four churches and nearly 200 other historic buildings; many of the residential 1920s wood-frame cottages are built in the Hawaiian Plantation style. There's also a lighthouse whose light was once one of the most powerful in the Pacific. This peaceful community and the quiet, oceanfront park nearby can only be explored with an organized tour, which must be arranged in advance.

At times, guided tours can be canceled. Check for updates from the park to avoid disappointment *(nps.gov/kala)*. If visitation restrictions are in place, views of the Kalaupapa Peninsula can still be enjoyed from the eucalyptus groves of Pālā'au State Park, a beautiful recreational area that rises 1,000 ft (300 m) above the coast.

There's also a lighthouse whose light was once one of the most powerful in the Pacific.

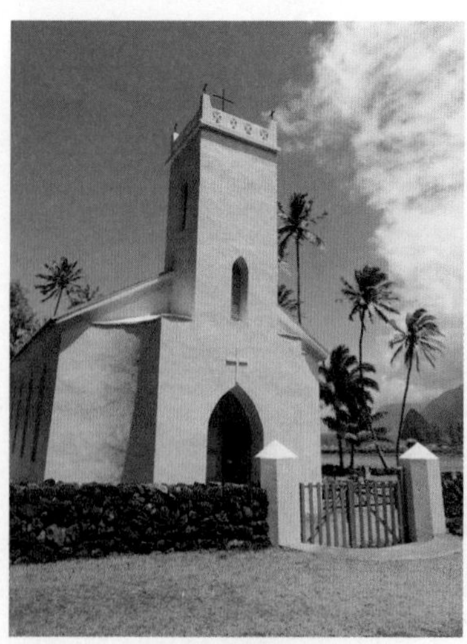

↑ Father Damien's St. Philomena Catholic Church, part of the Kalaupapa National Historical Park

LIFE AT THE SETTLEMENT

From 1866 to 1969, around 8,000 people were sent to the Kalaupapa Peninsula to live in isolation. In the beginning, food and medicine were in short supply, and condemnation to the peninsula was seen as a death sentence. However, things changed in 1873 when Father Damien *(below)*, a Belgian priest who came to Hawaii as a Roman Catholic missionary in 1864, volunteered to serve the colony. He built hospitals, churches, and homes, vastly improving the quality of life for the peninsula's residents. He also nursed patients without fear for his own life. After 12 years on the peninsula, he finally succumbed to leprosy in 1889.

By the 1930s, 40 years after Father Damien's death, life here had improved further: stores, water systems, and paved roads were constructed, as were buildings housing a cinema and a dining hall.

Did You Know?

At 3,600–3,900-ft (1,100–1,190-m) high, the Kalaupapa Cliffs are the tallest sea cliffs in the world.

→

The remote Kalaupapa Peninsula on the north shore of Moloka'i

EXPERIENCE MORE

Kaunakakai

Kamehameha V Hwy (Hwy 450) Moloka'i Visitors Association: (800) 800-6367

Kaunakakai, the main town on Moloka'i, was built at the end of the 19th century as an administrative center and port for the local sugar plantations.

The wooden boardwalks of its principal thoroughfare, Ala Malama Street, are lined with false-fronted stores, such as the Kanemitsu Bakery, and homey diners that reflect Moloka'i's multicultural community. At the eastern end of the street, tiny St. Sophia's Church is all but obscured behind an African tulip tree with its orange blossoms.

About half a mile (800 m) from the town center, the long stone jetty of Kaunakakai Harbor juts out into the ocean. It was built in 1898 with rocks taken from a destroyed *heiau* (temple). A break in the coral reef made it a natural place from which to launch canoes. The harbor is often busy with local fishers and divers.

Northeast of Kaunakakai, **Molokai Plumeria Farm** offers tours, u-pick flowers, and lei-making workshops. Further north, **Macadamia Nut Farm** offers tours and tastings.

GREAT VIEW
Kapuaiwa Coconut Grove

The soaring palms of this coconut grove, found 2 miles (3 km) west of Kaunakakai, between the highway and the ocean are a majestic sight to behold at sunset.

Molokai Plumeria Farm
1342 Mauna Loa Hwy, Kaunakakai 9am-noon Mon-Fri molokaiplumerias.com

Macadamia Nut Farm
2240 Lihi Pali Av, Ho'olehua (808) 567-6601 9:30am-3:30pm Mon-Fri, 10am-2pm Sat

Kamakou Preserve

Reached by 4WD road E of Maunaloa Hwy (Hwy 460), 4 miles (6.5 km) NW of Kaunakakai Moloka'i Visitors Association: (800) 800-6367

The remote mountaintop ridges of eastern Moloka'i protect one of the least spoiled tracts of rainforest in Hawaii – the Kamakou Preserve. It is reached by 4WD or mountain bike on a rutted dirt road.

The higher you climb, the wetter and lusher the forest becomes, and the more the road deteriorates. Native fauna and flora increasingly

← A group of towering palms reaching up toward the sky at Kapuaiwa Coconut Grove

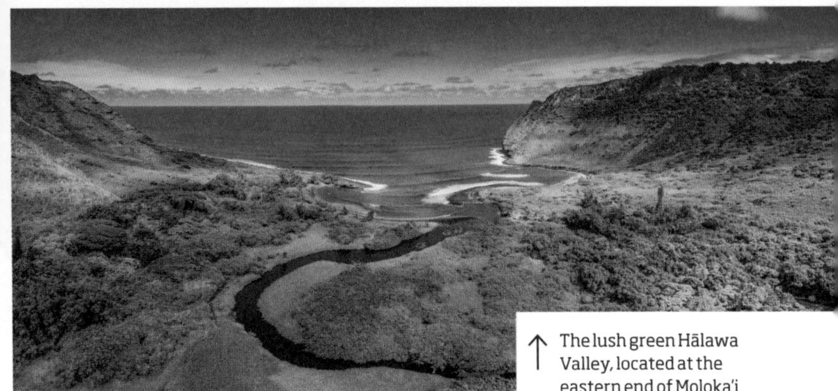

↑ The lush green Hālawa Valley, located at the eastern end of Moloka'i

predominate, with colorful *'ōhi'a* trees erupting amid vivid green foliage. Ten miles (16 km) from the entrance to the preserve, along a dirt road, superb views open out all the way to the north shore valleys. Here, Waikolu Lookout stands above the 3,700-ft (1,150-m) drop of valley.

Just beyond, the Pēpē'ōpae Trail climbs along a wooden walkway through rainforest. Every tree is festooned with hanging vines and spongy moss, while orchids glisten in the undergrowth. This misty wonderland is the last refuge of endangered birds like the Moloka'i thrush *(oloma'o)* and Moloka'i creeper *(kākāwahie)*. After crossing a windswept bog, the trail traverses a series of gulches to emerge at an excellent overlook above Pelekunu Valley.

Each month, the Nature Conservancy runs a guided hike through the preserve.

Hālawa Valley

End of Kamehameha V Hwy (Hwy 450), 27 miles (43 km) E of Kaunakakai Moloka'i Visitors Association: (800) 800-6367

Hawaii's original Polynesian settlers were established in beautiful Hālawa Valley by 650 CE, and for over 1,000 years they grew taro *(p171)* in an elaborate network of terraced fields. The ruins of nearly 20 ancient *heiau* (temples) lie hidden in the undergrowth on both sides of the valley. Hālawa was all but abandoned after the 1946 tsunami, but new generations of farmers now grow taro here.

Visitors get their first glimpse of Hālawa from an overlook near mile marker 26. Though its farthest reaches are often obscured by mountain mists, the dramatic shoreline lies spread out 750 ft (230 m) below. The placid, unhurried meanderings of the main stream as it approaches the ocean are in sharp contrast to the roaring surf just ahead.

The highway switchbacks down the hillside, reaching the valley floor at a quaint wooden chapel. A little farther along, the road ends at a low ridge of dunes, knitted together by *naupaka*, a white-flowered creeper. Surfers launch themselves into the waves from the small gray beach just beyond.

In summer, visitors wade across the river mouth to reach a nicer beach on the far side; in winter, it's safer to follow the dirt road that curves from beside the chapel. Shaded by imposing palm trees and sheltered from the full force of the sea by a stony headland, the beach is idyllic for swimming.

EAT

Kanemitsu Bakery

Since the 1920s, this bakery has been known for its late-night "hot bread," served with your choice of sweet or savory fillings.

79 Ala Malama St, Kaunakakai (808) 553-5855 Tue

Hiro's Ohana Grill

Dine on seafood and enjoy sunset views and live 'ukulele music at this hotel restaurant.

1300 Kamehameha V Hwy, Kaunakakai Mon hirosohanagrill.com

$$$

SHOP

Pu'u O Hoku Ranch Store

A biodynamic and organic cattle farm selling its own honey and other goodies.

Mile marker 25, Kaunakakai puuohoku.com

Did You Know?

Laka is thought of as being both the Goddess of Hula and the Goddess of the Forest.

6

Maunaloa

Maunaloa Hwy (Hwy 460), 16 miles (26 km) W of Kaunakakai
i Moloka'i Visitors Association: (800) 800-6367

In the days when the Moloka'i Ranch specialized in cattle and pineapples, tiny Maunaloa, situated on the flanks of the mountain of the same name, was the archetypal Hawaiian plantation village. The timber-frame houses belonging to its farm workers and *paniolo* (Hawaiian cowboys) faced out across the ocean to Waikīkī.

In the 1970s, the ranch switched to tourism, offering luxury camping, an upscale hotel, and outdoor activities; however, it closed in 2008. Today, a few homespun businesses still survive on the main street, including the **Big Wind Kite Factory**. The factory's owner, Jonathan Socher, is happy to show visitors around his manufacturing area and discuss the many kite designs. He also offers kite-flying lessons in the adjacent park.

INSIDER TIP
Marine Wildlife

Go wildlife spotting with UnCruise *(uncruise.com)*, one of the few cruises permitted to visit Moloka'i. See monk seals, humpback whales, and green sea turtles, among many other marine animals.

Moloka'i was renowned in ancient times as *Moloka'i pule o'o* (Moloka'i of strong prayers), the home of powerful priests and sorcerers. Dreaded "poisonwood gods" were said to have lived in the forests above Maunaloa; a sliver of wood cut from their favored trees could kill any foe. However, the *'ōhi'a* woods nearby played a more benign role in Hawaiian legend. Here the goddess Laka learned the hula and taught it to humans. This claim to be the birthplace of hula is disputed; Kē'ē Beach on Kaua'i boasts the same distinction *(p228)*.

Big Wind Kite Factory

120 Maunaloa Hwy (Hwy 460) **W** bigwindkites.com

7

Pāpōhaku Beach

Kalua Koi Rd, Moloka'i

The Pāpōhaku Beach, also known as Three Mile Beach, is one of Hawaii's largest white-sand stretches. Colossal waves here render the beach unsafe for swimming, especially between the months of October and March when the swells are at their most hazardous. There are also no lifeguards stationed at the beach.

Though the tides can be unruly, the pristine beach can be enjoyed on foot, especially at sunset. It often appears to be virtually uninhabited, offering a sense of romantic seclusion. The beach has excellent facilities, including campsites, indoor and outdoor showers, and picnic tables. In the past it was this beach, and several others, that supplied the sand for the almost entirely artificial Waikīkī Beach *(p96)*.

Located just beyond the southern end of Pāpōhaku is the secluded Dixie Maru Beach, named after a ship that was wrecked offshore in the 1920s. Today, it offers sheltered swimming and excellent snorkeling opportunities, though currents can be strong during high surf. To the north, the resort-community of Kaluako'i is fronted by the rocky Kepuhi Bay, which has a wide beach that is popular with surfers.

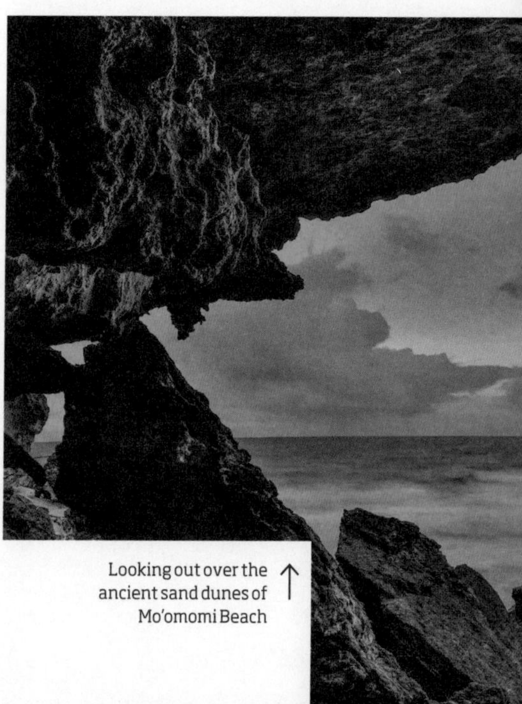

Looking out over the ancient sand dunes of Mo'omomi Beach ↑

STAY

Hotel Moloka'i
Moloka'i's only hotel resembles a traditional Polynesian village. Choose from modern, oceanfront suites or retro 1960s bungalows.

1300 Kamehameha V Hwy, Kaunakakai
hotelmolokai.com

$$$

Pālā'au State Park

Hwy 470, Kualapuu
7am-7pm daily dlnr.hawaii.gov

Around 4 miles (6.5 km) northeast of Kualapu'u, the Kala'e Highway (Hwy 470) comes to an end at Pālā'au State Park, which combines superb views over the Kalaupapa Peninsula *(p142)* with a legendary site. Stop at the viewpoint to gaze eastward along the awesome cliffs to Kalaupapa village and beyond. From the vista's parking lot, a hiking trail leads through the forest to Phallic Rock. As ancient legend has it, women who sleep beneath this outcrop will wake up pregnant. Its lifelike appearance has been partly crafted.

Kualapu'u

Maunaloa Hwy (Hwy 460), 9 miles (14 km) NW of Kaunakakai
Moloka'i Visitors Association: (800) 800-6367

The former plantation village of Kualapu'u is now home to Moloka'i's first coffee plantation, whose products can be tasted at the friendly, roadside espresso bar. Located 2 miles (3 km) northeast of town, the R. W. Meyer Sugar Mill preserves the remains of the area's short-lived dabble in the sugar business. The mill machinery, now restored, was in use for just 11 years from 1878 to 1889. These days it forms part of the adjoining **Moloka'i Museum and Cultural Center** (cash-only admission), an interesting collection of artifacts that illustrates the island's history.

Moloka'i Museum and Cultural Center
1795 Kala'e Hwy (Hwy 470) (808) 567-6436
10am-2pm Mon-Sat
Federal hols

Mo'omomi Beach

At the end of Mo'omomi Rd, 5 miles (8 km) NW of Ho'olehua

This beach, one of the few places along Moloka'i's north shore that is accessible to visitors, belongs to the drier western end of the island. The coastline here is made up of ancient sand dunes that have become lithified (turned to rock). The area is scattered with the bones of flightless birds, which may have been hunted to extinction by early Polynesian settlers.

A 5-mile (8-km) dirt road from Ho'olehua leads to Mo'omomi Bay, a surfing and fishing beach popular with locals.

A DRIVING TOUR
EAST MOLOKA'I

Length 30 miles (48km) **Stopping-off points** Refreshment stops are scarce, though there are a few restaurants and cafés in Kaunakakai, at the beginning of the drive **Terrain** Paved

The coastal highway that nestles beneath the peaks of eastern Moloka'i is among the most beautiful drives in Hawaii. Ancient sites and historic churches lie tucked away amid tropical flowers and luxuriant rainforest, while the picturesque slopes of West Maui are visible just across the water. Few people live in the area now, so the villages along the highway can often feel deserted – and amenities can be rare. At the end of the drive, the road finally twists to a halt at the ravishing Hālawa Valley, one of Hawaii's most stunning "amphitheater" valleys.

50

The number of ancient fishponds that line Moloka'i's southeast coast.

At **One Ali'i Beach Park,** *the small expanse of lawn, scattered with coconut palms, is ideal for picnics and also provides a perfect starting point for kayak trips. One Ali'i is a modern misspelling of the ancient Hawaiian name Oneali'i, meaning "Royal Sands."*

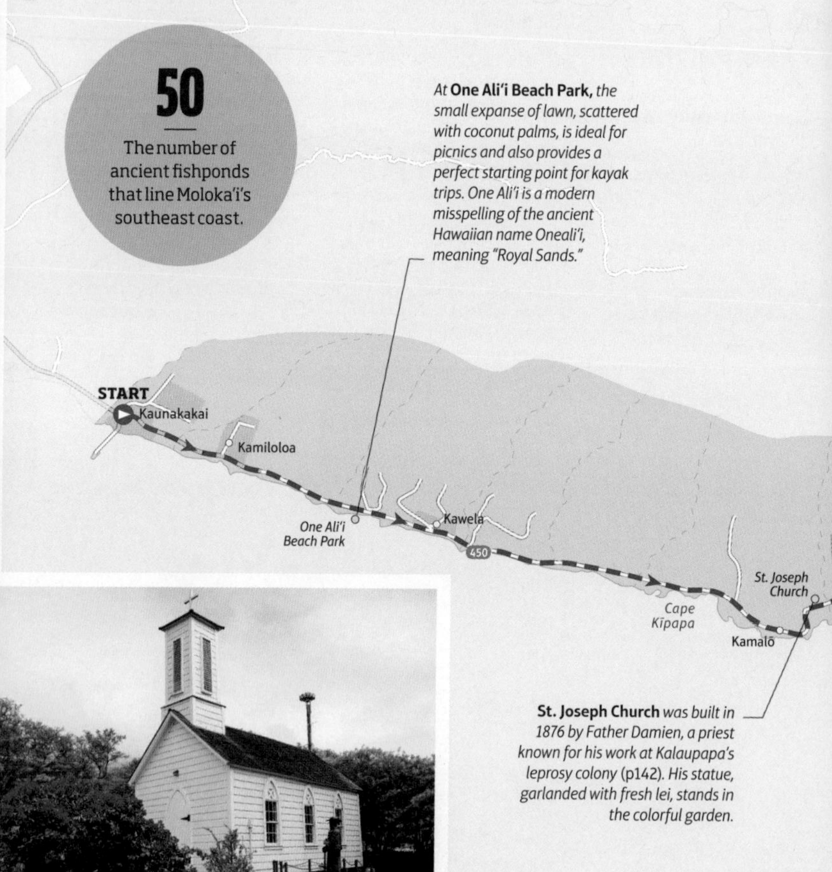

St. Joseph Church *was built in 1876 by Father Damien, a priest known for his work at Kalaupapa's leprosy colony* *(p142)**. His statue, garlanded with fresh lei, stands in the colorful garden.*

← St. Joseph Church, a quaint, wood-frame building

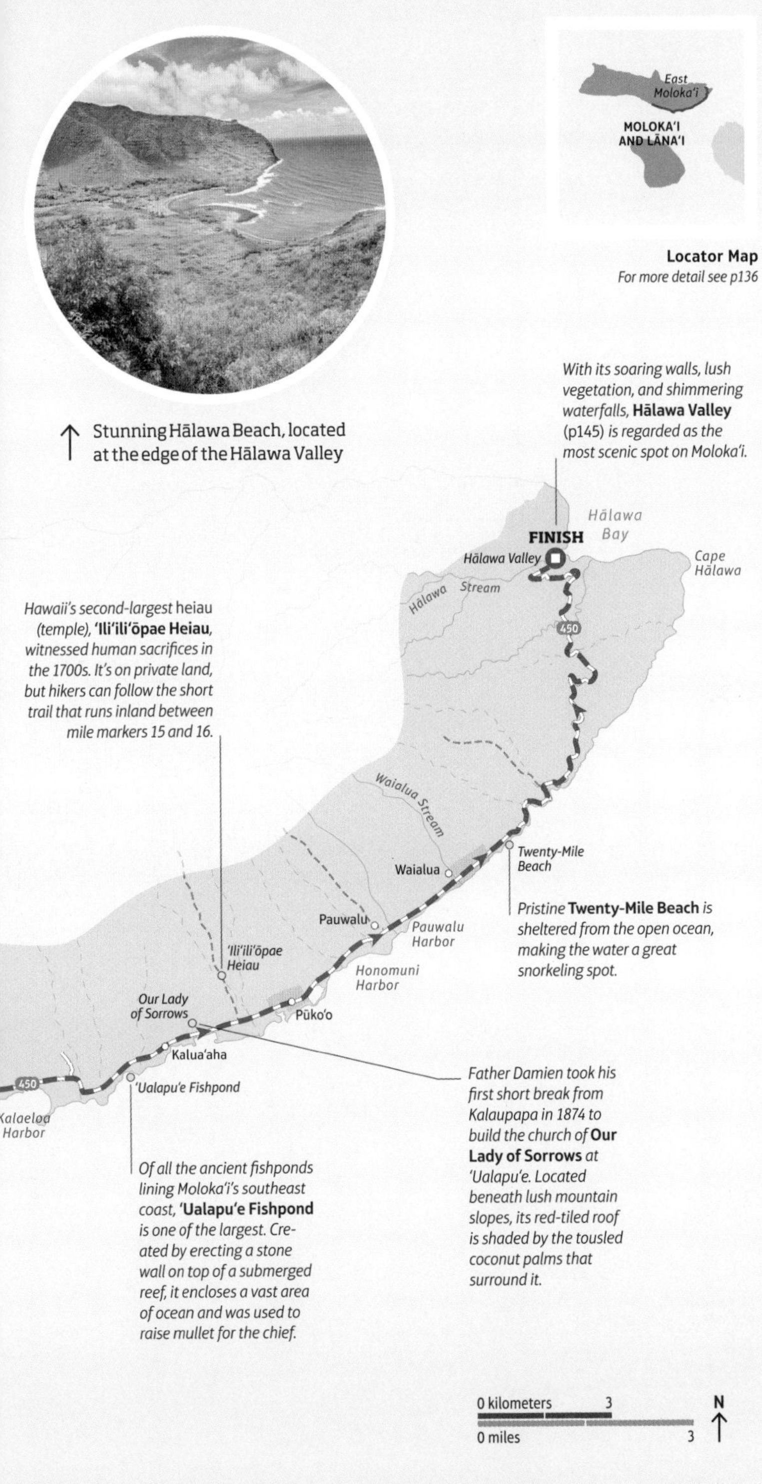

↑ Stunning Hālawa Beach, located at the edge of the Hālawa Valley

Locator Map
For more detail see p136

With its soaring walls, lush vegetation, and shimmering waterfalls, **Hālawa Valley** *(p145) is regarded as the most scenic spot on Moloka'i.*

Hawaii's second-largest heiau *(temple),* **'Ili'ili'ōpae Heiau**, *witnessed human sacrifices in the 1700s. It's on private land, but hikers can follow the short trail that runs inland between mile markers 15 and 16.*

Pristine **Twenty-Mile Beach** *is sheltered from the open ocean, making the water a great snorkeling spot.*

Father Damien took his first short break from Kalaupapa in 1874 to build the church of **Our Lady of Sorrows** *at 'Ualapu'e. Located beneath lush mountain slopes, its red-tiled roof is shaded by the tousled coconut palms that surround it.*

Of all the ancient fishponds lining Moloka'i's southeast coast, **'Ualapu'e Fishpond** *is one of the largest. Created by erecting a stone wall on top of a submerged reef, it encloses a vast area of ocean and was used to raise mullet for the chief.*

Humpback whale off the coast of Maui

MAUI

The second-largest Hawaiian island, Maui was formed by the convergence of two volcanoes at the isthmus known today as the Central Valley. The green 5,788-ft (1,764-m) West Maui Mountains are the eroded slopes of a single extinct volcano, while East Maui is composed of Haleakalā, an enormous 10,023-ft (3,055-m) dormant volcano crowned by a lunar landscape.

The earliest inhabitants are thought to have arrived from the Marquesas Islands in the 4th century CE, settling around modern-day Lāhainā and Hāna. Maui was split into rival chiefdoms until the 14th century, when Pi'ilani, a local chief, united the island. He built some of Maui's first roads, plus several extensive irrigation systems and the massive temple of Pi'ilanihale Heiau, near Hāna, whose ruins can still be seen today. Then, in 1795, Kamehameha I conquered Maui in his quest to unite the Hawaiian Islands, and in 1800, he established his royal seat at Lāhainā. Jean-François de Galaup, Comte de La Pérouse, was the first European to set foot on Maui, in 1786. Other foreigners followed during the 1800s, including missionaries, whalers, and contract laborers from Europe and Asia who came to work the growing sugar plantations. The communities they established retained the character of their homelands and created a multicultural heritage that is celebrated today in local holidays, customs, and food.

In 1946, Maui's first resort hotel opened in Hāna, and by the 1960s much of the island's west coast offered luxurious lodgings for tourists, who came to enjoy a game of golf along its glittering shores. Tourists continue to be drawn to Maui today, thanks to its stunning natural beauty and vibrant culture.

NĀKĀLELE POINT
Honokōhau
KAPALUA
Napili
Kahana
Honokōwai
Kapalua Airport
Honokōhau Valley
KAHAKULOA VILLAGE AND HEAD
KĀ'ANAPALI
West Maui Mountains
Waihe'e
Haleki'i-Pihana Heiau State Monument
Kanahā Beach Country Park
PĀ'IA
WAILUKU
Kanahā Pond
Kahului Airpo
Lahainaluna
'ĪAO VALLEY
KAHULUI
Lāhainā
Pu'unēnē
Hanaula 4,616 ft (1,406 m)
Waikapū
Launiupoko
Awalua Beach
Puu Anu 2,972 ft (905 m)
Central Valley
Olowalu
Keālia Pond NWR
Ukumehame
MĀ'ALAEA
'Au'au Channel
Mai Poina Beach Park
Mānele Bay
KĪHEI
Kama'ole
Keawakapu Beach
WAILEA
Mākena
Malu'aka Beach
MOLOKINI
MĀKENA STATE PARK
'ĀHIHI-KINA'U NATURAL AREA RESERVE
LA PÉROUSE BAY
Kaho'olawe
Pu'u Moa'ulaiki 1,421 ft (433 m)
Kaho'olawe Island Reserve
0 kilometers 10
0 miles 10
N

MAUI

Must Sees

1. Haleakalā National Park

Experience More

2. Kā'anapali
3. Kapalua
4. Nākālele Point
5. Kahului
6. Kahakuloa Village and Head
7. Wailuku
8. Kīhei
9. Mā'alaea
10. Molokini
11. 'Īao Valley
12. Mākena State Park
13. 'Āhihi-Kina'u Natural Area Reserve
14. La Pérouse Bay
15. Makawao
16. Wailea
17. Hāna
18. Pā'ia
19. Ke'anae Peninsula and Wailua Valley
20. Kaupō
21. Kahanu Garden
22. Upcountry Farms

The craggy peaks of Haleakalā silhouetted dramatically at sunrise, and *(inset)* visitors enjoying the Mars-like landscape ↑

HALEAKALĀ NATIONAL PARK

Haleakalā Crater Rd (Hwy 378) **24 hrs daily**
nps.gov/hale

Stretching from craggy peaks to coast, this magnificent national park covers the top of the vast Haleakalā shield volcano. The park's summit area is famous for its rugged, rocky peaks and Martian-like red deserts, while its southeast slope is home to lush and humid forest.

Crowned by a cratered landscape, the 10,023-ft (3,055-m) Haleakalā – meaning "House of the Sun" – dominates the island of Maui. While thought to have last erupted around 500 years ago, it is still considered an active volcano. Haleakalā's expansive and dusty Summit District, colored in tones of burned crimson and dark ash, is an otherworldly place, home to some of the world's rarest plants and animal species. Among them are the endangered *nēnē* bird and the endemic Haleakalā silversword, whose honey-scented blossoms can take up to 50 years to develop.

In contrast to the arid Summit District, the Kīpahulu District on Haleakalā's coastal southeastern slope is humid and deeply forested. This remote area is only accessible via the Road to Hāna *(p172)*. The hiking trails here wind past gushing waterfalls, freshwater streams and shimmering pools, as well as to remnants of ancient taro farms and fishing villages. From the many overlooks in this part of the park, you may spot humpback whales and dolphins out in the ocean, or green sea turtles and monk seals on Kīpahulu's rocky shores.

PICTURE PERFECT

Pu'u'ula'ula Summit

Climb up to the summit of the Pu'u'ula'ula (Red Hill), the highest point on Maui, to snap a photo of the entire Haleakalā volcano. A glassed-in shelter provides relief from the bitterly cold winds while you wait for the perfect shot.

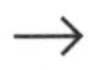

Stars illuminating the sky above Haleakalā National Park

Watching the sunset from the top of the crimson-hued Summit District

EXPLORING HALEAKALĀ NATIONAL PARK

Watching the Sunrise and Sunset

Haleakalā's high-altitude summit is perfect for observing the sun's rise and fall. The park requires a reservation to watch the sunrise; book via the website well in advance, although last-minute tickets are released online a few days ahead. Reservations are not needed for sunsets. Dress warmly as the temperature is below freezing during the night on the summit.

Stargazing

Haleakalā offers great stargazing thanks to its high altitude and lack of light pollution. As night falls, the skies begin to reveal an infinite number of stars – it's no wonder that the summit is home to so many observatories (closed to the public). Stargazing is especially spectacular when the moon is phasing out; the lack of moonlight makes the stars blaze brighter. To view them, rent a pair of binoculars from one of Maui's dive shops, pick up a stargazing map at the Park Headquarters Visitor Center or the Haleakalā Visitor Center, and park at an overlook. Remember to dress warmly.

Hiking

The numerous hiking trails offered here are suitable for most skill levels. You can opt to go out on your own or with a guide. Either way, make sure you are prepared – at over 10,000 ft (3,050 m) and highly exposed, Haleakalā can be windy, cold, hot, and even snowy during winter. Pack a proper backpack with a first-aid kit, snacks, and plenty of water.

Some of the best trails include Sliding Sands Trail *(p158)*, an 11-mile (17.8-km) hike that cuts across a crater with red cinder cones, and the 4-mile (6.5-km) Pīpīwai Trail that winds through a forest path home to ground-nesting owls. Or opt for the rocky 2.2-mile (3.6-km) Halemau'u Trail, across a natural land bridge and to a crater viewpoint.

Cycling

Switchbacking its way up to the summit of Pu'u'ula'ula *(p155)*, Crater Road is one of the most famous cycling climbs. The paved, two-lane road is well maintained, but due to its high altitude and length – 23 miles (37 km) – the route is difficult and is best left to experienced cyclists. But this doesn't mean you have to miss out: Bike Maui *(bikemaui.com)* offers downhill bikes to rent, and will drive you up to the summit, allowing you to whizz down on the paved main road.

Flora and Fauna Spotting

Haleakalā's Summit District is home to the rare and endemic Haleakalā silversword, which

STAY

Wilderness Cabins
Built in the 1930s, these three rustic cabins are accessible only by foot. From the park's visitor center, the first is a 3.7-mile (5.9-km) hike and the farthest is a 9.3-mile (15-km) trek. The cabins accommodate 12 people each, and have wood-burning stoves and outdoor pit toilets. Reservations can be made up to six months in advance.

recreation.gov

flourishes in the park's ashy and arid environment. The soft silvery hairs on this plant's in-curved leaves protect it from blazing hot days and harsh cold nights in the crater. The summit area is also home to the now endangered *nēnē*. A relative of the Canada goose, these zebra-striped birds were virtually extinct in the 1960s, but a conservation program improved their numbers.

You can also find tiny Hawaiian bats in the park, which are the only endemic Hawaiian land mammals in existence. In the Kīpahulu District you can spot the bright red *'apapane* bird and the *'i'iwi* bird. Full-day bird-watching treks are offered by Explore Maui Nature *(exploremaui nature.com)*.

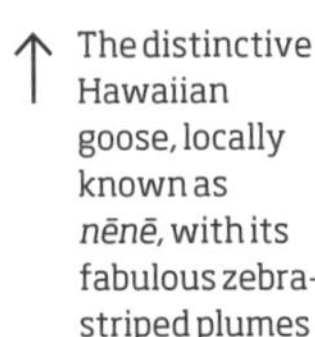

↑ The distinctive Hawaiian goose, locally known as *nēnē*, with its fabulous zebra-striped plumes

← A pathway leading into the densely forested Kīpahulu District

A LONG WALK KEONEHE'EHE'E TRAIL

Keonehe'ehe'e Trail
HALEAKALĀ
Locator Map

Length 17.6 miles (28.3 km) **Stopping-off points** Kapalaoa Cabin, if you reserve ahead **Terrain** Rocky dirt trail makes this hike difficult

Marked by stunning mountain scenery, the Keonehe'ehe'e ("sliding sands" in Hawaiian) Trail traverses rugged backcountry through a volcanic crater. From the trailhead, the trail quickly descends into the crater before regaining some of that elevation near the end. The trail is best suited to experienced hikers.

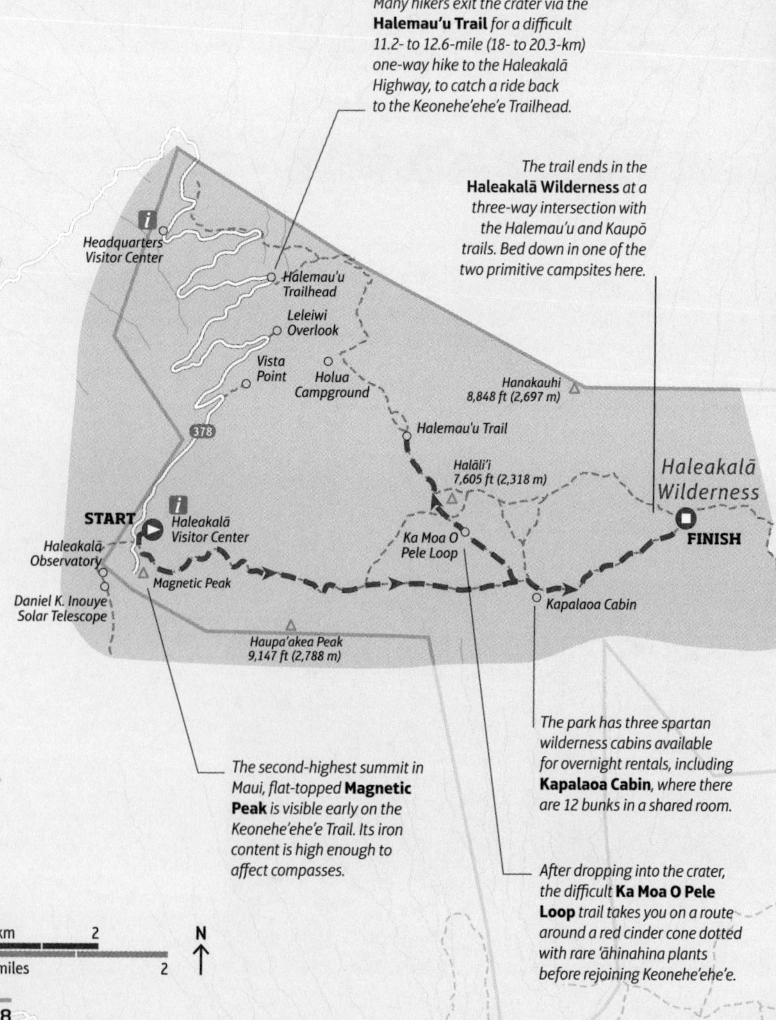

←

Silversword Plant in bloom at Haleakala National Park

EXPERIENCE MORE

Kā'anapali

Honoapi'ilani Hwy (Hwy 30) 29 kaana paliresort.com

Nestled between a 3-mile (5-km) beach and the West Maui Mountains, Kā'anapali is Maui's largest resort. It includes upscale beachfront hotels, sprawling condominiums, lush golf courses, and a large number of tennis courts. At the heart of Kā'anapali is **Whalers Village**, an upscale, oceanfront shopping center that has a large variety of stores and restaurants.

Despite all the hotels, the resort maintains a sense of community by staging events like Na Mele O Maui ("the songs of Maui"), a celebration of Hawaiian culture, and the Maui Onion Festival, which honors the local crop.

Through the ages, Kā'anapali was a special place, the site of a *heiau* (temple), a taro patch, and a royal fishpond. In the early 20th century, it developed as a playground for Hawaiian royalty, complete with a horse-racing track. Free tours of sites throughout the resort are conducted by employees of the hotel each week.

Pu'u Keka'a, which is better known as Black Rock, towers above long, white Kā'anapali Beach and overlooks one of the best snorkeling spots in Maui. Two centuries ago, when Maui chief Kahekili sought to encourage his troops, he would leap into the ocean from Black Rock. This involved spiritual, not physical, danger since it was believed that the dead jumped into the spirit world from here.

For morning jogs and evening sunset strolls, the Kā'anapali boardwalk is ideal. It extends over 3 miles (5 km) along the coast, weaving through resort grounds and beachfront restaurants.

Whalers Village

2435 Kā'anapali Pkwy 9am–9pm daily whalersvillage.com

LĀHAINĀ WILDFIRES

In 2023, the town of Lāhainā, 4 miles (6.5 km) south of Kā'anapali, was almost completely destroyed by wildfires during the summer. Nearly 100 people lost their lives and over 2,000 structures were heavily damaged. While the area remains closed and should not be disturbed or photographed, rebuilding efforts are underway and beloved Lāhainā attractions, like the Old Lāhainā Lū au, are operating again.

Kapalua

Honoapi'ilani Hwy (Hwy 30), 7 miles (11 km) N of Kā'anapali 29 kapalua.com

Pretty Kapalua is one of Maui's premier resort areas. Here, chic resorts and golf courses fronted by a series of

← Whalers Village, an outdoor shopping center on Kā'anapali's beachfront

exquisite crescent bays have taken the place of former pineapple plantations.

Two of the bays, Honolua and Mokulē'ia, have been designated marine life conservation districts, where divers and swimmers keep company with reef fish and green sea turtles. For spectacular views over these bays, the Mahana Ridge Trail, a lengthy day hike, takes trekkers from the coast to the verdant slopes of the West Maui Mountains. An easier hiking option is the network of Village Walking Trails that follow the old golf cart paths through a former golf course. From the top of the course there are some stunning panoramic views over Kapalua and there's a little duck-filled lake here, too.

PICTURE PERFECT
Dragon's Teeth

Centuries ago, a lava flow hardened as it reached the shores of Makaluapuna Point in Kapalua - the resulting jagged rocks resemble a dragon's teeth. Snap a shot at sunrise, when the "fangs" cast shadows over the ground.

↑ A jet of seawater erupting into the air from a blowhole set in the cliffs at Nākālele Point

4

Nākālele Point

Marker 38.5, Kahekili Hwy (Hwy 340), 13 miles (21 km) NE of Kā'anapali 427 Ala Makani St, Suite 101, Kahului; (808) 244-3530

This is the most northerly point on Maui. Vivid red-hued cliffs drop to the ocean and the trails along the bluffs offer terrific ocean views. There's an impressive blowhole here: when the surf is right, seawater is forced as high as 100 ft (30 m) into the air through a hole in this shoreline lava tube. It can be viewed from the road; avoid approaching it, as both the waves and the geysers are unpredictable.

EAT

Fish Market Maui

This popular spot serves up fresh seafood, including tasty fish tacos.

3600 Lower Honoapi'ilani Rd, Kā'anapali W fishmarketmaui.com

$$$

Monkeypod

Relaxed gastropub serving craft beers, pizzas, and burgers.

2435 Kā'anapali Pkwy, Kā'anapali W monkeypodkitchen.com

$$$

Sansei Seafood Restaurant & Sushi Bar

Open-concept Japanese hot spot serving award-winning sushi.

600 Office Rd, Kapalua W dkrestaurants.com

$$$

DRINK

Hali'imaile Distilling Company

Hali'imaile is known for smooth vodka made with pineapples. Tours and tastings are offered.

883 Hali'imaile Rd, Makawao haliimaile-distilling.com

Cafe O'Lei at the Plantation

Sip cocktails, made with local fruit and honey, on the patio of this lush farm.

1670 Honoapi'ilani Hwy, Wailuku cafe oleirestaurants.com

Paia Bay Coffee Bar

This café, filled with tropical plants, serves Maui-grown coffee.

120 Hāna Hwy, Pā'ia paiabaycoffee.com

STAY

Outrigger Kā'anapali Beach Hotel

Lovely beachfront spot, where all the modern rooms have balconies.

2525 Kā'anapali Pkwy, Kā'anapali outrigger.com

$$$

Montage Kapalua Bay

Gorgeous property with a great kids' club and spacious suites.

1 Bay Dr, Kapalua montage.com

$$$

5

Kahului

Honoapi'ilani Hwy (Hwy 30) 427 Ala Makani St, Suite 101, Kahului; (808) 244-3530

Kahului is the commercial and industrial center of Maui. The island's biggest airport and principal shipping harbor are located here. It also offers beaches, large parks, historic sites, and cultural attractions. The **Alexander and Baldwin Sugar Museum** is located 2 miles (5km) west of Kahului. Across from the Pu'unēnē Sugar Mill, built in 1902 by Alexander and Baldwin, the old supervisor's residence has been transformed into a museum that is about the industry that dominated Hawaii's economy for more than half a century. It features historical exhibits, narrated displays, and a model of a cane-crushing mill.

Once a royal fishpond, the **Kanahā Pond State Wildlife Sanctuary** is home to many migratory and native birds. These include two endangered species, the pink-legged Hawaiian stilt *(ae'o)* and the gray-black, duck-like Hawaiian coot *('alae keoke'o)*. There is an observation pavilion on the oceanside of Hāna Highway.

Alexander and Baldwin Sugar Museum

3957 Hansen Rd
10am–2pm Mon–Thu
Jan 1, Easter, Jul 4, Thanksgiving & Dec 25
sugarmuseum.com

Kanahā Pond State Wildlife Sanctuary

Off Hāna Hwy, between Kahului Airport and Kahului town Aug–Mar: dawn–dusk daily dlnr.hawaii.gov

Kahakuloa Village and Head

Kahekili Hwy (Hwy 340), 19 miles (31 km) NE of Kā'anapali 427 Ala Makani St, Suite 101, Kahului; (808) 244-3530

For nearly 1,500 years, families have inhabited Kahakuloa, growing taro on stone terraces and using aqueducts to irrigate crops from mountain streams.

Today, this isolated community is home to the direct descendants of the village's original inhabitants. In the village you'll find a pretty 19th-century church, local art galleries, and fruit stands where you can pick up freshly baked banana bread.

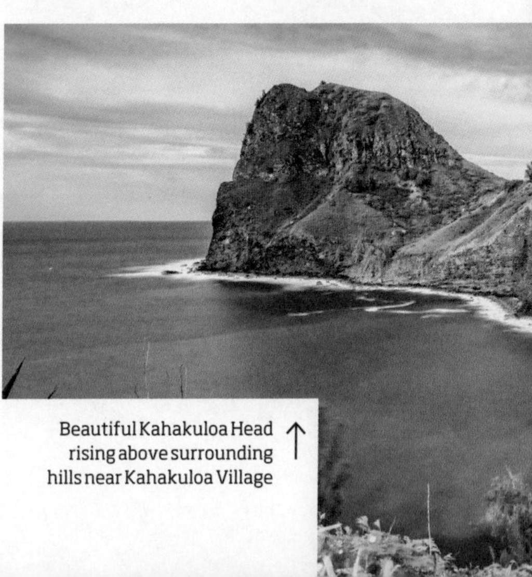

Beautiful Kahakuloa Head rising above surrounding hills near Kahakuloa Village ↑

GREAT VIEW
Waihe'e Ridge

Hike this moderate 5-mile (8-km) trail through a dense and bird-filled forest. At the end of the route you'll reach a picnic area with gorgeous views of the Waihe'e Valley and Wailuku below.

East of the village, the monolithic 636-ft (194-m) Kahakuloa Head rises majestically from the water's edge.

Wailuku

Honoapi'ilani Hwy (Hwy 30), 26 miles (42 km) SE of Kā'anapali 29 427 Ala Makani St, Suite 101, Kahului; (808) 244-3530

Located at the foothills of the West Maui Mountains, Wailuku was a royal center. Today, it is a county seat and a thriving community. It has a mix of architectural styles, with several notable buildings on High Street. The Market Street, has antique stores and the historic 'Iao Theater.

Headquarters of the Maui Historical Society, the **Bailey House Museum** is a time capsule of mission life in 19th-century Hawaii. The building housed the Wailuku Female Seminary, where missionary Edward Bailey taught. When the seminary closed, Bailey bought the house. The museum contains a collection of local artifacts, including *kapa* (tree bark) cloth, lei *(p53)*, and Bailey's own paintings of Maui.

Next door to the museum – and designed by Bailey – is the **Ka'ahumanu Church**, a Wailuku landmark that is listed on the National Register of Historic Places. The church, originally constructed in 1832, was rebuilt several times; the present New England-style structure and steeple were erected in the 1880s. Sunday services are conducted in Hawaiian.

Wailuku is also home to the **Maui Tropical Plantation and Country Store**. Some of the tropical plants displayed here, such as banana, taro, and breadfruit, were brought to the Hawaiian Islands by the ancient Polynesians. An open-air tram tour circles about half of the plantation. There's also a five-line zip-line, which soars over the lush groves and finishes with a zip over a lagoon.

The town is the site of the **Haleki'i-Pihana Heiau State Monument**, the most significant pre-contact *heiau* (temple) in the Central Valley. Important religious and civic affairs were conducted here. Haleki'i ("the House of Images") was probably a compound for chiefs. During religious ceremonies, *ali'i* (royalty) would reside in thatched houses whose walls are still visible on the temple's eastern face. A reconstructed section of wall is all that remains of Pihana ("Fullness"), a *luakini heiau* (temple that could be used for human sacrifices). Kamehameha I conducted a sacrifice here in order to give thanks for his victory in 'Iao Valley in 1790.

↑ The elegant exterior of the historic Ka'ahumanu Church

Bailey House Museum
2375A Main St
2pm Mon-Fri Jan 1, Thanksgiving & Dec 25
mauimuseum.org

Ka'ahumanu Church
103 S High St 9-10:30am Sun for services kaahumanchurch.org

Maui Tropical Plantation and Country Store
1670 Honoapi'ilani Hwy (Hwy 30), 2 miles (3 km) S of Wailuku
9am-4pm Tue-Sun mauitropicalplantation.com

Haleki'i-Pihana Heiau State Monument
Hea Place, off Kūhiō Pl, pedestrian access only from Waiehu Beach Rd
Dawn-dusk daily
dlnr.hawaii.gov

Lush valley with waterfall in the backdrop of mountains in ʻIao Needle Nation Park

8

Kīhei

Pi'ilani Hwy (Hwy 31) 10 427 Ala Makani St, Suite 101, Kahului; (808) 244-3530

One of the most populated areas on Maui, Kīhei lies on the island's sunny southwestern shore and has a vast stretch of white-sand beaches. Some of the island's best beaches for swimming, windsurfing, and snorkeling are found here, including Kalama Park and Kama'ole I, II, and III parks. Just south of Kama'ole III, there is a boat ramp from which many ocean activity charters depart.

The **Hawaiian Islands Humpback Whale National Marine Sanctuary** includes most of the ocean around Hawaii, but its administrative center is in Kīhei, at the edge of an ancient fishpond. Here there is an observation deck with a large viewing scope, allowing visitors to enjoy whale-watching at a distance.

Covering some of the last remaining natural wetland habitat in Hawaii, **Keālia Pond National Wildlife Refuge** is home to some 30 species of birds. Neighboring it is Keālia Beach, a nesting ground for the endangered hawksbill turtle.

Hawaiian Islands Humpback Whale National Marine Sanctuary

726 S Kīhei Rd 9:30am-2:30pm Mon-Fri hawaiihumpbackwhale.noaa.gov

Keālia Pond National Wildlife Refuge

Off Mokulele Hwy near Mile Marker 6  (808) 875-1582 Refuge: 6am-7pm daily; visitor center: 7:30am-4pm Mon-Fri During nesting season Mar-Aug

9

Mā'alaea

Honoapi'ilani Hwy (Hwy 30), 19 miles (31 km) SE of Kā'anapali 427 Ala Makani St, Suite 101, Kahului; (808) 244-3530

Nestled along the shoreline, Mā'alaea has oceanfront condominiums, many restaurants, a shopping plaza, and a small boat harbor, from which many snorkel and fishing boat charters depart, including the ferry to Lana'i *(p138)*. Mā'alaea Bay is popular with surfers and windsurfers. In winter, humpback whales frequent the bay and can be seen from the shore.

Maui Ocean Center, a huge aquarium and marine park, has

more than 60 indoor and outdoor displays. Exhibits include the Humpbacks of Hawai'i Exhibit & Sphere, Living Reef, Turtle Lagoon, and the Open Ocean. The thrilling Underwater Journey allows visitors to walk through a transparent tunnel set inside a huge tank full of colorful fish, sharks, rays, and other marine life.

Maui Ocean Center

 192 Mā'alaea Rd 9am-5pm daily mauioceancenter.com

WHALE-WATCHING

Although humpback whales can be spotted throughout the Hawaiian Islands, the shallow and protected 'Au'au Channel between Maui, Lāna'i, and Moloka'i is one of the best whale-watching destinations in the world. From about December through to May, the whales migrate here from Alaskan waters to breed, calve, and nurse their young. Visit *gohawaii.com* for more information on thrilling whale-watching tours.

10

Molokini

From Mā'alaea Harbor 427 Ala Makani St, Suite 101, Kahului; (808) 244-3530

Around 3 miles (5 km) off the coast of Maui, this crescent-shaped islet offers some of the best snorkeling and diving in Hawaii. The island (which is off-limits as a state seabird sanctuary) is all that's left of a large volcanic crater, its cove serving as a haven for marine life. The coral reef here attracts

↑ Scuba divers exploring the coral reef teeming with colorful fish, beneath Molokini

tropical fish, reef sharks, and humpback whales. Catamaran boat tours are run to Molokini's reef for snorkeling.

Around 6 miles (10 km) from Molokini is Kaho'olawe. This uninhabited island, once used by the US Navy for bomb testing, is home to several ancient sites. Access to the island is strictly limited.

ʻĪao Valley

'Īao Valley Rd, 28 miles (45 km) SE of Kā'anapali
427 Ala Makani St, Suite 101, Kahului; (808) 244-3530

The ʻĪao Valley Road leads into the West Maui Mountains. As the road begins to climb, the air becomes cooler, and traffic is replaced by the green of ʻĪao Valley – a sacred and historic site. In this valley in 1790, the forces of Kamehameha I trapped and annihilated those of Kahekili, the last independent chief of the island.

In a beautiful setting, about 2 miles (3 km) up the valley from Wailuku *(p163)*, is **Kepaniwai Heritage Gardens**. This county park is scattered with models showing architectural styles brought to the islands by various groups, such as a Japanese teahouse, a Portuguese villa, and a Hawaiian *hale*. Adjacent to the gardens, the **Hawai'i Nature Center** offers camps for kids.

The road ends at **ʻĪao Valley State Park**, at the foot of ʻĪao Needle, a pinnacle of volcanic rock towering 1,200 ft (365 m) above the valley floor. Trails continue into the valley, but this is one of the wettest places on earth, and hiking here can be dangerous.

Kepaniwai Heritage Gardens
870 ʻĪao Valley Rd
(808) 270-7980
7am–5:30pm daily

Hawai'i Nature Center
875 ʻĪao Valley Rd For events only, check website
hawaiinaturecenter.org

ʻĪao Valley State Park
ʻĪao Valley Rd, 3 miles (5 km) W of Wailuku
7am–6pm daily (reservations required)

SHOP

Tutu's Pantry
For Hawaii-made treats such as honey, jam, chocolate, and coffee, this shop is the ideal option.
2439 S Kīhei Rd, Kīhei
tutuspantry.com

Mahina
This local chain supplies beach-chic women's clothing in breezy fabrics and soft colors.
1913 S Kīhei Rd, Kīhei
shopmahina.com

808 Clothing Co.
A Maui-based company selling casual T-shirts for women and men, adorned with locally designed prints.
1941 S Kīhei Rd, Kīhei
808clothing.com

South Maui Gardens
An oasis with a Thursday artisan market, a plant nursery, and food truck. Hula shows are hosted on Wednesdays and Thursdays (advance booking required).
35 Auhana Rd, Kīhei
southmaui gardens.com

Farmer's Market Maui
This long-standing market is brimming with locally grown dragonfruit, lychee, passionfruit, soursop, and apple bananas. There is also a smoothie stand, and a souvenir booth.
61 S Kīhei Rd, Kīhei
Wed, Sat & Sun
farmersmarkets maui.com

Mākena State Park

Pi'ilani Hwy (Hwy 31), 11 miles (18 km) S of Kīhei Dawn-dusk hawaiistateparks.org

Still largely undeveloped, this state park contains three separate beaches backed by Pu'u Olai, a dormant volcanic cinder cone. When the weather is calm, all three are good for bodysurfing, boogie boarding, snorkeling, swimming, and sunbathing. On a clear day, they all have great views of the islands of Molokini *(p166)* and Kaho'olawe *(p167)*.

For more fine views, follow the 2-mile (3.2-km) trail that snakes up to the top of the Pu'u Olai cone. It's a hot and exposed trek so cover up and bring plenty of water.

'Āhihi-Kina'u Natural Area Reserve

At the end of Mākena Alanui, 5 miles (8 km) past Wailea 5:30am-7:30pm daily dlnr.hawaii.gov

This preserve is unique in Hawaii in that it protects both land and sea environments. To that end, it is illegal to damage or remove any of the natural habitat and some areas are closed to the public.

The section of the preserve on dry land is a dramatic lava landscape created by the last eruption of Haleakalā *(p154)* in 1790. Great snorkeling and diving is on offer.

La Pérouse Bay

Pi'ilani Hwy (Hwy 31), 14 miles (22 km) S of Kīhei 427 Ala Makani St, Suite 101, Kahului; (808) 244-3530

This bay, south of Mākena, was named for the first European to set foot on Maui, French explorer Jean-François de Galaup, comte de La Pérouse, who arrived here in 1786. There is a monument marking the spot on the *mauka* (mountain) side of the road. The dark and jagged lava flows here are from an eruption dating back to 1790 – the ruins of a Hawaiian village lie beneath it. Today the bay is known for its fantastic kayaking, snorkeling, and diving.

Makawao

Baldwin Av and Makawao Av, off Hwy 37, 20 miles (32 km) NE of Kīhei 427 Ala Makani St, Suite 101, Kahului; (808) 244-3530

Makawao has a distinctly Old West flavor, thanks to the wooden buildings that line its streets and the cattle ranches that surround it. It has been a cowboy town since the mid-19th century, but gradually the *paniolo* (Hawaiian cowboys) have made way for a growing artistic community. Today, art galleries showcasing local creations cluster around the crossroads at the town center. Glassblowing can be seen at Hot Island Glass on Baldwin Avenue throughout the day.

Wailea

Pi'ilani Hwy (Hwy 31), 7 miles (11 km) S of Kīhei gohawaii.com

Known for its five crescent-shaped golden beaches, the plush resort of Wailea is perfect for a day out on the leeward shores of south Maui. Opulent hotels, private homes, and

STAY

Hāna Kai Maui
Quiet and secluded oceanfront condo suites with full kitchens, laundry, and private balconies with stunning views.

4865 Uakea Rd, Hāna
hanakaimaui.com

$$$

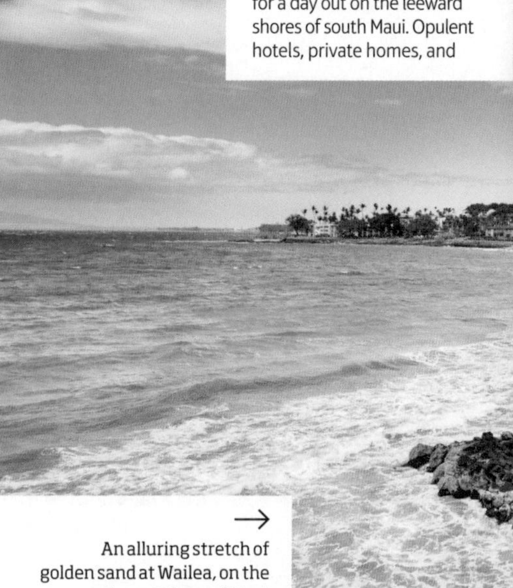

→ An alluring stretch of golden sand at Wailea, on the southwest shore of Maui

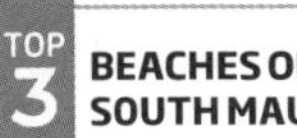

BEACHES OF SOUTH MAUI

Malu'aka
North of Mākena State Park, this sheltered beach is safe for families with small children.

Mai Poina
This long beach is a short drive from Wailea. Kids play on the north end, while the south is popular with windsurfers.

Keawakapu
Between Kīhei and Wailea, this beach offers good swimming, bodyboarding, and freshwater showers.

condominiums mingle with championship golf courses and high-end shopping.

Wailea Beach, a sheltered bay with calm waters, is ideal for swimming, snorkeling, and diving. A lovely paved path meanders parallel to the shore here. Kayak tours along Wailea's coast are popular, too.

17

Hāna

Hāna Hwy (Hwy 36, then Hwy 360), 51 miles (82 km) E of Kahului Hāna 427 Ala Makani St, Suite 101, Kahului; (808) 244-3530

The idyllic town of Hāna is known for its bucolic atmosphere. Its perfect round bay and dreamy climate have made it a prized settlement since ancient times and it is, perhaps unsurprisingly, known as Hawaii's "most Hawaiian town."

The **Hāna Cultural Center and Museum** presents a *kauhale* (residential compound) in the pre-contact style once unique to this area and exhibits artifacts that give a sense of local history. Built from blocks of coral in 1838, Wānanalua Church was erected by missionaries on top of an existing *heiau* (temple), thus symbolizing the triumph of Christianity over paganism.

Nearby Kaihalulu Bay is a hidden cove, owing its rust-colored sand to the Ka'uiki Head volcanic cinder cone behind it. The cliffs here are home to seabirds, including the *koa'e kea* whose feathers were prized by Hawaiian royals for making ceremonial objects. The trail down to the bay – which is unofficially clothing-optional – can be a challenge.

The scenic Hāna Belt Road *(p172)* twists along the coast to Pā'ia, with views of waterfalls, vegetation-clad gulches, taro fields, botanical gardens, rocky cliffs, and Honomanū Bay, with its black-sand beach.

Hāna Cultural Center and Museum
4974 Uakea Rd
10am-3pm Wed & Fri
Jan 1 & Dec 25 hanaculturalcenter.org

HIDDEN GEM
Take the Tube

About 4 miles (6 km) from Hāna, the Ka'eleku Cave, also known as the Hāna Lava Tube, is an easily accessible lava tube. The cave has handrails and informative signs, and the entry fee includes a flashlight.

Pā'ia

Hāna Hwy (Hwy 36), 8 miles (13 km) E of Kahului 427 Ala Makani St, Suite 101, Kahului; (808) 244-3530

Pā'ia is a bohemian beach town with offbeat stores, an international surfing reputation, and good, rustic restaurants. Back in the 1930s, though, this sugar town was the island's biggest population center. No longer in use, the sugar mill that once supported the town is on Highway 390, southeast of Pā'ia's only traffic light. The Mantokuji Buddhist Temple, east of town beside Hāna Highway *(p172)*, speaks eloquently of those who came to work the plantations.

To the west of town, H. A. Baldwin Beach County Park is good for bodysurfing and is popular with locals. Just east of Pā'ia on Hāna Highway is the world-famous windsurfing spot, Ho'okipa Beach County Park. Unique conditions allow windsurfers to perform aerial maneuvers over the breaking waves. With five surf breaks, it makes a great spectators' spot, especially in the afternoon when the wind is stronger.

Ke'anae Peninsula and Wailua Valley

Hāna Hwy (Hwy 36, then Hwy 360), 34 miles (55 km) E of Kahului 427 Ala Makani St, Suite 101, Kahului; (808) 244-3530

Between mile markers 16 and 20, drivers cross an area regarded by the state as a "cultural landscape." The star attraction, the ancient *lo'i* or taro ponds, can be seen from overlooks at mile markers 17 and 19.

Wailua's Coral Miracle Church, site of Our Lady of Fatima shrine, was built in 1860 with sea coral. A storm placed the coral on a nearby beach and locals gathered what they needed to build the church; later, another storm swept the unused coral away.

Kaupō

8 miles (13 km) past 'Ohe'o Gulch on Hwy 31 427 Ala Makani St, Suite 101, Kahului; (808) 244-3530

From 'Ohe'o Gulch, the Hāna Highway winds in and out of valleys with steep rock walls and via blind curves hugging the ocean cliffs to arrive at Kaupō.

Before the first Europeans arrived on Maui, thousands of people lived in the villages on this coast, sustaining themselves through farming and fishing. The missionary churches that still stand here, such as St. Joseph's Church (built in 1862), are evidence of the large Hawaiian population they once served. Built in 1859, Huialoha Church fell into disrepair during the last century. Volunteers repaired it and the church was reopened in 1978, adding extra meaning to its name Huialoha, "meeting of compassion."

From Kaupō, the landscape turns into dry desert as this area is in the lee of Haleakalā and gets little rain. The Kaupō Gap, visible from the road, was created when an erupting Haleakalā blew away a large section of the mountain's rim.

The 13-mile (21-km) Kaupō Gap Trail heads up the gap and is a challeng-ing hike up the steep and exposed side of the volcano. If you're not up for the task, even a quick jaunt on the rural trail affords beautiful views of the open ranchland. Be sure to carry water and other essentials when you visit this remote section of Maui.

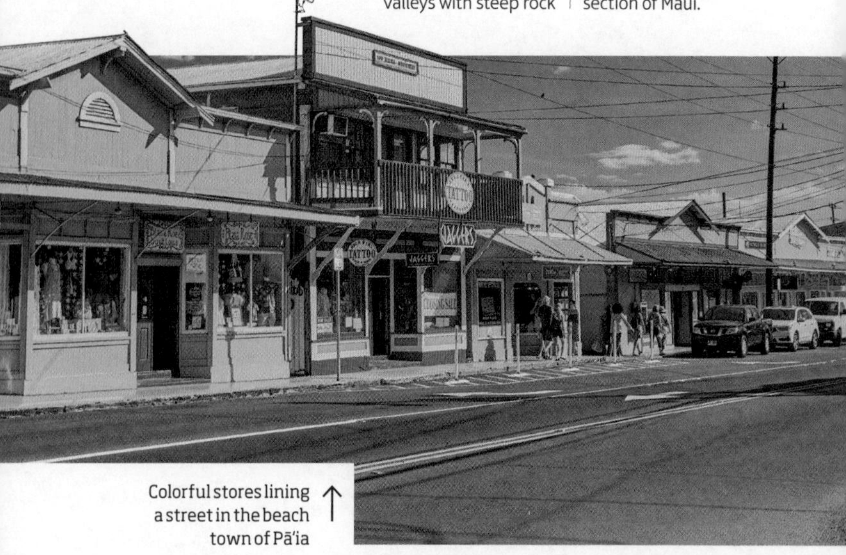

Colorful stores lining a street in the beach town of Pā'ia

St. Joseph's Church, one of Kaupō's several missionary churches

Kahanu Garden

650 Ulaino Rd 9am-4pm Mon-Fri, 9am-2pm Sat Thanksgiving & Dec 25 ntbg.org

This excellent garden is found within a native forest of *hala* (pandanus trees). It contains many species of flora representing the first plants brought over by Polynesian settlers, and explores the cultural relationships between people and these plants. Also found within the garden is Pi'ilanihale Heiau, Polynesia's largest ancient place of worship. The *heiau* was built in stages, beginning in the 13th century. Ceremonies and rituals dedicated to deities would have taken place here.

The *heiau* was all but forgotten until the 1970s, and was restored to its original state in the late 1990s. Follow the walking trail through the garden to the forest edge to admire the *heiau*, which is off-limits. Guided tours of the garden are also offered, providing an insight into both the plants and the *heiau*.

Upcountry Farms

Kula District 427 Ala Makani St, Suite 101, Kahului; (808) 244-3530

Upcountry is the term used to describe the fertile western slopes of Haleakalā. At these higher elevations you will find most of the island's farms and ranches, where an intriguing array of flowers, vegetables, fruits, and livestock flourish.

Run by two restaurant owners, **O'o Farm** features orchards where citrus fruits, tropical fruits, stone fruits, and apples are cultivated, as well as extensive herb and vegetable gardens. Visitors may tour the farm with a culinary specialist, hand-picking items for a one-of-a-kind lunch – you are welcome to bring your own wine.

Fragrant and pastoral, **Ali'i Kula Lavender** farm cultivates lavender (in full bloom during the summer months) and other tropical flowers. The little gift shop sells freshly baked lavender scones and lavender-infused drinks.

The **Surfing Goat Dairy** produces more than 20 different varieties of goat's cheese. Learn about the dairy's history and the cheese-making process on one of the daily tours. The **Thompson Ranch**, a working cattle ranch since 1902, takes various tours on horseback through fragrant eucalyptus forests and lush pastures along the upper slopes of Haleakalā.

O'o Farm
651 Waipoli Rd, Kula oofarm.com

Ali'i Kula Lavender
1100 Waipoli Rd, Kula 10am-4pm Fri-Mon aliikulalavender.com

Surfing Goat Dairy
3651 Omaopio Rd, Kula 9:30am-5pm Tue-Sat surfinggoatdairy.com

Thompson Ranch
1311 Waianu Rd, Kula 7am-7pm daily thompsonranchmaui.com

TARO IN HAWAII

Taro, the purplish-gray root (corm) of *Colocasia esculenta,* was the stuff of life in ancient Hawaii. It was believed that taro and humans had the same parents and that the gods had ordered the plant to care for humans, its siblings. This it did by providing nutrition, mostly in the form of *poi,* a pounded paste. It also acted as a symbol of the ideal *'ohana* (family): the plant grows in clumps of *'ohā* (stems), with the younger stems, like children, staying near the older core.

EAT

Ono Organic Farms Roadside Market

This stall sells organic, locally grown fruit, plus farm-made preserves.

Hāna Hwy, 10 miles (16 km) S of Hāna onofarms.com

Huli Huli Chicken

Enjoy chicken and ribs, with macaroni salad and rice, at this beachside tent. Cash only.

175 Haneoo Rd, Koki Beach (808) 639-2163

Coconut Glen's

Offers vegan ice cream, made with Maui coconuts. Cash only.

Mile marker 27.5 Hāna Hwy coconutglens.com

A DRIVING TOUR
ROAD TO HĀNA

Length 63 miles (101 km) **Stopping-off points** Hāmoa Beach, Pi'ilanihale Heiau, Maui Garden of Eden **Terrain** Mostly paved; unpaved sections between Hāna and Kaupō

Not until 1926 did the "Hāna Belt Road" connect the rest of Maui to its eastern shores. Running from beachy Pā'ia to remote Kaupō, this winding, wiggling route is widely regarded as one of the best drives in the world – and it's easy to see why. On the way you'll cruise past ancient sights and pretty beaches, and roll through swaths of lush rainforest cut through by cascading waterfalls and gulches brimming with tropical vegetation. The route can be tricky to drive: the road is notoriously twisting and narrow, with 620 curves and 59 narrow bridges to navigate; plus, it can get really busy. But you'll undoubtedly remember it as one of the most amazing drives of your life.

INSIDER TIP
Be Courteous

Alongside visitors, many locals use this road to go about their daily business. Check your mirrors regularly to see if someone wants to pass, only stop at designated viewpoints, and don't walk on the road.

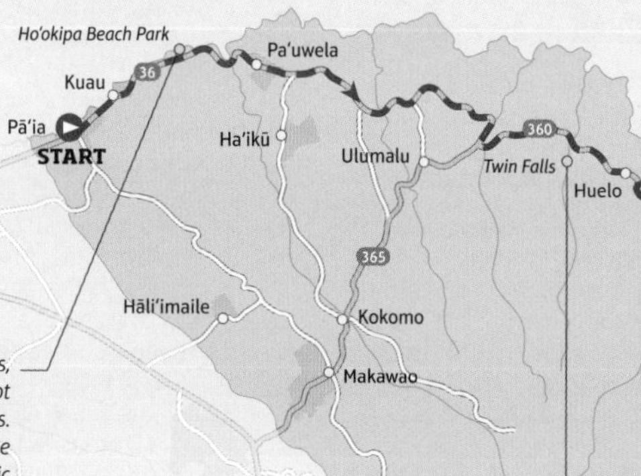

With its dramatic ocean waves, **Ho'okipa Beach Park** *is a hot spot for surfers and windsurfers. See the experts at work from the lookout area, which has picnic tables and public washrooms.*

An easily accessible but damp trail leads to **Twin Falls**, *two stunning waterfalls that plunge into a clear pool.*

← Surfers walking into the ocean at Ho'okipa Beach

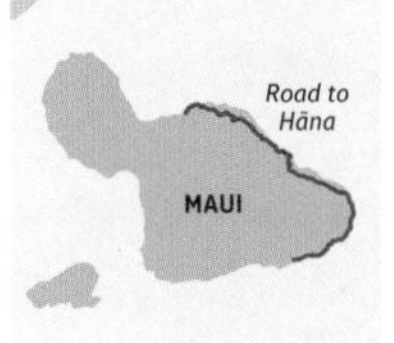

Locator Map
For more detail see p152

↑ Some of the tumbling waterfalls found at 'Ohe'o Gulch

An unmarked but obvious rest stop between mile markers 9 and 10 offers a picnic area. It's also the start for the **Waikamoi Ridge Trail***, an easy nature walk that passes through eucalyptus and bamboo groves.*

The family-friendly **Maui Garden of Eden** *features over 500 botanically labeled plants, a bamboo forest, views of waterfalls, and a café.*

Ke'anae Peninsula (p170) *has the remnants of an ancient taro-growing village.*

Dating from the 13th century, the beautifully preserved **Pi'ilanihale Heiau** (p171) *is Hawaii's largest ancient temple.*

Plan a stop at **Wai'ānapanapa State Park** *to explore sea caves, rocky cliffs, and a black-sand beach. Reservations for parking required.*

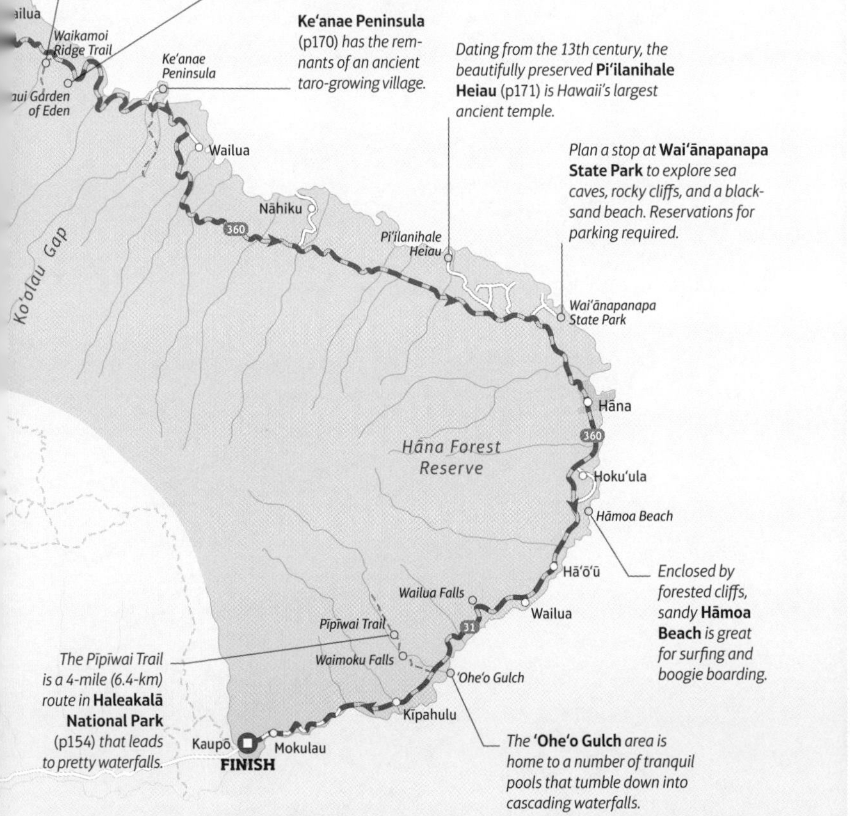

ailua
Waikamoi Ridge Trail
aui Garden of Eden
Ke'anae Peninsula
Wailua
Nāhiku
360
Ko'olau Gap
Pi'ilanihale Heiau
Wai'ānapanapa State Park
Hāna
360
Hāna Forest Reserve
Hoku'ula
Hāmoa Beach
Hā'ō'ū
Wailua Falls
Wailua
Pīpīwai Trail
31
Waimoku Falls
'Ohe'o Gulch
Kīpahulu
Kaupō
Mokulau
FINISH

Enclosed by forested cliffs, sandy **Hāmoa Beach** *is great for surfing and boogie boarding.*

The Pīpīwai Trail is a 4-mile (6.4-km) route in **Haleakalā National Park** (p154) *that leads to pretty waterfalls.*

The **'Ohe'o Gulch** *area is home to a number of tranquil pools that tumble down into cascading waterfalls.*

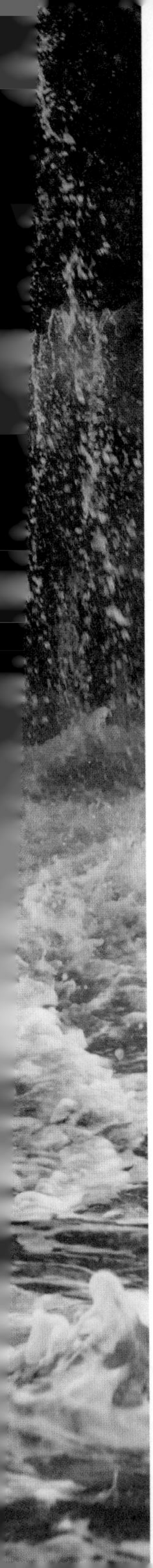

Molten lava flowing into the Pacific Ocean, Hawai'i Island

HAWAI'I ISLAND

Hawai'i Island – also known as the "Big Island" – is both the largest of the Hawaiian Islands and the youngest. It continues to be shaped by the turbulent activity of two of its five volcanoes; these overlapping fiery mountains have created a series of massive ridges down the center of Hawai'i, dividing the island into a dry and arid western side and a lush, rainforested eastern side.

Hawai'i saw some of the earliest Polynesian settlements, with migrants from the Marquesas Islands arriving as early as the 4th century. By the 13th century, a well-established class system existed on the island – as it did throughout the Hawaiian Islands – governed by royalty *(ali'i)* and high priests *(kahuna)*. During this time, strict laws, known as the *kapu* system, were put in place, land was divided according to hierarchy, and gods were revered. Around 1758, Kamehameha I was born here, spending most of his early life in the Waipi'o Valley. After defeating his cousin and rival, Kīwala'ō, in battle in 1782, he unified all the Hawaiian Islands under his rule by 1810. During this period, the British Captain James Cook visited the island twice; during his second visit, following a conflict with the local Hawaiians, he was killed.

Coffee plants from Brazil were planted in the island's Kailua-Kona area in 1828, and by the late 19th century hundreds of coffee plantations had appeared throughout the region. Coffee farming played an important role in the island's economy throughout the 20th century. During the latter half of the century, tourism boomed, with visitors drawn to the island's beachside towns and fiery volcanoes. Today, Hawai'i Island continues to grow in size thanks to regular volcanic activity, such as the eruption of Kīlauea, which adds land to the island.

HAWAI'I ISLAND

Must Sees

1. Hilo
2. Pu'uhonua O Hōnaunau National Historical Park
3. Hawai'i Volcanoes National Park
4. Waipi'o Valley
5. Mauna Kea

Experience More

6. Kailua-Kona
7. Kona Coffee Living History Farm
8. Hōlualoa
9. Kealakekua Bay State Historical Park
10. Ho'okena
11. Waikoloa Coast
12. Kekaha Kai State Park
13. Lapakahi State Historical Park
14. Kaloko Honokōhau National Historical Park
15. Pu'ukoholā Heiau National Historic Site
16. Kohala Mountain Road
17. Hāpuna Beach
18. Kohala Historical Sites State Monument
19. Waimea
20. Kapa'au
21. Honoka'a
22. Botanical World Adventures
23. Hawaii Tropical Botanical Garden
24. 'Akaka Falls State Park
25. Pāhoa
26. Kapoho
27. Puna Lava Flows
28. Ka'ū District
29. Ka Lae

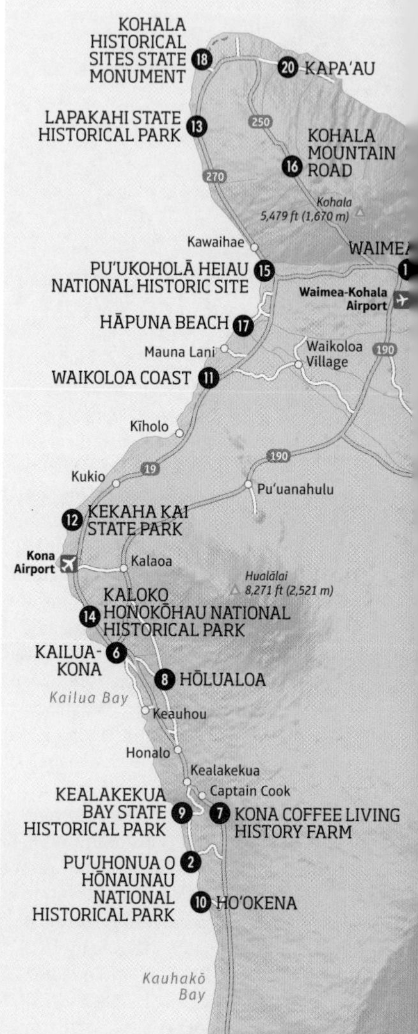

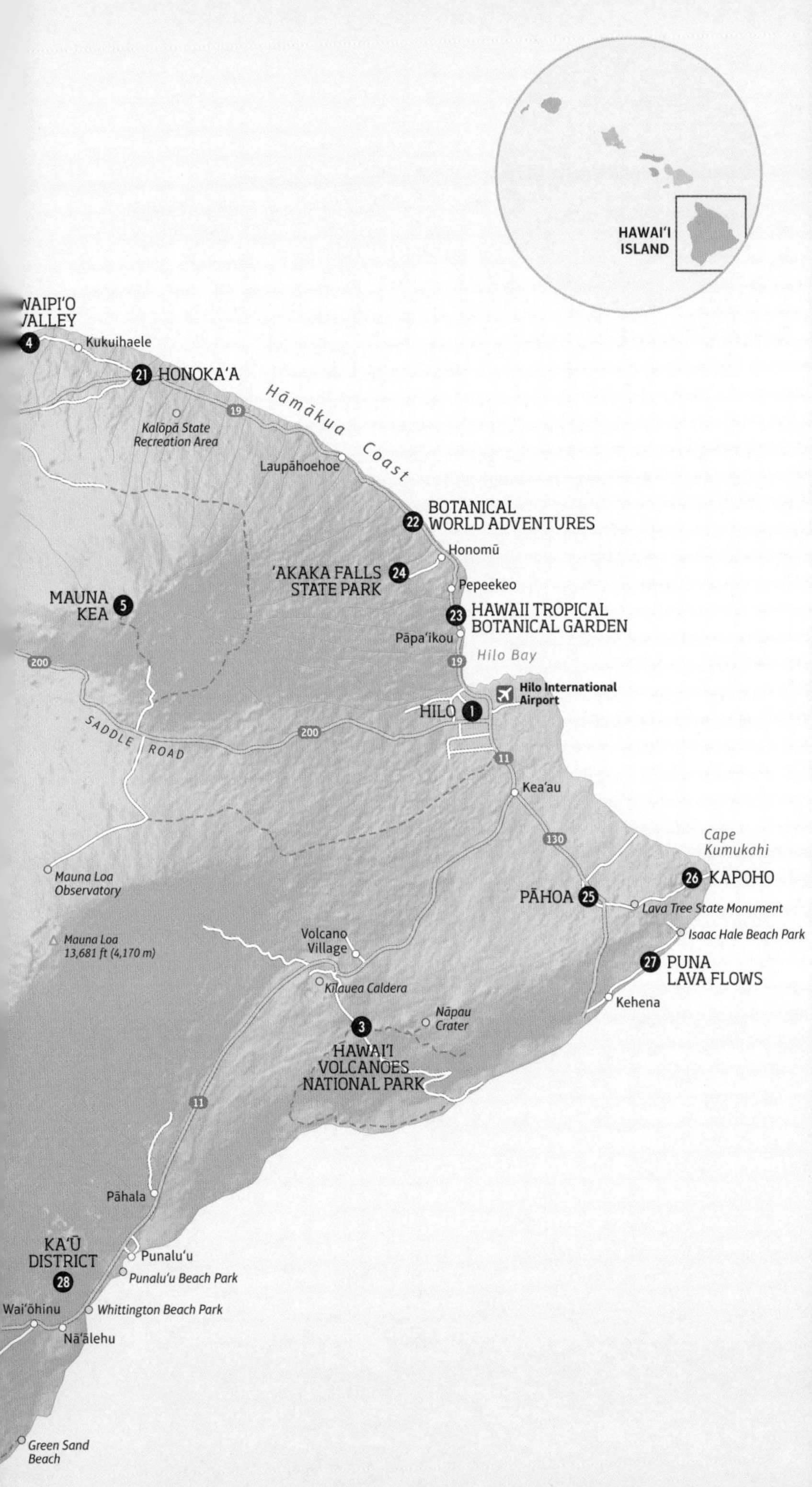

HAWAI'I ISLAND
WAIPI'O VALLEY
4
Kukuihaele
21 HONOKA'A
Hāmākua Coast
19
Kalōpā State Recreation Area
Laupāhoehoe
22 BOTANICAL WORLD ADVENTURES
Honomū
'AKAKA FALLS STATE PARK 24
Pepeekeo
MAUNA KEA 5
23 HAWAII TROPICAL BOTANICAL GARDEN
Pāpa'ikou
Hilo Bay
200
Hilo International Airport
HILO 1
SADDLE ROAD
11
Kea'au
130
Cape Kumukahi
26 KAPOHO
PĀHOA 25
Lava Tree State Monument
Isaac Hale Beach Park
Mauna Loa Observatory
Mauna Loa 13,681 ft (4,170 m)
Volcano Village
Kīlauea Caldera
27 PUNA LAVA FLOWS
Kehena
Nāpau Crater
3
HAWAI'I VOLCANOES NATIONAL PARK
Pāhala
KA'Ū DISTRICT
28
Punalu'u
Punalu'u Beach Park
Whittington Beach Park
Wai'ōhinu
Nā'ālehu
Green Sand Beach

HILO

Hawai'i Belt Rd (Hwy 19) 3 miles (5 km) E of Hilo Kamehameha Av, near Mamo St 62-3595 Āmaui Dr, Waimea; (808) 885-1655

With 47,000 residents, significant shipping and fishing industries out of its large bay, and a campus of the University of Hawai'i, Hilo rightfully deserves its designation as the state's second city. In spirit, though, "rainy old Hilo" couldn't be more different from sunny, urban Honolulu. The downtown buildings, many of them beautifully restored, were mostly constructed in the early 1900s; the streets are quiet, the pace is slow, and the atmosphere is low-key. Local attractions include gardens, waterfalls, beach parks, and fishponds.

Downtown

Many of the brightly colored, restored buildings of the old business district, clustered next to the Wailuku River, are listed with the National Register of Historic Places. Look out for the Hawaiian Telephone Company building, which combines aspects of the traditional Hawaiian house *(hale)* and Californian mission architecture; its designer, C. W. Dickey, is credited with developing Hawaiian Regional Architecture. Hilo Downtown Improvement Association offers visitor information.

One of the most notable historic buildings to be restored in Hilo is the Palace Theater (38 Haili St), which was built in 1925 in the Beaux Arts style. Today, this striking theater regularly hosts daily concerts, movies, and other special events, including musicals, theater performances, and comedy shows.

Mokupāpapa Discovery Center

76 Kamehameha Av 9am-4pm Tue-Sat Federal hols papahanaumokuakea.gov

The natural science, culture, and history of the remote northwest Hawaiian Islands, and that of the surrounding marine environment, is explained at this free exhibition center, which is housed in the century-old Koehnen Building. The center is a part of the Papahānaumokuākea Marine National Monument *(p47)*, a UNESCO World Heritage Site and one of the largest marine conservation areas in the world.

A 2,500-gallon (11,300-liter) saltwater aquarium at the Mokupāpapa Discovery Center provides a home for some of the fish that inhabit the region's coral reef, including the beautiful bandit angelfish and the orange anthias.

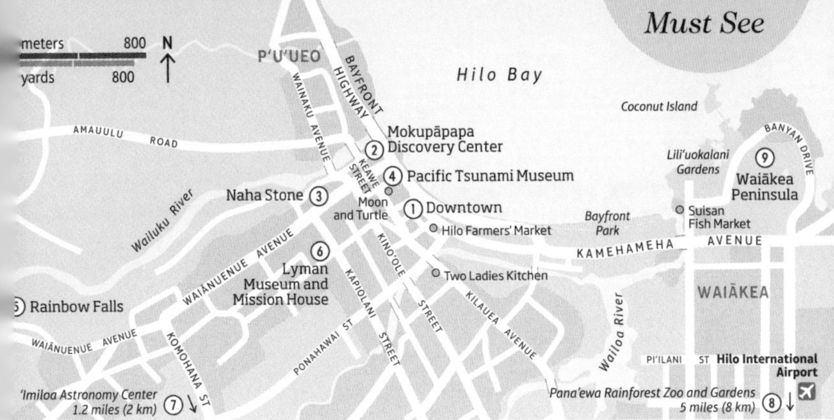

The center also features interactive educational exhibits, life-sized models of wildlife found in the northwestern Hawaiian Islands, artwork inspired by Hawaiian culture and the islands, and many interpretive panels in both Hawaiian and English.

③

Naha Stone

**300 Waiānuenue Av**

On the front lawn of the Hilo Public Library rests an estimated 7,000-lb (3,175-kg) rectangular volcanic rock known as the Naha Stone. Originating from Kaua'i, many legends surround the rock, including one that said that the person who could overturn the huge slab would be granted the power to be the first king of all the Hawaiian Islands. At the age of 14, it was King Kamehameha I who managed to overturn the stone. He subsequently did unify the Hawaiian Islands, fulfilling the legend.

④  

Pacific Tsunami Museum

130 Kamehameha Av 10am-4pm daily Federal hols tsunami.org

This museum is located in the historic First Hawaiian Bank Building, designed by C. W. Dickey. Built in 1930, the building survived both the 1946 and 1960 tsunamis and was donated to the museum in 1970.

Today, the museum is a memorial to the victims of past tsunamis that struck Hilo and promotes research and awareness programs that aim to reduce the devastation caused by future tsunamis. It features a range of multimedia and interactive displays, explaining how tsunamis (often called tidal waves) are formed and their effect on the Pacific Islands. The museum also teaches visitors about the Tsunami Warning System.

The oceanside city of Hilo, and *(inset)* restored buildings in Downtown

TSUNAMIS IN HILO

In 1946, an Alaskan earthquake triggered a tsunami that hit the unsuspecting Hawaiian Islands on the morning of April 1. Waves 56-ft (17-m) high tore Hilo's bayfront buildings off their foundations and swept them inland, killing 96 people. In 1960, another tsunami struck with a vengeance. Originating off the coast of Chile, it slammed Hilo on May 23 with three successive waves, causing damage worth $23 million. In spite of warnings, many locals refused to retreat, and 61 died.

↑ The tumbling cascade of pretty Rainbow Falls, and *(inset)* exploring the trails in the surrounding dense forest

⑤

Rainbow Falls

Waiānuenue Av, 2 miles (3 km) W of Downtown

Rainbow Falls ("Waiānuenue" in Hawaiian) earns its name when the morning sun filters through the mist generated by the 80-ft (24-m) waterfall, creating rainbows. A short climb via uneven stone steps is worth the effort as you will be treated to a bird's-eye view of the falls from above. The broad waterfall, nearly 100 ft (30.5 m) in diameter, plunges over a natural lava cave and into the river below.

The hollow at its base is the legendary home of Hina, the Hawaiian goddess of the moon and Maui's mother. The nearby trails provide many lookouts.

⑥

Lyman Museum and Mission House

276 Haili St 10am-4:30pm Mon-Fri Jan 1, Jul 4, Thanksgiving & Dec 25 lymanmuseum.org

Previously the home of the Reverend David and Sarah Lyman, missionaries who settled in Hilo in the early 1830s, the Lyman Mission House is the oldest standing wooden structure on the island of Hawai'i. It is well preserved with household items such as a cradle and quilts. The complex also includes a modern museum housing a varied collection, including a display of volcanic geology and artifacts from the years of immigration, such as a *braginha* – the Portuguese precursor to the ukulele.

The Lyman Museum also offers a wide range of educational programs, lectures, and workshops on Hawaiian arts and crafts throughout the year.

⑦ 

'Imiloa Astronomy Center

600 'Imiloa Pl 9am-4:30pm Tue-Sun imiloahawaii.org

The 'Imiloa Astronomy Center, which is part of the University of Hawai'i at Hilo, was built to showcase the connection between Hawaiian traditions and scientific ideas about the universe. The center, a great family attraction, offers kid-friendly interactive exhibits on the cultural and natural history of Mauna Kea *(p194)*, a full-dome planetarium with daily shows on space and volcanoes, and a Hawaiian outdoor garden where informative tours take place. Visitors can walk along the "Canoe Plants" pathway and see the plants that were brought to the islands by early Polynesians.

Did You Know?

It rains 272 days of the year on average in Hilo, due to the city's location on Hawai'i's windward side.

The gift shop stocks locally made crafts, books on local flora, and educational games for children. The restaurant is open for lunch and dinner and features traditional Hawaiian fare and American classics.

Pana'ewa Rainforest Zoo and Gardens

800 Stainback Hwy 10am–4pm daily Jan 1 & Dec 25 hilozoo.org

Nestled within the Pana'ewa Forest Reserve, this is the only naturally occurring tropical rainforest zoo in the US. The zoo has housed a unique flora and fauna collection since the 1970s. Over 60 species of animals can be found here, including giant anteaters, the Hawaiian *nēnē*, and two Bengal tigers, among other creatures.

Children will adore the playground and the butterfly house. Another highlight is the botanical gardens, filled with palm trees, bamboo groves, many varieties of *vireya* (tropical rhododendron), orchids, and serene water features. The zoo is free to visit but donations are warmly accepted.

Waiākea Peninsula

Banyan Dr

Jutting into Hilo Bay, Waiākea Peninsula supports a nine-hole golf course, a row of high-rise hotels, and the sprawling Lili'uokalani Gardens. The latter is a Japanese park that blends fishponds with small pagodas and arched bridges. A footbridge crosses to tiny Coconut Island, now a park and popular fishing spot but once a place of healing; the Hawaiians called it Moku Ola ("Island of Life"). Banyan Drive loops the peninsula under the dense shade of huge banyans planted by celebrities such as aviator Amelia Earhart and baseball player Babe Ruth.

Nearby Kalaniana'ole Avenue, which follows the east side of Hilo Bay, passes a number of beach parks interlaced with large fishponds. Carlsmith Beach Park offers excellent snorkeling and swimming on its sheltered eastern side. Another good swimming spot is Richardson Ocean Park, which nature has sculpted into protected, lagoon-like pools.

EAT

Hilo Farmers' Market

Find locally grown Kona coffee, fresh fruit, and macadamia nuts, as well as baked goods, at this large open-air market.

Corner of Mamo and Kamehameha Av 7am–3pm daily hilofarmersmarket.com

Two Ladies Kitchen

Grab a treat to-go at this confectionery shop, which sells pretty pastel-colored *mochi* - Japanese sweet, sticky rice cakes made with red bean paste.

274 Kilauea Av (808) 961-4766 Sun & Mon

Moon and Turtle

A relaxed restaurant serving outstanding and creative tapas, such as seared local tuna and local wild boar sausage.

51 Kalākaua St (808) 961-0599 5:30–9pm Tue-Sat

Suisan Fish Market

Pick up fresh poke bowls from Suisan, and then head next door to the Lili'uokalani Gardens to enjoy your meal.

93 Lihiwai St Sun & Wed suisan.com

The beautifully landscaped Lili'uokalani Gardens, with greenery and arched bridges

2

PU'UHONUA O HŌNAUNAU NATIONAL HISTORICAL PARK

Highway 160, off Hawai'i Belt Rd (Hwy 11) 8:15am-dusk daily nps.gov/puho

Pu'uhonua O Hōnaunau is one of Hawaii's most outstanding examples of a sacred sanctuary compound. Surrounded by high walls and a rough coast, this 16th-century sanctuary offered absolution to all those who managed to run or swim past the chief's warriors that stood guard.

From the 11th century onward, social interactions throughout the islands were regulated by the *kapu* (taboo) system. Infractions, ranging from stepping on a chief's shadow to women eating bananas, led to a violent death. Lawbreakers could escape punishment by reaching a *pu'uhonua* (sanctuary) such as Hōnaunau. However, reaching it was not easy; from the sea, you would have to swim through powerful waves that crashed onto the jagged lava rock, while from land, high walls needed to be climbed over.

Pu'uhonua O Hōnaunau was stripped of power in 1819 after the fall of the *kapu* system. Partially restored, this site now provides a glimpse into early Hawaiian culture. Visitors can wander the grounds and see a reconstructed *hālau*, a thatched A-frame structure, and wooden *Ki'i*, large, fierce-looking carvings of Hawaiian deities. Park-ranger-led walks are held daily, and the site has picnic facilities. The grounds are especially atmospheric just before sunset, so try to time your visit toward the end of the day.

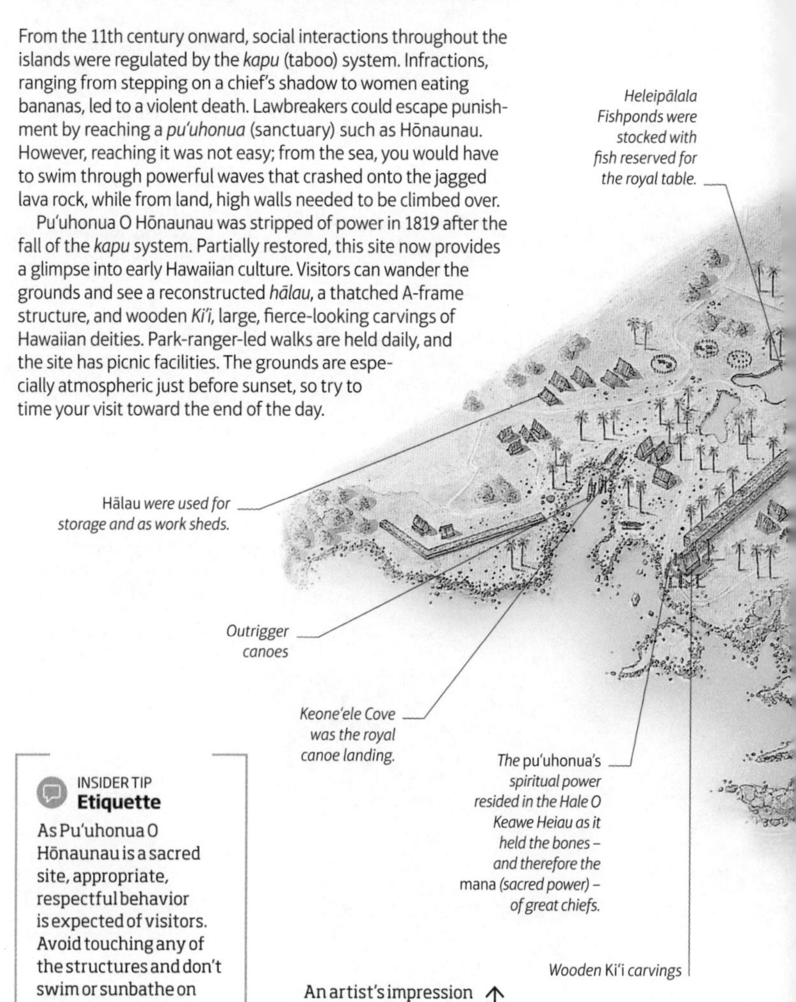

An artist's impression of Pu'uhonua O Hōnaunau National Historical Park ↑

INSIDER TIP
Etiquette

As Pu'uhonua O Hōnaunau is a sacred site, appropriate, respectful behavior is expected of visitors. Avoid touching any of the structures and don't swim or sunbathe on the park grounds.

↑ A Hawaiian sailing canoe on the shores of Pu'uhonua O Hōnaunau

23

The number of chiefs whose bones were once housed in Hale O Keawe Heiau.

The blazing Halema'uma'u Crater in Hawai'i Volcanoes National Park

HAWAI'I VOLCANOES NATIONAL PARK

Hawai'i Belt Rd (Hwy 11), 30 miles (48 km) SW of Hilo, 96 miles (155 km) SE of Kailua-Kona Route 11 from Hilo 24 hours daily nps.gov/havo

This national park is home to two majestic volcanoes: Mauna Loa, a huge shield volcano, and Kīlauea, one of the world's most active volcanoes. Two roads – Crater Rim Drive and Chain of Craters Road – wind through the park, offering visitors the chance to explore this fiery landscape up close. The park also has 150 miles (240 km) of hiking trails, and vast tracts of wilderness that preserve some of the world's rarest flora and fauna.

Kīlauea Caldera

This enormous caldera dominates the summit area of the highly active Kīlauea volcano, which last erupted in 2024. Many of the park's main sights, including Crater Rim Drive and Ha'akulamanu *(p187)*, are dotted around its rim. Sitting within the caldera, meanwhile, is the Halema'uma'u Crater, which measures more than 6,000 ft (1,828 m) across and around 1,600 ft (488 m) deep, and is home to a lava lake. The many fumaroles found both in the crater and along the rim continue to spew a large quantity of sulfur dioxide daily; those with respiratory problems should beware.

Kīlauea Visitor Center

1 Crater Rim Dr (808) 985-6011 9am-5pm daily

The Kīlauea Visitor Center offers fascinating information on the historical, cultural, and environmental features of the Hawai'i Volcanoes National Park. Exhibits give information about island formation, ecosystems, invasive species, and resource protection. A 25-minute film about volcanism and geology, "Born of Fire, Born of the Sea," is shown throughout the day.

Trail and lava viewing conditions can change rapidly – lava flow, sulfur dioxide gas, and other hazards may restrict access – so check with the park rangers at the center for the latest information. Overnight visitors must register here and

permits are issued on a first-come first-served basis.

The nearby village of Volcano has several accommodations and food options. However, due to mercurial weather and limited services elsewhere, visitors should pack their own food and water, have plenty of fuel, and dress in layers.

Volcano Art Center

Crater Rim Dr 9am-5pm daily volcanoartcenter.org

This center promotes Hawaii's rich culture through hula performances, exhibitions, and concerts. The center's Volcano Art Center Gallery is housed in the nearby 1877 Volcano House Hotel *(p186)*, listed as Hawaii's oldest visitor accommodations in the National Register of Historic Places. The gallery features works by more than 300 local artists inspired by Hawaii's environmental and cultural heritage. The center also offers classes on Hawaiian music, dance, crafts, writing, and language.

On Mondays, the center has free guided rainforest tours where visitors can learn about Kīlauea's last old-growth koa and *'ōhi'a lehua* rainforests.

Crater Rim Drive

This paved road was once a full loop encircling the Kīlauea Caldera but the western section has been closed indefinitely due to recent eruptions. Some of the park's main attractions are along the remaining parts of this scenic route, including the Thurston Lava Tube *(p186)* and the Kīlauea Overlook, which has views of the Kīlauea Caldera and Halema'uma'u Crater.

THE LEGEND OF PELE

In Hawaiian mythology, Pele is known as the goddess of lava and volcanoes. It is believed that she resides at the summit of Kīlauea Caldera, in the Halema'uma'u Crater, and that Kīlauea's eruptions are fueled by her mercurial nature. This respected deity is said to have occasionally appeared to people as a woman dressed in white, who wanders the roads and is sometimes accom-panied by a white dog.

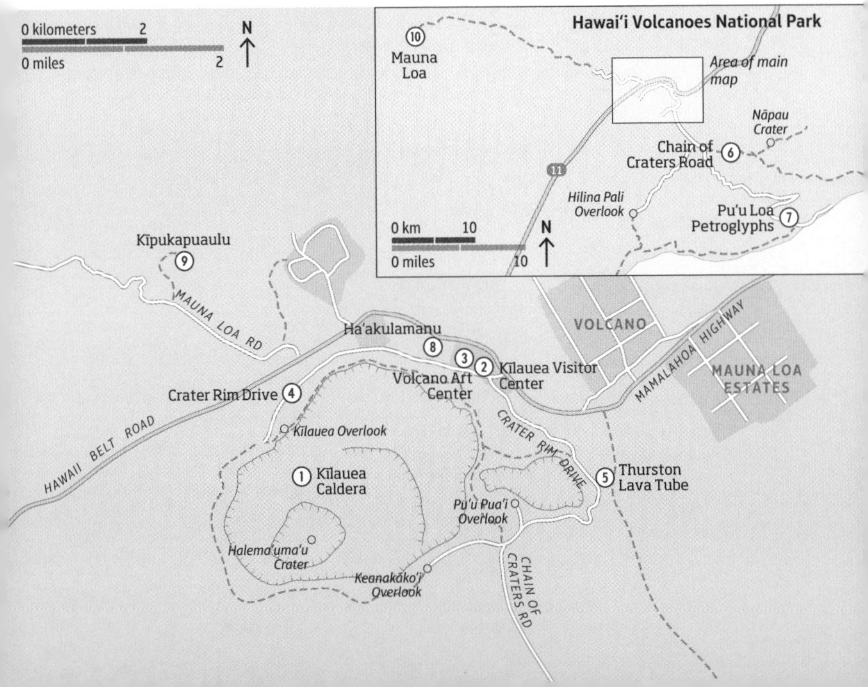

0 kilometers 2
0 miles 2
N

Hawai'i Volcanoes National Park
10 Mauna Loa
Area of main map
Nāpau Crater
Chain of Craters Road 6
11
Hilina Pali Overlook
Pu'u Loa Petroglyphs 7
0 km 10
0 miles 10
N

Kīpukapuaulu 9
MAUNA LOA RD
Ha'akulamanu 8
3 2 Kīlauea Visitor Center
Volcano Art Center
VOLCANO
MAMALAHOA HIGHWAY
MAUNA LOA ESTATES
Crater Rim Drive 4
Kīlauea Overlook
HAWAII BELT ROAD
CRATER RIM DRIVE
1 Kīlauea Caldera
5 Thurston Lava Tube
Pu'u Pua'i Overlook
Halema'uma'u Crater
Keanakāko'i Overlook
CHAIN OF CRATERS RD

Walking inside the giant tunnel of the Thurston Lava Tube

Thurston Lava Tube

8am-8pm daily

A popular stop along the Crater Rim Drive *(p185)*, the Thurston Lava Tube can be accessed via an easy 15-minute trail that begins with a steep descent into the rainforest. The trail is dense with towering green ferns and will lead you into a pit crater that is the entrance to the lava tube. Formed when the exterior of a lava flow cooled to a crust while the still-molten interior magma flowed out, the tube resembles a giant tunnel. The interiors are electrically lit, revealing glittering, multicolored, mineral-rich walls and the thin roots of *'ōhi'a* trees which dangle through the ceiling. Tours of the tube are self-guided; make sure to bring your own flashlight as a small section of about 150 ft (46 m) beyond the initial path is not lit.

Chain of Craters Road

To the south of Crater Rim Drive *(p185)*, the Chain of Craters Road veers off and heads toward the coast for 19 miles (30 km). As the road descends rapidly, you will experience a distinct change in landscape from rainforest to barren lava fields. The scenic view is studded with pit craters and recent lava flows. Stop at the Kealakomo Overlook along this route to admire the amazing panoramic view of lava fields extending out to the Pacific Ocean. Several hiking trails are found along the road too, including the trail to the Pu'u Loa Petroglyphs.

Pu'u Loa Petroglyphs

This coastal trail to these petroglyphs crosses old lava flows to reach an extensive petroglyph field located on the southern flank of Kīlauea. It is an easy to moderate 1.4-mile (2.25-km) round-trip hike, beginning at mile marker 16 on Chain of Craters Road, which takes about one and a half hours to complete. Hikers walk across rough basaltic lava to reach a wooden boardwalk that surrounds in excess of 23,000 petroglyph images etched on to the abundant lava surface. The majority of the images in this extensive field depict stylized human forms, but there are also representations of the moon, canoes, ships, insects, fish, and spears. Circles, spirals, dots, and other geometric designs are also common features.

Volcano House Hotel

This historic hotel offers cozy rooms, rustic cabins, and a campsite. Some rooms overlook the Halema'uma'u Crater.

1 Crater Rim Dr
hawaiivolcanohouse.com

8

Ha'akulamanu

A relatively easy 1.2-mile (2-km) round-trip path starting from the Kīlauea Visitor Center leads to Ha'akulamanu, also known as the Sulfur Banks. There is a boardwalk where you can view and smell the volcanic gases seeping from the vibrant mineral deposits. This area is particularly known for attracting birds, probably because of the warmth emitting from the volcanic ground. Visitors with respiratory problems, pregnant women, and young children should avoid this walk due to the gases.

Kīpukapuaulu

A *kīpuka* is a forested island untouched by surrounding lava flow. Vegetation has been spared by the lava flows and is therefore older and denser here. The lush green woodlands of Kīpukapuaulu bird park are home to one of the richest concentrations of rare native plants and bird life in Hawaii. The 1.2-mile (1.9-km) loop trail takes around one hour to complete. It begins with a gentle hike on an unpaved forest path, surrounded by recent lava flows from Mauna Loa. Native koa and *'ōhi'a lehua* trees grow at Kīpukapuaulu. It is also possible to spot endemic birds such as the *'elepaio* or *'apapane*, along with other species that include finches and Japanese white eyes. A bulletin board at the start of the trail provides descriptions of the diverse bird and plant species that are found here.

Mauna Loa

Mauna Loa, or "Long Mountain," is the world's largest active volcano. It is also one of five volcanoes that form Hawai'i Island. Covering the entire southern half of the island, Mauna Loa is 60 miles (95 km) long and 30 miles (50 km) wide, and rises to 13,681 ft (4,170 m) above sea level. It is a shield volcano, with gently sloping inclines that have been created from successive lava flows. Its summit is protected as part of Hawai'i Volcanoes National Park. The highly active Kīlauea volcano, with its impressive and vast caldera *(p184)*, lies on Mauna Loa's southeast flank.

Since its first documented eruption in 1843, Mauna Loa has erupted more than 33 times, with the last eruption occurring in 1984. The caldera at the summit, Moku'aweoweo (Hawaiian for "island of lurid burning"), is more than 3 miles (5 km) long and 1.5 miles (2.5 km) wide, with 600-ft (180-m) walls. Two trails within the park lead up to the summit area. Beginning at the Mauna Loa Observatory, the 6.4-mile (10.3-km) out-and-back Observatory Trail is a tough day hike across a rugged, lunar-like landscape. The 19.1-mile (30.8-km) Mauna Loa Trail begins amid rainforest at the end of the unpaved Mauna Loa Road. There is a lookout here that offers excellent views of the volcano; it can be visited even if you're not planning to tackle the hike. The Mauna Loa Trail takes several days to complete – accommodations on the route consist of the Pu'u'ula'ula Cabin and Summit Cabin (permits required). Both trails eventually intersect with the Summit Trail for the final approach to the peak. These trails are best left to experienced hikers, thanks to the high altitude and uneven terrain of rough lava rocks.

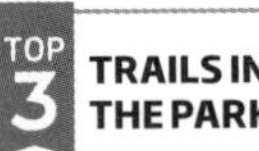

TRAILS IN THE PARK

Kūpina'i Pali Trail (Waldron Ledge)
An easy, 1-mile (1.5-km) round-trip along a paved path leads to a wide view of the Kīlauea Caldera.

Devastation Trail
This accessible paved path features remnants of the rainforest destroyed by the Kīlauea Ike eruption in 1959.

Halema'uma'u Trail
This moderate 1.8-mile (2.9-km) round-trip trail leads to the Kīlauea Caldera floor, first passing through a rainforest.

↑ Admiring the vast Mauna Loa volcano that stretches for miles

A stream of lava gushing into the sea, the heat and pressure causing a giant explosion ↑

A LONG WALK
CRATER RIM TRAIL

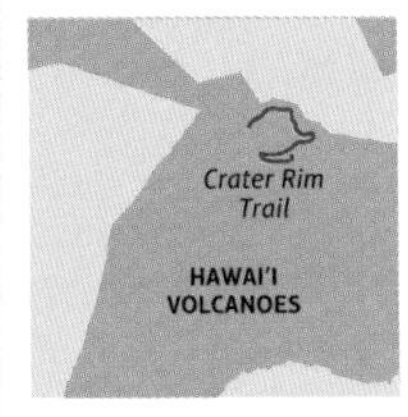

Locator Map

Length 8.3 miles (13.4 km) one-way **Stopping-off points** Volcano House **Terrain** Rocky dirt trail

Following the edge of the Kīlauea summit caldera, this hike is the best way to get a look at one of the most active volcanoes in the world. There are several trailheads along Crater Rim Dr., which roughly parallels the trail around the caldera, for hikers of all abilities to explore shorter sections of the trail. Stay on the marked trail at all times; the volcano is active and many areas can be dangerous.

Key

-- Walk route

Steam billows from ***Steaming Bluff*** *(Wahinepaku), a result of groundwater seeping into magma-heated formations deep underground.*

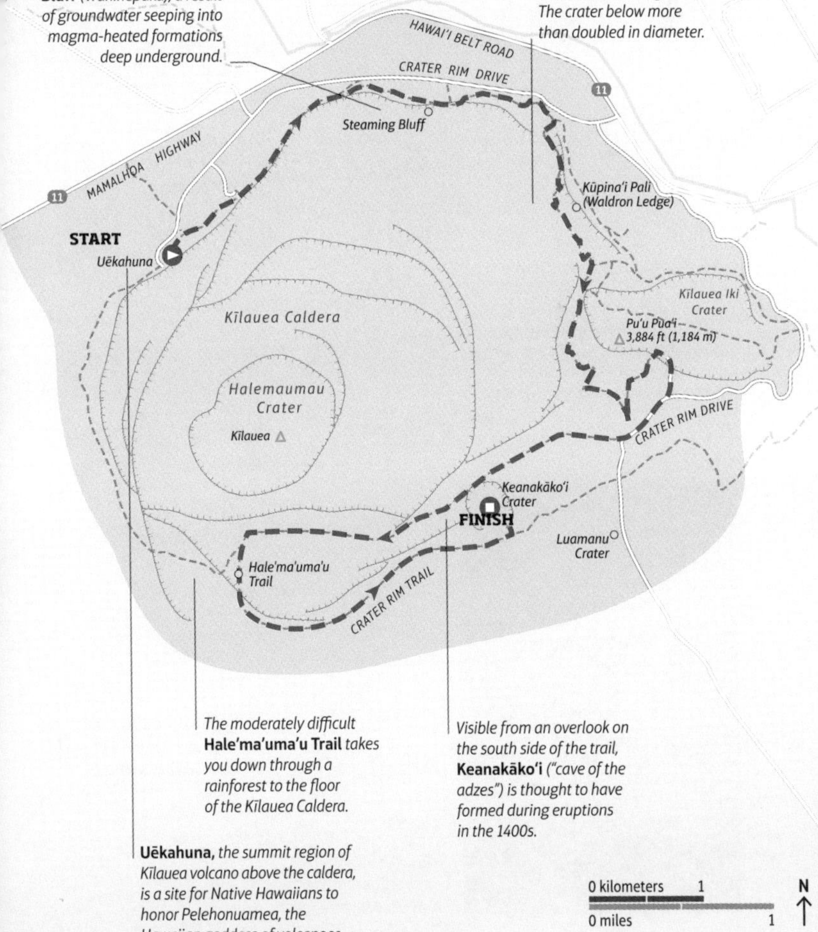

Observe the devastation wrought by the 2018 eruptions from ***Kūpina'i Pali*** *(Waldron Ledge). The crater below more than doubled in diameter.*

HAWAI'I BELT ROAD
CRATER RIM DRIVE
11
Steaming Bluff
MAMALHOA HIGHWAY
11
Kūpina'i Pali (Waldron Ledge)
START
Uēkahuna
Kīlauea Caldera
Kīlauea Iki Crater
Pu'u Pua'i 3,884 ft (1,184 m)
Halemaumau Crater
Kīlauea
CRATER RIM DRIVE
Keanakākoʻi Crater
FINISH
Luamanu Crater
Hale'ma'uma'u Trail
CRATER RIM TRAIL

The moderately difficult ***Hale'ma'uma'u Trail*** *takes you down through a rainforest to the floor of the Kīlauea Caldera.*

Visible from an overlook on the south side of the trail, ***Keanakāko'i*** *("cave of the adzes") is thought to have formed during eruptions in the 1400s.*

Uēkahuna, *the summit region of Kīlauea volcano above the caldera, is a site for Native Hawaiians to honor Pelehonuamea, the Hawaiian goddess of volcanoes.*

0 kilometers 1
0 miles 1
N

FORMATION OF THE HAWAIIAN ISLANDS

The Hawaiian Islands are the tips of a large chain of volcanoes stretching almost 3,100 miles (5,000 km) from Hawai'i Island to the Aleutian Trench in the north Pacific. Most are now underwater stumps, fringed by coral reefs, but many were once great shield (dome-shaped) volcanoes. Hawaii's oldest volcano is slowly disappearing into the Aleutian Trench, while its youngest volcano, Kīlauea, still spews out basaltic lava today, creating new land on Hawai'i Island. This cycle of destruction and creation, driven by the conveyor-belt movement of the Pacific plate over a stationary hot spot of magma, has been occurring for millions of years and will continue to happen for many more.

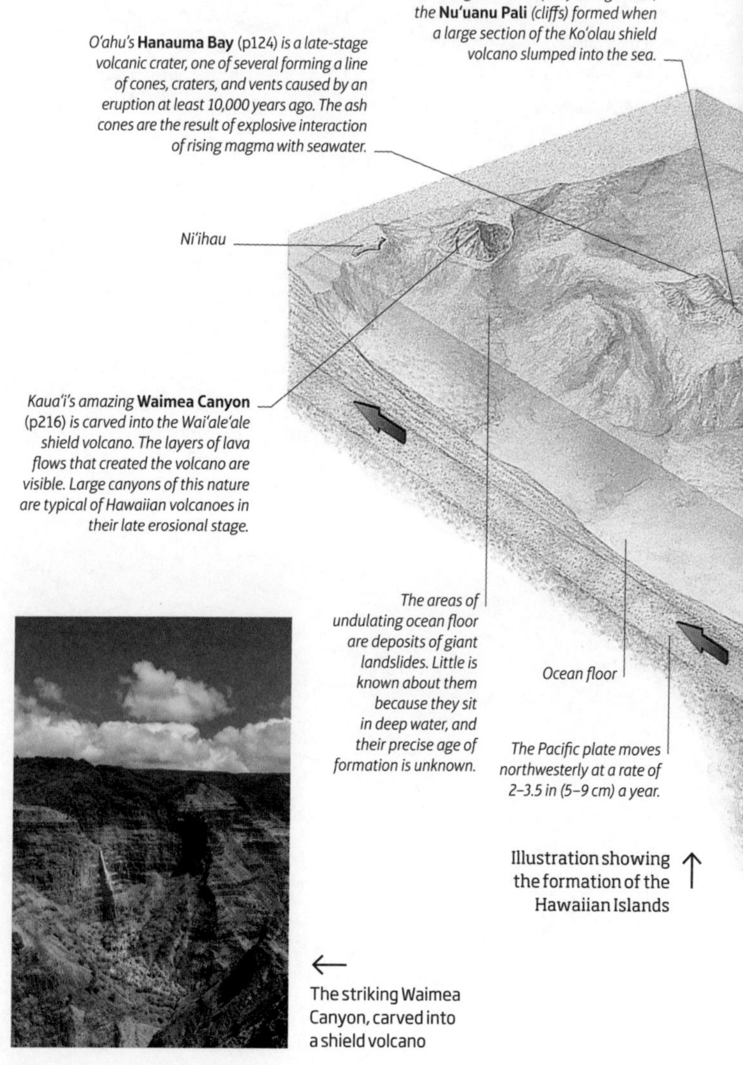

Illustration showing the formation of the Hawaiian Islands ↑

← The striking Waimea Canyon, carved into a shield volcano

CONVEYOR BELT

As it moves, the Pacific plate – the huge slab of earth's crust beneath the Pacific Ocean – rides over a stationary hot spot (mantle plume) that feeds heat and basaltic magma toward the surface. Mauna Loa, Kīlauea, and the "new" underwater volcano Lō'ihi are presently over the hot spot. As the plate moves to the northwest, volcanoes are gradually pulled off the hot spot while new volcanoes grow in their place.

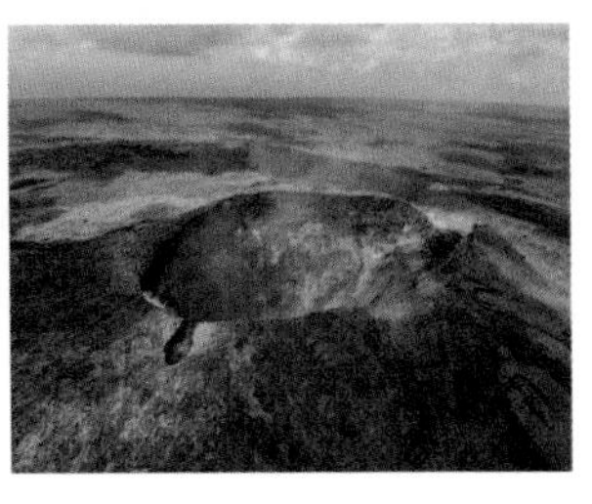

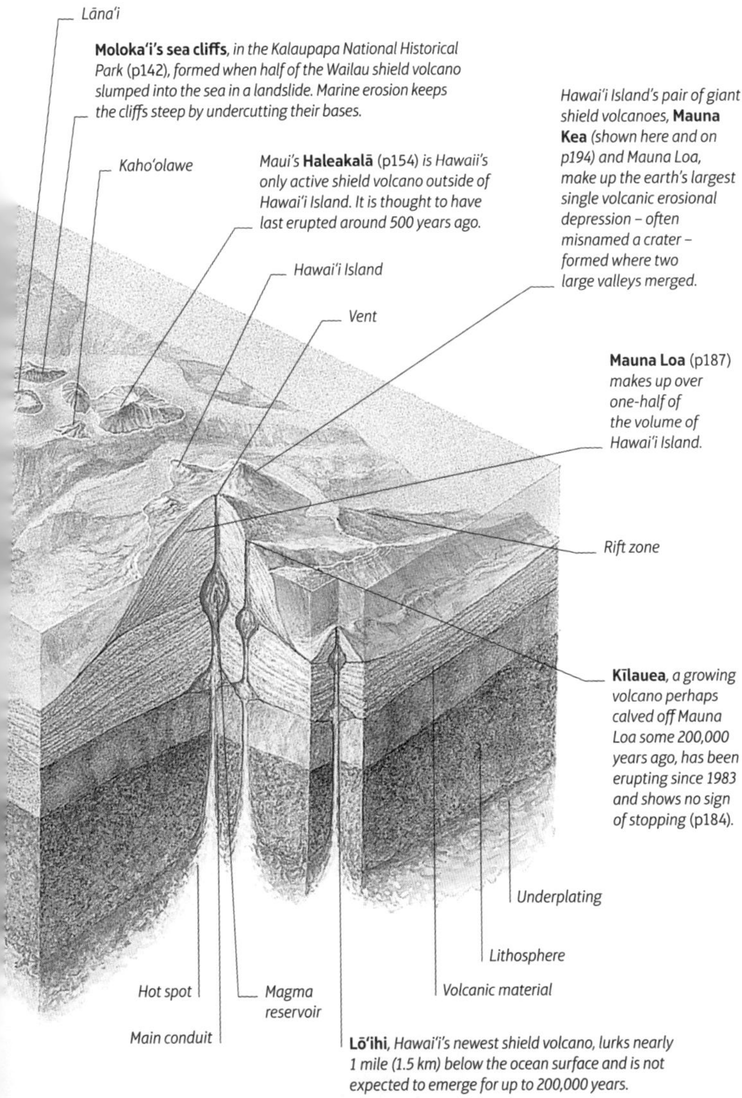

Lāna'i

Moloka'i's sea cliffs, *in the Kalaupapa National Historical Park (p142), formed when half of the Wailau shield volcano slumped into the sea in a landslide. Marine erosion keeps the cliffs steep by undercutting their bases.*

Kaho'olawe

Maui's **Haleakalā** (p154) *is Hawaii's only active shield volcano outside of Hawai'i Island. It is thought to have last erupted around 500 years ago.*

Hawai'i Island's pair of giant shield volcanoes, **Mauna Kea** *(shown here and on p194) and Mauna Loa, make up the earth's largest single volcanic erosional depression – often misnamed a crater – formed where two large valleys merged.*

Hawai'i Island

Vent

Mauna Loa (p187) *makes up over one-half of the volume of Hawai'i Island.*

Rift zone

Kīlauea, *a growing volcano perhaps calved off Mauna Loa some 200,000 years ago, has been erupting since 1983 and shows no sign of stopping* (p184).

Underplating

Lithosphere

Hot spot

Magma reservoir

Volcanic material

Main conduit

Lō'ihi, *Hawai'i's newest shield volcano, lurks nearly 1 mile (1.5 km) below the ocean surface and is not expected to emerge for up to 200,000 years.*

4

WAIPI'O VALLEY

62-3595 Āmaui Dr, Waimea; (808) 885-1655

If any spot could be designated the spiritual heartland of ancient Hawaii, it would have to be Waipi'o, or the "Valley of the Kings." Tours into this secluded, verdant valley are a wonderful way to experience the island's rich culture and stunning scenery.

The largest of seven valleys that punctuate this windward stretch of coast, Waipi'o measures 1 mile (1.5 km) wide at the sea and extends nearly 6 miles (10 km) inland. Its steep walls, laced with waterfalls, including the stupendous Hi'ilawe cascade, rise as high as 2,000 ft (600 m). Waipi'o Stream slices through the valley floor, coursing through fertile taro fields before emptying into the sea across a black-sand beach.

Centuries ago, this lush valley supported a population of over 10,000. A sacred place, the valley contained important *heiau* (temples), including a *pu'uhonua* (place of refuge) equal to that at Hōnaunau *(p182)*. The valley was Kamehameha I's boyhood playground. It was here, according to legend, that he received the sponsorship of Kūkā'ilimoku (the god of politics and war), and that he defeated his cousin and rival Kīwala'ō. Today, Waipi'o's few inhabitants cultivate taro, lotus, avocado, breadfruit, and citrus, and protect Hawaii's ancient spirit.

Access to the valley is limited. Due to road erosion and landslides, driving through the valley is only possible via a guided tour. Shuttle tours of the valley, run by Waipi'o Valley Shuttle, take visitors down into the majestic valley in an off-road vehicle while providing historical commentary on the area *(waipiovalleyshuttle.com)*. The Waipi'o Valley lookout offers breathtaking views of the valley and towering sea cliffs. The popular lookout has a picnic area and bathrooms. Parking spaces are often in high demand.

THE SHARK-MAN OF WAIPI'O VALLEY

According to Hawaiian legend, Nanaue was born to the shark king Kamohoalii and Kalei, a Hawaiian maiden. She was instructed by the king to never allow Nanaue to eat the flesh of any animal. However, as a boy, Nanaue was fed pork by his grandfather and he developed an appetite for meat, including human. Able to shape-shift into a shark like his father, Nanaue feasted on swimmers for years. He eventually escaped to Maui and then Moloka'i, where he was finally caught and killed.

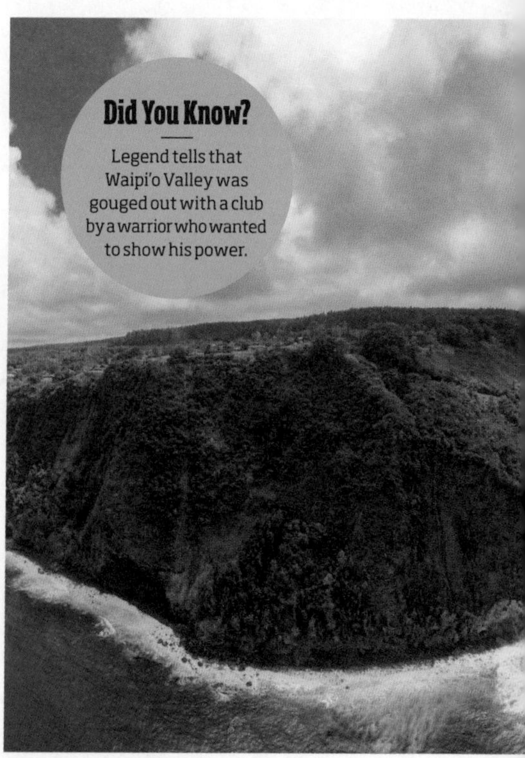

Did You Know?

Legend tells that Waipi'o Valley was gouged out with a club by a warrior who wanted to show his power.

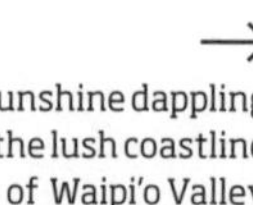

Sunshine dappling the lush coastline of Waipi'o Valley

1 The stunning cascades of the Kaluahine Falls make for a fantastic photo opportunity.

2 Admiring the sea cliffs from the Waipio Valley viewpoint in Hawai'i Island.

3 A beach in the valley, surrounded by dramatic cliffs running along the coastline of the island.

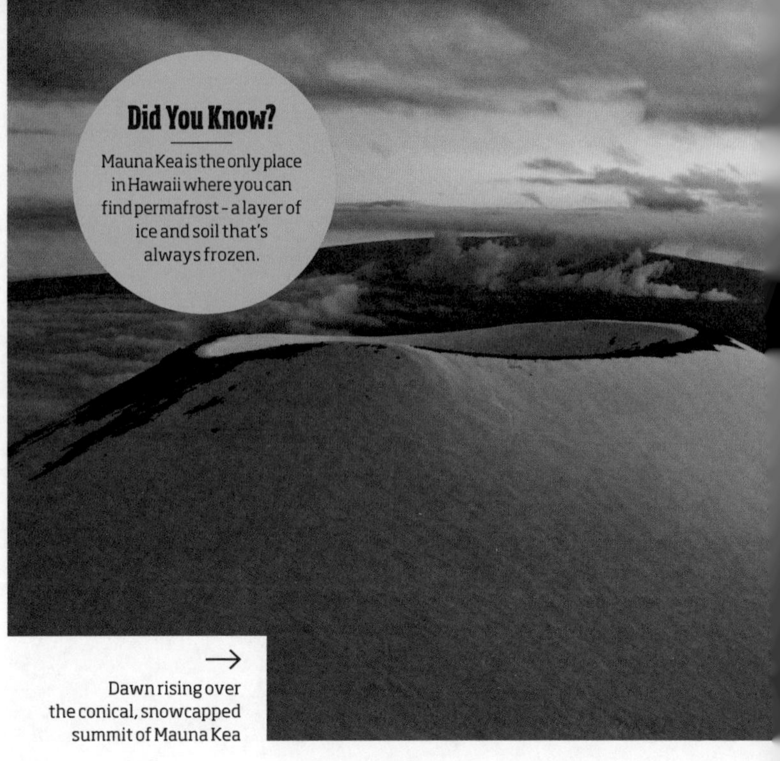

Did You Know?

Mauna Kea is the only place in Hawaii where you can find permafrost - a layer of ice and soil that's always frozen.

→ Dawn rising over the conical, snowcapped summit of Mauna Kea

5

MAUNA KEA

Off Saddle Rd (Hwy 200) at mile marker 28 62-3595 Āmaui Dr, Waimea; (808) 885-1655

Measured from its underwater base, Mauna Kea, a dormant volcano, is the tallest mountain on earth at 33,500 ft (10,200 m) in height. Regarded as sacred by Hawaiians, it has a peak dotted with crimson cinder cones and over a dozen observatories.

Midway between Hilo and Waimea, a road climbs up to the majestic summit of Mauna Kea ("White Mountain"). The first section of the road is well-paved and leads to the Onizuka Center for International Astronomy. Here, a visitor center, named after the Kona-born astronaut who died in the 1986 explosion of the space shuttle *Challenger*, has safety information, telescopes, and displays about the ecology of Mauna Kea, and offers free nightly stargazing sessions. There are impressive views, too, but the panorama is better from the summit. The second half of the road leading to the summit is a rougher gravel track that requires a 4WD vehicle to traverse. (Note that reaching the summit is often weather dependent.) This section of the route takes in several sites: the Mauna Kea Ice Age Natural Area Reserve, with a quarry where the ancient Hawaiians obtained the rock used for making their ax-like tools, or adzes; Moon Valley, where Apollo astronauts practiced driving their lunar rover in the 1960s; Lake Waiau, the third-highest lake in the US; and Pu'u Poli'ahu, the abode of Pele's sister Poli'ahu, the goddess of snow.

The summit itself offers panoramic views over the surrounding lunar-like landscapes, making it a popular place to watch the sunrise or sunset. Due to its elevation and absence of light and air pollution, it's also a premier site for astronomical observatories and one of the best places for stargazing. However, astronomy here is not without its controversy: between 2014 and 2022, a camp was set up opposing the construction of a telescope on land considered sacred by Hawaiians.

Hiking trails criss-cross Mauna Kea, including the Humu'ula-Manua Kea Summit Trail, a 4, 600-ft (1,400-m) climb along a 6-mile (10-km) alpine desert trail. In winter, snowboarders and skiers can frolic in the snow on the volcano's peak.

INSIDER TIP
Take it Slow

Mauna Kea's height means that altitude sickness is a real danger. Make sure you know the early symptoms, such as headaches and nausea, and acclimatize for an hour or so at the visitor center before heading up to the summit.

Mauna Kea's summit, due to its elevation and absence of light and air pollution, is a premier site for astronomical observatories and one of the best places for stargazing.

↓ Snowboarding on the snow-covered peak of Mauna Kea

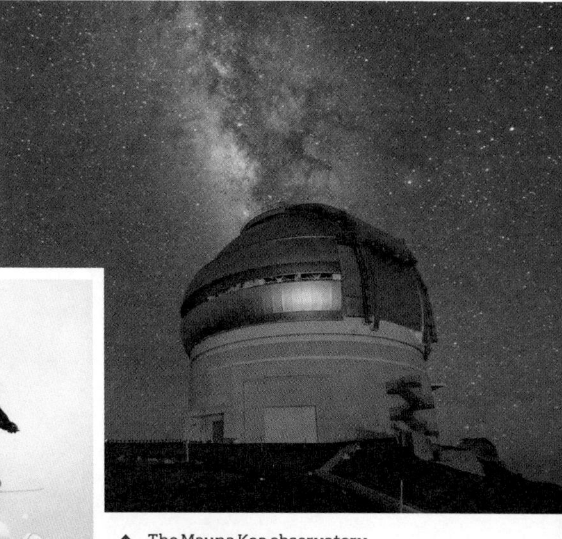

↑ The Mauna Kea observatory set against an awe-inspiring, star-studded night sky

EXPERIENCE MORE

Kailua-Kona

Hawai'i Belt Rd (Hwy 11 and 19) Ellison Onizuka International Airport (KOA) 62-3595 Āmaui Dr, Waimea; (808) 885-1655

This town is the center of the island's "Gold Coast." Within a two-block span along oceanfront Ali'i Drive are sites that played a role in some of the most important moments in Hawaii's history, from the unification of the islands to the advent of Christianity.

Built out into Kailua Bay is Ahu'ena Heiau, an ancient temple dedicated to the god Lono. Adjoining it is Courtyard King Kamehameha's Kona Beach Hotel, where the lobby has Hawaiian artifacts: tools, handicrafts, and a feather cape.

Missionaries built the **Moku'aikaua Church** on Ali'i Drive. The present lofty, granite church dates from 1837. A modest museum at the rear offers a scale model of the missionaries' brig, *Thaddeus.*

Across the street, **Hulihe'e Palace** was built at the same time and has similar rough-stone construction. It now serves as a museum that looks at the lifestyle of the monarchy.

Kailua-Kona is synonymous with sportfishing, and charter boats offer year-round opportunities to fish. The coastline is also dotted with small beaches, which are good for swimming, snorkeling, and diving.

Every month, Ali'i Drive hosts the Kokua Kailua Village Art Fair, which turns a section of the road into a pedestrian-only festive marketplace.

Moku'aikaua Church
75-5713 Ali'i Dr
Dawn-dusk daily
mokuaikaua.com

Hulihe'e Palace
75-5718 Ali'i Dr
10am-3:30pm Wed-Sat (to 2:30 Fri) Federal hols
daughtersofhawaii.org

Kona Coffee Living History Farm

82-6199 Mamalahoa Hwy, Captain Cook
10am-2pm Tue & Fri
konahistorical.org

Run by the Kona Historical Society, this historic farm tells the story of Kona coffee pioneers during the early 20th century. Visitors can wander around the coffee trees on

HIDDEN GEM
Flight of Fancy

Tickle your tastebuds in Kailua-Kona at the Kona Coffee & Tea Company (*konacoffeeandtea.com*). Here, you'll be served a tasting flight of various roasts, all of which have been grown on the slopes of Hualālai.

Canoeists enjoying the beautiful calm waters of Kailua Bay

the property as well as look inside the original 1920s farmhouse. Interpreters in period costumes are found demonstrating traditional craft-making and cooking methods, including how to make Spam *musubi* (a slice of Spam over a block of sticky rice) and coffee roasting. Coffee tastings take place and kids will enjoy visiting the farm's chickens and donkeys.

Hōlualoa

Hawai'i Belt Rd (Hwy 11), 3 miles (5 km) S of Kailua-Kona 62-3595 Āmaui Dr, Waimea; (808) 885-1655

A 15-minute drive up the winding and scenic Hualālai Road from Highway 19, on the slopes of Mount Hualālai, lies Hōlualoa. Set in the heart of the Kona coffee belt, coffee is its main focus, as attested by the annual Kona Coffee Cultural Festival in November.

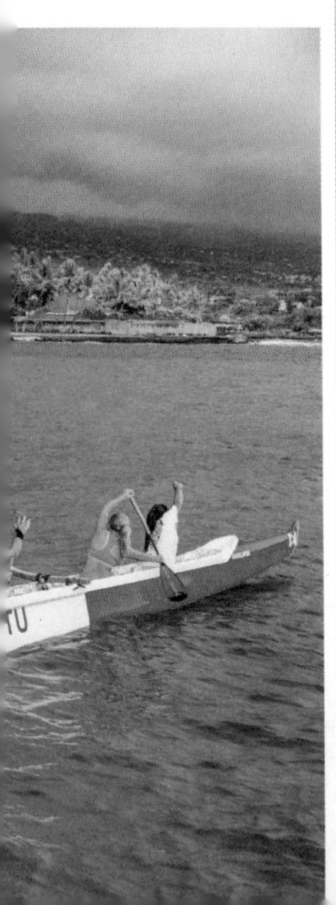

Long before tourism took hold, immigrants settled here to work on the many coffee plantations and vegetable farms. Hōlualoa turned into a thriving town packed with hotels, restaurants, and general stores to provide for their needs. Some of them still operate today, including **Kimura Lauhala Shop**. This place began as a general store in 1915, but became famous for its *lauhala* hats woven from the leaves of the pandanus tree.

Hōlualoa's main street is lined with galleries that present works by many of the island's well-known artists. **Studio 7** showcases the creations of local artists, including husband and wife Hiroki and Setsuko Morinoue. He is known for his large watercolors and wood-block prints; she is a ceramist. Works on display by other artists include turned bowls, wooden bracelets, and silk-screen prints. Over two dozen Hawai'i Island artists have their work exhibited at the **Glyph Art Gallery**; contemporary paintings, landscape photographs, and carved gourds are some of the artworks on display.

On the coast southwest of Hōlualoa, along Ali'i Drive, is La'aloa Bay Beach Park, also known as Magic Sands Beach. Here, the white-sand beach can disappear overnight after a storm, only to return again with the tides. It's a good spot for bodysurfing.

Kimura Lauhala Shop
77-996 Hualālai Rd (808) 324-0053 9am-5pm Mon-Fri (to 4pm Sat) Federal hols

Studio 7
76-5920 Mamalahoa Hwy Hours vary, check website studiosevenfinearts.com

Glyph Art Gallery
76-5933 Mamalahoa Hwy 11am-4pm Tue-Sat glyphartgallery.com

EAT

Keauhou Farmers Market
Locally grown honey, Kona coffee, macadamia nuts, and fruits are found at this market.

78-6831 Ali'i Dr, Kailua-Kona 8am-noon Sat keauhoufarmersmarket.com

Kona Brewing Company
Relax on the garden patio at this lively pub, accompanied by pizzas, fish tacos, and nachos.

74-5612 Pawai Pl, Kailua-Kona konabrewinghawaii.com

Da Poke Shack
A busy take-out spot by the beach offering amazing tuna poke and Hawaiian plate lunches.

76-6246 Ali'i Dr, Kailua-Kona dapokeshack.com

Island Lava Java
This café, offering beach views, is ideal for breakfast. Try the house-baked cinnamon rolls.

75-5801 Ali'i Dr, Kailua-Kona islandlavajava.com

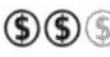

Ultimate Burger
A casual burger joint serving up grass-fed, Big Island beef burgers.

74-5450 Makala Blvd, Kailua-Kona ultimateburger.net

↑ The Captain Cook Monument in Kealakekua Bay, and *(inset)* colorful fish in the bay's waters

9

Kealakekua Bay State Historical Park

Nāpō'opo'o Rd, 4 miles (6 km) S of Captain Cook Captain Cook 7am-8pm daily dlnr.hawaii.gov

In 1779, Captain James Cook sailed into this protected bay – it was his first visit to Hawai'i Island (he had briefly visited Kaua'i in 1778). He had extensive contact with Hawaiians on the shores of this bay, and initially, Cook was welcomed by the local Hawaiians; however, relations grew hostile and, following a violent clash, Cook was killed.

Hikiau Heiau, a temple that Cook visited, is at the road's end. On the northern shore is the Captain Cook Monument, an obelisk marking where he died. The monument can't be reached by road, but is accessible either by boat (permit required) or by a moderate hike (the Ka'Awaloa Trail). Note that the trail descends rapidly. The bay – a State Marine Life Preserve with an abundance of fish, green sea turtles, and spinner dolphins – offers prime diving and snorkeling. The best way to explore it is by boat tour, which can take you to the best spots for swimming and diving.

10

Ho'okena

Hawai'i Belt Rd (Hwy 11), 24 miles (39 km) S of Kailua-Kona 62-3595 Āmaui Dr, Waimea; (808) 885-1655

In 1889, when author Robert Louis Stevenson asked to see a classic Hawaiian village, King Kalākaua sent him to Ho'okena. In those days, the small town had churches, a school, a courthouse, and a pier from which cattle were shipped to market in Honolulu. Today, other than weather-beaten houses and beach shacks, only lava walls and the ruined pier survive as reminders of its more prosperous past.

The center of life is beautiful Kauhakō Bay, with its gray-sand beach backed by long cliffs. The water teems with sea life, and there is excellent snorkeling and diving. The surf can be rough, and foot protection is recommended due to the sharp coral, lava rocks, and sea urchins that are found here.

11

Waikoloa Coast

W of Queen Ka'ahumanu Hwy (Hwy 19), 24 miles (39 km) N of Kailua-Kona 62-3595 Āmaui Dr, Waimea; (808) 885-1655

Waikoloa Beach Resort is built around one of this coast's best recreational areas, coconut-rimmed 'Anaeho'omalu Bay. The beach at "A-Bay" is calm, with a gradual, sandy bottom. Watersports equipment can

> **In 1889, when author Robert Louis Stevenson asked to see a classic Hawaiian village, King Kalākaua sent him to Ho'okena.**

INSIDER TIP
Under the Stars

Each month on Saturday evenings closest to a full moon, the Mauna Lani Resort on the Waikoloa Coast hosts Twilight at Kalahuipuaa, an event full of Hawaiian music, hula, and stories *(aubergeresorts.com)*.

be rented from the beach hut, and lessons in windsurfing and scuba diving are offered. Boat dives and cruises are also available. From the beach, coastal trails lead to fishponds, caves, and natural pools in which salt and fresh water mix to form unique ecosystems.

Kekaha Kai State Park

Off Queen Ka'ahumanu Hwy (Hwy 19), 9 miles (14 km) N of Kailua-Kona Division of State Parks; (808) 961-9540 8am-7pm daily

North of Kailua, a road runs through barren lava fields, the aftermath of an 1801 eruption of Mount Hualālai, all the way to Kekaha Kai State Park. With its picnic shelters and a beach of salt-and-pepper sand, the park is an oasis in this desolate wasteland. It is an ideal spot for swimming, snorkeling, diving, and, when the conditions are right, surfing. Before the park entrance, a rough road on the right leads to isolated Makalawena, a beautiful beach with dunes and coves.

Lapakahi State Historical Park

Off Akoni Pule Hwy (Hwy 270), 12 miles (19 km) N of Kawaihae (808) 961-9540 8am-4pm daily

The ruins of this large settlement provide a glimpse into the daily life of an old Hawaiian fishing village. Established in the 14th century, the village was inhabited for 500 years – until a falling water table and changing economic conditions caused the locals to abandon their homes.

Some thatched walls and roofs are gone; others have been restored to their original appearance. The lava foundations, *hālau* (canoe sheds), *kū'ula ko'a* (fishing shrines), and a *kōnane* stone board-game remain undamaged.

Kaloko Honokōhau National Historical Park

73-4786 Kanalani St, Kailua-Kona 8am-5pm daily nps.gov/kaho

Set along Kona's rocky shores, this park protects an ancient Hawaiian settlement. Plenty of hiking trails lead to petroglyphs, sacred temple ruins, and fishpond remains. The park is named for the two ancient *ahupua'a* (land subdivisions) that it covers, Kaloko and Honokōhau.

Here, you can venture along a coastal section of the Ala Kahakai National Historic Trail, and spot green sea turtles and waterbirds around the tidal pools. At Honokōhau Beach there are remnants of an old fish trap and an ancient *heiau* (temple). The harbor here is good for snorkeling.

A 15-minute trail from the visitor center toward the coast ends up at a petroglyph field, which includes over two dozen images etched into the lava rocks.

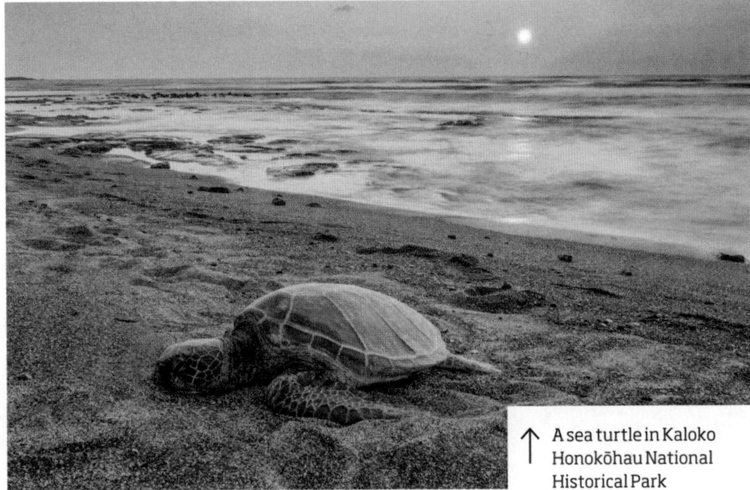

↑ A sea turtle in Kaloko Honokōhau National Historical Park

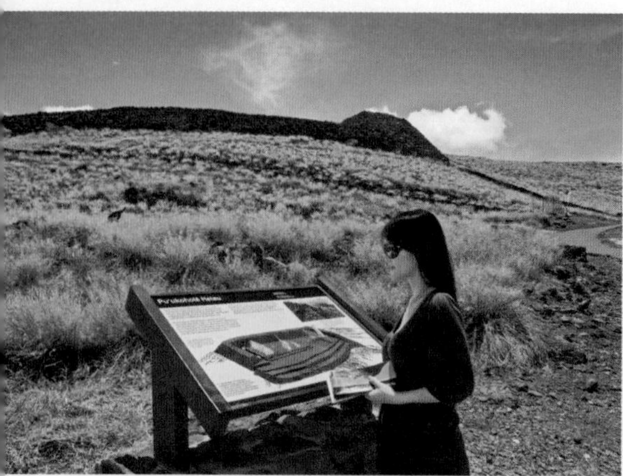

↑ An information panel on Pu'ukoholā Heiau, seen in the background

Pu'ukoholā Heiau National Historic Site

62-3601 Kawaihae Rd, Kawaihae 7:30am-5pm daily nps.gov/puhe

In 1790, Kamehameha I had reached an impasse in his drive to unify the island chain. On the advice of an oracle, he undertook the construction of Pu'ukoholā Heiau, a temple dedicated to Kūkā'ilimoku, the god of politics and war. It was destined to become the last such temple ever to be built.

Today, the massive monument stands undamaged on a hilltop overlooking Kawaihae Bay. Below it are the ruins of Mailekini Heiau, built for Kamehameha's ancestors. A third *heiau*, Haleokapuni, dedicated to shark gods, is believed to lie submerged in the waters below. An easy trail runs down past the first two *heiau* from the visitor center.

Just south of the *heiau* is the pretty Spencer Beach Park, a popular spot for camping, snorkeling, and diving. The clean beach and calm waters make it a great spot for kids.

Kohala Mountain Road

Hwy 250 62-3595 Āmaui Dr, Waimea; (808) 885-1655

The 20-mile (32-km) drive from Hāwī to Waimea follows the western ridge of low, worn Kohala Mountain. This twisting, tree-lined road provides wonderful vistas. The landscapes range from lush green hills and rolling pastures to black lava rock and distant beaches. A good place to stop and enjoy the panoramic views of the North Kohala coastline is at the Kohala Mountain Road lookout.

This is ranchland, and you will see ranch houses, and cattle and horses grazing. The area is dominated by the Parker Ranch, the largest operation in this area, and one of the largest cattle ranches in the United States. Its origins date right back to the early years of Western discovery and a young American adventurer named John Palmer Parker. He established a small dynasty here that shaped the history of the Kohala district. Today, the ranch covers a tenth of the island and supports 20,000 head of cattle.

INSIDER TIP
Ride into the Sunset

Paniolo Adventures offers horseback riding tours on its Ponoholo Ranch property, a working cattle ranch on the high slopes of the Kohala Mountain *(panioloadventures.com)*.

Hāpuna Beach

Off Queen Ka'ahumanu Hwy (Hwy 19), 7 miles (11 km) N of Waikoloa Coast

A stretch of white sand makes Hāpuna Beach the most popular beach on Hawai'i Island. With its clean, sandy bottom, the bay offers good swimming, snorkeling, and diving conditions. When the waves are active, surfers and bodyboarders flock here. The water should be treated with caution; strong currents have resulted in drownings. On the beach, there are places to rent snorkel sets and boogie boards, and posts staffed by lifeguards. **Hāpuna Beach State Recreation Area**, surrounding the beach, offers cabins for overnight stays, as well as a snack

bar and picnic tables. Just north of the bay, via the Mauna Kea Beach Hotel, is the crescent-shaped Kauna'oa Beach, one of the most photographed beaches on the island.

Hāpuna Beach State Recreation Area
Division of State Parks; (808) 882-6206 7am-8pm daily

Kohala Historical Sites State Monument

'Akoni Pule Hwy (Hwy 270), 53 miles (85 km) N of Kailua-Kona Dawn-dusk daily dlnr.hawaii.gov

Covering a stretch of coastline on the island's north shore, this is home to the Kamehameha Akahi 'Āina Hānau, thought by some to be the birthplace of Kamehameha I. A stone marks the place that this king, who united the Hawaiian Islands, was believed to be born. Found nearby is lichen-covered Mo'okini Heiau. Possibly dating from the 5th century CE, it is one of the oldest temples on the islands. In 1250, it was re-dedicated as a *luakini heiau* (temple that could be used for human sacrifice). In 1963, it became the first Hawaiian site to be listed in the National Historical Site Registry. Today, visitors to this massive *heiau* will discover a peaceful ruin. Nearby is Hāwī, a pleasant town with wooden sidewalks, painted storefronts, and trendy cafés.

Waimea

Hawai'i Belt Rd (Hwy 190), 38 miles (61 km) N of Kailua-Kona Waimea-Kohala Airport (MUE) 68-1330 Mauna Lani Dr, Suite 109A, Waimea; (808) 885-1655

Waimea's setting amid pasture land at an elevation of 2,700 ft (820 m) is a startling contrast to Hilo's rainforest and the Kona Coast's lava flats.

In the middle of town, the **Parker Ranch Center** recounts the history of *paniolo* (cowboy) culture and provides an insight into the area's influential Parker family. This story is further explored at the **Parker Ranch Historic Homes**, which include Puuopelu, a ranch house with a Regency interior and a collection of European art, and Mānā Hale, the Parkers' original home.

STAY

Kamuela Inn
A boutique hotel with breakfast included.

65-1300 Kawaihae Rd, Waimea the kamuelainn.com

Mauna Kea Beach Hotel
Luxury beachfront property with modern rooms, a lively bar, and lots of activities on-site.

62-100 Mauna Kea Beach Dr, Waimea maunakearesort.com

Parker Ranch Center
67-1185 Mamalahoa Hwy (Hwy 19) 9am-7pm Mon-Sat, 10am-5pm Sun Federal hols parkerranchcenter.com

Parker Ranch Historic Homes
66-1304 Mamalahoa Hwy (Hwy 190) 10am-2pm Mon-Wed (by appt only) Federal hols parkerranch.com

←
The rolling green pastures and forest of fertile Waimea

Looking out along the coast from the Pololū Valley, near Kapa'au

20

Kapa'au

'Akoni Pule Hwy (Hwy 270), 55 miles (88 km) N of Kailua-Kona 62-3595 Āmaui Dr, Waimea; (808) 885-1655

The small town of Kapa'au contains the original statue of Kamehameha I, a much-photographed replica of which stands in front of Ali'iōlani Hale in Honolulu. King Kalākaua commissioned the bronze sculpture in 1878. Cast in Paris, France, the statue was thought lost when the ship carrying it to Hawaii sank. A new statue was commi-ssioned and cast and this is the one that now stands in Honolulu. However, the origi-nal statue was found and arrived in the islands a few weeks after the first was installed on O'ahu. So it was brought to Kapa'au, thought by some to be the birthplace of Kamehameha I.

A large boulder known as Kamehameha Rock sits on the roadside heading east of town. Legend has it that the big chief once carried it to prove his strength; whole road crews have failed to move it since.

Nearby, the colorful Tong Wo Society building is the last of its kind on Hawai'i Island. This gathering place was built by Chinese immigrants in 1884.

At the end of Highway 270, a lookout has views of the Pololū Valley. Isolated by lush canyon walls, the valley's wide floor meets the sea at a black-sand beach. A 20-minute walk down a steep trail leads to the beach.

Did You Know?

Pololū means "long spear" in the Hawaiian language; the name accurately captures the valley's shape.

21

Honoka'a

Hawai'i Belt Rd (Hwy 19), 54 miles (87 km) NE of Kailua-Kona 62-3595 Āmaui Dr, Waimea; (808) 885-1655

This quaint rural town is actually one of the largest on the Hāmākua Coast. In 1881 plantation manager William Purvis sowed the first macadamia nut seeds here. The nut has since become an important crop for the islands, and there is a macadamia nut factory in town. Honoka'a has a handful of accommodation options, boutiques, shops, and restaurants, as well as art galleries, antique stores, and a nine-hole golf course.

This small community is home to the **Honoka'a People's Theater**. Built in 1930, the renovated theater shows movies on a big screen and also hosts concerts and dance performances.

Honoka'a People's Theater

45-3574 Mamane St, Honoka'a honokaapeople.com

HIDDEN GEM

Chocolate Tour

Honoka'a's Chocolate Company, an artisanal chocolate factory, offers farm tours of its cacao orchards and gardens where vanilla orchids, sugarcane, and fruit trees grow. Tastings are included *(honokaachocolateco.com)*.

Botanical World Adventures

31-240 Old Mamalahoa Hwy, Hakalau 8am-5:30pm daily botanicalworld.com

Located on an expanse of former sugarcane fields, Botanical World Adventures is a nature park that contains Hawaii's largest botanical garden. Featuring 5,000 species, the park's highlights include the pristine, 100-ft (30.5-m) Kamae'e Falls. These gushing cascades can be easily viewed via an overlook reached by a paved road within the park.

A selection of other family activities is available within the park, including zip-lines, segway tours, and a massive children's maze.

Hawaii Tropical Botanical Garden

27-717 Old Mamalahoa Hwy, Papaikou 9am-5pm daily htbg.com

Dedicated to the collection, protection, and display of tropical plants from around the world, the beautiful Hawaii Tropical Botanical Garden has over 2,000 species of flora growing along its paved pathways. Visitors can walk in the shades of the 100-year-old mango and coconut palm groves, admire scenic views of Onomea Bay and several waterfalls within the garden, and take in the delicate perfume of gingers and orchids. You can also bring a lunch to enjoy at one of the several picnic areas by the Onomea Stream and say hello to the resident macaws nesting at the Birdhouse.

'Akaka Falls State Park

Hwy 220, 3.5 miles (5.5 km) W of Honomū Honomū 8:30am-5pm daily Division of State Parks; (808) 961-9540

Two of the state's most hypnotic waterfalls can be found at 'Akaka Falls State Park, in the hills above the Hāmākua Coast. A loop trail, taking less than half an hour, links the 400-ft (120-m) Kahūnā Falls to 'Akaka Falls, an unbroken cascade of 420 ft (130 m). At the main lookout, the roar of water almost drowns out the incessant clicking of cameras. At the edge of the path, you can see the entire length of the falls from top to bottom, including the pool below, yet not get wet from the spray.

The waterfalls apart, the breezy park alone is worth the visit. Paths wind through trees, vines, bamboo, ginger, orchids, and exotic plants, accompanied by the sounds of rushing streams.

THE LEGEND OF 'AKAKA FALLS

Warrior chief 'Akaka led an unfaithful life. One day, overcome with shame for having lovers other than his wife, he threw himself over a cliff, transforming into the 'Akaka Falls. His wife rushed to the edge of the cliff but it was too late; she changed into the huge rock that sits at the top of the falls. 'Akaka's lovers, hearing of his death, wept and wept until they transformed into smaller waterfalls nearby.

The access road veers off Highway 19 at the welcoming old sugar town of Honomū, which has dwindled from its 1930s population of 3,000 to just over 500 today. The residents have kept the small main street alive, with Mr. Ed's Bakery (est. 1910) and several other weathered wooden buildings serving as cafés and gift shops.

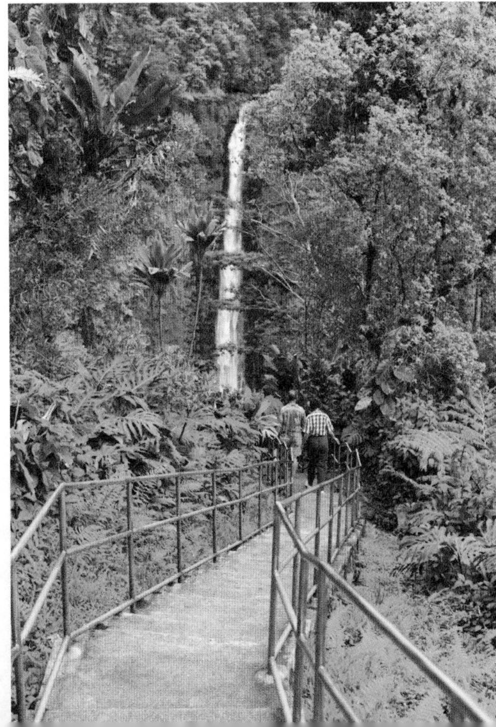

→ Walkway leading to the gracefully cascading 'Akaka Falls

EAT

Punalu'u Bake Shop
The southernmost bakery in the US, this shop is known for its fluffy Hawaiian sweetbreads.

95-5642 Mamalahoa Hwy, Nā'ālehu
bakeshophawaii.com

Hana Hou Restaurant
This casual diner serves delicious home-baked pies and cakes.

95-1148 Nā'ālehu Spur Rd, Nā'ālehu Tue
naalehu restaurant.com

Tex Drive-In
Local diner famous for its *malasadas* (donuts) and Hawaiian lunches.

45-690 Pakalana St, Honoka'a
texdrivein-hawaii.com

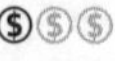

Island Naturals
Excellent health-food store with great take-out options from its deli.

15-1870 Akeakamai Loop, Pāhoa
islandnaturals.com

DRINK

What's Shakin'
Take-out shack for smoothies made with locally grown fruit.

27-999 Mamalahoa Hwy, Pepeekeo Sun & Mon whatsshakin bigisland.com

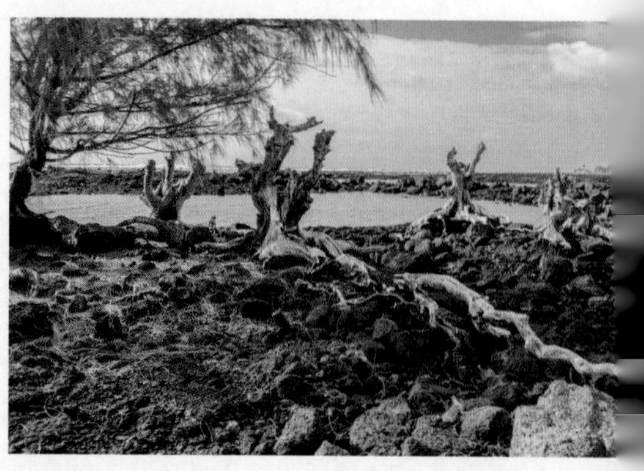

↑ The unusual "lava trees" that can be seen near Kapoho

Pāhoa

Hwy 130, 20 miles (32 km) S of Hilo 62-3595 Āmaui Dr, Waimea; (808) 885-1655

The main strip of Pāhoa offers "Wild West"-style buildings with raised boardwalks and low awnings that have been reinterpreted along psychedelic themes. Shops sell hemp products, espresso coffee, and New Age books.

In 2018, the eruption of Kīlauea caused lava flows to descend just east of Pāhoa, swallowing up nearly 700 homes. Fortunately, there were no injuries or deaths.

Kapoho

Hwy 132, 27 miles (43 km) S of Hilo 62-3595 Āmaui Dr, Waimea; (808) 885-1655

The town of Kapoho has been destroyed twice by Kīlauea's eruptions; once in 1960 and most recently in 2018. Countless luxury homes, built after the first destruction, now lie buried under lava flows that have added over 520 acres (210 ha) of new land to Kapaho's coastline.

In 1790, a wave of lava cut through a nearby forest, leaving *'ōhi'a* trunks sheathed in black stone. Today, only the hollowed-out casts, or "lava trees," remain, but new trees have grown back. Together they make up the **Lava Tree State Monument**, a shady park with a trail around the casts.

Lava Tree State Monument
Hwy 132, 2.5 miles (4 km) E of Pāhoa Dawn-dusk daily Division of State Parks; (808) 961-9540

Puna Lava Flows

Hwy 137, SW of Kapoho for 14 miles (23 km) County Parks & Recreation; (808) 961-8311

Narrow Highway 137 traces the Puna coastline along the base of Kīlauea's East Rift Zone. Here, the dense foliage occasionally breaks into solidified lava flows, mute reminders that Puna residents live by the grace of Madam Pele, the Hawaiian goddess of volcanoes *(p185)*.

Isaac Hale Beach Park features a black-sand beach, also known as Pohoiki Beach, created by Kīlauea's 2018 eruption. **MacKenzie State Recreation Area**, a clifftop park set in an ironwood forest, gives access to an old Hawaiian coastal trail and a long lava tube. The area is said to be haunted due to its dark history, which includes convict labor working here in the 1850s.

Southwest of here the Puna coastal road ends abruptly where the roadway, and the entire countryside, has been obliterated by congealed lava.

Isaac Hale Beach Park
Junction of Hwy 137 and Pāhoa-Pohoiki Rd Daily

MacKenzie State Recreation Area
Hwy 137, 2 miles (3 km) S of junction with Pāhoa-Pohoiki Rd Daily

Ka'ū District

Hawai'i Belt Rd (Hwy 11), 53 miles (85 km) SW of Hilo Pāhala, Punalu'u, Nā'ālehu, and Wai'ōhinu 62-3595 Āmaui Dr, Waimea; (808) 885-1655

The long southern arc of the Hawai'i Belt Road (Hwy 11) between Volcano Village and Kailua-Kona traverses the vast and sparsely populated Ka'ū district. Three small towns are located here. Agricultural Pāhala, where macadamia nuts, sugarcane, and oranges are grown, is a quiet place where the only noise might be the occasional crowing of roosters. Nā'ālehu, the most southerly town in the US, is Ka'ū's largest town, with a few shops. Wai'ōhinu is known for a monkeypod tree that Mark Twain planted in 1866. The original tree fell in a storm in 1957 but has since grown again from shoots.

The gem of the south coast is **Punalu'u Beach Park**, where a pure black-sand beach is crowded with coconut trees. The beach is known for its rare Hawksbill turtles and green sea turtles that nest here and bask in the sun. These turtles are protected in Hawaii by federal and state laws so visitors should not touch or feed them. Visitors may camp at Punalu'u and at Whittington Beach Park, 5 miles (8 km) farther south.

Punalu'u Beach Park
Off Hwy 11, 5 miles (8 km) SW of Pāhala Daily Dept of Parks and Recreation, Hilo; (808) 961-8311

Ka Lae

S Point Rd, off Hwy 11, 6 miles (10 km) W of Wai'ōhinu 62-3595 Āmaui Dr, Waimea; (808) 885-1655

Also known as South Point, Ka Lae is as far south as you can travel inside the US. Fierce winds drive against a battered grassland that gives way finally to a rocky shoreline. It all feels like the ends of the earth. Although the powerful waves are daunting, these have long been prime fishing grounds. The mooring holes that Hawaiians drilled into the rocks so they could keep their canoes safe while fishing are still visible, providing early evidence of Polynesian settlement.

HIDDEN GEM
Green Sands

Northeast of Ka Lae is the unusual Green Sand Beach (Papakōlea), composed of olivine sand. It's a pleasant but exposed and hot 2.5-mile (4-km) hike along a 4WD road to reach the beach.

↑ Surf pounding the rocky shoreline of Ka Lae, the southernmost point in Hawaii

A DRIVING TOUR HĀMĀKUA COAST

Length 55 miles (88 km) **Stopping-off points** Kalōpā State Recreation Area, Hawaii Tropical Botanical Garden, Laupāhoehoe Point Beach Park **Terrain** Paved

The verdant cliffs lining the island's windward coast are stunning company on the drive along the Hawai'i Belt Road (Hwy 19), which traces the edge of the Hāmākua Coast. With dozens of side roads begging investigation, you can easily spend a day traveling the 55 miles (88 km) between the *paniolo* (Hawaiian cowboy) town of Waimea and lively Hilo, the state's second-largest city. This stretch has been designated the Hilo-Hāmākua Heritage Coast due to the area's historic and cultural significance. Look out for brown-and-white signs on the Hawai'i Belt Road as these indicate specific points of interest situated along the way.

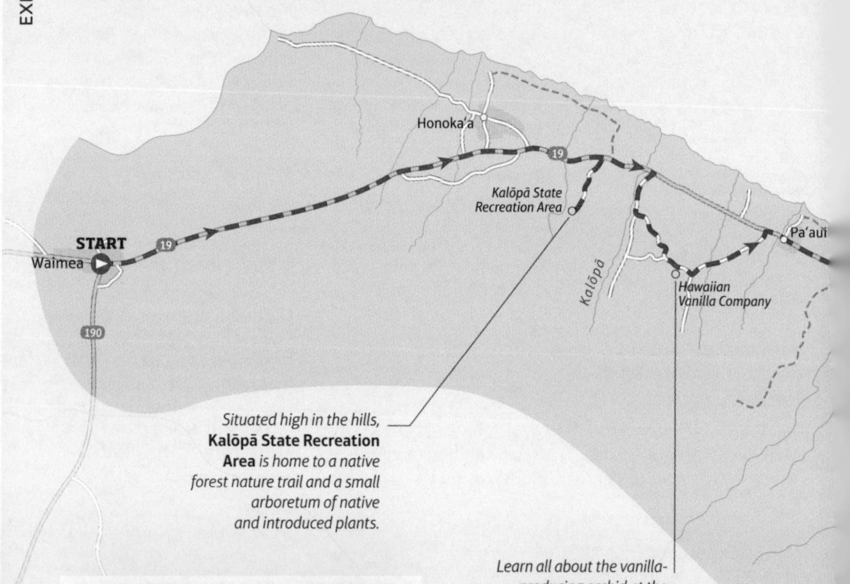

Honoka'a
19
Kalōpā State Recreation Area
START
Waimea
19
190
Kalōpā
Hawaiian Vanilla Company
Pa'auilo

Situated high in the hills, **Kalōpā State Recreation Area** *is home to a native forest nature trail and a small arboretum of native and introduced plants.*

Learn all about the vanilla-producing orchid at the **Hawaiian Vanilla Company**, *a family farm that offers tours of the grounds and factory. Tastings and a vanilla-infused lunch are also offered.*

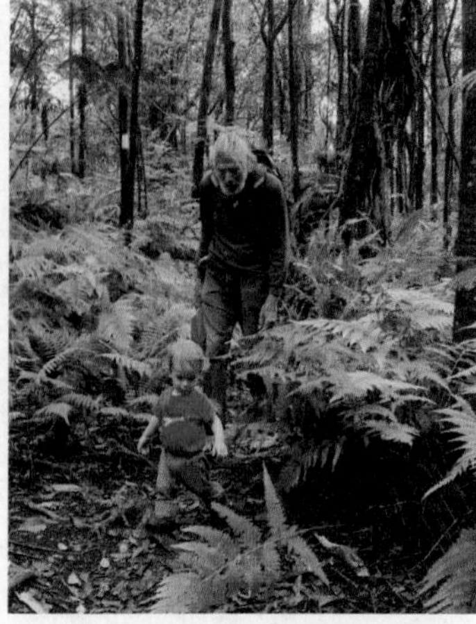

← Taking a walk along the native forest nature trail at Kalōpā State Recreation Area

←
Surf breaking on the rocky coast at Laupāhoehoe Point Beach Park

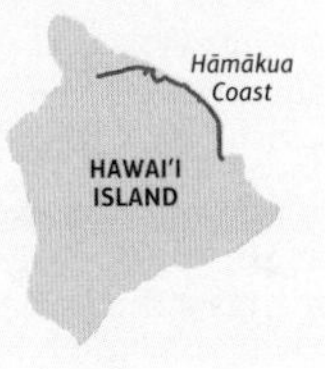

Locator Map
For more detail see p176

0 kilometers 10
0 miles 10
N

Reached via a short forest trail, **Hikiau Falls** *is a beautiful veil of water that rushes down into a deep clear pool, home to rainbow trout.*

Hikiau Falls
'Ō'ōkala

Laupāhoehoe Point Beach Park *provides stupendous views over a lush lava outcrop that juts into the pounding sea.*

Laupāhoehoe
Pāpa'aloa
19
Nīnole

At **Kolekole Beach County Park**, *south of mile marker 15, a delightful stream tumbles into the ocean, making this a popular spot for picnics.*

Hakalau
Kolekole Beach Country Park
Honomū
Kolekole
220
'Akaka Falls State Park
Pepe'ekeo
Hawaii Tropical Botanical Garden
Pāpa'ikou
Kapehu
Pauka'a
19
Wainaku
Hilo Bay
Wailuku River
200
Hilo
FINISH
Kaumana
200
2000

The trails in the **Hawaii Tropical Botanical Garden** (p203) *pass through a patch of rain-forest that includes a lily pond and an array of tropical plants. The bottom of the garden has views of the sea.*

A DRIVING TOUR
SADDLE ROAD

Length 70 miles (112km) **Stopping-off points** Pick up refreshments in Hilo as amenities are rare on the road. Mauna Kea's visitor center has a small shop.

To drive Saddle Road is to drive along the shoulders of giants. This scenic route cruises through the trough where two mountains, Mauna Kea and Mauna Loa, collide. Though it was once a hazardous route banned by many car rentals, Saddle Road is now safer and fully paved. Along the way, drivers get a close-up look at the island's interior make-up: cool rainforests cover the Hilo district, lava fields stretch across the road's 6,500-ft (2,000-m) summit, and parched grasslands await at Waimea.

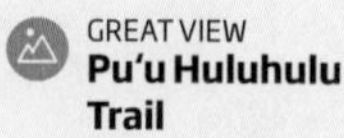

GREAT VIEW
Pu'u Huluhulu Trail

This easy, forested trail offers wonderful views of Mauna Kea as it climbs to the top of an old cinder cone. The trail parking lot is near mile marker 28 on Saddle Road.

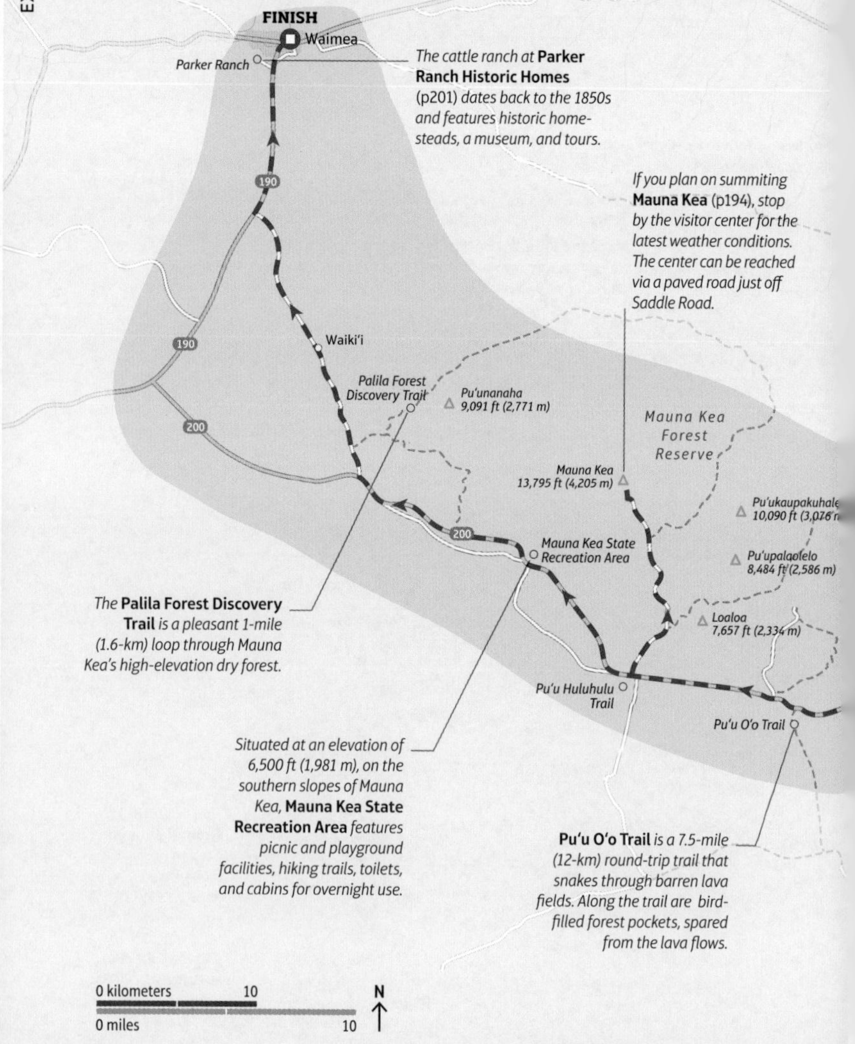

The cattle ranch at **Parker Ranch Historic Homes** *(p201) dates back to the 1850s and features historic homesteads, a museum, and tours.*

If you plan on summiting **Mauna Kea** *(p194), stop by the visitor center for the latest weather conditions. The center can be reached via a paved road just off Saddle Road.*

The **Palila Forest Discovery Trail** *is a pleasant 1-mile (1.6-km) loop through Mauna Kea's high-elevation dry forest.*

Situated at an elevation of 6,500 ft (1,981 m), on the southern slopes of Mauna Kea, **Mauna Kea State Recreation Area** *features picnic and playground facilities, hiking trails, toilets, and cabins for overnight use.*

Pu'u O'o Trail *is a 7.5-mile (12-km) round-trip trail that snakes through barren lava fields. Along the trail are bird-filled forest pockets, spared from the lava flows.*

0 kilometers 10
0 miles 10
N

↑ Cascading Rainbow Falls, located near the beginning of the drive

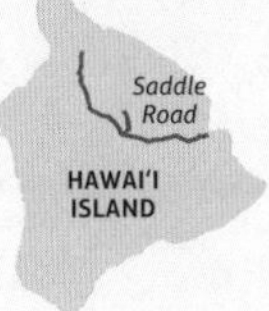

Locator Map
For more detail see p176

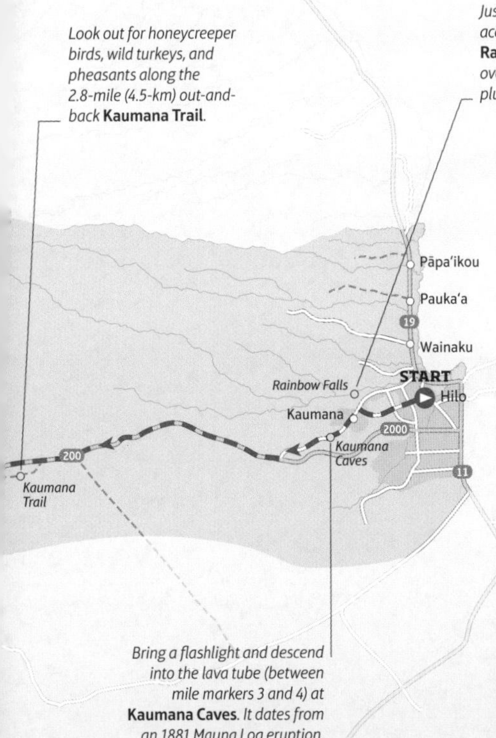

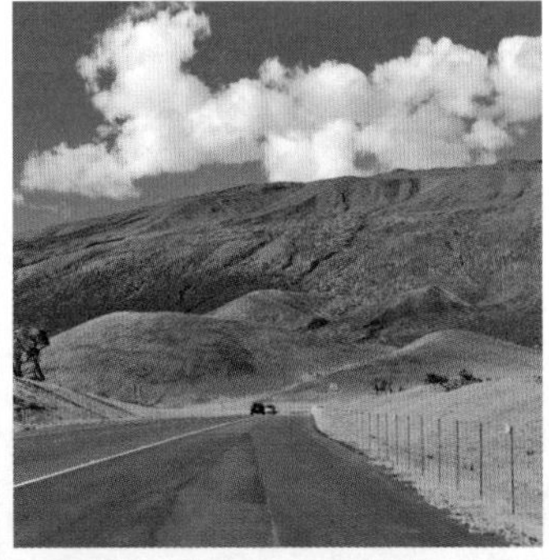

↑ Mauna Kea's ridges looming over Saddle Road

Kalalau Valley in the Nāpali Coast State Wilderness Park

KAUA'I

Formed over five million years ago, Kaua'i is the oldest of all the Hawaiian Islands. The outline of the volcano that created this verdant isle has all but vanished, leaving in its place a roughly circular island on which nowhere is more than 12 miles (19 km) from the ocean.

Polynesian voyagers, most likely Marquesas islanders, may have first arrived on Kaua'i as early as 1,500 years ago, with a second wave of settlers, possibly from today's Tahiti, arriving several centuries later. Taro, sweet potato, and sugarcane were grown successfully by these settlers, who also fished in the island's seafood-rich waters. Temples were built during this time as well, remnants of which can still be seen along the Wailua River.

In 1778, Captain James Cook became the first European to set foot on the Hawaiian Islands when he landed at Kaua'i's Waimea Bay. His arrival paved the way for the islands to engage in trade with Europe. During the late 18th to early 19th centuries, King Kamehameha I – who was determined to unify the Hawaiian Islands – twice failed to bring Kaua'i under his control, once due to a storm and the other due to an epidemic. In 1810, Kaua'i's ruler Kaumuali'i, possibly wishing to avoid future bloodshed, undertook peaceful negotiations with Kamehameha I and agreed to join the Hawaiian Kingdom.

During the 19th century, sandalwood and sugar industries – established during Cook's trading era – thrived on the island. However, by the 1950s, tourism had become the mainstay of the economy, spurred on by the construction of the airport in Līhu'e. Today, visitors continue to flock to Kaua'i, thanks to this "Garden Isle's" lush rainforest, tumbling waterfalls, pristine beaches, and sharply fluted mountain peaks.

KAUA'I

Must Sees

1. Līhu'e
2. Waimea Canyon and Kōke'e State Parks
3. Nāpali Coast State Wilderness Park

Experience More

4. Wailua
5. Wailua Falls
6. Fern Grotto
7. Wailua Complex of Heiaus
8. Sleeping Giant
9. Kīlauea Point
10. Mount Wai'ale'ale
11. Kapa'a
12. Anahola
13. Kalihiwai Beach
14. Hanalei
15. Hā'ena and Kē'ē Beaches
16. Lumaha'i Beach
17. Princeville
18. Limahuli Garden
19. Waimea
20. Allerton Garden
21. Polihale Beach
22. Ni'ihau
23. Hanapēpē
24. Kauai Coffee Company Visitor Center
25. Po'ipū

HĀ'ENA AN
KĒ'Ē BEACHE
18 LIMAHUL GARDEN
KALALAU TRAIL
NĀPALI COAST STATE WILDERNESS PARK 3
Kalalau Lookout
Pu'u o Kila Lookout
Nāpali Coast
550
Koke'e Museum
2 KŌKE'E STATE PARK
Alaka'i Swamp
Mākaha Valley
Kohua Ridge 3,776 ft (1,151 m)
Púu Lua 3,478 ft (1,060 m)
POLIHALE BEACH 21
Barking Sands Beach
Waimea Canyon Lookout
WAIMEA CANYON STATE PARK 2
Waimea
Kaulakahi Channel
50
552
550
Kekaha
19 WAIMEA
Ni'ihau 12 miles (20 km) 22
Russian Fort Elizabeth
Pākalā
Kaumakani
HANAPĒPĒ 23
Ele'ele
Salt Pond Beach County Park
24 KAUAI COFFEE COMPANY VISITOR CENTER
0 kilometers 6
0 miles 6
N

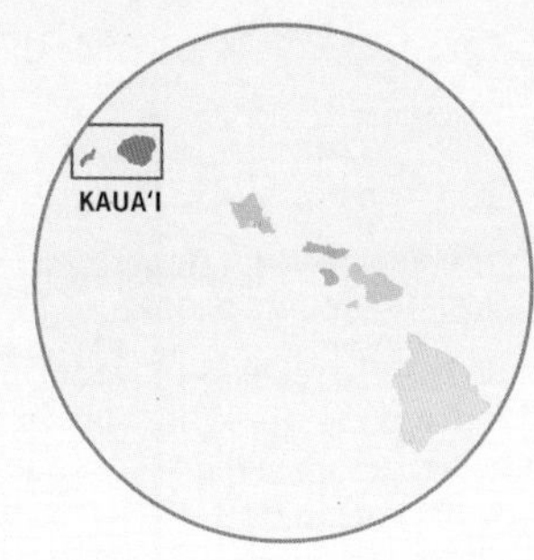
KAUA'I
PRINCEVILLE
'Anini Beach
Secret Beach
9 KĪLAUEA POINT
16 LUMAHA'I BEACH
17
Princeville Airport
13 KALIHIWAI BEACH
Larsen's Beach
56
Kīlauea
Moloa'a Bay
14 HANALEI
Hanalei National Wildlife Refuge
Wai'oli
Lumaha'i
Hanalei
Anahola Mountains
56
Anahola Bay
12 ANAHOLA
Makaleha Mountains
Namolokama 4,413 ft (1,345 m)
Donkey Beach
Keālia
MOUNT WAI'ALE'ALE
10
581
11 KAPA'A
Keahua Arboretum
SLEEPING GIANT 8
580
Waipouli
Kawaikini 5,243 ft (1,598 m)
Wailua Homesteads
4 WAILUA
7 WAILUA COMPLEX OF HEIAUS
6
Lydgate State Park
WAILUA FALLS 5
FERN GROTTO
Wailua
583
56
Kapala'oa 3,314 ft (1,010 m)
Hanamā'ulu
51
Līhu'e Airport
1 LĪHU'E
Puhi
50
Nāwiliwili Bay
Hulē'ia National Wildlife Reserve
Kalāheo
50
'Ōma'o
Hā'upu Ridge
Lāwa'i
530
Kōloa
Kaua'i Channel
Māhā'ulepū Beach
20 ALLERTON GARDEN
25 PO'IPŪ

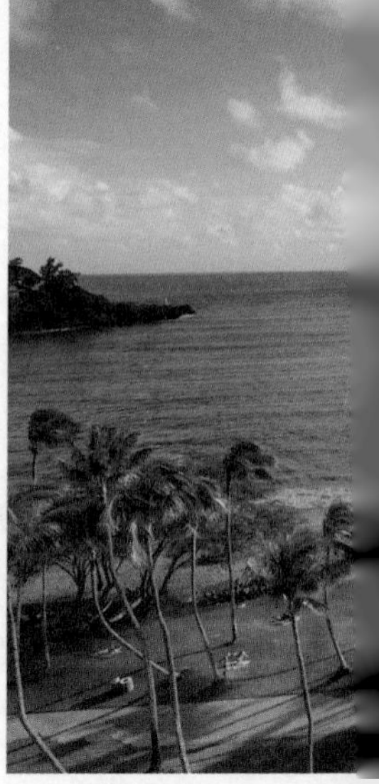

1

LĪHU'E

✈ 2 miles (3 km) E of Līhu'e 🚌 Rice St ℹ KVB, 4473 Pahe`e St, Suite F; (808) 245-3971

Līhu'e is the administrative and business center of Kaua'i and also the site of the island's air and sea ports. The town grew up in the 1860s to serve a nearby sugar plantation; the latter drew many immigrant workers to settle in the town. Today, Līhu'e's multicultural heritage is reflected in its vibrant shops and restaurants.

① Kaua'i Museum

4428 Rice St 9am-4pm Mon-Sat Jan 1, Labor Day, Jul 4, Thanksgiving & Dec 25 kauaimuseum.org

This two-part museum focuses on the island's history and its Indigenous people. The Wilcox Building features traditional artifacts gathered by the missionary Wilcox family, including koa-wood bowls and *kāhili*, feathered standards once used as a sign of royalty in Hawaii. Connected to the Wilcox Building via a courtyard, the Rice Building tells *The Story of Kaua'i* through ancient weapons and videos on geology.

② Grove Farm Homestead

4050 Nāwiliwili Rd Mon, Wed & Thu Federal hols grovefarm.org

No settlement existed on the site of modern Līhu'e until 1864, when George Wilcox, the son of early missionaries, established the Grove Farm Plantation for sugarcane harvesting.

Although Wilcox lived in a humble cottage, his heirs built the imposing mansion, paneled in dark koa wood, that is now the centerpiece of the homestead. The two-hour guided tour takes guests through the house, servants' quarters, and the orchard. Reservations for the tour are necessary and should be booked in advance. There are tours at 10am and 1pm.

Kalapakī Beach

Off Wa'apā Rd (Hwy 51), at Royal Sonesta Kaua'i Resort

This is one of the safest beaches in the area, making it a good choice

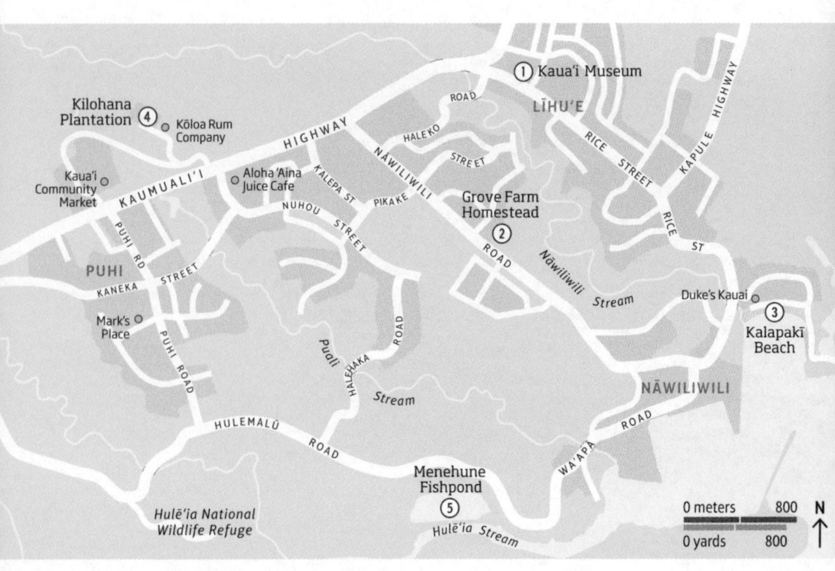

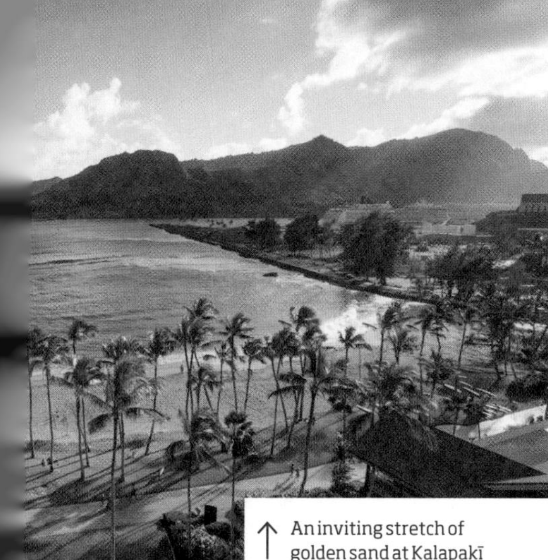

An inviting stretch of golden sand at Kalapakī Beach in Līhu'e

for families. It is also home to the top-class Royal Sonesta Kaua'i Resort and a handful of restaurants. Expert surfers swirl right out into the bay, but the inshore waters are sheltered enough for children. On the far side, the palm-fringed lawns of Nāwiliwili Beach County Park are ideal for picnics.

A ten-minute walk east of Kalapakī Beach lies Ninini Beach with its two secluded sandy coves and an automated lighthouse that's been in operation since 1897.

Kilohana Plantation

3-2087 Kaumuali'i Hwy (Hwy 50), 1.5 miles (2.5 km) W of Līhu'e 9:30am-9:30pm daily kilohanakauai.com

This grand house dates back to the 1930s. Its resemblance to a Tudor-style country estate makes it the perfect home for one of Kaua'i's most elegant restaurants, as well as a bar and several gift boutiques and art galleries. The train offers a comfortable way of exploring the vast plantation, and allows visitors to discover Kilohana's agricultural past and present.

Menehune Fishpond

Lookout on Hulemalū Rd, 1.5 miles (2.5 km) S of Līhu'e To the public, except by guided kayak tours

Ancient Hawaiians exploited a natural bend in the Hulē'ia Stream by building a 900-ft (275-m) dam of rounded boulders to create the Alekoko ("Rippling Blood") Fishpond. The Hawaiians used it to fatten mullet for the royal table; as the fish grew, they could not pass through the latticed sluices through which they had entered the enclosure.

This ancient structure is more commonly referred to as the Menehune Fishpond. Its prehistoric stonemasonry is credited, as so often in Hawaii, to the little *Menehune*. These mythical figures are described by popular legend as a magical people already hard at work in Hawaii when the first Polynesian settlers arrived. Now privately owned, the fishpond can be seen only from afar.

Unless you rent a kayak, the same goes for the Hulē'ia National Wildlife Refuge just upstream, where former taro and rice terraces are set aside for the exclusive use of a population of waterbirds.

EAT

Kaua'i Community Market

Find farm-fresh harvests and food trucks at this market.

3 Kaumuali'i Hwy 9:30am-1pm Sat kauaigrown.org

Mark's Place

This take-out spot offers generous portions of Hawaiian plate lunches.

1610 Haleukana St 10:30am-2:30pm Mon-Fri marksplacekauai.com

Aloha 'Aina Juice Cafe

Try delicious açai bowls and healthy fresh juices at this little café.

4454 Nuhou St 8am-4pm Mon-Fri, 9am-3pm Sat alohaainajuice.com

DRINK

Kōloa Rum Company

This distillery offers complimentary tastings of their award-winning rums.

3-2087 Kaumuali'i Hwy 10am-5pm Mon-Sat koloarum.com

Duke's Kauai

Soak up sunset views while sipping fruity cocktails at this popular beachside bar.

3610 Rice St 11am-10pm Mon-Sat, 9am-10pm Sun dukeskauai.com

2

WAIMEA CANYON AND KŌKE'E STATE PARKS

Kōke'e Rd (Hwy 550) Parks: dawn-dusk daily; Kōke'e Museum: 9am-4pm daily dlnr.hawaii.gov

These neighboring national parks are two of the island's most spectacular. Dubbed the "Grand Canyon of the Pacific," Waimea is a landscape of plunging gorges swathed in lush vegetation. Kōke'e – reached via a road that runs through Waimea – is home to precious ecosystems and offers excellent hiking trails.

Waimea Canyon was created by earth movements that almost split Kaua'i in two. Over time, heavy rains have helped form a gorge 3,600 ft (1,100 m) deep that is still being eroded today, as occasional landslides slash away layers of rich green vegetation and the Waimea River carries the red mud into the ocean. Several lookouts found along Kōke'e Road offer incredible vistas, or you can delve into the park on foot: the hikes will take you past feral goats, flowing waterfalls, and to amazing views of the canyon itself.

At the north end of Waimea Canyon is the equally stunning Kōke'e State Park. At around 3,200–4,200 ft (975–2,180 m) above sea level, this park brims with native flora and fauna. The watery Alaka'i Swamp has some of Hawaii's rarest birds, such as the *'i'iwi*, or scarlet honeycreeper. It is also laced with incredible hiking trails and has lookouts that offer sweeping views of the Kalalau Valley stretching toward the ocean. The tiny Koke'e Museum offers information on trails in the park, as well as a shop and exhibits on natural history.

Taking in the dramatic splendor of the Waimea Canyon

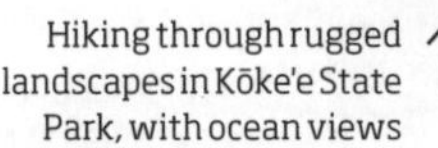

Hiking through rugged landscapes in Kōke'e State Park, with ocean views

TOP 3

HIKES IN KŌKE'E

Poomau Canyon Lookout Trail
An easy, half-hour forest hike that finishes at a dramatic ridgeline with views of several stunning waterfalls plunging down the canyon walls.

Alaka'i Swamp Trail
A half-day trek through one of the highest rainforests in the world, following boardwalks through shallow bogs to reach a gorgeous coastal lookout.

Awa'awapuhi Trail
A difficult but richly rewarding 6-mile (9.5-km) round-trip day hike that ends at a high cliff offering jaw-dropping views over the coast, with its fluted peaks and blue sea.

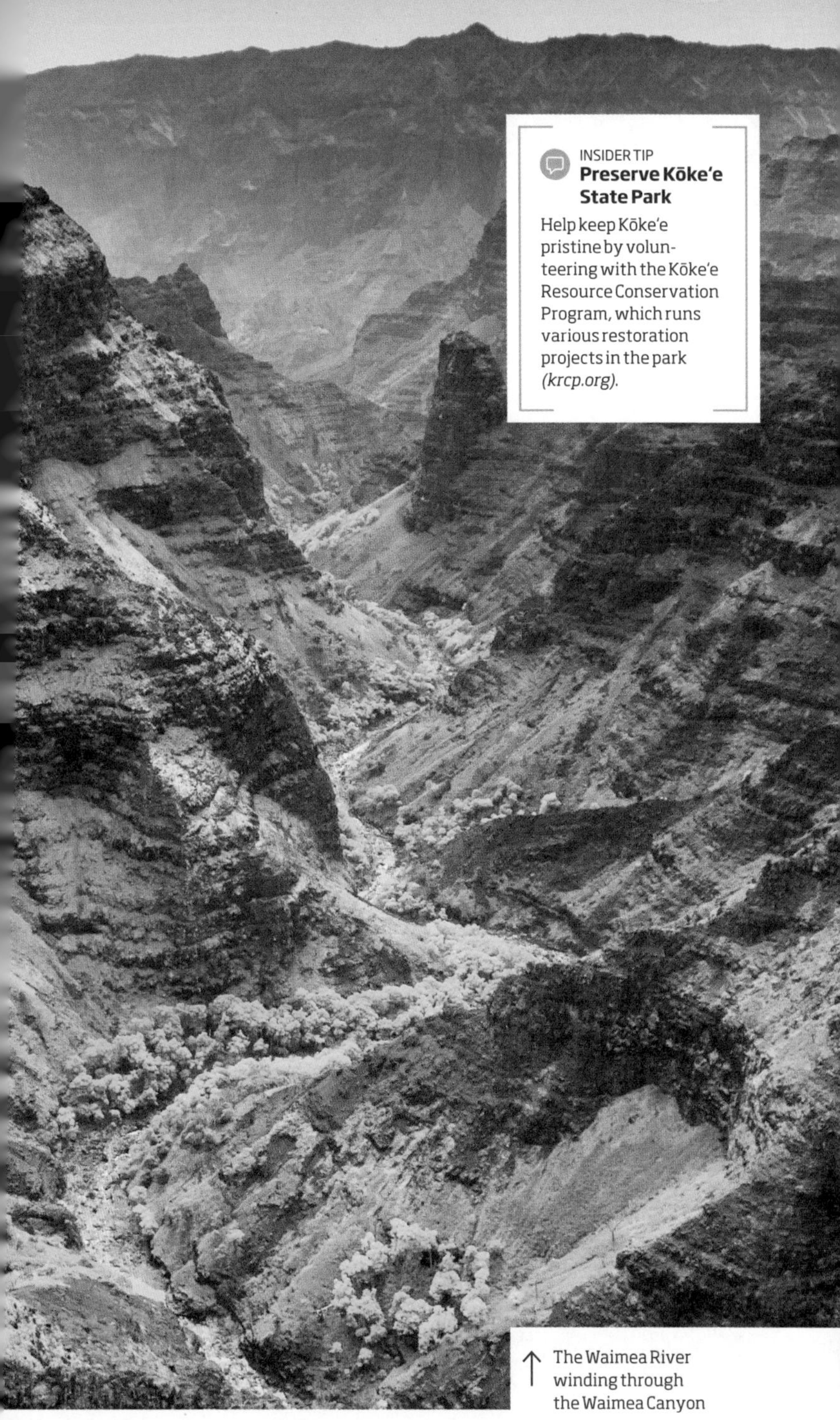

INSIDER TIP
Preserve Kōke‘e State Park

Help keep Kōke‘e pristine by volunteering with the Kōke‘e Resource Conservation Program, which runs various restoration projects in the park *(krcp.org)*.

↑ The Waimea River winding through the Waimea Canyon

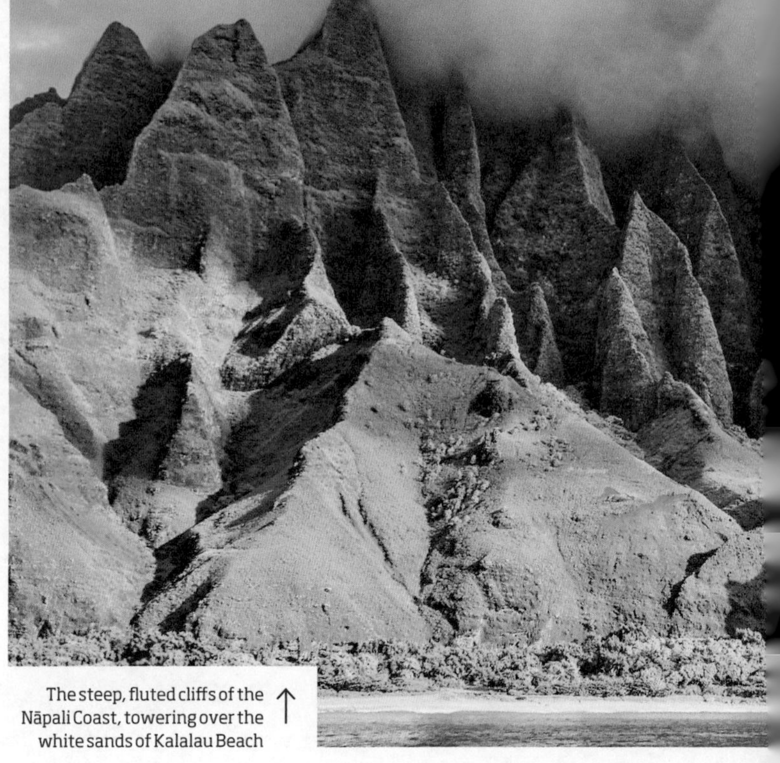

The steep, fluted cliffs of the Nāpali Coast, towering over the white sands of Kalalau Beach

3

NĀPALI COAST STATE WILDERNESS PARK

Kuhio Highway (Hwy 560), 38 miles (61 km) NW of Līhu'e Dawn-dusk daily dlnr.hawaii.gov

This remote park on Kaua'i's northwestern shore is a place of otherworldly natural beauty. Here, towering, razor-edged cliffs – thickly draped in lush rainforest and interspersed by shadowy valleys rife with gushing waterfalls – plummet steeply down to meet the deep-blue ocean and the occasional sandy beach.

Around eight centuries ago, the Nāpali Coast was populated by Polynesian settlers who were lured here by its fish-abundant waters and gorges full of game. They left behind evidence of their existence in the form of stone terraces and temple ruins that are still found along its shores. Today, this area – now uninhabited – is a protected park due to the uniqueness of its flora and fauna, which have evolved here in relative isolation. You might spy delicate little bog orchids and scarlet-colored *'i'iwi* honeycreeper birds.

The park also features the world-renowned 22-mile (36-km) Kalalau Trail *(p220)*, which only experienced hikers should undertake. This challenging one-way trail –starting near Ke'e Beach and ending at Kalalau Beach – passes through thick tropical brush, over streams, and across valleys, as well as scaling steep cliffs. While hiking this multi-day route, you may be able to spot the tiny *'anianiau* bird, the smallest honeycreeper in Hawaii. Apart from this hiking route, much of the park is impossible to explore on foot, so take to the skies and seas instead. Helicopter trips here soar over high fluted peaks, dip into wide canyons, and get up close to cascading waterfalls. Catamarans sail along the park's pristine coast, offering the chance to snorkel and spot dolphins.

↑ The small *'anianiau* honeycreeper, a bird endemic to the forests of Kaua'i

↑ Watching a dolphin jumping out of the water on a boat trip off the Nāpali Coast

TOP 4 SEA CAVES TO SEE ON A BOAT TRIP

Open Ceiling
This hollowed-out lava tube cave is also known as Pukalani, meaning, "hole into the heavens."

Wai'ahu'akua
The longest cave on the Nāpali Coast has two entrances and a gushing waterfall.

Honopū Arch
This high sea arch between two white-sand beaches has appeared in many Hollywood movies.

Honeymooners
Dark and narrow upon entry, this cave opens up onto a white-sand beach with a waterfall streaming down next to it.

A LONG WALK
KALALAU TRAIL

Length 11 miles (18 km) **Stopping-off points** Ke Ahu A Laka, Hanakāpī'ai Falls, Hanakoa Falls **Terrain** Dirt track, which can be muddy, rocky, and slippery

The precipitous cliffs of the Nāpali Coast make it impossible for the road to continue west of Kē'ē Beach, but hardy hikers can follow the narrow Kalalau Trail a further 11 miles (18 km) to the isolated Kalalau Valley. One of the most dramatic hikes in the world, it threads its way through a lush, rugged, and almost primeval-looking landscape. While this is not an expedition to undertake lightly, a half-day round-trip to Hanakāpī'ai Valley is within most people's capabilities and provides an unforgettable wilderness experience. The trail gets drier as it heads west, but the initial stretches can be very muddy, with dense vegetation. Negotiating this tangled forest of *hala* (pandanus) trees often requires scrambling over rock falls, or picking your way among slippery tree roots.

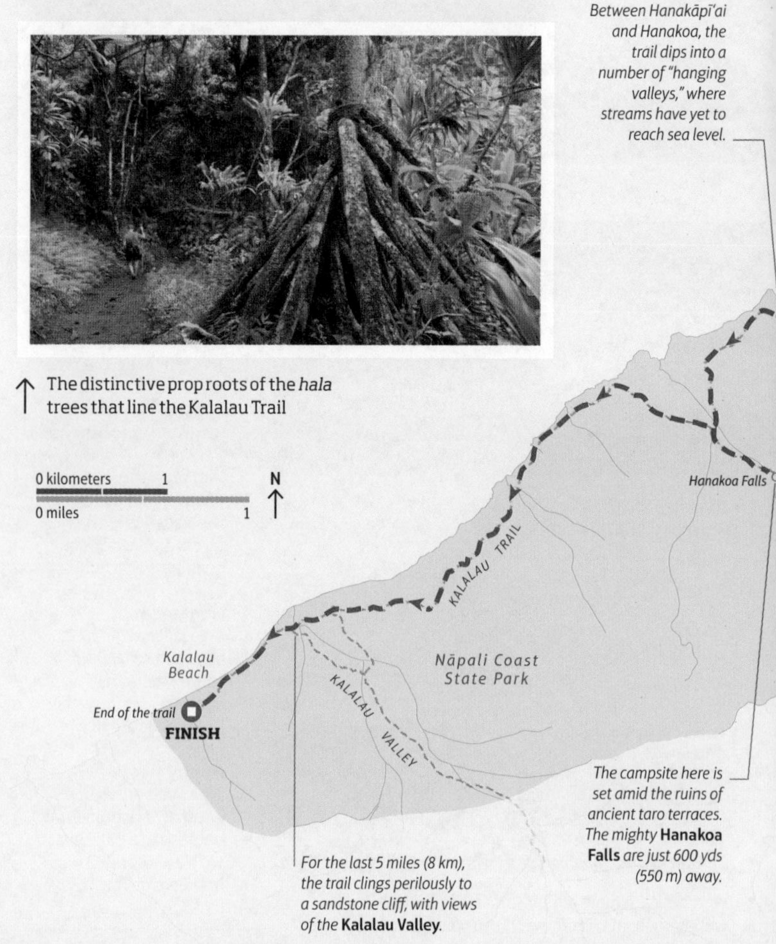

↑ The distinctive prop roots of the *hala* trees that line the Kalalau Trail

Between Hanakāpī'ai and Hanakoa, the trail dips into a number of "hanging valleys," where streams have yet to reach sea level.

The campsite here is set amid the ruins of ancient taro terraces. The mighty **Hanakoa Falls** *are just 600 yds (550 m) away.*

For the last 5 miles (8 km), the trail clings perilously to a sandstone cliff, with views of the **Kalalau Valley**.

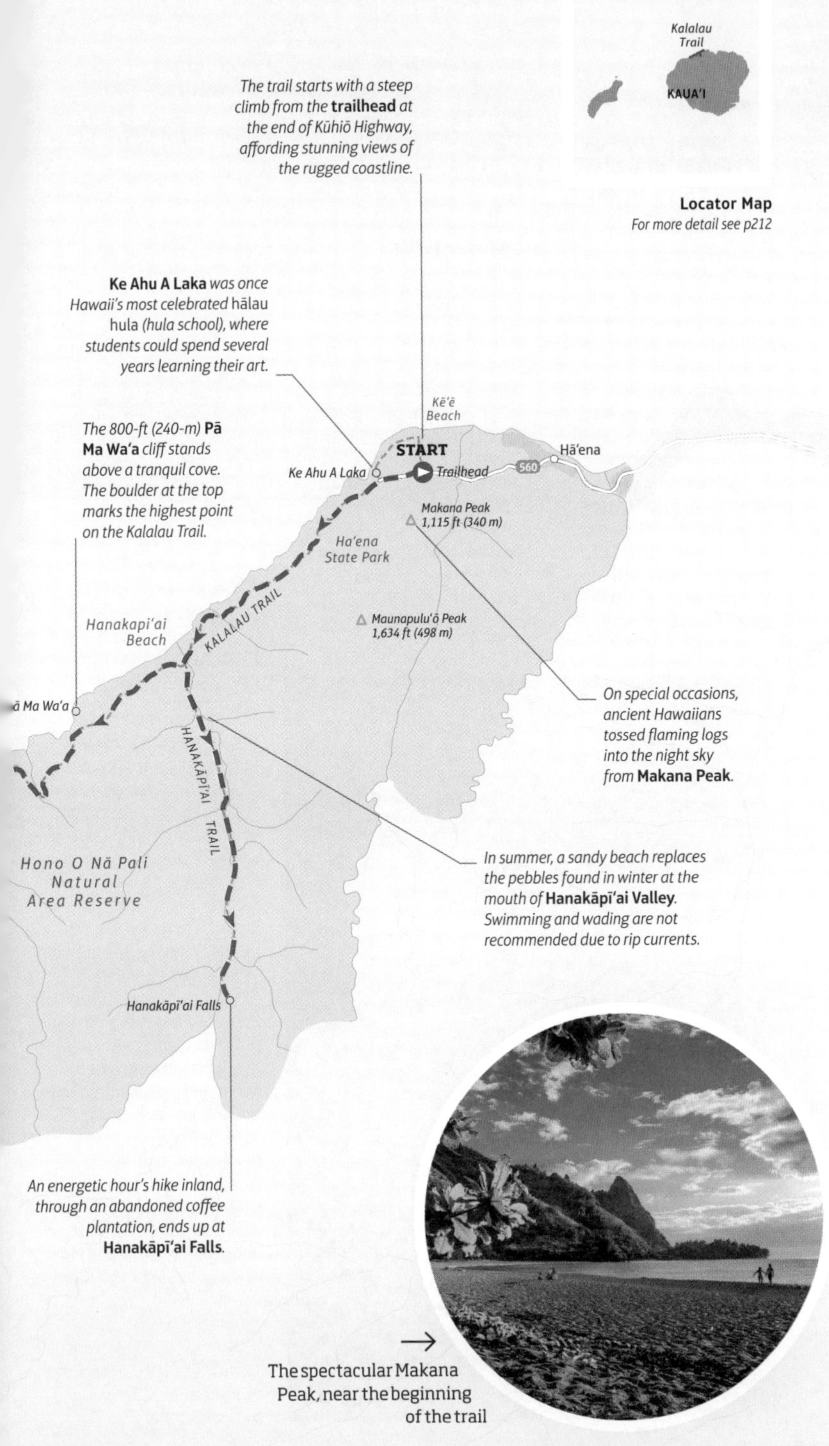

Locator Map

For more detail see p212

The trail starts with a steep climb from the ***trailhead*** *at the end of Kūhiō Highway, affording stunning views of the rugged coastline.*

Ke Ahu A Laka *was once Hawaii's most celebrated* hālau hula *(hula school), where students could spend several years learning their art.*

The 800-ft (240-m) **Pā Ma Wa'a** *cliff stands above a tranquil cove. The boulder at the top marks the highest point on the Kalalau Trail.*

On special occasions, ancient Hawaiians tossed flaming logs into the night sky from **Makana Peak**.

In summer, a sandy beach replaces the pebbles found in winter at the mouth of **Hanakāpī'ai Valley**. *Swimming and wading are not recommended due to rip currents.*

An energetic hour's hike inland, through an abandoned coffee plantation, ends up at **Hanakāpī'ai Falls**.

→

The spectacular Makana Peak, near the beginning of the trail

EXPERIENCE MORE

4

Wailua

**Kūhiō Hwy (Hwy 56), 6 miles (10 km) N of Līhu'e**
4473 Pahe`e St, Suite F, Līhu'e; (808) 245-3971

On Kaua'i's Coconut Coast (eastern shore), the town of Wailua is an ideal base for the outdoor recreational activities found along the Wailua River and up the Sleeping Giant mountain range. Several upscale resorts and casual restaurants and cafés line Wailua Beach, a sandy, windy strand suitable for surfers, kiteboarders, and bodyboarders. South of Wailua Beach is Lae Nani Beach, a small crescent with rocky tidal pools that are frequented by green sea turtles. A human-made enclosed beach area is ideal for kids to swim.

5

Wailua Falls

**Mā'alo Rd (Hwy 583), 5 miles (8 km) N of Līhu'e**
Līhu'e

The one winding road through old sugarcane fields, which branches left from the main highway a mile (1.5 km) north of Līhu'e, leads directly to the 80-ft (24-m) Wailua Falls.

From the roadside parking lot, you can admire the white cascade as it tumbles from a sheer ledge. After heavy rain, the river also bursts from a couple of natural tunnels hollowed into the rock wall below. If possible, try to visit the falls in the morning when the sun glistens off the pool below. Visitors should note that the steep and slippery trail that leads down to the pool is closed due to the instability of the cliffside.

Wailua Falls has been used for many movie backdrops, as well as the TV series *Fantasy Island* from the late 1970s. Legend has it, the falls were also used by Hawaiian royalty to test their endurance by jumping into the pool below, though many didn't survive.

Fern Grotto

Wailua River
Waipouli **Daily**

This large cave behind a fern-draped rock face is famous for its beauty. A paved path, lined with lush foliage, leads to the grotto, where you may end up being serenaded with the *Hawaiian Wedding Song* – it's a popular spot for wedding ceremonies. Pleasure barges make trips up the Wailua River to the grotto from a marina 2 miles (3 km) downstream. The hour-long narrated cruise passes by some pretty scenery; the riverbanks are covered in palm-like pandanus plants and piri grass.

Farther up the river are the magnificent Uluwehi Falls. To access these 120-ft (37-m) cascades you have to kayak upriver and then trek along a dense rainforest trail; caution is advised as it can be slippery.

The tumbling twin cascades of Wailua Falls, surrounded by lush greenery

The popular golden sandy beach at Lydgate State Park ↑

Did You Know?

A bridge makes it impossible to sail up the Wailua River from the ocean.

Wailua Complex of Heiaus

Kūhiō Hwy (Hwy 56) Waipouli 4473 Pahe`e St, Suite F; (808) 245-3971

This trail of sacred sites, also known as the King's Highway, runs through the Wailua Valley, which was once the seat of power in ancient Kaua'i. Along it lie four *heiaus* (temples) and a *pu'uhonua* (place of refuge), as well as several other important sites.

The highway started south of the Wailua River in what is now Lydgate State Park, known for its popular beach. Only vestiges survive here of the mighty stone walls of the Hikinaakalā Heiau (the name means "Rising of the Sun"), a temple where worshipers would greet the dawn. Farther along the King's Highway, up Kuamo'o Road (Hwy 580), lies a pair of boulders known as the Birthing Stones; as per tradition, only chiefs whose mothers gave birth while wedged between them could ever rule Kaua'i.

Sleeping Giant

1.5 miles (2.5 km) NW of Wailua Waipouli

Overlooking the ocean is the undulating ridge of Nounou Mountain. This long, low hillock is more commonly known as the Sleeping Giant, thanks to an outline resembling a huge human figure lying on its back.

Three distinct hiking trails climb from its east, west, and south sides. They are reached from Kūhiō Highway (Hwy 56), Kāmala Road (Hwy 581), and Kuamo'o Road (Hwy 580) respectively. They converge to follow the alarmingly narrow crest, arriving at a meadow-like clearing in the forest at the top, which is a prime picnic spot offering panoramic coastal views.

STAY

Kauai Shores Hotel
Beachside budget hotel with colorful rooms, a pool, and yoga classes.

420 Papaloa Rd, Wailua kauaishoreshotel.com

Fern Grotto Inn
Plantation-style cottages with modern interiors and coconut grove views. Free use of bicycles, kayaks, and beach gear.

4561 Kuamoo Rd, Wailua kauaicottages.com

Waipouli Beach Resort
Elegant beachfront suites with kid-friendly pools and a spa.

4-820 Kūhiō Hwy, Wailua outrigger.com

$$$

9

Kīlauea Point

Kīlauea Rd, off Kūhiō Highway (Hwy 56), 10 miles (16 km) NW of Anahola Kīlauea 4473 Pahe`e St, Suite F, Līhu'e; (808) 245-3971

The Hawaiian name Kīlauea ("much spewing") applies not only to the southernmost volcano on Hawai'i Island but also to the northernmost spot on the Hawaiian archipelago, Kaua'i's Kīlauea Point. Here the name refers not to spouting lava, but rather to the raging waves that foam around the base of this rocky promontory. Together with a couple of tiny offshore islets, the windswept clifftop has been set aside as the **Kīlauea Point National Wildlife Refuge**, a sanctuary for Pacific seabirds. Here, birdwatchers can see frigatebirds, Laysan albatrosses, and many other species.

A short walk beyond the visitor center leads to the red-and-white Kīlauea Lighthouse, which marks the beginning of Kaua'i's North Shore. When erected in 1913, the lighthouse held the largest clamshell lens in the world, but that has now been supplanted by a much smaller structure on its far side. Tours take place on Wednesdays and Saturdays.

As you approach the tip of the headland, extensive views open up to the west beyond Secret Beach and Princeville to the emerald-hued Nāpali cliffs, which are widely thought to be one of the most beautiful places on earth. The exposed oceanfront slopes to the east, meanwhile, are flecked with thousands of white seabirds and can be explored on ranger-led walking tours.

The most dramatic views of Kīlauea Lighthouse and, in winter especially, of the mighty waves that pound northern Kaua'i are from the vast shelf of glorious yellow sand known as Secret Beach. To reach it, turn right onto Kalihiwai Road,

INSIDER TIP
Spot Marine Life

From the headland near Kīlauea Lighthouse, you have the chance of spotting humpback whales in winter, dolphins in spring and summer, and green sea turtles in fall. Rare monk seals can also be observed here throughout the year.

Looking down on the rocky, vegetation-clad cliffs at Kīlauea Point, and *(inset)* the red-and-white Kīlauea Lighthouse

half a mile (800 m) west of the Kīlauea turnoff, then follow a red-dirt track that cuts away to the right. From its far end, a trail zig-zags through woods, coming out at a luscious tropical cove. Even in summer the sea tends to be too rough for swimming. However, it is worth walking the length of the beach to see the white surf crashing against the black lava rocks, and the glorious waterfall at the far end, nearest the lighthouse.

Kīlauea Point National Wildlife Refuge
Kīlauea Point
(808) 828-1413 10am-4pm Wed-Sat (book in advance) Federal hols

Mount Wai'ale'ale

11 miles (18 km) W of Wailua

Mount Wai'ale'ale, meaning "overflowing water," is one of the wettest places on earth. Some 36.5 ft (11 m) of rain each year cascades down its green-velvet walls. The summit is normally wreathed in mists.

Unless you take a helicopter tour, Wai'ale'ale can only be glimpsed from below. Follow Kuamo'o Road (Hwy 580) past 'Ōpaeka'a Falls and the Keahua Forestry Arboretum, and if the clouds clear you will be confronted by astonishing views of a sheer, pleated cliff face. Dirt roads lead through the forest to its base, where the Wailua River thunders down from the 5,148-ft (1,570-m) peak. These roads are dangerous, if not impassable, after heavy rain.

Kapa'a

Kūhiō Hwy (Hwy 56), 10 miles (16 km) N of Līhu'e
4473 Pahe`e St, Suite F, Līhu'e; (808) 245-3971

Tourist development along Kaua'i's East Shore is mostly concentrated into the 5-mile (8-km) coastal strip that runs north of the Wailua River. Maps mark distinct communities at Wailua and Waipouli, but the only real town here is Kapa'a, farther north, home of the annual Coconut Festival in October. Most of the false-front buildings that line its wooden boardwalks hold restaurants, souvenir stores, or equipment rental outlets, but Kapa'a still maintains the look of a late 19th-century plantation village. The fringe of sand at the ocean's edge is divided into a number of beach parks.

On the first Saturday of every month, the Kapa'a Art Walk takes place in Old Town Kapa'a. Shops, restaurants, and cafés stay open late, while artists showcase their work and live music and fire dancing performances entertain.

The first of the more appealing beaches north of Kapa'a is tucked out of sight half a mile (800 m) from the highway and is reached by a forest trail that drops to the right not far past mile marker 11. This uncrowded, pretty stretch of sand is known as Donkey Beach.

DRINK

Moloa'a Sunrise Fruit Stand

Stop for smoothies at this shack found on the road between Anahola and Kīlauea Point. Try the Tropical Treat, made with mango, banana, guava, pineapple, and papaya.

6011 Koolau Rd, Anahola Sat-Mon moloaasunrisefruitstand.com

Anahola

Kūhiō Hwy (Hwy 56), 14 miles (22 km) N of Līhu'e
4473 Pahe`e St, Suite F, Līhu'e; (808) 245-3971

The small, scattered village of Anahola overlooks the sweeping, palm-fringed curve of Anahola Bay, an ancient surfing site. North of town, just inland of the highway, is the picturesque Anahola Baptist Church. Set against a beautiful mountain backdrop, the church makes a lovely photograph.

Nearby Anahola Beach is not too crowded, despite its combination of beautiful setting, safe swimming, and convenient access. Reached by a spur road looping down from Kūhiō Highway (Hwy 56) shortly after mile marker 13, the beach faces the most sheltered section of Anahola Bay. The area nearest the showers is reserved for family swimming, while the slightly more turbulent waters farther north are enjoyed by surfers.

EAT

Fresh Bite
A food truck offering farm-to-table eats, including organic salads, wraps, and sandwiches.

5100 Kūhiō Hwy, Hanalei Sat & Sun freshbitekauai.com

Hanalei Bread Company
Busy little café that's great for a hearty breakfast sandwich and strong coffee.

5-5161 Kūhiō Hwy, Hanalei hanaleibreadco.com

Hanalei Gourmet
Relaxed spot with pub-style dishes and great cocktails. The fresh catch-of-the-day fish dish is always good.

5-5161 Kūhiō Hwy, Hanalei Sat & Sun hanaleigourmet.com

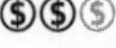

Tahiti Nui
Casual spot serving Polynesian dishes. Nightly live music adds to the atmosphere.

5-5134 Kūhiō Hwy, Hanalei Sat thenui.com

Bar Acuda
Great tapas and wine bar with a patio and top service. Reservations recommended.

5-5161 Kūhiō Hwy, Hanalei Sun & Mon cudahanalei.com

The sweeping crescent-shaped bay at Hanalei, enclosed by green hills ↑

Kalihiwai Beach

Kūhiō Hwy (Hwy 56), 26 miles (42 km) NW of Līhu'e 4473 Pahe`e St, Suite F; (808) 245-3971

Shielded behind a grove of ironwood trees, this lovely, crescent-shaped beach is located at the mouth of the Kalihiwai River. In winter, it's a good spot for surfing and bodysurfing, although the waves here can be powerful and are best left to experts. In summer, it's a good beach for swimming, although this is often dependent upon the conditions. The river here also offers excellent opportunities for kayaking.

Around 5 miles (8 km) west of Kalihiwai beach is the quiet 'Anini Beach. Here, you'll find around 3 miles (5 km) of golden sand, perfect for lounging on. Between the beach and the coral reef that lies 200 yds (180 m) offshore, shallow turquoise waters provide the safest swimming on Kaua'i's North Shore. There is also excellent snorkeling on the coral reef itself, as well as an idyllic campsite set among the trees. You can access 'Anini Beach from Anini Road or via a 30-minute scenic walking trail from Princeville, beginning at the Westin Princeville Ocean Resort Villas.

Did You Know?

By law, no building on Kaua'i is allowed to be built taller than a palm tree.

Hanalei

Kūhiō Hwy (Hwy 56), 31 miles (50 km) NW of Līhu'e 4473 Pahe`e St, Suite F; (808) 245-3971

Nowhere deserves the name Hanalei, or "crescent bay," more than this half-moon inlet, fringed with golden sand and cradled by soaring green cliffs, that lies west of Princeville.

The flat valley floor of the Hanalei River is dominated by taro, planted under the auspices of the **Hanalei National Wildlife Refuge** to re-create the preferred habitat of the state's endangered waterbirds. Criss-crossed by irrigation channels and scattered with inaccessible islands that poke from the mud, it is home to an ever-changing population of coots, herons, stilts, and transient migratory birds. The valley's lush, green landscape is best seen from a viewpoint on Kūhiō Highway, just west of

PICTURE PERFECT
Hanalei Pier at Sunrise

Capture a perfect sunrise or sunset photo from Hanalei Bay. Angle your camera to catch the sun's rays illuminating Hanalei Pier in the foreground, while high, fluted green mountain ridges rise behind.

the Princeville turnoff as the refuge is closed to the public.

The slender bridge across the Hanalei River is the first of a series of one-lane bridges that slow North Shore traffic to a virtual crawl, helping to protect the region from overdevelopment. The village of Hanalei, set on the far side, is still recognizably a plantation settlement but is kept busy these days catering to the needs of a community of surfers and Nāpali adventurers. A trio of stunning mountains forms a magnificent backdrop – Hīhīmanu to the east, Māmalahoa to the west, and, in the center, the sublime Nāmolokama, furrowed with over 20 waterfalls that combine to form Wai'oli Stream.

At first glance, Hanalei Bay might look like an ideal harbor, but many ships have come to grief on its submerged reefs and only shallow-draft pleasure yachts now use the jetty. There are several attractive spots for sunbathing or camping, but swimming is only advisable from Waikoko Beach at the western end.

Hanalei's most visible relic of the past is the missionary complex, set on landscaped lawns west of the town center and backed by high, tree-clad mountains. The town's earliest Christian edifice, Wai'oli Church, was put up in 1841. This large wooden structure now functions as a social hall, set back to the right of its successor, the 1912-vintage **Wai'oli Hui'ia Church**. With its vivid green shingles, stained glass, and gray-capped belfry, nestled beneath a spreading palm tree, Wai'oli Hui'ia is one of the loveliest buildings on Kaua'i. Tucked away behind it, the **Wai'oli Mission House** was home to generations of two missionary families, including the Wilcoxes, whose descendants lived here until the late 1970s. Although some of the original furnishings have gone, period replacements provide a sense of 19th-century Hanalei.

KAUA'I IN THE MOVIES

The fabulous scenery of Kaua'i has served as a backdrop in many Hollywood blockbusters, from a Caribbean paradise in *Islands in the Stream* (1977) to South America in *Raiders of the Lost Ark* (1981). The island has starred alongside the big screen's biggest names. Frank Sinatra's war-torn Pacific-island beach in *None but the Brave* (1965) was Pīla'a Beach, east of Kīlauea. Elvis Presley's greatest box-office hit, *Blue Hawaii* (1961), climaxed with a kitsch wedding ceremony at the former Coco Palms Resort. The Honopū Valley on the Nāpali Coast stood in as Skull Island in the 1977 remake of *King Kong* and much of *Jurassic Park* (1993) was shot in Hanapēpē Valley. Kaua'i is probably best remembered for its role in Rodgers and Hammerstein's musical *South Pacific* (1958). More recent movies that have used Kaua'i as a backdrop include *Jurassic World* (2015) and *Jungle Cruise* (2021).

Hanalei National Wildlife Refuge
Ohiki Rd Viewpoint: 9am-3pm Tue-Sat fws.gov

Wai'oli Hui'ia Church
5 Kūhiō Hwy (Hwy 56) 10am-2pm Mon & Wed-Fri, 9:30am-noon Sun waiolihuiiachurch.org

Wai'oli Mission House
Kūhiō Hwy (Hwy 56) (808) 245-3202 9am-3pm Tue, Thu & Sat Federal hols

15

Hā'ena and Kē'ē Beaches

Off Kūhiō Hwy (Hwy 56), 7 miles (11 km) W of Hanalei **dlnr.hawaii.gov**

Two beach parks with similar names are located near the end of the highway along the North Shore. The first one, Hā'ena Beach Park, offers a pleasant campsite in a coconut grove where the shoreline is too exposed for safe swimming. Ten minutes' walk east from here is Tunnels Beach, whose extensive reef is one of Kaua'i's most popular snorkeling sites. The name refers to the tubular waves that lure the surfers in winter.

Immediately west of here, the second park, Hā'ena State Park, is mostly inaccessible to casual visitors (advance reservations are necessary), having been set aside to spare this part of the coast from development rather than make it available for public use. Kē'ē Beach, at the end of the road but still within the state park, is one of the most beautiful of all the North Shore beaches, its glowing yellow sands all but engulfed by rampant tropical vegetation. The turquoise inshore lagoon provides an irresistible cooling-off spot for hikers back from the Kalalau Trail *(p220)*, plus a much-loved swimming and snorkeling site. However, the often turbulent waters around and beyond the reef can be dangerous.

A legend identifies this beach as the original birthplace of hula. Pele the volcano goddess is said to have been enticed here in a dream by the sweet music of a Kauaian warrior, and they promptly fell in love. The raised headland just west of the beach holds the remains of Hawaii's first *hālau hula* (hula school).

16

Lumaha'i Beach

Off Kūhiō Hwy (Hwy 56), 2 miles (3 km) W of Hanalei  **Hanalei**

Shortly beyond Hanalei Bay, a small roadside pull-off marks the top of a steep trail down to the spellbinding Lumaha'i Beach. Thanks to its appearance in the movie *South Pacific* *(p227)*, this is declared to be the most romantic beach in Hawaii. Its long and broad golden sands are perfect for an evening walk.

The mountain peak of Bali Hai dominated the beach on screen, but that was due to technical trickery; in fact, it's a tiny outcrop called Makana at the end of a ridge, 4 miles (6.5 km) farther west.

↑ A dramatic sunset over the sandy shore of Tunnels Beach, near Hā'ena State Park

17

Princeville

Kūhiō Hwy (Hwy 56), 30 miles (48 km) NW of Līhu'e  **Hanalei-Lihue** **4473 Pahe`e St, Suite F; (808) 245-3971**

The former sugar plantation of Princeville, set on the rolling meadows of a headland above Hanalei Bay, has been developed as Kaua'i's most exclusive resort. Its centerpiece, the chic 1 Hotel Hanalei Bay, offers long-range views of the North Shore mountains, which are now shared by a golf course, as well as more hotels, condominiums, vacation homes, and a small shopping mall.

Below the bluffs, Princeville features some delightful little beaches. The best of the bunch, Pu'upōā Beach, is reached by trails that drop from both 1 Hotel Hanalei Bay and the Hanalei Bay Resort next door. Its wide sands offer dramatic views across Hanalei Bay, as well as over the wetlands to the peaks that tower behind Hanalei *(p226)*, and there's excellent family swimming in the shallow waters. Pu'upōā Beach stretches as far as the

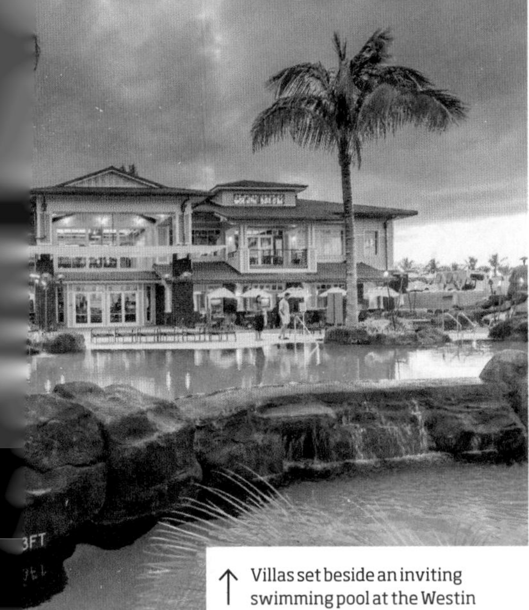

↑ Villas set beside an inviting swimming pool at the Westin Princeville Ocean Resort

mouth of the Hanalei River, so rented kayaks can easily be paddled upstream.

Princeville-based surfers and snorkelers flock to Pali Ke Kua Beach, also called Hideaways Beach, by way of a trail down from the Pali Ke Kua condominiums buildings 1 and 2.

Tucked away in the jungle valleys of Princeville are the **Princeville Botanical Gardens**. The gardens offer an excellent tour of the verdant property, which includes honey, fruit, and chocolate tastings.

Princeville Botanical Gardens
3840 Ahonui Pl
9:30am Mon, Tue, Thu & Fri (by appt only) kauai botanicalgardens.com

INSIDER TIP
Princeville Ranch

For an adventurous day away from the coast, visit the Princeville Ranch *(princeville ranch.com)*. It offers horseback riding lessons and horseback trail rides for children.

18 

Limahuli Garden

5-8291 Kūhiō Hwy (Hwy 56), 6 miles (10 km) W of Hanalei 8:30am-4pm Tue-Sat Jan 1, Thanksgiving & Dec 25 ntbg.org

The lush Limahuli Garden (reservations mandatory) is located a quarter of a mile (400 m) before the end of Kūhiō Highway, in a steep, high valley. In ancient times, the Limahuli Valley was part of a self-sufficient *ahupua'a* (a wedge-shaped division of land running from mountain to sea). Since then, it has barely been occupied, with the exception of the notorious "Taylor Camp," a commune that was run from 1969 to 1977 on land owned by actress Elizabeth Taylor's brother.

Part of the valley remains in sufficiently good condition to have been set aside as a botanical sanctuary, protecting both indigenous Hawaiian plants and species brought to the islands by early Polynesian settlers. The sanctuary's aim is to preserve the native species and increase their numbers. Visitors can explore only a small portion that begins at the road and stretches inland, supporting reconstructed ancient taro terraces that climb the hillside. A network of trails allows you to meander through a mixed forest of unusual trees, such as the Polynesian-introduced *kukui* or candlenut, once prized for its oil, and the native *'ōhi'a 'ai* or mountain apple. From the higher slopes there are wonderful views of the coastline, as well as glimpses of the Nāpali cliffs to the west. Inland, the strangely eroded mountains loom above Limahuli Stream, overshadowing the off-limits Limahuli Preserve.

STAY

Hanalei Bay Resort
Gorgeous garden setting with views of Hanalei Bay and condo-style rooms.

5380 Honoiki Rd, Princeville
hanaleibayresort.com

$$

Westin Princeville Ocean Resort Villas
Upscale resort ideal for couples and families, with roomy suites and lovely pools.

3838 Wyllie Rd, Princeville
marriott.com

$$$

1 Hotel Hanalei Bay
Luxurious beachfront property with excellent dining options, a golf course, and a kids' club.

5520 Ka Haku Rd, Princeville
1hotels.com

$$$

Sunrise over the dramatic Makawehi Bluff near Poʻipū

Waimea

Kaumuali'i Hwy (Hwy 50), 24 miles (39 km) W of Līhu'e 4473 Pahe`e St, Suite F; (808) 245-3971

It was here in 1778 that the crewmen of Captain Cook's third Pacific voyage set foot on Hawaiian soil. A plaque marks the site of the landfall and a statue of Cook can be found in the town center. The beach where he landed, however, is named not in his honor but after Lucy Wright, Waimea's first Hawaiian teacher. Situated west of the Waimea River, the black-sand beach is lined with coconut palms, trees, and swaths of grassy areas.

Waimea's Theater, dating back to 1938, is in full Art Deco restored splendor and has single movie screenings several times a week.

Just across Waimea River, a headland holds what's left of Russian Fort Elizabeth. This star-shaped edifice was built by George Schäffer in 1816. A German doctor, pretending to be a naturalist but working as a spy for the Russian-American Company, he had gained the confidence of Kaumuali'i, the chief of Kaua'i, and decided to double-cross his employers. He and Kaumuali'i hatched a plot to conquer the archipelago and divide it between the Tsar of Russia and the chief. Within a year, fooled into thinking that the US and Russia were at war, Schäffer fled the islands. His fort served the government for 50 more years but is now dilapidated.

Did You Know?

Waimea's Captain Cook statue is a replica of one found in the seaside town of Whitby in the UK.

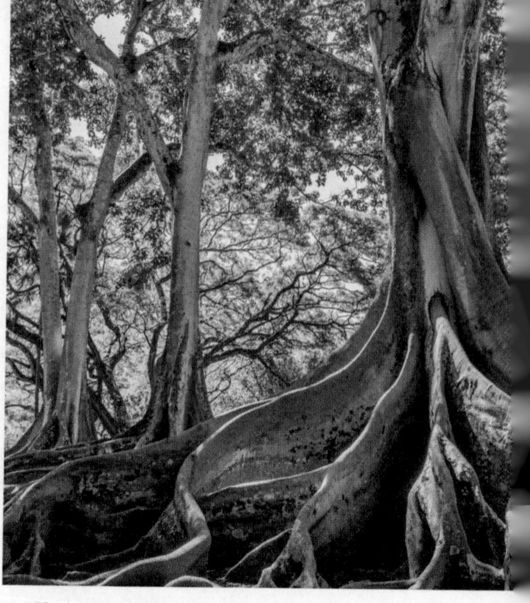

The impressive Moreton Bay fig trees, found in Allerton Garden

Allerton Garden

4425 Lawa'i Rd, Kōloa Hours vary, check website Federal hols ntbg.org

Lāwa'i Valley stretches back from the pretty little cove of Lāwa'i Kai, 2 miles (3 km) west of Po'ipū. Occupied in antiquity by taro farmers and later used by Chinese immigrants to grow rice, the valley became Queen Emma's favorite retreat in the 1870s. In the 1930s, it was bought by the Allertons, a Chicago banking family, and a plot near the sea was exquisitely landscaped to create Allerton Garden.

Bequeathed to the National Tropical Botanical Garden by the last of the Allerton family in 1987, the valley, sadly, was devastated by Hurricane Iniki in 1992. The Allertons' oceanfront home and Queen Emma's cottage have been fully restored, however, and the Allerton Garden is once more a wonderful showpiece. Unlike its counterpart at Limahuli *(p229)*, the garden aims to delight the eye rather than concentrate on native plants. Visitors are transported from the visitor center near Kōloa to the otherwise out-of-reach site via a mandatory 15-minute shuttle ride, and from there tour the garden on foot. The Allertons conceived the design as a series of separate "rooms," and each section, such as the serene Diana Fountain or the lovely Italianate Art Deco Mermaid Fountain, has its own character. The plants are the real stars, however, from heliconias and bromeliads to assorted tropical fruits in the orchards. Species familiar as houseplants in chillier climes run riot, while graceful palms line the placid stream that glides through the heart of the valley. Note the towering roots of the Moreton Bay fig trees, which featured in blockbusters like *Jurassic Park* and *Pirates of the Caribbean*.

Serious botanists will appreciate the chance to see rare species in the nursery, including *Kanaloa kahoolawensis*, a woody shrub whose only two known wild specimens were first identified on the uninhabited island of Kaho'olawe during the 1980s. Prior reservation is required to join the tour. Next door to the Allerton Garden is the McBryde Garden, which has a focus on native Hawaiian flora. The tours can combine both gardens or you can go on a self-guided tour of McBryde only. You can also opt for a sunset tour of the Allerton Garden, which incorporates a light dinner out on the *lanai* of the Allerton home, with views of the sun as it dips below the horizon on the Pacific.

DEPARTURE TO THE UNDERWORLD

Peppered with sea caves and home to an ancient Hawaiian temple within the base of the sea cliff, the area around Polihale Beach is said to be the departure point for the *'uhane* (souls) of the dead. They are thought to leave from here for Po, the Hawaiian underworld, out in the depths of the ocean. The *'uhane* would stay in the temple found here before making their final leap to meet the god Kanaloa, the ruler of the underworld, who is often in the shape of an octopus or squid.

21

Polihale Beach

 **5 miles (8 km) beyond the end of Kaumuali'i Hwy (Hwy 50), off Lower Saki Mana Rd**

The westernmost region of Kaua'i, shielded from the ocean winds in the rain shadow of the central mountains, is characterized by long, flat expanses of sand. A sizable chunk of the area has been taken over by the US military, whose installations include systems that would give early warning of another attack on Pearl Harbor.

Skirt the security fences by following the dirt roads inland, and 15 miles (24 km) northwest of Waimea you come to the vast expanse of Polihale Beach. The surf is far too ferocious for swimming, but it's a wonderful place for a walk, with the cliffs of the Nāpali Coast rising to the north. Head west from the end of the road and you'll reach the dunes known as the Barking Sands, whose hollow grains are said to groan and howl when disturbed by wind or a heavy footfall.

22

Ni'ihau

 **15 miles (24 km) SW of Kaua'i**

Just visible from the coast at Waimea, Ni'ihau is the smallest populated island in the chain, with 150 inhabitants. Owned by the Robinson family – descendants of Elizabeth Sinclair, who paid Kamehameha V $10,000 for the island in 1864 – it has few tourists. There is no hotel, airport, or cars; you can visit only by a costly helicopter tour that avoids the inhabited areas.

The isolation has since turned the island into an important stronghold of Hawaiian culture – Hawaiian is still the first language here. Locals support themselves with fishing, farming, and threading necklaces of the delicate *pūpū* (shells) that wash up on the beaches – Ni'ihau shell lei can sell for thousands of dollars. With annual rainfall of just 12 in (300 mm), Ni'ihau is able to support only minimal agriculture. The only town, Pu'uwai ("heart"), is on the west coast, and consists of a grid of dirt roads that are dotted with bungalows and colorful gardens.

↑ Remote Polihale Beach, with the soaring Nāpali cliffs providing a scenic backdrop

Hanapēpē

Kaumuali'i Hwy (Hwy 50), 18 miles (29 km) W of Līhu'e 4473 Pahe`e St, Suite F; (808) 245-3971

Between Waimea and Po'ipū, "Kaua'i's Biggest Little Town," as the locals call it, is an intriguing detour off Kaumuali'i Highway. Although taro was once grown in the valley, the village owes its late 19th-century look to the Chinese workers who farmed rice here.

Later, Hanapēpē was all but abandoned, but several of its timber-frame buildings have now reopened as galleries and craft shops, and there are several attractive restaurants catering to the visitors. On Friday nights Hanapēpē hosts an open art walk where galleries, shops, and restaurants open their doors till late and vendors line the streets selling locally made artwork.

Hanapēpē is also home to a famous swinging bridge, constructed in the early 1900s so that residents could cross the Hanapēpē River. On the town's shores is the unique Glass Beach, made entirely of sea glass smoothened over time by the crashing waves.

Kauai Coffee Company Visitor Center

870 Halewili Rd, Kalaheo 9am-5pm Mon-Fri, 10am-4pm Sat & Sun kauaicoffee.com

The largest coffee farm in the US, the Kauai Coffee Estate covers 3,100 acres (1,255 ha) and has over 4 million coffee trees. The estate takes pride in following environmentally friendly and sustainable farming practices, including running an efficient irrigation system and a composting program. Visitors can wander around on a free and informative walking tour, and sample the coffee at the visitor center shop, where coffee, ice cream, and other goodies are for sale.

GREAT VIEW

Maha'ulepu Heritage Trail

Running from Po'ipū's Shipwreck Beach to Punahoa Point, the 2-mile (3-km) coastal Maha'ulepu Heritage Trail offers stunning views over rolling dunes, rugged cliffs, and rocky shores.

Po'ipū

Hwy 520, 12 miles (19 km) SW of Līhu'e Kōloa Shuttle (twice a day from Shops at Kukui'ula mall) poipubeach.org

Sprawling to either side of the mouth of the Waikomo Stream, at the southern tip of Kaua'i, Po'ipū remains the island's most popular beach resort. In 1992, Hurricane Iniki ripped the roofs off its plush oceanfront hotels and filled their lobbies with sand and

Exploring the rock pools at Po'ipū Beach, while the tide is out ↑

ruined cars. Apart from the odd derelict property, Po'ipū is now back to normal.

The prime spot in the center of the beach is Po'ipū Beach Park, complete with lifeguards and a kids' playground. There's safe swimming offshore, and great snorkeling at its western end. To the east, Brennecke's Beach is more of a haunt for young surfers, while farther along, beyond Makahū'ena Point, the shoreline becomes a wilderness of sand dunes. Fossilized bones of long-extinct flightless birds have been found in this area, and many native plant species survive here and nowhere else. Another popular beach is the one known locally as Shipwreck Beach. A short walk east along the coast lie the lithified cliffs of the Makawehi Bluff.

The rudimentary jetty at the mouth of Waikomo Stream has been in use since the mid-1800s. Known as Kōloa Landing, it was built to serve Hawaii's first sugarcane plantation, established inland at Kōloa in 1835. Kōloa itself, with its wooden boardwalks and false-fronted stores, is a pleasant place for a stroll.

West of Po'ipū, the coast road ends at Spouting Horn, a natural blowhole in a ledge of black lava just back from the sea. It is dangerous, so don't get closer than the lookout.

Extending from Po'ipū to Kōloa is the Kōloa Heritage Trail – a 10-mile (16-km) route that can be walked, biked, or driven. The route includes 14 points of interest, starting with the Spouting Horn blowhole and ending at the Kōloa Missionary Church. A free map is available from the Po'ipū Beach Foundation's website.

Did You Know?

The fountains of white spume expelled from Spouting Horn can reach a height of 50 ft (15 m).

EAT

Puka Dog

This place offers hot dogs with a Hawaii-inspired twist, such as pineapple and mango relish.

2100 Hoone Rd, Po'ipū
pukadog.com

Little Fish Coffee

Fuel up with organic coffee, smoothies, açai bowls, and bagels from this cute café.

2294 Po'ipū Rd, Po'ipū
littlefishcoffee.com

Tidepools

Overlooking a lagoon, this restaurant at the Grand Hyatt serves decadent seafood dishes including polenta-crusted scallops.

1571 Po'ipū Rd, Po'ipū
hyatt.com

Sueoka Store

This century-old Asian grocery store serves snacks such as chicken bento lunch boxes.

5392 Kōloa Rd, Kōloa
sueokastore.com

SHOP

Warehouse 3540

Artist studios, home decor boutiques, and food trucks form this great marketplace.

3540 Kōloa Rd, Kaleheo
warehouse-3540.com

NEED TO KNOW

Interstate H-3 on the island of O'ahu

BEFORE YOU GO

Things change, so plan ahead to make the most of your trip. Be prepared for all eventualities by considering the following points before you travel.

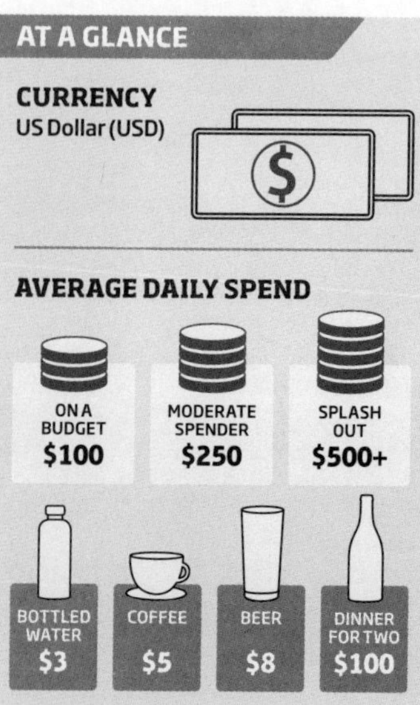

ESSENTIAL PHRASES

Hello	Aloha
Good morning	Aloha kakahiaka
Good evening	Aloha ahiahi
Thank you	Mahalo
You're welcome	'A'ole pilikia
Excuse me	E Kala mai

ELECTRICITY
Standard electric current is 120 volts and 60 Hz. Power sockets are types A (two flat prongs) and B (two flat prongs plus a round prong).

Passports and Visas

For entry requirements, including visas, consult your nearest US embassy or check with the **US Department of State**. Canadian visitors require a valid passport to enter the US. Citizens of the 41 countries that are part of the US Visa Waiver Program, including the UK, do not need a visa for stays of up to 90 days, but must apply in advance for the Electronic System for Travel Authorization (**ESTA**) and have a valid passport. All other visitors will need a passport and tourist visa to enter. A return airline ticket is required to enter the US.

ESTA
W esta.cbp.dhs.gov/esta
US Department of State
W travel.state.gov

Government Advice

It is important to consult both your and the US government's advice before traveling. The **US State Department**, the **UK Foreign, Commonwealth and Development Office** and, the **Australian Department of Foreign Affairs and Trade** offer the latest information on security, health, and local regulations.

Australian Department of Foreign Affairs and Trade
W smartraveller.gov.au
UK Foreign, Commonwealth & Development Office
W gov.uk/foreign-travel-advice
US State Department
W travel.state.gov

Customs Information

You can find information on the laws relating to goods and currency taken in or out of Hawaii on the **Go Hawaii** official tourist board website.

Go Hawaii
W gohawaii.com

Insurance

We recommend that you take out a comprehensive insurance policy covering theft, loss

of belongings, medical care, cancellations, and delays, and read the small print carefully. Insurance is important when traveling in Hawaii as there is no universal health care in the US and so the cost of medical care is high. If you have a mainland health insurance plan, check to see if it's valid in Hawaii.

Vaccinations

No inoculations are required unless you come from, or have stopped in, an area suffering from an epidemic, particularly cholera or yellow fever.

Money

Credit and debit cards, including contactless, can be used for most transactions. ATMs are easily found and visitors can use their cards to withdraw cash. Have cash on hand for roadside stands, tips, and the occasional cash-only establishment.

Tipping is the norm. Around 15–20 per cent of the check is usual for waitstaff or $1 per drink for bartenders. When traveling by taxi, 10–15 per cent of the fare is expected. Tip luggage handlers $1–2 a bag and housekeeping $2–5 a day.

Booking Accommodations

There is an abundance of accommodation options in Hawaii, including luxury resorts and homey hotels. Camping can be an appealing prospect if you're on a budget. The Christmas holiday period, summer (particularly June to August), and spring break are the busiest times of year and prices rise accordingly. Book early to get the cheapest deals.

A hotel tax of at least 10 per cent is levied, which is often higher for certain resort areas like Waikīkī, plus parking and resort fees of $30 and $40 respectively.

Travelers with Specific Requirements

Most hotels, restaurants, and attractions provide wheelchair ramps, designated parking places, and accessible restrooms. Braille translations of important signs are also commonplace. The **Disability and Communication Access Board** website provides downloadable factsheets detailing access to parks, beaches, and other attractions.

Many of Hawaii's main attractions, including Pearl Harbor *(p110)* and Haleakalā National Park *(p154)*, offer services such as park brochures and signage in braille, wheelchair-accessible sights and areas, and the ability to request American Sign Language interpreters. Several beaches offer all-terrain wheelchairs; check the Go Hawaii website *(p238)* for further information.

Disability and Communication Access Board
W health.hawaii.gov/dcab

Language

Hawaii is the only US state with two official languages – English and Hawaiian, or 'Ōlelo Hawai'i. Roughly 0.1 per cent of Hawaii's population can speak the latter fluently, but this is on the rise.

Opening Hours

Situations can change quickly and unexpectedly. Always check before visiting attractions and hospitality venues for up-to-date opening hours and booking requirements.

Mondays Many museums and restaurants close.
Sundays Most banks close, and many businesses and attractions open only in the afternoon.
State Holidays Hours tend to vary or are limited for many attractions and businesses; most places close on Christmas and New Year's Day.

STATE HOLIDAYS

Jan 1	New Year's Day
3rd Mon in Jan	Martin Luther King Jr. Day
3rd Mon in Feb	Presidents' Day
Mar 26	Prince Kūhiō Day
Mar/Apr	Good Friday
Last Mon in May	Memorial Day
Jun 11	King Kamehameha I Day
Jul 4	Independence Day
3rd Fri in Aug	Statehood Day
1st Mon in Sep	Labor Day
Nov 11	Veterans Day
4th Thu in Nov	Thanksgiving
Dec 25	Christmas

GETTING AROUND

Whether you are visiting just one island or hopping around the archipelago, discover how best to reach your destination and travel like a pro.

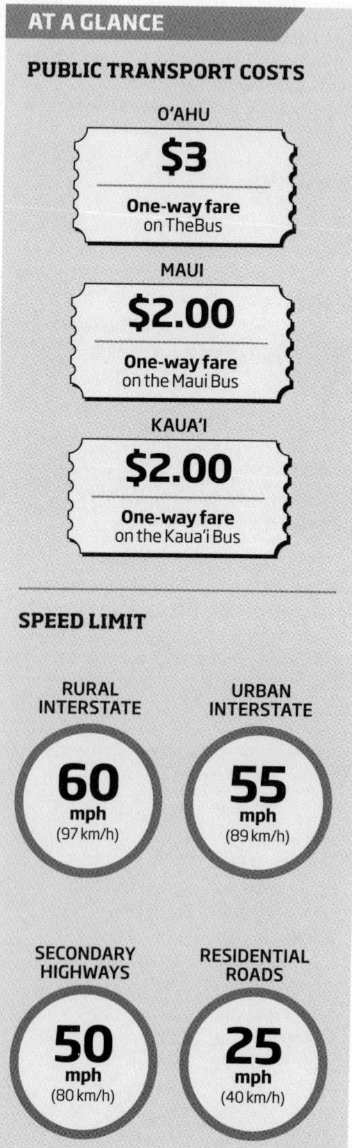

Arriving by Air

Hawaii's main transportation hub is the Honolulu International Airport, 10 miles (16 km) west of Honolulu on O'ahu. Its three terminals handle international, domestic, and interisland flights. Long-haul and interisland flights also land at Kahului Airport on Maui, Ellison Onizuka Kona International Airport on Hawai'i Island, and Līhu'e Airport on Kaua'i.

The majority of nonstop flights from the US to Hawaii depart from the US West Coast. Flights to Hawaii from other mainland cities and from Canada often involve a stop on the West Coast.

United Airlines and Air Canada are just two of the airlines that fly from Europe to Hawaii, stopping in the mainland US or Canada en route. Nonstop flights to Honolulu are possible from Sydney, Australia and Auckland, New Zealand with Qantas and Air New Zealand respectively.

Arriving by Sea

The **Norwegian Cruise Line** offers week-long cruises around Hawaii. A number of luxury liners, including **Royal Caribbean**, also stop off here.

Norwegian Cruise Line
W ncl.com

Royal Caribbean
W royalcaribbean.com

Interisland Travel

Interisland Air Travel

Flying between the islands is straightforward, with plentiful connections, but it can be expensive. The main airlines offering interisland flights are Hawaiian Airlines, Southwest, and Mokulele Airlines. Interisland flights run between the main airports on O'ahu, Maui, Hawai'i Island, and Kaua'i, as well as Hilo International Airport on Hawai'i Island and Kapalua Airport on Maui. Moloka'i Airport on Moloka'i is served only by interisland flights from Honolulu International Airport and Maui's Kahului airport, and little Lāna'i Airport on Lāna'i is serviced by flights from Honolulu International Airport, Moloka'i Airport, and Kahului Airport.

GETTING TO AND FROM THE AIRPORT

Airport	Distance to City	Taxi Fare	Public Transport	Journey Time
Kahului Airport (Maui)	3.5 miles (5.5 km) to Kahului Town	$13	Bus	10 min
Kona International Airport (Hawai'i Island)	8 miles (13 km) to Kailua-Kona	$25	Bus	15 min
Hilo International Airport (Hawai'i Island)	3 miles (5 km) to Hilo	$15	Bus	10 min
Honolulu International Airport (O'ahu)	10 miles (16 km) to Waikīkī	$40–50	Bus	15–30 min
Līhu'e Airport (Kaua'i)	2 miles (3 km) to Līhu'e	$10	Bus	5 min
Moloka'i Airport	8 miles (13 km) to Kaunakakai	$25–30	n/a	20 min

FLIGHT JOURNEY PLANNER

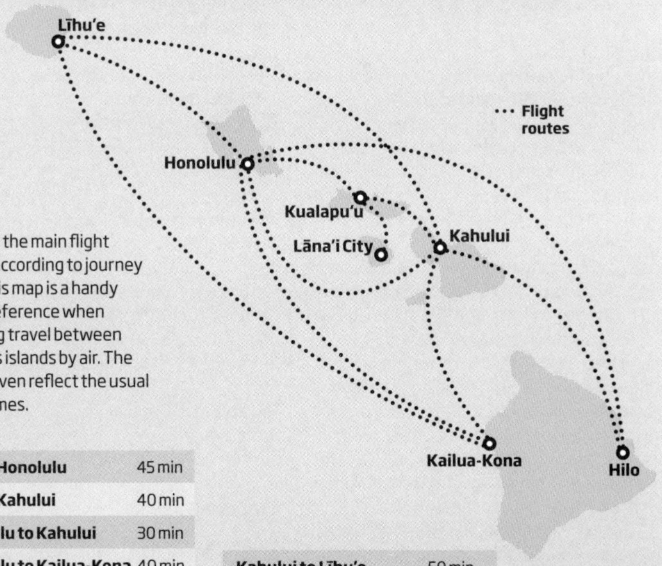

Plotting the main flight routes according to journey time, this map is a handy visual reference when planning travel between Hawaii's islands by air. The times given reflect the usual flight times.

Hilo to Honolulu	45 min
Hilo to Kahului	40 min
Honolulu to Kahului	30 min
Honolulu to Kailua-Kona	40 min
Honolulu to Līhu'e	35 min
Honolulu to Kualapu'u	25 min
Kahului to Kailua-Kona	35 min
Kahului to Līhu'e	50 min
Kahului to Kualapu'u	25 min
Kailua-Kona to Līhu'e	55 min
Kualapu'u to Lāna'i City	20 min

Interisland Ferry Travel

Expeditions runs Hawaii's only interisland ferry service, which connects Mā'alaea Harbor on Maui with Manele Harbor on Lāna'i. It sails multiple times per day, with the crossing taking about an hour; the trip doubles as a whale-watching cruise in winter. Fares start at $30/20 adult/child.

Expeditions
W go-lanai.com

Public Transportation

Public transportation options vary across the islands, with O'ahu's **TheBus** the most comprehensive system, followed by Maui's **Maui Bus**, Hawai'i Island's **Hele-On Bus**, and Kaua'i's **Kaua'i Bus**. All of these companies provide safety and hygiene measures, timetables, ticket information, and transport maps on their websites. Honolulu, on O'ahu, also has a trolley service, and a rail system is currently under construction. Moloka'i and Lāna'i don't have public transportation systems so car rentals are necessary on these islands, with shuttle buses and taxis as alternatives.

TheBus
W thebus.org
Maui Bus
W mauicounty.gov
Kaua'i Bus
W kauai.gov
Hele-On Bus
W heleonbus.hawaiicounty.gov

Buses

On O'ahu, TheBus covers most of the island, with several routes calling at the airport. You can purchase a one-way fare ($3), a one-day fare ($7.50), or a monthly pass ($80), either paid by cash in exact change as you board the bus or by a reloadable **HOLO card**. The latter is a convenient option if you plan on using TheBus frequently. HOLO cards can be picked up for free and loaded up at local retailers such as 7-Elevens, ABC Stores, and at TheBus Pass Office, as well as online. DaBus2 is a handy free app that provides information on TheBus times and routes.

On Maui, the Maui Bus runs 12 different routes covering the western half of the island, where the main towns and sights are. Tickets are bought onboard the bus using cash only (exact change). One-way fares are $2 and day fares $4. The buses run from about 7am till about 9pm every day, depending on the route.

The Kaua'i Bus follows the main island road all the way from Hanalei in the north to Kekaha in the west. It runs hourly Monday to Saturday, with more limited service on Sundays. Tickets are purchased onboard using exact change in cash. A one-way fare is $2 and a day fare is $5.

On Hawai'i Island, the Hele-On Bus runs various routes connecting Kailua-Kona with Hilo (via Waimea and Honoka'a), Kailua-Kona with the Kohala resorts, and Hilo with Hawai'i Volcanoes National Park. Tickets can be bought using cash only (exact change) onboard the bus. Fares are free until the end of 2025, after that they may go back to $2 per ride. Schedules are not ideal for sightseers but it is budget-friendly.

HOLO card
W holocard.net

Trolleys

On O'ahu, the open-air trolleys rolling around Honolulu are a fun way to get around. Run by **Waikīkī Trolley**, the four routes cover Chinatown and the historic sights (red line), Diamond Head area (green line), ocean viewpoints (blue line), and shopping destinations (pink line). Tickets can be purchased at tour desks or through the website. Day passes are available for all lines, costing $5.50 for the pink line, $19 for the green line, and $31.50 for the blue and red lines. One-, four-, and seven-day all-line tickets are available.

Waikīkī Trolley
W waikikitrolley.com

Train

The long-awaited **Honolulu Rail Transit** project, Skyline will consist of a 20-mile (32-km) rail system, connecting the airport to the city. The first stage of the project opened in 2023, linking the Aloha Stadium with East Kapolei. The second stage will link Pearl Harbor to the airport and is slated to open in 2025. The third and final stage will continue the line to Downtown Honolulu, with a completion date of 2031.

Honolulu Rail Transit
W honolulutransit.org

Taxis

Taxis can be found at airports, most major shopping centers, and outside major hotels. Rather than hail a cab on the street, it's often easier to head to a taxi stand or call for pick-up, especially outside of Honolulu. Some remote areas have limited or no taxi service. Ride-hailing apps such as **Uber** and **Lyft** operate in major centers.

Lyft
W lyft.com
Uber
W uber.com

Driving

Although Honolulu suffers with the traffic congestion of any major US city, driving in Hawaii is generally a pleasure, and it is often a great way to explore the islands. Local people are seldom in a hurry, so allow plenty of time for journeys. Residents never use their horns – it's considered rude to do so unless in an emergency – so on narrow roads check your mirrors regularly and pull over to let cars pass. Always check the weather, since roads can be flooded and temporarily impassable during or after heavy rain. If you ask for directions, locals will often suggest landmarks as reference points. Around Honolulu, you're likely to be told "Go ewa" (northwest) or "Go diamondhead" (southeast), and on all the islands you'll hear the words *mauka* (toward the mountain) and *makai* (toward the sea).

Car Rental

To rent a vehicle in Hawaii, you must be over 21 (surcharges may apply for those under 25). All drivers require a valid passport, credit card, and driver's license; if the license is not in English, an International Driving Permit is required. Large rental companies have desks at the airports on the four main islands. They offer vehicles of all sizes, including 4WD vehicles. It's usually easy to rent a car for a day or two from local agencies in Waikīkī, but you should book well in advance elsewhere in Hawaii.

Most visitors pay extra for a Loss Damage Waiver (LDW). This protects you from Hawaii's "no fault" policy, which holds the driver responsible for damage to the rental car, regardless of fault. Your insurance policy or credit card may cover damage costs to rental cars; always check. Most rental firms forbid the use of unpaved roads.

Parking

Some hotels offer free parking, and major hotels and many restaurants also provide valet parking. The chief exception is in Waikīkī, where hotels and parking lots can charge $30 or more to park overnight. When booking accommodations, check whether parking is included.

Free parking in Honolulu fills up quickly, especially on weekends. Your other options are parking lots or metered street parking; carry a stash of coins for the latter and note that it is usually free on Sundays. Be sure to heed all parking signs to avoid getting ticketed or your car towed.

Rules of the Road

Drive on the right, use the left lane only for passing, and give way to traffic from the right. Drivers must yield to pedestrians, even if they are crossing illegally. Seat belts are required for all passengers, in the front and back. Texting while driving is illegal but drivers can use a hand-free device when talking on a cell phone. Hawaii has one of the lowest maximum speed limits in the US; limits are clearly signed and strictly enforced.

It's illegal to drive under the influence of drugs or alcohol in Hawaii, and to carry open containers of alcohol inside a car. The blood-alcohol limit is 0.08 per cent (0.02 per cent for drivers under 21). Drunk driving will lead to fines and/or jail time.

Cycling

Bicycle routes can be found all over the islands, but come with challenges. Be aware of traffic, weather conditions, and narrow roads.

Measures to improve cyclist safety in urban areas are ongoing. In Honolulu, a protected bike lane runs 2 miles (3 km) along South King Street, from Moiliili to Downtown. However, traffic can be bothersome to a leisurely ride. Many cyclists take advantage of the front-loading bike racks on TheBus (available for no extra charge) and get out of the city before they start pedaling.

The other islands also have a number of cycle routes. On Kaua'i, the **Kauai Path** is a scenic 7-mile (11-km) shared cycling and walking path on the east coast of the island. On Maui, the exhilarating 25-mile (40-km) ride down Haleakalā *(p154)* is a popular option for cyclists; there's also a family-friendly, car-free path between Kahului and Pā'ia on Maui's north shore. Over on Hawai'i Island, adventurous mountain bikers head to Mana Road, a 40-mile (64-km) dirt path high up on the slopes of Mauna Kea *(p194)*. With sparse traffic, the roads on both Moloka'i and Lāna'i are ideal for cycling.

Kauai Path
W kauaipath.org

Bike Sharing and Rentals

Bike-sharing schemes are found on O'ahu and Hawai'i Island. In Honolulu, **Biki** has 1,300 bikes at 130 docking stations around town. Operating in Kona and Hilo, **HIBIKE** also offers bike-sharing, although on a smaller scale. There are multiple bike rental companies, many offering a variety of bikes, including road, mountain, and e-bikes.

Biki
W gobiki.org
HIBIKE
W hawaiiislandbike.com

Walking and Hiking

Hawaii's main cities and towns generally have walkable centers. Many areas of Honolulu are easily navigable on foot, including Waikīkī *(p92)*, Chinatown *(p80)*, and Kaka'ako *(p88)*; plus, the city is home to several walkable gardens and parks. In addition, a number of trails can be found close by, including the Diamond Head crater trail *(p117)*.

Beyond the towns and cities, the islands are awash with excellent hiking opportunities, in particular the national parks. Hike across volcanic landscape in Hawai'i Volcanoes National Park *(p184)*, walk among rainforest in Waimea Canyon and Kōke'e State Parks *(p216)*, or tackle the Kalalau Trail *(p220)*, one of the most dramatic coastal walks in the world, in the Nāpali Coast State Wilderness Park *(p218)*.

PRACTICAL INFORMATION

A little local know-how goes a long way in Hawaii. Here you will find all the essential advice and information you will need during your stay.

AT A GLANCE

EMERGENCY NUMBERS

GENERAL EMERGENCY

911

TIME ZONE

HST, Hawaii Standard Time (GMT-10). Hawaii does not use daylight saving time.

TAP WATER

Tap water in Hawaii is safe. Never drink from freshwater sources such as creeks.

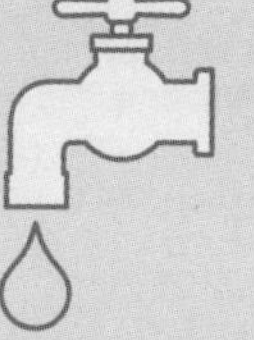

WEBSITES AND APPS

Go Hawaii

Hawaii's official tourist information website *(gohawaii.com)*, with detailed information on each island.

HAWAI'I Magazine

The state's national magazine *(hawaiimagazine.com)*, also available in print form.

Hawaii News Now

Hawaii's main and current online news source *(hawaiinewsnow.com)*.

KHON2 WX

A free and accurate weather app.

DaBus2

An app providing up-to-date information on times and routes for TheBus.

Personal Security

Hawaii is generally remarkably safe, and violent crime is rare. Use common sense and it's unlikely you'll come up against any problems. The main likelihood is theft from a rented vehicle. Never leave any valuables in the car; thieves are skilled at dealing with door and trunk locks. While crime in Honolulu is not nearly the problem it is in some other major US cities, Hawaii's capital city has its share of less salubrious neighborhoods; check with your hotel concierge about areas to avoid, especially late at night. Hitchhiking is illegal and it is recommended not to go on hikes alone due to the risk of an accident or of getting lost.

Hawaii is the only US state not to have a statewide police service. Instead each county – in effect, each island – runs its own police department. If you have anything stolen, report the crime within 24 hours to the nearest police station and take ID with you. Get a copy of the crime report in order to claim on your insurance. Contact your embassy if you have your passport stolen, or in the event of a serious crime or accident.

As a rule, Hawaii's people are very accepting of all persons, regardless of their race, gender, or sexuality. Hawaii was the first US state to consider legalizing same-sex marriage, a ruling that became official in 2013. Honolulu, especially Waikīkī, has LGBTQ+-friendly accommodations, restaurants, and bars; Queen's Surf Beach, part of the larger Waikīkī Beach, is popular with the local LGBTQ+ community.

Health and Safety

Despite its location in the tropics, Hawaii carries few health risks. Sun exposure and the ocean pose the biggest threats. To protect yourself from the powerful rays, wear a hat, sunglasses, and reef-safe sunblock; note that the sale of sunblock containing reef-damaging oxybenzone and octinoxate is illegal in Hawaii. Avoid being out during the heat of midday and in high temperatures for long periods, and drink plenty of fluids.

When swimming in the ocean, pay close attention to conditions, regardless of how experienced you are. Many beaches can be safe in

summer but dangerous in winter. If you've never surfed before, don't try it without proper instruction. A lifeguard is often stationed at the most popular beaches; always ask about current conditions, and heed posted warnings. Be wary of using unguarded beaches. For more information visit the **Hawaii Ocean Safety** website, which provides up-to-date information on such things as current and wind conditions.

Watch out for scorpions in the arid regions, centipedes and mosquitoes in the rainforests, and box jellyfish and Portuguese man-of-war in the sea.

Hawaii Ocean Safety
W oceansafety.hawaii.gov

Smoking, Alcohol, and Drugs

Smoking, including e-cigarettes, is prohibited in all public spaces, such as shops, theaters, nightclubs, bars, and restaurants. Tobacco products can be purchased by those over 21 years old.

The minimum legal age for drinking is 21. It is illegal to drink in a state or national park, and to carry an open container of alcohol in your vehicle.

Possession of up to 0.1 oz (3 g) of cannabis can result in a small fine. Possession of larger amounts, or of other illegal drugs, is prohibited and can result in heavy fines or even a prison sentence.

ID

Visitors to Hawaii should carry ID with them at all times. Besides requiring ID for entry into Hawaii and when traveling between the islands, you will need it for accommodation reservations, as proof of age to purchase alcohol and cigarettes, and for vehicle, watersport, and bicycle rentals.

Local Customs

Locals are seldom in a hurry. Use your car horn only in an emergency. Clothing is casual, too. Always take your shoes off before entering someone's home. Call tropical-print shirts aloha shirts, not Hawaiian shirts – these shirts are proudly worn by locals and aren't merely tourist souvenirs.

Trespassing is illegal on Hawaii. When exploring the island watch out for signs marked *kapu* (forbidden) as they often mean no trespassing. If you want to enter private property, always seek permission from the landowner first. All beaches are public access.

Responsible Tourism

The climate crisis is impacting Hawaii, with water shortages and wildfires increasingly frequent. Do your bit to help protect Hawaii's fragile ecosystem. Shop locally, and respect sacred sites and natural areas. Stick to marked paths, and don't remove lava rocks, sand, or shells. You can also travel Pono (consciously and respectfully) by picking tour operators certified by **Sustainable Tourism Association of Hawai'i**, volunteering with **Sustainable Coastlines Hawaii**, and donating to the **Lāhainā Restoration Foundation**.

Lāhainā Restoration Foundation
W lahainarestoration.org
Sustainable Coastlines Hawaii
W sustainablecoastlineshawaii.org
Sustainable Tourism Association of Hawai'i
W sustainabletourismhawaii.org

Cell Phones and Wi-Fi

Many cafés and bars offer free Wi-Fi to customers, and most hotels offer Wi-Fi in guest rooms.

Local SIM cards are available from T-Mobile, Verizon, and other network providers. While cellphone coverage tends to be excellent in resort and urban areas, it may be unreliable in more remote spots. Hikers should not depend on their cell phones for emergency use.

Post

The US Post Service branches can be found in major centers, and service is good.

Taxes and Refunds

There is a 4 per cent sales tax on all goods and services; further county surcharges can add an extra 0.7 per cent. You will also need to factor in hotel tax *(p239)*. Tax refunds are not offered to foreign visitors.

Discount Cards

On O'ahu, the **Go Oahu** pass includes entry to over 40 attractions, including the Polynesian Cultural Center and Pearl Harbor. Single- and multi-day passes can be purchased.

Go Oahu
W gocity.com/oahu

INDEX

Page numbers in **bold** refer to main entries.

GLOSSARY OF HAWAIIAN TERMS

Closely related to Tahitian, Samoan, and other Polynesian languages, Hawaiian, or ʻŌlelo Hawaiʻi, began as an oral language. It was first put into written form by the missionaries who arrived in the 1820s. The teaching and speaking of Hawaiian was banned from the early 1900s, and by the time the Hawaiian cultural renaissance began in the 1970s, the language was almost totally lost. Today, roughly 0.1 per cent of Hawaii's population can speak it fluently, though this percentage is on the rise thanks to Hawaiian language immersion programs, which are producing new generations of Hawaiian speakers.

SUMMARY OF PRONUNCIATION

The Hawaiian language has just 12 letters: the five vowels plus h, k, l, m, n, p, and w.

unstressed vowels:

a	*as in "**a**bove"*
e	*as in "b**e**t"*
i	*as y in "cit**y**"*
o	*as in "s**o**le"*
u	*as in "f**u**ll"*

stressed vowels:

ā	*as in "f**a**r"*
ē	*as in "p**a**y"*
ī	*as in "s**ee**"*
ō	*as in "s**o**le"*
ū	*as in "m**oo**n"*

consonants:

h	*as in "**h**at"*
k	*as in "**k**ick"*
l	*as in "**l**aw"*
m	*as in "**m**ow"*
n	*as in "**n**ow"*
p	*as in "**p**in"*
w	*as in "**w**in" or "**v**ine"*

The *ʻokina* (glottal stop) is found at the beginning of some words starting with vowels or between vowels. It is pronounced like the sound between the syllables in the English "uh-oh."

aliʻi	*ahlee-ee*
likoʻi	*leeleekoh-ee*
ʻohana	*oh-hahnah*

The *kahakō* (macron) is a mark found only above vowels, indicating vowels that should be stressed.

kāne	***kah**-nay*
kōkua	***koh**-koo-ah*
pūpū	***poo-poo***

EVERYDAY WORDS

ʻāina	***aye**-nah*	land
aloha	*ah-loh-ha*	hello; goodbye; love
hale	*ha-leh*	house
haole	*how-leh*	foreigner; Caucasian
hula	*who-la*	Hawaiian dance
kāhiko	***kaa**-hee-koh*	old; traditional
kamaʻāina	*kah-mah-**aye**-nah*	familiar; resident
kāne	***kah**-nay*	man
kapa	*kah-pah*	bark cloth
keiki	*kay-kee*	child
kōkua	***koh**-koo-ah*	help
kumu	*kooh-mooh*	teacher
lānai	***luh**-nigh*	porch; balcony
lei	*layh*	garland
lua	*looah*	bathroom; toilet
mahalo	*muh-ha-low*	thank you
muʻumuʻu	*moo-oo-moo-oo*	long billowing dress
ʻohana	*oh-hahnah*	family
ʻono	*oh-noh*	delicious
pau	*pow*	done
puka	*poo-kah*	hole
wahine	*w(v)ah-he-nay*	woman
wikiwiki	*w(v)eek-ee-w(v)eekee*	quickly

GEOGRAPHICAL AND NATURE TERMS

ʻaʻā	*ah-**aah***	rough, jagged lava
kai	*kaee*	ocean
koholā	*koh-hoh-**laah***	humpback whale
kona	*koh-nah*	leeward side
koʻolau	*koh-oh-lowh*	windward side
kukui	*kuh-kooh-eeh*	candlenut tree
makai	*muh-kaee*	toward the sea
mauka	*mau-kuh*	toward the mountains
mauna	*mau-nah*	mountain
nēnē	***nay-nay***	Hawaiian goose
pāhoehoe	***pah**-hoy-hoy*	smooth lava
pali	*pah-lee*	cliff
puʻu	*poo-oo*	hill
wai	*w(v)hy*	fresh water

HISTORICAL TERMS

ahupuaʻa	*ah-hoo-poo-ah-ah*	a division of land, from mountains to sea
aliʻi	*ahlee-ee*	chief; royalty
heiau	*hey-yow*	ancient temple
kahuna	*kah-hoo-nah*	priest; expert
kapu	*kah-poo*	forbidden; taboo
kupuna	*koo-poo-nah*	elders; ancestors
luakini	*looh-ah-kee-nee*	human sacrifice temple
makaʻāinana	*mah-kah-**aye**-nanah*	commoner
mana	*mah-nah*	supernatural power
mele	*meh-leh*	song
moʻo	*moh-oh*	lizard
oli	*oh-leeh*	chant
pili	*pih-leeh*	grass for thatching
puʻuhonua	*pooh-ooh-hoh-nuah*	place of refuge

FOOD WORDS

ʻahi	*ah-hee*	yellowfin tuna
aku	*ah-koo*	skipjack; bonito
aʻu	*ah-oo*	swordfish; marlin
haupia	*how-peeah*	traditional coconut pudding
imu	*ee-moo*	underground oven
kalo	*kah-loh*	taro
kālua	***kah**-looah*	food baked slowly in underground oven
kiawe	*key-ah-veh*	wood used for grilling
laulau	*lau-lau*	steamed filled ti-leaf packages
lilikoʻi	*lee-lee-koh-ee*	passion fruit
limu	*lee-moo*	seaweed
lomi-lomi salmon	*low-me low-me*	raw salmon pieces with onion and tomato
lūʻau	***loo**-ow*	Hawaiian feast
mahimahi	*muh-hee-muh-hee*	dorado; dolphin fish
ono	*oh-no*	wahoo
opah	*oh-pah*	moonfish
ʻōpakapaka	***oh**-pah-kah-pah-kah*	pink snapper
poi	*poy*	pounded taro root
pūpū	***poo-poo***	appetizer
uku	*oo-koo*	gray snapper
ulua	*oo-looah*	jackfish; pompano

PIDGIN

Hawaii's unofficial conglomerate language is commonly heard on playgrounds, in shopping malls, and backyards throughout Hawaii. Here are some words and phrases you may hear:

brah	*brother, pal*
broke da mout'	*great food*
buggah	*pal or pest*
fo' real	*really*
fo' what	*why*
grinds	*food; also to grind*
howzit?	*how are you?; how is everything?*
kay den	*okay then*
laydahs	*later; goodbye*
li' dat	*like that*
li' dis	*like this*
no can	*cannot*
no mo' nahting	*nothing*
shoots!	*yeah!*
stink eye	*dirty look*
talk story	*chat; gossip*

ACKNOWLEDGMENTS

The publisher would like to thank the following for their contribution to the previous edition: Gerald Carr, Bonnie Friedman, Kathryn Glendenning, Rita Goldman, Hinahina Gray, Gabrielle Innes Clemence Mclaren, Melissa Miller, Alex Salkever, Stephen Self, Greg Ward, Paul Wood

The publisher would like to thank the following for their kind permission to reproduce their photographs:

(Key: a-above; b-below/bottom; c-centre; f-far; l-left; r-right; t-top)

4Corners: Susanne Kremer 2-3; 6-7.

Alamy Stock Photo: AB Forces News Collection / Ens. Britney Duesler 59tr; Album 61tr, / British Library 60clb; All Canada Photos / Steve Ogle 22-23ca; tomas del amo 25tr; ART Collection 63bc; Scott Barclay 39tr; Debra Behr 196-97b; Russ Bishop 30-31ca; Steve Bly 219bl; Dimitry Bobroff 24tl; 58cla; Robert Bush 160-61; Cannon Photography LLC / BrownWCannonIII 130br; Cavan Images 39b, / Aurora Photos / Sean Davey 72crb / Julia Cumes 49crb, / Logan Mock-Bunting 42b; CPA Media Pte Ltd / Pictures From History 61tl; 62tl; CPC Collection 60t; Cultura Creative Ltd / Rosanna U 31tr; Cultura Creative RF / Pete Saloutos 26-27ca; Curved Light USA 203br; Ian Dagnall 62clb; Danita Delimont / Daisy Gilardini 45crb; Danita Delimont / Rob Tilley 205b; Jim DeLillo 51bl; Design Pics Inc / Hawaiian Legacy Archive / Pacific Stock 64bc; Design Pics Inc / Pacific Stock / Alvis Upitis 185t, / James Crawford 109bl, / Peter French 30-31tc, 193tl, / Ron Dahlquist 40b, 45cla, 140b, 154t, 173tl; Reinhard Dirscherl 141tl; Beth Dixson 224cl; Douglas Peebles Photography 91br, 113t, 116br, 142bl, 143, 200-01b, 219clb; dpa picture alliance archive 42tl, 58crb; John Elk III 142bc; Craig Ellenwood 33cla; Greg Balfour Evans 87t; Everett Collection Historical 64cla, 64clb; Michele Falzone 20cr, 162-63t; David Fleetham 35tl, 45tr, 47cl, 149tl, 168-69t, Florilegius 61br, Dennis Frates 35cla (Subalpine), 228bl; Granger Historical Picture Archive NYC 62br, 63tr; Jeffrey Isaac Greenberg 19+, 100cr; Michael Greenfelder 198cla; Gerold Grotelueschen 216bl; H. Mark Weidman Photography 55br; Kelly Headrick 83b; Historic Images 63crb; Alpha Historica 64tl; 97br; George H. H. Huey 60br; Marshall Ikonography 85tl; Doug James 8cla; Mark A. Johnson 38clb; Niels van Kampenhout 51crb; Don Landwehrle 11t; 228-29t; Angus McComiskey 26–27tc, 156tr; 209br; Henk Meijer 222bl; David L. Moore 36b; 49cla; 126-27b; National Geographic Image Collection 41cla, 145t, 146-47b; NOAA 44b, 47tr; David Olsen 52-53b, 163bl; PBpictures 127tl; Jamie Pham 35clb; Photo Resource Hawaii / David Franzen 57br, 103bl, / David Schrichte 125cra, / Franco Salmoiraghi 36cra, 50bl, / Jack Jeffrey 34cla, / Tami
Kauakea Winston 58cra, 58cl, 59cl, 206bl; Photononstop / Tibor Bognar 59tl; The Picture Art Collection 63cra; Susanne Pommer 24-25ca; Prisma by Dukas Presseagentur GmbH / Heeb Christian 199b, / Sonderegger Christof 41crb; Sergi Reboredo 183bl; RGB Ventures / SuperStock / Alvis Upitis 36tl; robertharding / Christian Kober 216cra, / Michael DeFreitas 8cl, 43clb, 194-95t, 202t; C. Storz 191tr; Travel Pix 101tl; Greg Vaughn 17bl, 134-35; David Wa 54-55t; David Wall 24tr, 125ca; WaterFrame_mus 200tl; Jim West 182cl; Westend61 GmbH / Michael Runkel 86bl; Olivera White 188; wonderlandstock 48-49b; Yvette Cardozo 27tl; Regula Heeb-Zweifel 167tr.

AWL Images: Danita Delimont Stock 31tc, 114-15b; Michele Falzone 71t, 92-93; 159; Christian Heeb 164-165; James Montgomery 16c, 66-67.

Bridgeman Images: 101crb.

Dreamstime.com: Debra Reschoff Ahearn 221br; Dmitry Akhmetov 32b; Valentin Armianu 55tr; Bennymarty 99b; Bhofack2 11br; Ralf Broskvar 148bl; George Burba 28cr; Sorin Colac 10-11b; 96-97b; James Crawford 37t; Dirkr 131tl, 180-81b; Eric Broder Van Dyke 74bl; Eddygaleotti 234-35b; Maria Luisa Lopez Estivill 193cra; Galyna Andrushko 22tl; Giuseppemasci 84t; Haveseen 37clb; Ibrester 193tr; Industryandtravel 35cla; Rico Leffanta 20crb; 43t; Madrabothair 4, 48-49t; Maria1986nyc 23tr; Markpittimages 57tr; Martinmark 28bl, 50-51t, 71bl, 106-07, 161cla, 218-19t; Mav100 39crb; Leigh Anne Meeks 83cr; Mickem 156-57b; MNStudio 27tr; Joseph Morelli 204tr; Shane Myers 28crb; 46cla; Yooran Park 105tl; Photoquest 20t; Picturemakersllc 12-13b; Marek Poplawski 54br; Ppy2010ha 75cl; Robertplotz 18, 150-51; Prasit Rodphan 46-47b; Robin Runck 35cl; Daniel Shumny 72bl; Silvestrovairina 59cra; Tommy Song 214-15t; Steveheap 22-23t, 190bl; Paul Topp 13br, 59clb; Jeff Whyte 20bl, 56tl; Dr. Victor Wong 65tr; Wpd911 198t.

Getty Images: AFP / George F. Lee 65bc; Alan Behr / MCT / Tribune News Service 41tr; Archive Photos / PhotoQuest 64crb; Corbis Historical / David Pollack 64-65t, / Ralf-Finn Hestoft 65crb; David Fleetham / VW PICS / Universal Images Group 8clb; De Agostini / DEA Picture Library 61cla; DigitalVision / Colin Anderson Productions pty ltd 8-9; Icon Sports Wire / Kirk Aeder 195bl; Moment / © 2011 Brandon S. Olmstead 125tr, / Christopher Chan 186-87t, / Dusty Pixel photography 12clb, / Kjell Linder 100-01b, / M Swiet Productions 128-29; 226-27t, / Michael Orso 195br; Moment Mobile / Schafer & Hill 163crb; Moment Open / Carl Larson Photography 175tl; Photodisc / Michele Falzone 161br; Stockbyte / Barry Winiker 85bl; Stone / Art Wolfe 11crb; Stone / Jon Hicks 102-03t, / Peter Unger 172b; Universal Images Group / Jeff Greenberg 86-87t, / Jumping Rocks 220cl; Westend61 10clb, 207tl.

Getty Images / iStock: agaliza 19tl, 176-77; Matt Anderson 138t; anouchka 72t; Joel Carillet 12t, 87br; CoreyFord 168bl; Phil Davis 132-33b; E+ / Art Wager 236-37, / JamesBrey 209tl, / Joel Carillet 62-63t; 70c; 76-77, / JTSorrell 32tr, / pawel.gaul 192-93b, / Saturated 52-53t, / wingmar 13cr; Gim42 89crb; GlowingEarth 19cb, 210-11, 230-31; gregobagel 104b; HaizhanZheng 34-35b, 118-19; The Image Bank / Jupiterimages 37cr; jewhyte 88t; jimfeng 112-13b; Kyle Kempf 131tr; kokkai 74-75t; Sreejith Kurup 144b; mihtiander 17t, 120-21; mizoula 13t; PB57photos 124-25b; Png-Studio 182t; RugliG 10ca; sphraner 117t; Adam-Springer 224-25b; The World Traveller 223t; theartist312 33tr; tropicalpixsingapore 96cl; wallix 233b; YinYang 26tl, 44tr, 170-71b, 181clb.

Hawai'i Food & Wine Festival: 58clb.

Honolulu Department of Parks and Recreation: 53cla.

Kapalua Wine and Food Festival: 58cr.

Photo Resource Hawaii: © 2013 Ann Cecil 108-09t; © 2015 Mike Krzywonski 109br.

The Polynesian Cultural Center: 25tl.

Robert Harding Picture Library: David Cornwell 111; Reinhard Dirscherl 40t; Dana Edmunds 53b; Douglas Peebles 33crb, 39cla, 57clb, 59crb; Ed Robinson 22cla; Michael Runkel 28t; Alexandra Simone 38t; Masa Ushioda 216-17.

Shutterstock.com: Richie Chan 56-57b; Yi-Chen Chiang 72cr; Danita Delimont 174bl, 232tr; gg-foto 30t; ja-images 82tr; Christian Mueller 98-99t; Nagel Photography 89bl; Susanne Pommer 166-67b; Theodore Trimmer 80-81t.

Waikiki Artfest- Handcrafters and Artisans Alliance: 43br.

WorkPlay: 75b.

Cover images: *Front and Spine*: **Getty Images:** Matteo Colombo
Back: **Alamy Stock Photo:** David Wall cla; **Dreamstime.com:** Madrabothair c; **Getty Images:** Matteo Colombo b; **Getty Images / iStock:** HaizhanZheng tr; *Front Flap*: **4Corners:** Susanne Kremer cra; **Alamy Stock Photo:** Craig Ellenwood cla; **Dreamstime.com:** George Burba br; Martinmark cb; **Getty Images:** Stone / Jon Hicks t; **Getty Images / iStock:** RugliG bl.

All other images © Dorling Kindersley Limited

Illustrators:
Robert Ashby, Richard Bonson, Gary Cross, Chris Forsey, Stephen Gyapay, Claire Littlejohn, Chris Orr & Associates, Robbie Polley, Mike Taylor, John Woodcock

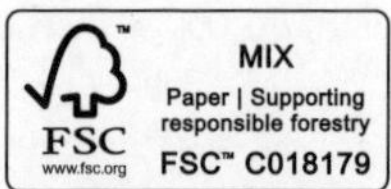

This book was made with Forest Stewardship Council™ certified paper – one small step in DK's commitment to a sustainable future.
Learn more at **www.dk.com/uk/information/sustainability**

A NOTE FROM DK

The rate at which the world is changing is constantly keeping the DK travel team on our toes. While we've worked hard to ensure that this edition of DK travel guide Hawaii is accurate and up-to-date, we know that opening hours alter, standards shift, prices fluctuate, places close, and new ones pop up in their stead. So, if you notice we've got something wrong or left something out, we want to hear about it. Please get in touch at travelguides@dk.com

This edition updated by
Contributor Lisa Voormeij
Senior Editors Dipika Dasgupta, Zoë Rutland
Senior Art Editors Laura O'Brien, Vinita Venugopal
Project Editors Sarah Allen, Abhijit Dutta, Anuroop Sanwalia
Assistant Art Editor Bineet Kaur
Proofreader Susanne Hillen
Indexer Helen Peters
Assistant Picture Research Administrator Manpreet Kaur
Senior Picture Researcher Nishwan Rasool
Deputy Manager, Picture Research Virien Chopra
Publishing Assistant Simona Velikova
Jacket Designer Laura O'Brian
Senior Cartographer Mohammad Hassan
Cartography Manager Suresh Kumar
DTP Designer Rohit Rojal
Production Controller Kariss Ainsworth
Managing Editors Beverly Smart, Hollie Teague
Managing Art Editor Gemma Doyle
Senior Managing Art Editor Priyanka Thakur
Art Director Maxine Pedliham
Publishing Director Georgina Dee

First edition 1998
Published in Great Britain by Dorling Kindersley Limited, 20 Vauxhall Bridge Road, London SW1V 2SA
The authorized representative in the EEA is Dorling Kindersley Verlag GmbH. Arnulfstr. 124, 80636 Munich, Germany
Published in the United States by DK Publishing, 1745 Broadway, 20th Floor, New York, NY 10019, USA

24 25 26 27 10 9 8 7 6 5 4 3 2 1

A CIP catalog record for this book is available from the British Library.
A catalog record for this book is available from the Library of Congress.
ISSN: 1542 1554
ISBN: 978 0 2417 0939 9
Printed and bound in China.
www.dk.com